Prominent African Leaders Since Independence

Bridgette Kasuka, Editor

Source: Wikipedia:
http://en.wikipedia.org/
and other sources.

Bridgette Kasuka, Editor
April 2013

First Edition

ISBN 978-9987-16-026-6

New Africa Press
Dar es Salaam, Tanzania

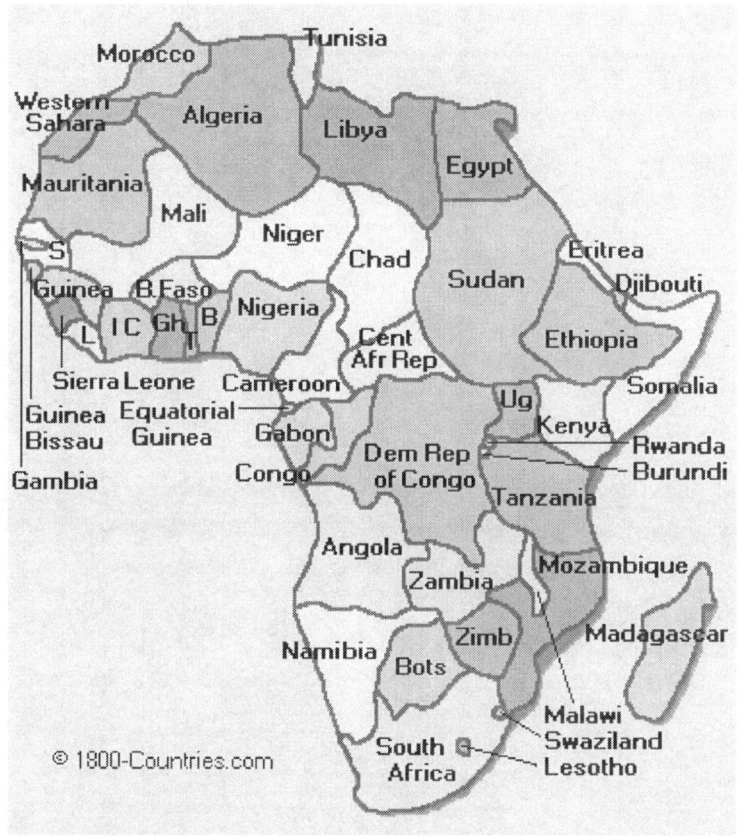

Contents

Sekou Toure

William Tubman

Ellen Johnson Sirleaf

Felix Houphouet-Boigny

Kwame Nkrumah

Jerry Rawlings

Sylvanus Olympio

Thomas Sankara

Nnamdi Azikiwe

Abubakar Tafawa Balewa

Odumegwu Ojukwu

Yakubu Gowon

Kenneth Kaunda

Kamuzu Banda

Samora Machel

Robert Mugabe

Seretse Khama

Agostinho Neto

Sam Nujoma

Nelson Mandela

Thabo Mbeki

Winnie Madikizela Mandela

Acknowledgements

I WISH to express my profound gratitude to all those who have contributed to the articles in Wikipedia about the African leaders featured in this work.

Without their contributions, I would not have been able to compile this volume.

I have played only one role: editing the material for clarity.

I have also excluded some material I felt was not necessary to provide comprehensive profiles of the leaders covered here.

Therefore there is not a single article about an African leader in this book which appears in its entirety the way it was published in Wikipedia.

And whatever shortcomings there are in terms of factual content can not be attributed to a single person.

Compilation of Wikipedia articles is a collective enterprise; so are any errors that readers may be able to find in this volume which is a product of many individuals who have contributed to the online encyclopaedia to add to the pool of human knowledge for the betterment of mankind.

There is more that can be learned about these leaders. But that is beyond the scope of this work.

Introduction

THIS IS a profile of the most influential African leaders during the post-colonial period.

The order in which the profiles of these leaders appear in the book is not determined by the degree of influence they had or have in different areas.

I have started with Haile Selassie in northeast Africa followed by the leaders of a region that is known as East Africa comprising Kenya, Uganda, Tanzania and Rwanda and Burundi; then Central Africa, West Africa, and finally southern Africa.

Therefore the arrangement is geographical.

The work focuses on leaders who have had an impact not only on their countries but on the continent as a whole in terms of influence, good or bad, or both. I have also added some material here and there from other sources including myself to complement this work.

Leaders such as Nkrumah, Nyerere, and Sekou Toure were known to be ardent Pan-Africanists and some of the most prominent advocates of African unity and liberation.

They had profound influence on the continent.

Idi Amin was known not only for his antics but for the role he played in shaping the course of some of the most important events in the history of post-colonial Africa including the ouster of President Milton Obote and the invasion of Tanzania and annexation of 710 square miles of Tanzanian territory by Uganda during his reign of terror as the country's military head of state.

He was extremely dangerous. But he also had a "soft" spot, with a "tender" heart. As one journalist described him, one minute he could be playful as a kitten, and next, lethal as a lion.

Odumegwu Ojukwu may not have been a head of state of a sovereign entity recognised by the international community except by five countries. But there is no question that when his home region of Eastern Nigeria seceded and declared independence as the Republic of Biafra under his leadership, he was thrust into the spotlight as the leader of a secessionist movement which not only threatened to destroy the Nigerian federation; it also threatened to encourage secession in other parts of Africa. Many African leaders feared that the secession of Biafra would have encouraged others to secede had Biafra survived as a nation.

Ojukwu also remained a hero to his people, the Igbo, even decades after the war ended. And when he died, he was given a state funeral. The Nigerian president, Goodluck Jonathan, described him as a national hero.

Like Idi Amin, Mobutu Sese Seko also gained notoriety but in a different way. He will always be remembered for the role he played in the assassination of Patrice Lumumba and for impoverishing his country, leaving it an empty shell after 32 years of kleptocratic rule in spite of the fact that Congo, called Zaire during his reign, is potentially one of the richest countries in Africa and in the world, richer than South Africa in terms of mineral wealth.

It was Mobutu who had Lumumba arrested; and it was he who sent Lumumba to Elisabethville, renamed Lubumbashi, the capital of secessionist Katanga Province, knowing full well that Lumumba's arch-enemy, Moise Tshombe, would have him killed in collusion with the Belgians and the Americans who also wanted Lumumba dead.

In fact, it was the Americans and the Belgians who engineered and masterminded Lumumba's assassination.

Winnie Madikizela Mandela was not a president. But she earned credentials as one of the most prominent leaders within South Africa during the struggle against apartheid. She mobilised blacks against the racist regime when her husband Nelson Mandela was in prison.

She could even have become the first female president of South Africa, and the first female head of state on the continent, had her political career not been derailed by scandals.

Yet she stands out as one of the most influential African leaders because of her prominent role in the liberation struggle against white minority rule and deserves inclusion in the pantheon of African leaders featured in this work.

Many leaders featured in the book were not only some of the most prominent and most influential during the colonial and post-colonial years; they were also the founding fathers of their nations. And they shaped the destinies of their countries.

Those who were not the founding fathers, for example Jerry Rawlings of Ghana and Yoweri Museveni of Uganda, left an indelible mark on their countries as well. They changed the destinies of their countries and stand out, together with the founding fathers, as some of the most important leaders Africa has ever produced since the advent of colonial rule.

Many African leaders have been left out of the book, not because they are not important but because their impact and influence is minimal.

Many people, including a significant number of Africans who are knowledgeable about African affairs, have never even heard of them. Or they know very little about them. And there are many examples to illustrate this point.

Who was Hubert Maga?

He was the first president of Dahomey when the country won independence from France on 1 August 1960. Dahomey was renamed the People's Republic of Benin on 30 November 1975.

Hubert Maga was overthrown in October 1963 by Colonel Christophe Soglo but served again as president of Dahomey from May 1970 to May 1972.

What about Leon M'ba and Maurice Yameogo?

They were also the first presidents of their countries. Leon M'ba became president of Gabon when the country won independence from France on 17 August 1960. And Maurice Yameogo became president of Upper Volta when the country won independence, also from France, on 5 August 1960. Upper Volta was renamed Burkina Faso in August 1984.

How many people know about or remember Hamani Diori?

He was the first president of Niger when the country won independence from France on 3 August 1960. He was re-elected in 1965 and 1970 and stayed in power until he was overthrown in a military coup on 15 April 1974. He also played a mediating role during the Nigerian civil war when the leaders of the two sides in the war met in Niamey, Niger's capital, under his stewardship.

Yet he's not known like Sekou Toure, Milton Obote, or even Milton Margai, the first prime minister of Sierra Leone whose influence beyond his country Sierra Leone was equally insignificant.

Who was the first president of Chad after the country won independence from France on 11 August 1960?

Francois Tombalbaye.

He was assassinated at the presidential palace on 13 April 1975 in a military coup led by the commander of the army, General Felix Malloum, who became president.

Who was Hassan Gouled Aptidon?

He was the first president of Djibouti.

Even some educated Africans don't know that Djibouti is a country on their continent. They don't even know where it is.

What about Luis Cabral?

He became the first president of Guinea-Bissau when the country declared independence from Portugal on 24 September 1973.

So was Nkrumah, and so was Azikiwe, Nyerere, Sekou Toure, Kenyatta, Obote and Kaunda. They were also the first presidents of their countries.

The contrast is obvious.

That's the point.

Haile Selassie

Haile Selassie, a name which in Ge'ez means "Power of the Trinity," was born Tafari Makonnen on 23 July 1892. He died on 27 August 1975. He was 83. He was Ethiopia's regent from 1916 to 1930 and Emperor of Ethiopia from 1930 to 1974.

The heir to a dynasty that traced its origins to the 13th century, and from there by tradition back to King Solomon and Queen Makeda, Empress of Axum, known in the Abrahamic tradition as the Queen of Sheba, Haile Selassie is a defining figure in both Ethiopian and African history.

At the Lleague of Nations in 1936, Emperor Haile Selassie condemned the use of chemical weapons by Italy against his people.

His internationalist views led to Ethiopia becoming a charter member of the United Nations, and his political thought and experience in promoting multilateralism and collective security have proved seminal and enduring.

His suppression of rebellions among the nobles

(*mekwannint*), as well as what some perceived to be Ethiopia's failure to modernise adequately, earned him criticism among some contemporaries and historians.

Haile Selassie is revered as the returned Messiah of the Bible, God incarnate, by Rastafarians. The Rastafari movement, which is strongest in the Caribbean especially Jamaica, has a significant number of members estimated to be between 200,000 and 800,000.

The Rastafari movement started in Jamaica in the 1930s. Its members believe that Haile Selassie is a messianic figure who will lead a future golden age of eternal peace, righteousness, and prosperity. They don't believe that he died because God never dies.

He himself remained a member of the Ethiopian Orthodox Christian Church throughout his life. He never said he was a messiah. But he did not discourage Rastafarians, either, from believing that he was one, although he was reportedly embarrassed when he visited Jamaica and saw Rastafarians who really believed that he was God incarnate.

Name

Haile Selassie was born Tafari Makonnen (Amharic pronunciation *lij teferī mekōnnin*). "Lij" in Amharic literally means "child" and indicates that a youth is of noble blood.

He would later become Ras Tafari Makonnen. "Ras" literally means "head" and is the equivalent of "duke," although it is often rendered in translation as "prince."

Tafari, his given name, in Amharic means "one who is respected", while *Haile* literally means in Ge'ez "Power of" and Selassie means "trinity" (i.e. Haile Selassie "Power of the Trinity"), which was his coronation name in 1930. *Haile Selassie* was also his Christian baptismal name as an infant.

In 1916 during the reign of the Empress Zauditu, the empress gave him the position of a regent. In 1928, this position was elevated and Empress Zauditu granted him the throne of Shoa. His title was then elevated to Negus which means "King."

On 2 November 1930, after the death of Empress Zauditu, Ras Tafari Makonnen was crowned emperor. Upon his ascension to the position of emperor, he took as his regnal name (reign name), "Haile Selassie", meaning "Power of the Trinity."

Haile Selassie's full title in office was "His Imperial Majesty Haile Selassie I, King of Kings, Lord of Lords, Conquering Lion of the Tribe of Judah, and Elect of God" (Ge'ez - *girmāwī ḳadāmāwī 'aṣē ḥaile śelassie, mō'ā 'ambassā ze'imneggede yehūda negus negast ze'ītyōp̓p̓yā, tsehume 'igzī'a'bihēr*). This title reflects Ethiopian dynastic traditions which hold that all monarchs must trace their lineage back to Menelik I who in the Ethiopian tradition was the offspring of King Solomon and the Queen of Sheba.

To Ethiopians Haile Selassie has been known by many names, including Janhoy, Talaqu Meri, and Abba Tekel. The Rastafari employ many of these appellations, also referring to him as HIM, Jah, and Jah Rastafari.

Biography

Early life

Haile Selassie's direct male line originated from the Amhara people. But he also had Oromo, Tigray, and Gurage roots.

He was born on 23 July 1892 in the village of Ejersa Goro in the Harar province of Ethiopia. His mother was Woizero ("Lady") Yeshimebet Ali Abajifar, daughter of Dejazmach Ali Abajifar, the renowned ruler of Wollo province.

Haile Selassie's father was Ras Makonnen Woldemikael Gudessa, the governor of Harar. Ras Makonnen served as a general in the First Italo-Ethiopian War, playing a key role at the Battle of Adwa. He inherited his imperial blood through his paternal grandmother, Princess Tenagnework Sahle Selassie, who was an aunt of Emperor Menelik II, and as such asserted direct descent from Makeda, the Queen of Sheba, and King Solomon of ancient Israel.

Ras Makonnen arranged for Tafari as well as his first cousin, Ras Imru Haile Selassie to receive instruction in Harar from Abba Samuel Wolde Kahin, an Ethiopian capuchin monk, and from Dr. Vitalien, a surgeon from Guadeloupe.

Tafari was named Dejazmach (literally "commander of the gate," roughly equivalent to "count") at the age of 13 on 1 November 1905. Shortly thereafter, his father Ras Makonnen, died at Kulibi in 1906.

Governorship

Tafari assumed the titular governorship of Selale in 1906, a realm of marginal importance but one that enabled him to continue his studies. In 1907, he was appointed governor of a part of the province of Sidamo. It is alleged that during his late teens, Haile Selassie was married to *Woizero* Altayech, and that from this union, his daughter Romanework Haile Selassie was born.

Following the death of his brother Yelma in 1907, the governorship of Harar was left vacant and its administration was left to Menelik's loyal general, *Dejazmach* Balcha Safo. Balcha Safo's administration of Harar was ineffective, and so during the last illness of Menelik II, and the brief reign of Empress Taitu Bitul, Tafari was made governor of Harar in 1910 or 1911.

On 3 August he married Menen Asfaw of Ambassel,

niece of heir to the throne Lij Lyasu.

Regency

The extent to which Tafari Makonnen contributed to the movement that would come to depose Iyasu V is unclear. Iyasu V, or Lij Iyasu, was the designated but uncrowned Emperor of Ethiopia from 1913 to 1916. Iyasu's reputation for scandalous behavior and a disrespectful attitude towards the nobles at the court of his grandfather, Menelik II, damaged his reputation. And his flirtation with Islam was considered treasonous among the Ethiopian Orthodox Christian leadership of the empire. On 27 September 1916, Iyasu was deposed.

Contributing to the movement that deposed Iyasu were conservatives such as Fitawrari Habte Giyorgis, Menelik II's longtime minister of war. The movement to depose Iyasu preferred Tafari, as he attracted support from both progressive and conservative factions. Ultimately, Iyasu was deposed on the grounds of conversion to Islam. In his place, the daughter of Menelik II (the aunt of Iyasu) was named Empress Zewditu.

Zewditu wa made regent for Tafari during his early years. Tafari was elevated to the rank of *Ras* and was made heir apparent and crown prince. In the power arrangement that followed, Tafari accepted the role of regent plenipotentiary (*Balemulu 'Inderase*) and became the *de facto* ruler of the Ethiopian empire (*Mangista Ityop'p'ya*). Zewditu would govern while Tafari would administer.

While Iyasu had been deposed on 27 September 1916, on 8 October the coup d'etat went awry. Iyasu managed to escape into the Ogaden Desert and his father, *Negus* Mikael of Wollo, had time to come to his aid. On 27 October, *Negus* Mikael and his army met an army under *Fitawrari* Habte Giyorgis loyal to Zewditu and Tafari. During the Battle of Segale, *Negus* Mikael was defeated and captured. Any chance that Iyasu would regain the throne was ended and he went into hiding. On 11 January 1921, after avoiding capture for about five years, Iyasu was taken into custody by Gugsa Araya Selassie.

On 11 February 1917, the coronation for Zewditu took place. She pledged to rule justly through her regent, Tafari. While Tafari was the more visible of the two, Zewditu was far from an honorary ruler. Her position required that she arbitrate the claims of competing factions. In other words, she had the last word. Tafari carried the burden of daily administration but, because his position was relatively weak, this was often an exercise in futility for him. Initially his personal army was poorly equipped, his finances were limited, and he had little leverage to withstand the combined influence of the empress, the minister of war, or the provincial governors.

During his regency, the new crown prince developed the policy of cautious modernisation initiated by Menelik II. He secured Ethiopia's admission to the League of Nations in 1923 by promising to eradicate slavery; each emperor since Tewodros II had issued proclamations to end slavery, but without effect: the internationally scorned practice persisted well into Haile Selassie's reign.

Travel abroad

In 1924, *Ras* Tafari toured Europe and the Middle East visiting Jerusalem, Cairo, Alexandria, Brussels, Amsterdam, Stockholm, London, Genevva, and Athens. With him on his tour was a group that included *Ras* Seyum Mangasha of western Tigre Province, *Ras* Hailu Tekle Haymanot of Gojjam Province, *Ras* Mulugeta Yeggazu of Illubabor Province, *Ras* Makonnen Endelkachew, and Blattengeta Heruy Welde Sellase.

The primary goal of the trip to Europe was for Ethiopia to gain access to the sea. In Paris, Tafari was to find out from the French foreign ministry that this goal would not be realised. However, failing this, he and his retinue inspected schools, hospitals, factories, and churches.

Although patterning many reforms after European models, Tafari remained wary of European pressure. To guard against economic imperialism, Tafari required that all enterprises have at least partial local ownership. Of his modernisation campaign, he remarked, "We need European progress only because we are surrounded by it. That is at once a benefit and a misfortune."

Throughout *Ras* Tafari's travels in Europe, the Levant, and Egypt, he and his entourage were greeted with enthusiasm and fascination. He was accompanied by Seyum Mangasha and Hailu Tekle Haymanot who, like Tafari, were sons of generals who contributed to the victorious war against Italy a quarter century earlier at the Battle of Adwa. Another member of his entourage, Mulugeta Yeggazu, actually fought at Adwa as a young man.

The "Oriental Dignity" of the Ethiopians and their "rich, picturesque court dress were sensationalised in the media; among his entourage he even included a pride of lions which he distributed as gifts to President Alexandre Millerand and Prime Minister Raymond Poincaré of France; to King George V of the United Kingdom, and to the Zoological Garden (*Jardin Zoologique*) of Paris. As one historian noted, "Rarely can a tour have inspired so many anecdotes".

In return for two lions, the United Kingdom presented *Ras* Tafari with the imperial crown of Emperor Tewodros II for its safe return to Empress Zewditu. The crown had been taken by Robert Napier during the 1868 Expedition of Abyssinia. Napier was the British commander of the expedionary force against Emperor Tewodros II.

During the same period, the crown price (Ras Tafari, later to known as Haile Selassie) visited the Armenian monastery of Jerusalem. There, he adopted 40 Armenian orphans (*Arba Lijoch* – "forty children") who had lost their parents in Ottoman massacres. *Ras* Tafari arranged for the musical education of the youths and they came to form the imperial brass band.

The Arba Lijoch arrived in Addis Ababa in 1924 and, along with their bandleader Kevork Nalbandian, became the first official orchestra of the nation. Nalbandian also composed the music for *Marsh Teferi* (words by Yoftehé Negusé) which was the Imperial National Anthem from 1930 to 1974.

King and Emperor

In 1928, the authority of *Ras* Tafari Makonnen was challenged when Dejazmatch Balcha Safo went to Addis Ababa with a sizeable armed force. When Tafari consolidated his hold over the provinces, many of Menilek's appointees refused to abide by the new regulations.

Balcha Safo, who was governor (*Shum*) of the coffee-rich Sidamo Provence, was particularly troublesome. The revenues he remitted to the central government did not reflect the accrued profits and Tafari recalled him to Addis Ababa. The old man came in high dudgeon and, insultingly, with a large army. The *Dejazmatch* paid homage to Empress Zewditu, but snubbed *Ras* Tafari.

On 18 February, while Balcha Safo and his personal bodyguard were in Addis Ababa, *Ras* Tafari had *Ras* Kassa Haile Darge buy off his army and arrange to have him displaced as the *Shum* of Sidamo Province by Birru Wolde Gabriel who himself was replaced by Desta Damtew.

Even so, the gesture of Balcha Safo empowered Empress Zewditu politically and she attempted to have Tafari tried for treason. He was tried for his benevolent dealings with Italy including a 20-year peace accord which was signed on 2 August.

In September, a group of palace reactionaries, including some of the courtiers of the empress, made a final bid to get rid of Tafari. The attempted coup d'etat was tragic in its origins and comic in its end. When confronted by Tafari and a company of his troops, the ringleaders of the coup took refuge on the palace grounds in Menilek's mausoleum. Tafari and his men surrounded them only to be surrounded themselves by the personal guard of Empress Zewditu.

More of Tafari's khaki clad soldiers arrived and, with superiority of arms, decided the outcome in his favour. Popular support, as well as the support of the police, remained with Tafari. Ultimately, Empress Zewditu relented and, on 7 October 1928, she crowned Tafari as *Negus* which in Amharic means "King."

The crowning of Tafari (Haile Selassie) as king of Ethiopia was controversial. He occupied the same territory as the empress rather than going off to a regional kingdom of the empire. Two monarchs, even with one being the vassal and the other the emperor (in this case empress), had never occupied the same location as their seat in Ethiopian history.

Conservatives agitated to redress this perceived insult to the dignity of the crown, leading to the rebellion of Ras Gugsa Welle.

Gugsa Welle was the husband of the Empress Zewditu and the *Shum* of Begemder Province. In early 1930, he raised an army and marched it from his provincial headquarters at Gondar towards Addis Ababa. On 31 March 1930, Gugsa Welle was met by forces loyal to *Negus* Tafari and was defeated at the Battle of Anchem. He was killed in action.

News of Gugsa Welle's defeat and death had hardly spread through Addis Ababa when the Empress Zewditu died suddenly on 2 April 1930.

Although it was long rumoured that the empress was poisoned upon the defeat of her husband, or alternately that she died from shock upon hearing of the death of her estranged yet beloved husband, it has since been documented that she succumbed to a flu-like fever and complications from diabetes.

With the passing of Zewditu, Tafari himself became emperor and was proclaimed *Neguse Negest ze-'Ityopp'ya*, "King of Kings of Ethiopia". He was crowned on 2 November 1930 at Addis Ababa's Cathedral of St. George. The coronation was by all accounts "a most splendid affair", and it was attended by royals and dignitaries from all over the world.

Among those in attendance were George V's son Prince Henry, Marshal Franchet d'Esperey of France, and the Prince of Udine representing Italy. Emissaries from the United States, Egypt, Turkey, Sweden, Belgium, and Japan were also present. British author Evelyn Waugh was also present, penning a contemporary report on the event, and American travel lecturer Burton Holmes shot the only known film footage of the event.

One newspaper report suggested that the celebration may have incurred a cost in excess of $3,000,000. Many of those in attendance received lavish gifts; in one instance, the Christian Emperor even sent a gold-encased Bible to an American bishop who had not attended the coronation but who had dedicated a prayer to the Emperor on the day of the coronation.

Haile Selassie introduced Ethiopia's first written constitution on 16 July 1931, providing for a bicameral legislature. The constitution kept power in the hands of the nobility but it did establish democratic standards among the nobility, envisaging a transition to democratic rule: it would prevail "until the people are in a position to elect themselves."

The constitution limited the succession to the throne to the descendants of Haile Selassie, a restriction that met with the disapproval of other dynastic princes including the princes of Tigrai and even the Emperor's loyal cousin,

26

Ras Kassa Haile Darge.

In 1932, the Kingdom of Jimma was formally absorbed into Ethiopia following the death of King Abba Jifar II of Jimma.

Conflict with Italy

Ethiopia became the target of renewed Italian imperialist designs in the 1930s. Benito Mussolini's fascist regime was keen to avenge the military defeats Italy had suffered to Ethiopia in the First Italo-Abyssinian War and to efface the failed attempt by "liberal" Italy to conquer the country, as epitomised by the defeat of Italian forces at Adowa.

A conquest of Ethiopia could also empower the cause of fascism and embolden its rhetoric of empire. Ethiopia would also provide a bridge between Italy's Eritrean and Italian Somaliland possessions.

Ethiopia's position in the League of Nations did not dissuade the Italians from invading Ethiopia in 1935; the "collective security" envisaged by the League proved useless, and a scandal erupted when the Hoare-Laval Pact revealed that Ethiopia's League allies were scheming to appease Italy.

Mobilisation

Following the December, 5th, 1934 Italian invasion of Ethiopia at Walwal, Ogeden Province, Haile Selassie joined his northern armies and set up headquarters at Desse in Wollo province. He issued his famous mobilisation order on 3 October 1935:

"If you withhold from your country Ethiopia the death from cough or head-cold of which you would otherwise die, refusing to resist (in your district, in your patrimony, and in your home) our enemy who is coming from a distant country to attack us, and if you persist in not shedding your blood, you will be rebuked for it by your Creator and will be cursed by your offspring. Hence, without cooling your heart of accustomed valour, there emerges your decision to fight fiercely, mindful of your history that will last far into the future...

If on your march you touch any property inside houses or cattle and crops outside, not even grass, straw, and dung excluded, it is like killing your brother who is dying with you...

You, countryman, living at the various access routes, set up a market for the army at the places where it is camping and on the day your district-governor will indicate to you, lest the soldiers campaigning for Ethiopia's liberty should experience difficulty. You will not be charged excise duty, until the end of the campaign, for anything you are marketing at the military camps: I have granted you remission...

After you have been ordered to go to war, but are then idly missing from the campaign, and when you are seized by the local chief or by an accuser, you will have punishment inflicted upon your inherited land, your property, and your body; to the accuser I shall grant a third of your property...."

On 19 October 1935, Haile Selassie gave more precise orders for his army to his Commander-in-Chief, Ras Kassa:

1. When you set up tents, it is to be in caves and by trees and in a wood, if the place happens to be adjoining to these—and separated in the various platoons. Tents are to be set up at a distance of 30 cubits from each other.

2. When an aeroplane is sighted, one should leave large open roads and wide meadows and march in valleys and trenches and by zigzag routes, along places which have trees and woods.

3. When an aeroplane comes to drop bombs, it will not suit it to do so unless it comes down to about 100 metres; hence when it flies low for such action, one should fire a volley with a good and very long gun and then quickly disperse. When three or four bullets have hit it, the aeroplane is bound to fall down. But let only those fire who have been ordered to shoot with a weapon that has been selected for such firing, for if everyone shoots who possesses a gun, there is no advantage in this except to waste bullets and to disclose the men's whereabouts.

4. Lest the aeroplane, when rising again, should detect the whereabouts of those who are dispersed, it is well to remain cautiously scattered as long as it is still fairly close. In time of war it suits the enemy to aim his guns at adorned shields, ornaments, silver and gold cloaks, silk shirts and all similar things. Whether one possesses a jacket or not, it is best to wear a narrow-sleeved shirt with faded colours. When we return, with God's help, you can wear your gold and silver decorations then. Now it is time to go and fight. We offer you all these words of advice in the hope that no great harm should befall you through lack of caution. At the same time, We are glad to assure you that in time of war We are ready to shed Our blood in your midst for the sake of Ethiopia's freedom..."

Compared to the Ethiopians, the Italians had an advanced, modern military which included a large air force. The Italians would also come to employ chemical weapons extensively throughout the conflict, even targeting Red Cross field hospitals in violation of the Geneva Convention.

Progress of the war

Starting in early October 1935, the Italians invaded Ethiopia. On 6 October, Italian honor was avenged when Adwa fell. But, by November, the pace of invasion had slowed appreciably and Haile Selassie's northern armies were able to launch what was known as the "Christmas Offensive. During this offensive, the Italians were forced back in places and put on the defensive. However, by early in 1936, the First Battle of Tembien stopped the progress of the Ethiopian offensive and the Italians were ready to continue their onslaught.

Following the defeat and destruction of the northern Ethiopian armies at the Battle of Amba Aradam, the Second Battle of Tembien, and the Battle of Shire, Haile Selassie took the field with the last Ethiopian army on the northern front. On 31 March 1936, he launched a counterattack against the Italians himself at the Battle of Maychew in southern Tigray. The Emperor's army was defeated and retreated in disarray. As Haile Selassie's army withdrew, the Italians attacked from the air along with rebellious Raya and Azebo tribesmen on the ground who were armed and paid by the Italians.

Haile Selassie made a solitary pilgrimage to the churches at Lalibela at considerable risk of capture before returning to his capital. After a stormy session of the council of state, it was agreed that because Addis Ababa could not be defended, the government would relocate to the southern town of Gore, and that in the interest of preserving the Imperial house, the Emperor's wife Menen Asfaw and the rest of the Imperial family should immediately depart for Djibouti and from there continue on to Jerusalem.

Exile debate

After further debate as to whether Haile Selassie should go to Gore or accompany his family into exile, it was agreed that Haile Selassie should leave Ethiopia with his family and present the case of Ethiopia to the League of Nations at Geneva. The decision was not unanimous and several participants, including the nobleman Page (*Blatta*) Tekle Wolde Hawariat, objected to the idea of an Ethiopian monarch fleeing before an invading force._ Haile Selassie appointed his cousin Ras Imru Haile Selassie as prince regent in his absence and left with his family for Djibouti on 2 May 1936.

On 5 May, Marshal Pietro Badoglio led Italian troops into Addis Ababa and Mussolini declared Ethiopia an Italian province. Victor Emanuel III was proclaimed as the new emperor of Ethiopia.

However, on the previous day, the Ethiopian exiles had left Djibouti aboard the British cruiser HMS *Enterprise*. They were bound for Jerusalem in the British Mandate of Palestine where the Ethiopian royal family maintained a residence. The Imperial family disembarked at Haifa and then went on to Jerusalem. Once there, Haile Selassie and his retinue prepared to make their case at Geneva.

The choice of Jerusalem was highly symbolic, since the Solomonic Dynastry claimed descent from the House of David.

Leaving the holy Land, Haile Selassie and his entourage sailed for Gibraltar aboard the British cruiser HMS *Capetown*. From Gibraltar, the exiles were transferred to an ordinary liner. By doing this, the government of the United Kingdom was spared the expense of a state reception.

Collective security and the League of Nations, 1936

Mussolini, upon invading Ethiopia, had promptly declared his own "Italian Empire"; because the League of Nations afforded Haile Selassie the opportunity to address the assembly, Italy even withdrew its League delegation on 12 May 1936. It was in this context that Haile Selassie walked into the hall of the League of Nations, introduced by the president of the Assembly as "His Imperial Majesty, the Emperor of Ethiopia" (*Sa Majesté Imperiale, l'Empereur d'Ethiopie*).

The introduction caused a great many Italian journalists in the galleries to erupt into jeering, heckling, and whistling. As it turned out, they had earlier been issued whistles by Mussolini's son-in-law, Count Galeazzo Ciano.

Haile Selassie waited calmly for the hall to be cleared and responded "majestically" with a speech sometimes considered among the most stirring of the 20th century.

Although fluent in French, the working language of the League, Haile Selassie chose to deliver his historic speech in his native Amharic. He asserted that, because his "confidence in the League was absolute", his people were now being slaughtered. He pointed out that the same European states which found in Ethiopia's favour at the League of Nations were refusing Ethiopia credit and *matériel* while helping Italy which was using chemical weapons on military and civilian targets alike:

"It was at the time when the operations for the encircling of Makale were taking place that the Italian command, fearing a rout, followed the procedure which it is now my duty to denounce to the world.

Special sprayers were installed on board aircraft so that they could vaporise, over vast areas of territory, a fine, death-dealing rain. Groups of nine, fifteen, eighteen aircraft followed one another so that the fog issuing from them formed a continuous sheet.

It was thus that, as from the end of January 1936, soldiers, women, children, cattle, rivers, lakes, and pastures were drenched continually with this deadly rain. In order to kill off systematically all living creatures, in order to more surely poison waters and pastures, the Italian command made its aircraft pass over and over again. That was its chief method of warfare."

Noting that his own "small people, 12 million inhabitants, without arms, without resources" could never withstand an attack by a large power such as Italy, with its 42 million people and "unlimited quantities of the most death-dealing weapons", he contended that all small states were threatened by the aggression, and that all small states were in effect reduced to vassal states in the absence of collective action. He admonished the League that "God and history will remember your judgment."

"It is collective security: it is the very existence of the League of Nations. It is the confidence that each State is to place in international treaties... In a word, it is international morality that is at stake. Have the signatures appended to a Treaty value only in so far as the signatory Powers have a personal, direct and immediate interest involved?"

The speech made the Emperor Haile Selassie an icon for anti-fascists around the world, and *Time* magazine named him "Man of the Year".

He failed, however, to get what he most needed: the League agreed to only partial and ineffective sanctions on Italy, and several members even recognised the Italian conquest of Ethiopia.

Exile

Haile Selassie spent his exile years (1936–1941) in Bath, United Kingdom, in Fairfield House, which he bought. The Emperor and Kassa Haile Darge took morning walks together behind the high walls of the 14-room Georgian house. Haile Selassie's favourite reading was "diplomatic history." But most of his serious hours were occupied with the 90,000-word story of his life which he was laboriously writing in Amharic.

Before moving into Fairfield House, he briefly stayed at Warne's Hotel in Worthing and in Parkside, Wimbledon. A bust of Haile Selassie is in nearby Cannizaro Park to commemorate this time and is a popular place of pilgrimage for London's Rastafarian community.

Haile Selassie stayed at the Abbey Hotel in Malvern in the 1930s and his granddaughters and daughters of court officials were educated at Clarendon School in North Malvern.

During his time in Malvern, he attended services at Holy Trinity Church in Link Top. A blue plaque, commemorating his stay in Malvern, was unveiled on Saturday, 25 June 2011. As part of the ceremony, a delegation from the Rastafari movement gave a short address and a drum recital.

Haile Selassie's activity in this period was focused on countering Italian propaganda as to the state of Ethiopian resistance and the legality of the occupation. He spoke out against the desecration of houses of worship and historical artifacts (including the theft of a 1,600-year old imperial obelisk), and condemned the atrocities suffered by the Ethiopian civilian population.

He continued to plead for intervention by the League of Nations and to voice his certainty that "God's judgment will eventually visit the weak and the mighty alike," although his attempts to gain support for the struggle against Italy were largely unsuccessful until Italy entered World War II on the German side in June 1940.

The Emperor's pleas for international support did take root in the United States, particularly among African American organisations sympathetic to the Ethiopian cause.

In 1937, Haile Selassie was to give a Christmas Day radio address to the American people to thank his supporters when his taxi was involved in a traffic accident, leaving him with a fractured knee. Rather than cancelling the radio appearance, he proceeded in much pain to complete the address in which he linked Christianity and goodwill with the Covenant of the League of Nations and asserted that "War is not the only means to stop war":

"With the birth of the Son of God, an unprecedented, an unrepeatable, and a long-anticipated phenomenon occurred. He was born in a stable instead of a palace, in a manger instead of a crib. The hearts of the Wise men were struck by fear and wonder due to His Majestic Humbleness. The kings prostrated themselves before Him and worshipped Him. 'Peace be to those who have good will'. This became the first message.

Although the toils of wise people may earn them respect, it is a fact of life that the spirit of the wicked continues to cast its shadow on this world. The arrogant are seen visibly leading their people into crime and destruction. The laws of the League of Nations are constantly violated and wars and acts of aggression repeatedly take place... So that the spirit of the cursed will not gain predominance over the human race whom Christ redeemed with his blood, all peace-loving people should cooperate to stand firm in order to preserve and promote lawfulness and peace."

During this period, Haile Selassie suffered several personal tragedies. His two sons-in-law, Ras Desta Damtew and Dejazmach Beyene Merid, were both executed by the Italians. The Emperor's daughter, Princess Romanework, wife of Dejazmach Beyene Merid, was herself taken into captivity with her children and died in Italy in 1941. His daughter Tsehai died during childbirth shortly after the imperial restoration in 1942.

After his return to Ethiopia, he donated Fairfield House to the city of Bath as a residence for the aged, until modified in the 1990s; it is now used as a residential meeting centre.

1940s and 1950s

British forces, which consisted primarily of Ethiopian-backed African and South African colonial troops under the "Gideon Force" of Colonel Orde Wingate" coordinated the military effort to liberate Ethiopia. The Emperor himself issued several imperial proclamations in this period, demonstrating that, while authority was not divided up in any formal way, British military might and the Emperor's populist appeal could be joined in a concerted effort to liberate Ethiopia.

On 18 January 1941, during the East African campaign, Haile Selassie crossed the border between Sudan and Ethiopia near the village of Um Iddla. The standard of the Lion of Judah was raised again. Two days later, he and a force of Ethiopian patriots joined Gideon Force which was already in Ethiopia and preparing the way. Italy was defeated by a force of the United Kingdom, the Commonwealth of Nations, Free France, Free Belgium, and Ethiopian patriots. On 5 May 1941, Haile Selassie entered Addis Ababa and personally addressed the Ethiopian people, five years to the day since his 1936 exile:

"Today is the day on which we defeated our enemy. Therefore, when We say let us rejoice with our hearts, let not our rejoicing be in any other way but in the spirit of Christ. Do not return evil for evil. Do not indulge in the atrocities which the enemy has been practising in his usual way, even to the last.

Take care not to spoil the good name of Ethiopia by acts which are worthy of the enemy. We shall see that our enemies are disarmed and sent out the same way they came. As St. George who killed the dragon is the Patron

Saint of our army as well as of our allies, let us unite with our allies in everlasting friendship and amity in order to be able to stand against the godless and cruel dragon which has newly risen and which is oppressing mankind."

After World War II, Ethiopia became a charter member of the United Nations. In 1948, the Ogaden, a region disputed with Somalia, was granted to Ethiopia by the UN. On 2 December 1950, the UN General Assembly adopted Resolution 390 (V), to incorporate Eritrea (the former Italian colony) into Ethiopia in order to form a federation. Eritrea was to have its own constitution which would provide for ethnic, linguistic, and cultural balance, while Ethiopia was to manage its finances, defence, and foreign policy.

Despite his centralisation policies that had been made before World War II, Haile Selassie still found himself unable to push for all the programmes he wanted. In 1942, he attempted to institute a progressive tax scheme, but this failed due to opposition from the nobility, and only a flat tax was passed; in 1951, he agreed to reduce this as well.

Ethiopia was still "semi-feudal", and the emperor's attempts to alter its social and economic form by reforming its modes of taxation met with resistance from the nobility and the clergy who were eager to resume their privileges in the postwar era. Where Haile Selassie actually did succeed in effecting new land taxes, the burdens were often passed by the landowners to the peasants. Despite his wishes, the tax burden remained primarily on the peasants.

Between 1941 and 1959, Haile Selassie worked to establish the autocephaly of the Ethiopian Orthodox Church. The Ethiopian Orthodox Church had been headed by the *abuna*, a bishop who answered to the Partriarchate in Egypt. Haile Selassie applied to Egypt's Holy Synod in 1942 and 1945 to establish the independence of Ethiopian bishops and, when his appeals were denied. he threatened to sever relations with the See of St. Mark.

Finally, in 1959, Pope Kyrillos VI elevated the Abuna to Patriarch-Catholicos. The Ethiopian Church remained affiliated with the Alexandrian Church. In addition to these efforts, Haile Selassie changed the Ethiopian church-state relationship by introducing taxation of church lands and by restricting the legal privileges of the clergy who had formerly been tried in their own courts for civil offences.

In keeping with the principle of collective security, for which he was an outspoken proponent, he sent a contingent under General Mulugueta Bulli, known as the Kagnew Battalion, to take part in the Korean War by supporting the United Nations Command. It was attached to the American 7th Infantry Division and fought in a number of engagements including the Battle of Pork Chop Hill. In a 1954 speech, Emperor Haile Selassie spoke of Ethiopian participation in the Korean War as a redemption of the principles of collective security:

"Nearly two decades ago, I personally assumed before history the responsibility of placing the fate of my beloved people on the issue of collective security, for surely, at that time and for the first time in world history, that issue was posed in all its clarity. My searching of conscience convinced me of the rightness of my course and if, after untold sufferings and, indeed, unaided resistance at the time of aggression, we now see the final vindication of that principle in our joint action in Korea, I can only be thankful that God gave me strength to persist in our faith until the moment of its recent glorious vindication."

During the celebrations of his Silver Jubilee in November 1955, Haile Selassie introduced a revised constitution under which he retained effective power, while extending political participation to the people by allowing the lower house of parliament to become an elected body. But party politics were not allowed.

Modern educational methods were more widely spread throughout Ethiopia and the country embarked on a development scheme and plans for modernisation, tempered by Ethiopian traditions and within the framework of the ancient monarchical structure of the state.

Haile Selassie compromised when practical with the traditionalists in the nobility and the church. He also tried to improve relations between the state and ethnic groups and granted autonomy to Afar lands that were difficult to control. Still, his reforms to end feudalism were slow and weakened by the compromises he made with the entrenched aristocracy.

The revised constitution of 1955 has been criticised for reasserting "the indisputable power of the monarch" and maintaining the relative powerlessness of the peasants.

Haile Selassie Charity Experience

His Majesty Emperor Haile Selassie I had sent aid to the British Government in 1947 when Britain was affected by heavy flooding. In a letter sent written by His Imperial Majesty addressed to Lord Meork National Distress Fund London,He said, "even though We are busy of helping our people who didn't recover from the crises of the war, we heard that your fertile and beautiful country is devastated by the unusually heavy rain, and your request for aid. Therefore, We are sending small amount of money, about one thousand pounds through our embassy to show our sympathy and cooperation." Source: *Addis Zemen* newspaper, Addis Ababa, Ethiopia, 3 October 1947.

1960s

Haile Selassie contributed Ethiopian troops to the United Nations operation in the Congo peacekeeping force in 1960 during the Congo crisis to consolidate Congolese integrity and independence.

On 13 December 1960, while Haile Selassie was on a state visit to Brazil, his Imperial Guard forces staged an unsuccessful coup, briefly proclaiming Haile Selassie's eldest son Asaf Wossen as the new emperor. The coup was crushed by the regular army and police forces. The coup attempt lacked broad popular support, was denounced by the Ethiopian Orthodox Church, and was unpopular in the army, the police and the air force. Nonetheless, the effort to depose Haiale Selassie had support among students and the educated classes.

The coup attempt has been characterised as a pivotal moment in Ethiopian history, the point at which Ethiopians "for the first time questioned the power of the king to rule without the people's consent."

Student populations began to empathise with the peasantry and the poor and to advocate on their behalf. The coup spurred Haile Selassie to accelerate reforms which manifested in the form of land grants to military and police officials. But the reforms were not enough to bring about fundamental change to improve the lives of ordinary Ethiopians most of whom were peasants.

The Emperor continued to be a staunch ally of the West, while pursuing a firm policy of decolonisation in Africa, which was still largely under European colonial rule.

The United Nations conducted a lengthy inquiry regarding the status of Eritrea, with the superpowers each vying for a stake in the state's future. Britain, the administrator at the time, suggested the partition of Eritrea between Sudan and Ethiopia, separating Christians and Muslims. The idea was instantly rejected by Eritrean political parties, as well as the UN.

A UN plebiscite voted 46 to 10 to have Eritrea federated with Ethiopia, which was later stipulated on 2 December 1950 in a UN resolution. Eritrea would have its own parliament and administration and would be represented in what had been the Ethiopian parliament which would become the federal parliament.

However, Haile Selassie would have none of European attempts to draft a separate constitution under which Eritrea would be governed, and wanted his own 1955 constitution protecting families to apply in both Ethiopia and Eritrea.

Eritreans would have none of that, either.

In 1961 the 30-year Eritrean struggle for independence began, followed by Haile Selassie's dissolution of the federation and shutting down of Eritrea's parliament. The struggle was inevitable because of tensions between independence-minded Eritreans and the Ethiopian authorities.

The Emperor declared Eritrea the fourteenth province of Ethiopia in 1962.

The war would continue for 30 years, as first Haile Selassie, then the Soviet-backed junta that succeeded him, attempted to retain Eritrea by force.

In 1963, Haile Selassie presided over the establishment of the Organisation of African Unity (OAU), with the new organisation establishing its headquarters in the Ethiopian capital Addis Ababa. As more African states won their independence, the Emperor played an important role as a Pan-Africanist and, together with President Modibo Keita of Mali, was successful in negotiating the Bamako Accords which brought an end to the border conflict between Morocco and Algeria.

Also in 1963, on October 6th, Emperor Haile Selassie addressed the General Assembly of the United Nations, referring in his address to his earlier speech to the League of Nations:

"Twenty-seven years ago, as Emperor of Ethiopia, I mounted the rostrum in Geneva, Switzerland, to address the League of Nations and to appeal for relief from the destruction which had been unleashed against my defenceless nation, by the Fascist invader. I spoke then both to and for the conscience of the world. My words went unheeded, but history testifies to the accuracy of the warning that I gave in 1936. Today, I stand before the world organisation which has succeeded to the mantle discarded by its discredited predecessor. In this body is enshrined the principle of collective security which I unsuccessfully invoked at Geneva. Here, in this Assembly, reposes the best — perhaps the last — hope for the peaceful survival of mankind."

On 25 November 1963, Haile Selassie was among other heads of state, including French President Charles de Gaulle, who travelled to Washington, D.C., to attend the funeral of assassinated President John F. Kennedy.

In 1966, Haile Selassie attempted to create a modern, progressive tax that included registration of land which would significantly weaken the nobility. Even with alterations, this law led to a revolt in Gojjam which was repressed although enforcement of the tax was abandoned. The revolt, having achieved its design in undermining the tax, encouraged other landowners to defy Haile Selassie.

Student unrest became a regular feature of Ethiopian life in the 1960s and 1970s. Marxism took root in large segments of the Ethiopian intelligentsia, particularly among those who had studied abroad and had thus been exposed to radical and left-wing sentiments that were becoming popular in other parts of the globe.

Resistance by conservative elements at the Imperial Court and Parliament, and by the Ethiopian Orthodox Church, made Haile Selassie's land reform proposals difficult to implement, and also damaged the standing of the government, costing Haile Selassie much of the goodwill he had once enjoyed. This bred resentment among the peasant population. Efforts to weaken unions also hurt his image.

As these issues began to pile up, Haile Selassie left

much of domestic governance to his prime minister, Akilu Habte Wold, and concentrated more on foreign affairs.

1970s

Outside Ethiopia, Haile Selassie continued to enjoy enormous prestige and respect. As the longest-serving head of state in power, Haile Selassie was often given precedence over other leaders at state events such as the state funerals of John F. Kennedy and Charles de Gaulle, the summits of the Non-Aligned Movement, and the 1971 celebration of the 2,500 years of the Persian Empire. His high profile and frequent travels around the world raised Ethiopia's international image.

Wollo Famine

Famine mostly in Wollo, northeastern Ethiopia, as well as in some parts of Tigray is estimated to have killed 40,000 to 80,000 Ethiopians between 1972 and 1974. Although the region is infamous for recurrent crop failures and continuous food shortage and starvation risk, this episode was remarkably severe. It led to the 1973 production of the ITV programme, *The Unknown Famine*, by Jonathan Dimbleby. Dimbleby's report suggested a far higher death toll than the figure given by the Ethiopian leaders, stimulating a massive influx of aid while at the same time destabilising Haile Selassie's regime.

Some reports suggest that the Emperor was unaware of the extent of the famine, while others assert that he was well aware of it but was ashamed to admit his people were starving.

In addition to the exposure of attempts by corrupt local officials to cover up the famine from the Imperial government, the Kremlin's depiction of Haile Selassie's Ethiopia as backwards and inept (relative to the purported utopia of Mrxism-Leninism) contributed to the popular uprising that led to its downfall and the rise of Mengistu Haile Mariam. The famine and its image in the media undermined popular support for the government and Haile Selassie's once unassailable personal popularity fell.

The crisis was exacerbated by military mutinies and high oil prices, the latter a result of the 1973 oil crisis. The international economic crisis triggered by the oil crisis caused the costs of imported goods, gasoline, and food to skyrocket, while unemployment spiked.

Revolution

In February 1974, four days of serious riots in Addis Ababa against a sudden economic inflation left five dead. The Emperor responded by announcing on national television a rollback of gasoline prices and a freeze on the cost of basic commodities. This calmed the public, but the promised 33% military wage hike was not substantial enough to pacify the army, which then mutinied, beginning in Asmara and spreading throughout the country.

The mutiny led to the resignation of Prime Minister Aklilu Habte Wold on 27 February 1974. Haile Selassie again went on television to agree to the army's demands for still greater pay and named Endelkachew Makonnen as his new prime minister. However, despite Endalkatchew's many concessions, discontent continued in March with a four-day general strike that paralysed the nation.

Imprisonment

The Derg, a committee of low-ranking military officers and enlisted men, set up in June to investigate the military's demands, took advantage of the government's disarray to depose Haile Selassie on 12 September 1974. General Aman Mikael Andom, a Protestant of Eritrean origin, served briefly as provisional head of state pending the return of Crown Prince Asfa Wossen who was then receiving medical treatment abroad.

Haile Selassie was placed under house arrest briefly at the 4th Army Division in Addis Ababa, while most of his family was detained at the late Guke Harrar's residence in the north of the capital. The last months of the emperor's life were spent in imprisonment in the Grand Palace.

Later, most of the Imperial family was imprisoned in the Addis Ababa prison Kerchele, also known as "Alem Bekagne", or "Goodbye, cruel world".

On 23 November 1974, 60 former high officials of the Imperial government, known as "the Sixty", were executed without trial. The executed included Haile Selassie's grandson and two former prime ministers. These killings, known to Ethiopians as "Bloody Saturday," were condemned by Crown Prince Asfa Wossen; the Derg responded to his rebuke by revoking its acknowledgment of his imperial legitimacy and announced the end of the Solomonic dynasty.

Death and interment

On 28 August 1975, the state media officially reported publicly that the "ex-monarch" Haile Selassie had died on 27 August of "respiratory failure" following complications from a prostate operation. His doctor, Asrat Woldeyes, denied that complications had occurred and rejected the government version of his death.

Some imperial loyalists believed that the Emperor had in fact been assassinated, and this belief remains widely held.

One Western correspondent in Ethiopia at the time commented:

"While it is not known what actually happened, there are strong indications that no efforts were made to save him. It is unlikely that he was actually killed. Such rumors were bound to arise no matter what happened, given the atmosphere of suspicion and distrust prevailing in Addis Ababa the time."

Court testimony given by the emperor's servants however indicate that they were ordered to leave the Emperor's rooms for the night and that they returned in the morning to find him dead in his bed, with a strong chemical smell in the room.

They further testified that the Emperor had been in perfect health the night before when they had left him. Professor Asrat Woldeyes also testified that his patient had completely recovered from the effects of the surgery and that there had been no complications.

There were also reports that he was suffocated under a pillow by the soldiers.

The Soviet-backed Derg fell in 1991. In 1992, the Emperor's bones were found under a concrete slab on the palace grounds; some reports suggest that his remains were discovered beneath a latrine.

For almost a decade thereafter, as Ethiopian courts attempted to sort out the circumstances of his death, his coffin rested in Bhata Church near his great uncle Menelik II's imperial resting place.

On 5 November 2000, Haile Selassie was given an Imperial funeral by the Ethiopian Orthodox church. The post-communist government refused calls to declare the ceremony an official imperial funeral.

Although such prominent Rastafarian figures as Rita Marley, the wife of Bob Marley, and others participated in the grand funeral, most Rastafari rejected the event and refused to accept that the bones were the remains of Haile Selassie.

There remains some debate within the Rastafari movement as to whether Haile Selassie actually died in 1975.

Children

Emperor Haile Selassie had six children with his wife, Empress Menen Asfaw, who was born on 25 March 1889 and died on 15 February 1962. Her baptismal name was Wolete Giyorgis.

The children were Princess Tenagnework, Crown Prince Asfaw Wossen, Princess Tsehai, Princess Zenebework, Prince Makonnen, and Prince Sahle Selassie.

There is some controversy as to Haile Selassie's eldest daughter, Princess Romanework Haile Selassie. While the living members of the royal family state that Romanework is the eldest daughter of Empress Menen, it has been asserted that Princess Romanework is actually the daughter of a previous union of the emperor with Woizero Altayech.

The emperor's own autobiography makes no mention of a previous marriage or having fathered children with anyone other than Empress Menen.

Prince Asfaw Wossen was first married to Princess Wolete Israel Seyoum and then following their divorce to Princess Medferiashwork Abebe. Prince Makonnen was married to Princess Sara Gizaw. Prince Sahle Selassie was married to Princess Mahisente Habte Mariam. Princess Romanework married Dejazmatch Beyene Merid.

Princess Tenagnework first married Ras Desta Damtew and, after she was widowed, married Ras Andargachew Messai. Princess Zenebework married Dejazmatch Haile Selassie Gugsa. Princess Tsehai married Lt. General Abiye Abebe.

Rastafari Messiah

Today, Haile Selassie is worshipped as Jesus incarnate by Rastafarians. The Rastafari movement takes its name from Haile Selassie's pre-imperial name *Ras* – meaning *Head*, a title equivalent to Duke – Tafari Makonnen.

The movement started in Jamaica during the 1930s, coincidentally, during the same period when the Nation of Islam – of Black Muslims – started in the city of Detroit in the state of Michigan in the United States.

The Rasfari movement was heavily influenced by a Jamaican black nationalist, Marcus Garvey, who was a strong proponent of Pan-Africanism, a philosophy and ideolgy aimed at uniting all blacks in the world and encouraging those in the diaspora to return to Africa to help build a strong black African homeland or empire.

Haile Selassie is viewed as the messiah who will lead the people of Africa and of the African diaspora to freedom. His official titles are *Conquering Lion of the Tribe of Judah* and *King of Kings and Elect of God.* His traditional lineage is thought to be from King Solomon and the Queen of Sheba who is known as Makeda in Ethiopian history and tradition.

These notions are perceived by Rastafarians as proof and confirmation of the return of the Messiah in the prophetic Book of Revelation in the New Testament: *King of Kings, Lord of Lords, Conquering Lion of the Tribe of Judah,* and *Root of David.*

The Rastafari faith in the incarnate divinity of Haile Selassie began after news reports of his coronation reached Jamaica, particularly via the two *Time* magazine articles on the coronation the week before and the week after the event. Haile Selassie's own perspectives permeate the philosophy of the movement.

Not all Rastafarian mansions – branches of the Rastafari movement – consider Haile Selassie as Jesus Christ incarnate. One example is The Twelve Tribes of Israel who consider him a divinely anointed king, thus Christ in his kingly character and defender of the Christian faith.

In 1961, the Jamaican government sent a delegation composed of both Rastafari and non-Rastafari leaders to Ethiopia to discuss the matter of repatriation, among other issues, with the Emperor. He reportedly told the Rastafarian delegation which included Mortimer Planno: "Tell the Brethren to be not dismayed, I personally will give my assistance in the matter of repatriation."

Haile Selassie visited Jamaica on 21 April 1966. Approximately one hundred thousand Rastafari from all over Jamaica descended on Palisadoes Airport in Kingston, having heard that the man whom they considered to be their Messiah was coming to visit them. Spliffs and chalices were openly smoked, causing "a haze of ganja smoke" to drift through the air.

Haile Selassie arrived at the airport but was unable to come down the mobile steps of the airplane, as the crowd rushed the tarmac. He then returned into the plane, disappearing for several more minutes. Finally, Jamaican authorities were obliged to request Ras Mortimer Planno, a well-known Rasta leader, to climb the steps, enter the plane, and negotiate the Emperor's descent. Planno re-emerged and announced to the crowd: "The Emperor has instructed me to tell you to be calm. Step back and let the Emperor land."

That day is widely held by scholars to be a major turning point for the movement. And it is still commemorated by Rastafarians as Grounation Day, the anniversary of which is celebrated as the second holiest holiday after November 2nd, the Emperor's Coronation Day.

From then on, as a result of Planno's actions, the Jamaican authorities were asked to ensure that Rastafarian representatives were present at all state functions attended by His Majesty. And Rastafarian elders also ensured that they obtained a private audience with the Emperor where he reportedly told them that they should not emigrate to Ethiopia until they had first liberated the people of Jamaica. This dictum came to be known as "liberation before repatriation."

Haile Selassie defied expectations of the Jamaican authorities and never rebuked the Rastafari for their belief in him as the returned Jesus. Instead, he presented the movement's faithful elders with gold medallions – the only recipients of such an honour on this visit.

During PNP leader (later Jamaican Prime Minister) Michael Manley's visit to Ethiopia in October 1969, the Emperor allegedly still recalled his 1966 reception with amazement and stated that he felt that he had to be respectful of their beliefs. This was the visit when Manley received the Rod of Correction or Rod of Joshua as a present from the Emperor, which is thought to have helped him to win the 1972 election in Jamaica.

Rita Marley, Bob Marley's wife, converted to the Rastafari faith after seeing Haile Selassie on his Jamaican trip. She claimed in interviews (and in her book *No Woman, No Cry*) that she saw a *stigmata* print on the palm of Haile Selassie's hand as he waved to the crowd which resembled the markings on Christ's hands from being nailed to the cross – a claim that was not supported by other sources but was used as evidence for her and other Rastafarians to suggest that Haile Selassie was indeed their messiah.

She was also influential in the conversion of Bob Marley, who then became internationally recognised as a Rastafarian besides being an icon of reggae music. As a result, Rastafari became much better known throughout much of the world. Bob Marley's posthumously released song , *Iron Lion Zion*, refers to Haile Selassie.

Haile Selassie's attitude to the Rastafari

According to Robert Earl Hood, Haile Selassie "never denied or affirmed his divinity." In *Reggae Routes: The Story of Jamaican Music*, Kevin Chang and Wayne Chen state:

"It's often said, though no definite date is ever cited, that Selassie himself denied his divinity. Former senator and *Gleaner* editor, Hector Wynter, tells of asking him, during his visit to Jamaica in 1966, when he was going to tell Rastafarians he was not God. 'Who am I to disturb their belief?' replied the emperor."

After his return to Ethiopia, he dispatched Archbishop Abuna Yesehaq Mandefro to the Caribbean to help draw Rastafarians and other West Indians to the Ethiopian church and, according to some sources, denied his divinity.

In 1948, Haile Selassie donated a piece of land at Shashamane, 155 miles south of Addis Ababa, for the use of people of African descent from the West Indies. Numerous Rastafari families settled at Shashamane. And many of them still live there as a community.

Jomo Kenyatta

Jomo Kenyatta (*c.* 1894 – 22 August 1978) served as the first prime minister (1963–1964) and president (1964–1978) of Kenya.

Some biographers say he was born in 1889. Others say he was born in 1891. What is probably not in dispute is that he was born in the 1890s, most likely in the early nineties.

He is considered to be the founding father of Kenya

and one of the most prominent leaders of post-colonial Africa together with Kwame Nkrumah, Julius Nyerere, Nnamdi Azikiwe, Ahmed Sekou Toure, Kenneth Kaunda, Milton Obote, Leopold Sedar Senghor, Patrice Lumumba, and a few others.

In Kenya, Nairobi's Jomo Kenyatta International Airport, Kenyatta International Conference Centre, Nairobi's main street and main streets in many Kenyan cities and towns, numerous schools, two universities (Kenyatta University and Jomo Kenyatta University of Agriculture and Technology), the country's main referral hospital, markets, and housing estates are named after him. Also, a statue in downtown Nairobi and monuments all over Kenya stand in his honour.

Kenya observed a public holiday every October 20th in his honour until the new 2010 constitution abolished Kenyatta Day and replaced it with Mashujaa (Heroes') day.

Also, Kenyatta's face adorns Kenyan currency notes and coins of all denominations. But this is expected to change as the new constitution bans the use of the portrait of any person on Kenya's currency.

Early life

Jomo Kenyatta was born Kamau wa Muigai. His father was Muigai, and his mother, Wambui.

He was born in the village of Gatundu in what was then known as British East Africa before the country was renamed Kenya. He was a member of the Kikuyu ethnic group, the largest in the country.

His date of birth, sometime in the early to mid 1890s, is unclear, and was unclear even to him, as his parents were almost certainly not literate, and no formal birth records of Africans were kept in Kenya at that time.

His father died while Kamau was very young after

52

which, as per custom, he was adopted by his uncle Ngengi, who also inherited his mother, to become Kamau wa Ngengi. When his mother died during childbirth, young Kamau moved from Ng'enda to Muthiga to live with his grandfather Kũngũ wa Magana, to whom he became very close.

He then left home to become a resident pupil at the Church of Scotland Mission (CSM) at Thogoto, close to Kikuyu Town, about 12 miles northwest of Nairobi. He studied amongst other subjects: the Bible, English, mathematics, and carpentry. He paid the school fees by working as a houseboy and as a cook for a white settler living nearby.

In 1912, having completed his mission school education, he became an apprentice carpenter. The following year he underwent initiation ceremonies, including circumcision, to become a member of the *kihiumwiri* age group.

In 1914, he converted to Christianity, assuming the name John Peter, which he then changed to Johnstone Kamau. He left the mission later that year to seek employment.

He first worked as an apprentice carpenter on a sisal farm in Thika under the tutelage of John Cook who had been in charge of the building programme at Thogoto. During the First World War, the Kikuyu were forced into work by the British authorities. To avoid this, Kamau went to live with Maasai relatives in Nnarok where he worked as a clerk for an Asian contractor.

In 1919 he married Grace Wahu under Kikuyu customs. When Grace got pregnant, his church elders ordered him to get married before a European magistrate and undertake the appropriate church rites.

Kamau's first son, Peter Muigai, was born on 20 November 1920.

Kamau served as an interpreter in the Nairobi High Court and had a shop (store) at his Dagoreti home during that period. He eventually married Grace Wahu in a civil ceremony in 1922. Grace Wahu lived in the Dagoreti home until her death in April 2007 at the age of around 100.

In 1922 Kamau began working as a store clerk and water-meter reader for the Nairobi Municipal Council Public Works Department, once again under John Cook who was the Water Superintendent. Meter reading helped him meet many Kenyan-Asians at their homes who would become important allies later on.

He entered politics after taking interest in the political activities of James Beauttah and Joseph Kang'ethe, the leaders of the Kikuyu Central Association (KCA). He joined the KCA in 1924 and rose up the ranks of the association. Eventually he began to edit the KCA's Kikuyu newspaper. By 1928 he had become the KCA's general secretary.

In 1928 he launched a monthly Kikuyu-language newspaper called *Mwĩgwithania* (*Reconciler*) which aimed to unite all sections of the Kikuyu. The paper, supported by an Asian-owned printing press, had a mild and unassuming tone, and was tolerated by the colonial government. He also made a presentation on Kikuyu land problems before the Hilton Young Commission in Nairobi in the same year.

Overseas

In 1929 the KCA sent Kenyatta to London to present African grievances before the Colonial office. One of the main subjects was land which had been taken from the Kikuyu by the colonial settlers. He wrote articles to British newspapers about the matter.

Indian leader Mr. Isher Dass, who was also a member of Kenya's Legislative Council (commonly known as Legco), collected the funds for Kenyatta's trip to Britain.

Kenyatta returned to Kenya on 24 September 1930 and

was welcomed at Mombasa by his wife Wahu and James Beauttah.

He then took part in the debate on the issue of female circumcision – female genital mutilation of girls – a common practice among the Kikuyu. Kenyatta sided with the traditionalists to defend the practice which was an integral part of Kikuyu culture. He later worked for Kikuyu Independent Schools in Githunguri.

He returned to London in 1931 and enrolled as a student at Woodbrooke Quaker College in Birmingham.

From 1932 to 1933, he briefly studied economics in Moscow at the Comintern School, KUTVU (University of the Toilers of the East) before his sponsor, the Trinidadian communist and Pan-Africanist George Padmore, fell out with his Soviet hosts, forcing Kenyatta to move back to London.

In 1934, Kenyatta enrolled at University College London. And from 1935, he studied social anthropology under Bronislaw Malinowski at the London School of Economics (LSE). He published his revised LSE thesis as *Facing Mount Kenya* in 1938 under his new name, Jomo Kenyatta. The name "Jomo" is translated in English to "Burning Spear", while the name "Kenyatta" was said to be a reference to the beaded Masai belt he wore, and later to "the Light of Kenya."

During this period, he was also an active member of a group of African, Caribbean and American intellectuals who included Trinidadians C.L. R. James and Eric Williams, W.A. Wallace Johnson, a Sierra Leonean; Paul Robeson and Ralph Bunche, both black Americans. During his presidency, a number of streets in Nairobi were named after those early black-emancipation intellectuals.

Kenyatta acted as an extra in the film *Sanders of the River* (1934) directed by Alexander Korda and starring Paul Robeson.

During World War II, he worked as a labourer at an English farm in Sussex and lectured on Africa for the

Workers' Educational Association.

In 1942, he married an Englishwoman, Edna Clarke. He also published *My People of Kikuyu* and *The Life of Chief Wang'ombe, a history shading into legend.* Edna gave birth to their son, Peter Magana, in 1943. The son was named after Kenyatta's grandfather.

In 1945, with other prominent African nationalists, Kenyatta helped organise the fifth Pan-African Congress held in Manchester, England. He and Nkrumah served as secretaries.

He left Edna Clarke behind in Britain when he returned to Kenya in 1946.

Return to Kenya

Kenyatta returned to Kenya in 1946, after almost 15 years abroad.

He married for the third time, to Grace Wanjiku, Senior Chief Koinange's daughter, and sister to Mbiyu Koinange who later became a lifelong confidant and one of the most powerful politicians during Kenyatta's presidency.

Kenyatta then went into teaching, becoming principal of Kenya Teachers' College, Githunguri.

In 1947, he was elected president of the Kenya African Union (KAU). He began to receive death threats from white settlers after his election.

From 1948 to 1951 he toured and lectured around the country condemning idleness, robbery, urging hard work while campaigning for the return of the land taken by the white settlers and for independence within three years.

His wife, Grace Wanjiku, died in childbirth in 1950 as she gave birth to daughter Jane Wambui, who survived.

In 1951 Kenyatta married Ngina Muhoho, daughter of Chief Muhoho. She was popularly referred to as Mama Ngina and was independent Kenya's First Lady when Kenyatta was elected president.

The Mau Mau uprising began in 1951 and KAU was banned. A state of emergency was declared on 20 October 1952.

Trial and imprisonment

Kenyatta was arrested in October 1952 and indicted with five others on the charges of "managing and being a member" Mau Mau. Mau Mau was an anti-colonial movement.

The accused were known as the "Kapenguria Six." They were Bildad Kaggia, Kung'u Karumba, Jomo Kenyatta, Fred Kubai, Paul Ngei, and Achieng' Oneko.

The trial lasted five months. Rawson Macharia, the main prosecution witness, turned out to have perjured himself. The judge – who had only recently been awarded an unusually large pension and who maintained secret contact with the then colonial Governor of Kenya Evelyn baring during the trial – was openly hostile to the defendants' cause.

The defence, led by British lawyer Dennis Pritt, argued that the white settlers were trying to scapegoat Kenyatta and that there was no evidence tying him to Mau Mau.

The court sentenced Kenyatta on 8 April 1953 to seven years imprisonment with hard labour and indefinite restriction thereafter. Appeal was denied by the British Privy Council in 1954.

Kenyatta remained in prison at Kapenguria in the arid northern part of Kenya until 1959, after which he was detained in Lodwar, another remote part of the country. His compatriots were also imprisoned at Kapenguria.

The state of emergency was lifted on 12 January 1960.

On 28 February 1960, a public meeting of 25,000 in Nairobi demanded Kenyatta's release.

On 15 April 1960, more than one million signatures for a plea to release him were presented to the British governor of Kenya.

On 14 May 1960, Kenyatta was elected *in abstentia* – he was still in confinement – as president of the Kenya African National Union (KANU), the leading nationalist party in the country demanding independence.

On 23 March 1961, Kenyan leaders, including Daniel arap Moi, later his long time vice president and successor as president, visited him at Lodwar.

On 11 April 1961, he was moved to Maralal with his daughter Margaret where he met with the world press for the first time in eight years.

On 14 Augusr 1961, he was released and brought to Gatundu to a hero's welcome.

While contemporary opinion linked Kenyatta to Mau Mau, historians have questioned his alleged leadership of the radical movement.

Kenyatta was a political moderate. Also, his marriage to the daughters of chiefs who served colonial interests, his post-independence allies (mostly fellow Kikuyus) mainly being former colonial collaborators, and his mistreatment of former Mau Mau fighters after he came to power, all strongly suggest that he had very little regard for Mau Mau. Yet he used it, even if indirectly or simply by association (guilty by association), to build himself as the leading African nationalist in colonial Kenya; which he was.

Leadership

Pre-independence

Kenyatta was admitted into the Legislative Council (Legco) after his release in August 1961, and after Kariuki Njiiri, the son of late Chief Njiiri, gave up his Kigumo seat for him.

In 1961 and 1962, Kenyatta led the KANU delegation

to the first and second Lancaster conferences in London where Kenya's independence constitution was negotiated.

Elections were held in May 1963, pitting Kenyatta's KANU against KADU which was led by Ronald Ngala from the Coast Province. Kenyatta came from the Central Province which was and still is overwhelmingly Kikuyu.

KANU wanted Kenya to be a unitary state. KADU (Kenya African Democratic Union) wanted Kenya to be an ethnic federal state, fearing that smaller tribes would be dominated by the larger ones, especially the Kikuyu and the Luo.

KANU beat KADU by winning 83 seats out of 124.

On 1 June 1963, Kenyatta became prime minister of the autonomous Kenyan government, with Queen Elizabeth II remaining as head of state (after independence, styled as *Queen of Kenya*), represented by a governor-general. He consistently asked white settlers not to leave Kenya and supported reconciliation.

Post-independence

Kenyatta retained the role of prime minister after independence was declared and jubilantly celebrated on 12 December 1963.

On 1 June 1964, Kenyatta became president when he successfully had parliament amend the constitution to make Kenya a republic with his office becoming executive president: the head of state, head of government, and commander-in-chief of the armed forces.

His policy was that of continuity and gradual Africanisation of the government, keeping many colonial civil servants in their old jobs as they were gradually replaced by Kenyans.

He also asked for British troops' help against Somali rebels, known as *Shiftas*, in the northeast and in ending an army mutiny in Nairobi in January 1964.

On 10 November 1964, KADU officially dissolved and

its representatives joined KANU, forming a single party.

Kenyatta was re-elected unopposed in 1966, and the next year had the constitution amended to expand his powers. This term of his presidency featured border conflicts with Somalia and more political opposition.

He made KANU, dominated by members of his tribe the Kikuyu, practically the only political party in the country. He consolidated his power greatly and placed several of his Kikuyu tribesmen in most of the powerful state and security offices and posts.

State security forces harassed dissidents and were suspected of complicity in several murders of prominent personalities deemed as threats to his regime, including Pio Gama Pinto, Tom Mboya, and J. M. Kariuki. MP and Lawyer C.M.G. Argwings-Kodhek and former KADU leader and minister, Ronald Ngala, also died in suspicious car accidents.

In 1968 he published his biography *Suffering Without Bitterness*.

In the 1969 elections, Kenyatta banned the only other party, the Kenya People's Union (KPU), formed and led by his former vice president, Jaramogi Oginga Odinga, who had been forced to quit KANU along with his left-leaning allies. He detained its leaders and called elections in which only KANU was allowed to participate.

On 29 January 1970, he was sworn in as president for a further term. For the remainder of his presidency, Kenya was effectively a one-party state, and Kenyatta made use of detention, appeals to ethnic loyalties, and careful appointment of government jobs to maintain his commanding position in Kenya's political system.

However, his advancing age kept him from the day-to-day management of government affairs. He intervened only when necessary to settle disputed issues. His relative isolation resulted in increasing domination of Kenya's affairs by well-connected Kikuyus who acquired great wealth as a result.

Kenyatta was again re-elected as president in 1974 in elections in which he, again, ran alone. He was sworn in as president for a third term on 5 November 1974. His increasingly feeble health meant that his inner circle effectively ruled the country and greatly enriched themselves, in his name.[12] He remained president until his death four years later in 1978.

Death

President Kenyatta had suffered a heart attack in 1966. He would in the mid-seventies lapse into periodic comas lasting from a few hours to a few days from time to time. In April 1977, then well into his 80s, he suffered a massive heart attack.

On 14 August 1978, he hosted his entire family, including his son Peter Magana who flew in from Britain with his family, to a reunion in Mombasa.

On 22 August 1978, President Kenyatta died in Mombasa of natural causes attributable to old age.

Mzee Jomo Kenyatta was buried on 31 August 1978 in Nairobi in a state funeral at a mausoleum on Parliament grounds.

He was succeeded as president after his death by his vice-president Daniel arap Moi.

Legacy

Mzee Jomo Kenyatta, as he was popularly known, was an important and influential statesman in Africa. He is credited with leading Kenya to independence and setting up the country as a relatively prosperous capitalist state. He pursued a moderate pro-Western, anti-Communist economic philosophy and foreign policy. He oversaw the setting up of the institutions of independent Kenya, and also oversaw Kenya's admission into the United Nations.

But his land-reform policy was a failure. The biggest beneficiaries of "land reform" were his fellow Kikuyus and his own family.

During his reign, the country was reasonably well-governed, peaceful and stable, the economy developed and grew rapidly and attracted high levels of foreign investment, and a black Kenyan professional and business middle class was created.

However, Kenyatta was not without major flaws, and did bequeath Kenya some major problems which continue to bedevil the country today, hindering its development, and threatening its existence as a peaceful unitary multi-ethnic state. He failed to mould Kenya, being its founding father, into a homogeneous multi-ethnic state. Instead, the country became and remains a de-facto confederation of competing tribes.

That is in sharp contrast with neighbouring Tanzania where under the leadership of Julius Nyerere, the country was able to virtually conquer tribalism and build a solidly united nation almost without parallel on the continent in spite of the fact that it has about 130 different tribes, in addition to significant numbers of members of racial minorities, especially of Asian and Arab origin, unlike Kenya which has only about 50 tribes although it has a fairly large number of Asians, Arabs and Europeans mostly of British origin.

In fact, one of the main reasons why the majority of Tanzanians are opposed to an East African federation – envisaged to comprise Kenya, Uganda, Tanzania, Rwanda and Burundi – is tribalism in Kenya and in the other countries which they fear will spread to Tanzania if the countries unite under one government.

Also, Kenyatta's resettlement of many Kikuyu tribesmen in the country's Rift Valley Province is widely considered to have been done unfairly.

His authoritarian style, with elements of patronage, favouritism, tribalism and/or nepotism drew criticism and dissent, and set a bad example followed by his successors. He had the constitution radically amended to expand his powers, consolidating executive authority.

He has also been criticised for ruling through a post-colonial clique consisting largely of his relatives, other Kikuyus, mostly from his native Kiambu district, and African Kikuyu colonial collaborators and their offspring, while giving scant reward to those whom most consider the real fighters for Kenya's independence.

This clique became and remains the wealthiest, most powerful and most influential class in Kenya to date, and has held the country back, blocking reform and change, and the emergence of fresh progressive leadership, in its manoeuvres to maintain its power and wealth.

Kenyatta has further been criticised for encouraging the culture of wealth accumulation by public officials using the power and influence of their offices, thereby deeply entrenching corruption in Kenya.

Family

Kenyatta had two children from his first marriage with Grace Wahu: son Peter Muigai Kenyatta (born 1920), who later became a deputy minister; and daughter Margaret Kenyatta (born 1928). Margaret served as mayor of Nairobi between 1970–76 and then as Kenya's ambassador to the United Nations from 1976 -86. Their mother Grace Wahu died in April 2007.

Kenyatta also had one son, Peter Magana Kenyatta (born 1943), from his short marriage with Edna Clarke in Britain.

His third wife, Grace Wanjiku, died when giving birth in 1950. Daughter Jane Wambui survived.

His fourth wife, the best known due to her role as First Lady, was Ngina Kenyatta (née Muhoho), also known as Mama Ngina. She often accompanied him in public and has some streets in Nairobi and Mombasa named after her. She bore Kenyatta four children: Christine Wambui (born 1952), Uhuru Muigai Kenyatta (born 1961), Anna Nyokabi (also known as *Jeni*) and Muhoho Kenyatta (born 1964).

At this writing on 23 December 2011, Mama Ngina was still living quietly as a wealthy widow in Kenya.

Uhuru Kenyatta, Mzee Kenyatta's political heir, unsuccessfully vied for the Kenyan presidency as President Moi's preferred successor in 2002 and is today the Kenyan deputy prime minister and minister for finance.

Muhoho Kenyatta runs his mother's vast family business but lives out of the public limelight.

Jomo Kenyatta was the uncle of Ngethe Njoroge, Kenya's first representative to the United Nations and the great uncle of Tom Morello, the guitarist for Rage Against the Machine. His niece, Beth Mugo, married to a retired ambassador, is a member of parliament and currently serves as Minister for public health.

Books by Jomo Kenyatta

- *Facing Mount Kenya* (1938)
- *My people of Kikuyu and the life of Chief Wangombe* (1944)
- *Suffering Without Bitterness* (biography 1968)
- *Kenya: The land of conflict* (1971)
- *The challenge of Uhuru;: The progress of Kenya, 1968 to 1970* (1971)

Julius Nyerere

Julius Kambarage Nyerere (13 April 1922 – 14 October 1999) was the first president of Tanzania, and previously Tanganyika. He led the country for 24 years since independence in 1961. He stepped down from the presidency in 1985. He was one of the most influential leaders in the history of post-colonial Africa, and one of the longest- ruling. Kenyan scholar Professor Ali Mazrui described Nyerere as "one of the giants of the twentieth century."

Born in Tanganyika to Nyerere Burito (1860–1942), chief of the Zanaki, Julius Nyerere was known by the Swahili name *Mwalimu* or 'teacher', his profession prior to politics. He was also referred to as *Baba wa Taifa*, which in Swahili, or Kiswahili, means Father of the Nation.

He was first named Kambarage when he was born and took the name Julius after he started primary school and later converted to Christianity.

He received his higher education at Makerere University College, which later became a full-fledged university, in Kampala, Uganda, and at the University of Edinburgh in Scotland. He went to Edinburgh to study for his master's degree in October 1949. That was also the first time he went to the UK.

After he returned to Tanganyika in October 1952, he worked as a secondary school teacher. In July 1954, he helped form the Tanganyika African Union (TANU) which led the struggle for independence from Britain.

He became Tanganyika's first prime minister after the country won independence on 9 December 1961. He became president in 1962 when Tanganyika became a republic.

Tanganyika united with Zanzibar on 26 April 1964 to form Tanzania. The new country was first known as the United Republic of Tanganyika and Zanzibar. It changed its name to Tanzania on 29 October 1964. Nyerere became the first president of the United Republic.

Nyerere was first elected as president in 1965. It was also in the same year that Tanzania became a one-party state.

Two years later, Tanzania adopted the Arusha Declaration on 5 February 1967. It was the country's political and economic blueprint which outlined Nyerere's socialist vision of *ujamaa* which means "familyhood" in Kiswahili. *Ujamaa* was Nyerere's version of African socialism.

Nyerere retired in 1985 but remained chairman of the ruling party known in Kiswahili as Chama Cha Mapinduzi which means the Party of the Revolution or Revolutionary Party. He continued to wield enormous influence in that position. Even after he stepped down and was no longer chairman of the ruling party, he still exerted a lot of influence and national leaders often sought his advice.

Nyerere died of leukemia in London in 1999. In 2009, he was named "World Hero of Social Justice" by the president of the United Nations (UN) General Assembly.

Early life and education

Kambarage Nyerere was born on 13 April 1922 in the village of Butiama in what is now Mara Region on the shores of Lake Victoria in northern Tanganyika.. He was one of 26 children of Nyerere Burito.

He began attending Government Primary School in Musoma in 1934 at the age of 12 where he completed the four-year programme in three years and went on to Tabora Government School in 1937. He later described Tabora School as being "as close to Eton as you can get in Africa."

In 1943 he was baptised as a Catholic, taking the baptismal name of Julius.

He received a scholarship to attend Makerere University College where he founded the Tanganyika Welfare Association which eventually merged with the Tanganyika African Association (TAA). TAA was formed in 1929 as an advocacy group seeking better working conditions for African civil servants; it was more social than political in orientation.

Nyerere received his teaching diploma from Makerere in 1947. He returned to Tanganyika and taught for 3 years at St. Mary's Secondary School in Tabora. He taught Biology and English.

In 1949 he got a government scholarship to attend the University of Edinburgh. He was the first Tanganyikan to study at a British university. When he was in Edinburgh, he encountered Fabian thinking and began to develop his particular vision of connecting socialism with African communal living.

He obtained a Master of Arts (M.A.) degree in Economics and History in 1952 and returned to Tanganyika in October the same year.

Political career

On his return to Tanganyika, Nyerere took a position teaching History, English and Kiswahili, at St. Francis' College, near Dar es Salaam, the capital.

In 1953 he was elected president of the TAA, a civic organisation dominated by civil servants, that he had been involved with while a student at Makerere.

In 1954 he transformed TAA into the politically oriented Tanganyika African National Union (TANU). TANU's main objective was to achieve national sovereignty for Tanganyika.

A campaign to register new members was launched and, within a year TANU, had become the leading political organisation in the country.

Nyerere's activities attracted the attention of the colonial authorities. He was forced to make a choice between his political activities and teaching. He was reported as saying that he was a "schoolmaster by choice and a politician by accident."

He resigned from teaching and travelled throughout the country speaking to common people and tribal chiefs, trying to garner support for the movement towards independence. He also spoke on behalf of TANU to the Trusteeship Council and the Fourth Committee of the United Nations in New York, demanding independence for Tanganyika.

His oratorical skills and integrity helped Nyerere achieve TANU's goal of winning independence without war or bloodshed. The cooperative British governor, Sir Richard Turnbull, was also a factor in the struggle for independence.

Nyerere entered the colonial Legislative Council (Legco) following the country's first elections in 1958–59 and was elected chief minister following fresh elections in 1960. In 1961 Tanganyika was granted self government and Nyerere became its first prime minister on 9 December 1961.

A year later, Nyerere became president.

He was instrumental in forming the union between the islands of Zanzibar and the mainland Tanganyika to create Tanzania about two months and a half after a coup in Zanzibar on 12 January 1964 which toppled Jamshid bin Abdullah who was the Arab sultan of Zanzibar.

The coup leader, a stonemason from Lira, Uganda, named John Okello, had intended Zanzibar to join Kenya. Nyerere, unnerved by the Tanganyika Army mutiny a few days later, ensured that Okello was barred from returning to Zanzibar after a visit to the mainland.

Economic policies

When in power, Nyerere implemented a socialist economic programme enunciated in the Arusha Declaration and introduced a policy of collectivisation in the country's agricultural system known as ujamaa or "familyhood."

Although some of his policies can be characterised as

socialist, Nyerere was first and foremost an African, and secondly a socialist. He was what is often called an African socialist. He had tremendous faith in rural African people and their traditional values and ways of life unlike some of his socialist contemporaries such as Nkrumah who espoused Marxism-Leninism. He believed that life should be structured around *ujamaa*, or the extended family found in traditional Africa. He believed that in these traditional villages, *ujamaa* had for centuries existed before the continent was colonised.

He believed that Africans were already socialists and that all that they needed to do was return to their traditional mode of life and they would recapture it.

That would be a true repudiation of capitalism, since his society would not rely on capitalism to exist, survive and thrive.

Unfortunately for Nyerere and for Tanzania, *ujamaa* caused agricultural output to plummet. The deficit in cereal grains was more than 1 million tons between 1974 and 1977. Only loans and grants from the World Bank and the IMF in 1975 prevented Tanzania from going bankrupt. By 1979, *ujamaa* villages contained 90% of the rural population but only produced 5% of the national agricultural output.

Subsequently, the country fell on hard economic times, exacerbated by the war against Idi Amin and the six-year drought which hit the country.

Tanzania went from being one of the largest exporters of agricultural products in Africa to being one of the largest importers of those products. The country couldn't even grow enough to feed itself.

A number of reasons have been given to explain why *ujamaa* failed, including hostility by the capitalist West towards Tanzania to make sure that socialism did not succeed. It is claimed that Western countries imposed hard conditions on Tanzania, forcing prices of her export commodities to go down among other things, because they did not want her to become a role model for other African countries and others in the Third World had she succeeded in building a vibrant socialist nation.

It was the era of the Cold War when the East and the West were locked in an ideological rivalry to prove which system was the best, capitalism or communism (or socialism), and the big powers competed for clients in the Third World.

Western hostility towards Tanzania was also attributed to the country's strong support for the liberation movements in the countries of southern Africa still under white minority rule, regimes which were ideologically and economically an integral part of the West.

But there are others, including many Africans, who contend that Tanzania's socialist policies failed because there was no such thing as socialism in traditional societies across the continent. Nyerere was trying to build on something that did not exist. Communal farms and ownership, one of the cornerstones of *ujamaa*, simply don't exist in traditional Africa. Most Africans own their own farms even if they live in closely-knit communities.

Whatever the case, Tanzania's attempt at socialist transformation of the country was probably the most daring experiment in social engineering in Africa during the post-colonial era. And it has left a legacy which continues to inflame passions and fuel debate among many people, not just intellectuals, across the continent and elsewhere around the world.

One internationally renowned African intellectual, Nigerian writer Wole Soyinka, has called for a return to *ujamaa* and for the revival of the Arusha Declaration which was buried when Tanzania adopted free-market policies. He wants that to be done in other African countries as well, not just in Tanzania. He also greatly admires Nyerere as a leader.

Nyerere announced that he would retire after presidential elections in 1985, leaving the country to enter its free market era – forced to do so by structural adjustment programmes (SAP's) imposed by International Monetary Fund (IMF) and World Bank – under the leadership of Ali Hassan Mwinyi.

He was also instrumental in putting both Ali Hassan Mwinyi and Benjamin Mkapa in power. Mwinyi served as president from 1985 to 1995, and Mkapa from 1995 to 2005.

Nyerere remained the chairman of the ruling Chama Cha Mapinduzi (CCM) for five years following his presidency until 1990, and is still recognised as the *Father of the Nation.*

Foreign policy

Nyerere's foreign policy emphasised nonalignment during the Cold War. Under his leadership, Tanzania enjoyed friendly relations with both the Western world and the Eastern bloc, although there were some problems in relations with some Western countries at different times, especially with the United States, Britain, Germany and France, the biggest supporters of white minority regimes in the countries of southern Africa.

Nyerere, along with several other Pan-Africanist leaders founded the Organisation of African Unity (OAU) in Addis Ababa, Ethiopia, in May 1963.

He supported several liberations movements involved in the struggle against white minority rule in the countries of southern Africa. They included the African National Congress (ANC) and the Pan-Africanist Congress (PAC) of South Africa; the Front for the Liberation of Mozambique (Portuguese acronym, FRELIMO) in its fight against Portuguese colonial rule; the Zimbabwe African National Union (ZANU) and the Zimbabwe African People's Union (ZAPU) in their war against the white minority regime of Ian Smith in Rhodesia; and the Popular

71

Movement for the Liberation of Angola (MPLA) in its struggle against Portuguese colonial rule.

Tanzania was the headquarters of all the liberation movements in Africa under the umbrella of the OAU Liberation Committee which also had its headquarters in Tanzania's capital Dar es Salaam.

From the mid-1970s onwards, Nyerere was the chairman of the Frontline States – Tanzania, Zambia, Mozambique, and Botswana – which spearheaded the struggle against white minority rule in the southern part of the continent.

And in 1978, he led Tanzania in the war with Uganda which started when Ugandan military dictator Idi Amin invaded Tanzania and annexed 710 square miles of its territory in the northwestern region of Kagera which borders Uganda. Tanzania won the war and Amin fled into exile, first to Libya and then to Saudi Arabia where he spent the rest of his life.

Nyerere was also instrumental in the 1977 coup in the Seychelles which brought France-Albert René to power. René, a socialist, was president of the Seychelles from 1977 to 2004.

Outside Africa, Nyerere was an inspiration to Walter Lini, the prime minister of Vanuatu, whose theories on Melanesian socialism owed much to the ideas he got from Tanzania, which he visited.

Lecturers inspired by Nyerere also taught at the University of Papua New Guinea in the 1980s, helping educated Melanesians familiarise themselves with his ideas.

Post-presidential activity

After the Presidency, Nyerere remained the chairman of CCM until 1990 when Ali Hassan Mwinyi took over. Nyerere also remained vocal about the extent of corruption and corrupt officials during the Mwinyi administration. He also blocked Jakaya Kikwete's nomination for the presidency, citing that he was too young to run a country. Nyerere was instrumental in getting Benjamin Mkapa elected. Mkapa had been minister of foreign affairs for a time during Nyerere's presidency. Kikwete later became president in 2005.

In one of his famous speeches during the CCM general assembly, Nyerere said *"Ninang'atuka,"* meaning that he was pulling out of politics for good. It is term in the Zanaki language spoken by Nyerere's tribe, one of the smallest in Tanzania. The word has become a part of the Swahili vocabulary, although it has not yet entered the dictionary.

Nyerere kept to his word that Tanzania would be a democratic country. He moved back to his childhood home village of Butiama in northern Tanzania.

During his retirement, he continued to travel the world meeting various heads of government as an advocate for poor countries and especially the South Centre institution. He travelled more widely after retiring than he did when he was president of Tanzania.

One of his last high-profile actions was when he acted as the chief mediator in the Burundi conflict in 1996. He died in a London hospital of leukaemia on 14 October 1999. He was 77.

Positions he held after his presidency:

Chairman of Chama Cha Mapinduzi (1985–1990), Chairman of the independent International South Commission (1987–1990), and Chairman of the South Centre in the Geneva and Dar es Salaam Offices (1990–1999).

In January 2005, the Catholic diocese of Musoma, in his home region of Mara, opened a cause for the beatification of Julius Nyerere. Nyerere was a devout Catholic who attended Mass daily throughout his public life and was known for fasting frequently.

He has received honorary degrees from the University of Edinburgh (UK), Duquesne University (USA), the University of Cairo (Egypt), the University of Nigeria, Nsukka (Nigeria), the University of Ibadan (Nigeria), the University of Liberia (Liberia), the University of Toronto (Canada), Howard University (USA), Jawaharlal Nehru University (India), the University of Havana (Cuba), the National University of Lesotho (Lesotho), the University of the Philippines (the Philippines), Fort Hare University (South Africa), Sokoine University of Agriculture (Tanzania), and Lincoln University (USA).

He received the Nehru Award for International Understanding in 1976, the Third World Prize in 1982, the Nansen Medal for outstanding services to Refugees in 1983, the Lenin Peace Prize in 1987, the International Simón Bolívar Prize in 1992, and the Gandhi Peace Prize in 1995.

President Yoweri Museveni of Uganda awarded Nyerere the Katonga, Uganda's highest military medal, in honour of his opposition to colonialism and Idi Amin's government in 2007.

Cultural influences

Nyerere continued to influence the people of Tanzania after he stepped down as president. His influence lasted for the rest of life.

His ideas of socialism, his humility, his high ethical standards and high moral integrity continue to resonate in many areas of national life in Tanzania. One of those areas is music. One genre of music in which his ideas are articulated is hip hop.

Nyerere believed socialism was an attitude of mind that barred discrimination and entailed equality of all human beings. Therefore, *ujamaa* can be said to have created the social environment for the development of hip hop culture.

Like in other countries, hip hop emerged in post-colonial Tanzania when divisions among the population were prominent, whether by class, ethnicity or gender. Rappers' broadcast messages of freedom, unity, and family, topics that are all reminiscent of the spirit Nyerere put forth in *ujamaa*.

In addition, Nyerere supported the presence of foreign cultures in Tanzania saying, "a nation which refuses to learn from foreign cultures is nothing but a nation of idiots and lunatics...[but] to learn from other cultures does not mean we should abandon our own."

Under his leadership, the ministry of national culture and youth was created to help preserve and promote the country's customs and traditions and national way of life which also reflected the nation's identity.

Publications

- *Freedom and Unity*
- *Freedom and Socialism. A Selection from Writings & Speeches, 1965–1967* (1968)
    - Includes "The Arusha Declaration"; "Education for self-reliance"; "The varied paths to socialism"; "The purpose is man"; and "Socialism and development."
- *Freedom & Development, Uhuru Na Maendeleo* (1974)
    - Includes essays on adult education; freedom and development; relevance; and ten years after independence.
- *Ujamaa — Essays on Socialism'* (1977)
- *Crusade for Liberation* (1979)
- *Julius Kaisari* (a Swahili translation of William Shakespeare's *Julius Caesar*)

- *Mabepari wa Venisi* (a Swahili translation of William Shakespeare's play, *The Merchant of Venice*).

Milton Obote

Apollo Milton Obote (28 December 1925 – 10 October 2005) was the first prime minister and first president of Uganda. He served as prime minister from 1962 to 1966, and as president from 1966 to 197; then again as president from 1980 to 1985.

He led the country to independence from Britain in October 1962.

He was overthrown by Idi Amin in 1971 but regained power in 1980. His second rule was marred by repression and by the deaths of many civilians as a result of a civil war known as the Ugandan Bush War.

Early life

Milton Obote was born at Akokoro village in Apac District in northern Uganda. He was the son of a local chief of the Lango ethnic group, one of the largest in Uganda.

He began his education in 1940 at the Protestant Missionary School in Lira. He later attended Gulu Junior Secondary School, Busoga College and eventually Makerere University College in Kampala, Uganda's capital.

He wanted to study law. But Makerere did not have a faculty of law. Therefore he decided to study arts or social sciences. The subjects he studied included English and geography. His interest in English literature led him take another name, Milton as his middle name, because of his great admiration for English poet Milton who wrote

Paradise Lost, a poetic work Obote liked very much.

He worked in Buganda kingdom in southern Uganda before moving to Kenya where he worked as a construction worker at an engineering firm. While in Kenya, Obote became involved in the Kenyan independence movement. Upon returning to Uganda in 1956, he joined a political party, Uganda National Congress (UNC), and was elected to the colonial Legislative Council (Legco) in 1957.

In 1959, the UNC split into two factions, with one faction under the leadership of Obote merging with Uganda People's Union to form the Uganda People's Congress (UPC).

Prime Minister

In the run up to independence elections, Obote formed a coalition with the Buganda royalist party, Kabaka Yekka. The two parties controlled a parliamentary majority and Obote became prime minister in 1962. He assumed the post on 25 April 1962, appointed by Sir Walter Coutts, then governor-general of Uganda. The following year, the position of governor-general was replaced by a ceremonial presidency to be elected by parliament. Frederick Edward Mutesa, the Kabaka (King) of Buganda, became the ceremonial president, with Obote as executive prime minister.

In January 1964, there was a mutiny at the military barracks at Jinja, Uganda's second-largest city and home to a burgeoning military.

There were similar mutinies in two other eastern African countries, Kenya, and Tanzania where they started on 20 January; all three countries requested the support of troops from the British military. Before the Nritish troops arrived, however, Obote sent Defence Minister Felix Onama to negotiate with the mutineers. Onama was held hostage and agreed to many demands, including significant pay increases for the army and the rapid promotion of many officers. One of the officers who was fast promoted was Idi Amin, future president of Uganda.

In 1965, Kenyans had been barred from leadership positions within the government, and this was followed by the removal of Kenyans *en masse* from Uganda in 1969 under Obote's guidance.

As prime minister, Obote was implicated in a gold smuggling plot, together with Idi Amin, then deputy commander of the Ugandan armed forces. When the parliament demanded an investigation of Obote and the ousting of Amin, he suspended the constitution and declared himself president in March 1966, allocating to himself almost unlimited power under state of emergency rulings.

Several members of his cabinet who were leaders of rival factions in the party were arrested and detained without charge.

In May 1966, the Buganda regional parliament passed a resolution declaring Buganda's incorporation into Uganda to be *de jure* null and void after the suspension of the constitution. Obote responded with armed attack upon Mutesa's palace which ended with Mutesa fleeing into exile Britain.

In 1967, Obote's power was cemented when parliament passed a new constitution which abolished the federal structure of the independence constitution and created an executive presidency.

Presidency

In 1969 there was an attempt on Obote's life. In the aftermath of the attempt, all opposition political parties were banned, leaving Obote as an effectively absolute ruler. A state of emergency was in force for much of the time and many political opponents were jailed without trial for life.

In 1969-70, Obote published a series of pamphlets which were supposed to outline his political and economic policy. The Common Man's Charter was a summary of his approach to socialism. The government took over a 60% share in major private corporations and banks in the country in 1970.

Obote was overthrown in January 1971 by the army while attending a Commonwealth conference in Singapore, and Amin became president. In the two years before the coup, Obote's relations with the West had become strained. Some have suggested that Western Governments were at least aware of, and may have aided, the coup. Obote fled to Tanzania.

The fall of Obote's regime was welcomed and celebrated by many Ugandans. But after Amin took over and unleashed terror, many of the same people who celebrated the downfall of Obote wished he had stayed in power. Amin was worse than Obote.

Second term

In 1979, Idi Amin was ousted by Tanzanian forces aided by Ugandan exiles.

By 1980, Uganda was governed by an interim presidential commission. At the time of the 1980 elections, the chairman of the commission was a close associate of Obote, Paulo Muwanga.

Muwanga was the *de facto* President of Uganda for only a few days from 12 May to 20 May in 1980. He was the third of three presidents who served for short periods of time between Amin's ouster and the setting up of the presidential commission. The other two presidents were Yusuf Lule and Godfrey Binaisa.

The elections in 1980 were won by Obote's Uganda

People's Congress (UPC). But the results were disputed by the opposition whose members believed the elections were rigged. This led to a guerrilla rebellion led by Yoweri Museveni's National Resistance Army (NRA) and several other military groups.

It has been estimated that approximately 100,000 people died as a result of fighting between Obote's Uganda National Liberation Army (UNLA) and the guerrillas.

On 27 July 1985, Obote was deposed again. As in 1971, he was overthrown by his own army commanders in a military coup. This time the commanders were Brigadier Brazilio Olara-Okello and General Tito Okello. The two men briefly ruled the country through a military council. But after a few months of near chaos, Museveni's NRA seized control of the country.

Death in exile

After his second removal from power, Obote fled to Tanzania and later to Zambia. For some years it was rumoured that he would return to Ugandan politics.

In August 2005, however, he announced his intention to step down as leader of the UPC. In September 2005, it was reported that Obote would return to Uganda before the end of 2005.

On 10 October 2005, Obote died of kidney failure in a hospital in Johannesburg, South Africa.

He was given a state funeral attended by President Museveni in the Ugandan capital Kampala in October 2005, to the surprise and appreciation of many Ugandans, since he and Museveni were bitter rivals.

Other groups, such as the Baganda survivors of the Luwero Triangle massacres were bitter that Obote was given a state funeral.

He was survived by his wife and five children. On 28 November 2005, his wife Miria Obote was elected UPC party president.

One of his sons, Jimmy Akena, was elected a member of parliament for Lira municipality, a constituency in northern Uganda which is the ancestral home of the Obote clan.

Idi Amin

Idi Amin Dada (c. 1925 – 16 August 2003) was a military leader and president of Uganda from 1971 to 1979.

Amin joined the British colonial regiment, called the King's African Rifles, in 1946, and eventually held the rank of major-general and commander of the Ugandan army before seizing power in the military coup of January 1971, deposing President Milton Obote. He later promoted himself to field marshal while he was the military head of state.

Amin's rule was characterised by human rights abuses, political repression, ethnic persecution, extra-judicial killings, nepotism, tribalism, regionalism, corruption and gross economic mismanagement. The number of people killed during his reign of terror is estimated by international observers and human rights groups to range from 100,000 to 500,000.

During his years in power, Amin was backed by Libya's ruler Muammar al-Gaddafi as well as the Soviet Union and East Germany, although he seized power with the help of Israel and Britain.

In 1975–1976, Amin became the chairman of the organisation of African Unity (OAU).

In 1977, after the last two British diplomats withdrew from Uganda, Amin declared he had beaten the British and added "CBE," for "Conqueror of the British Empire," to his title. Radio Uganda then announced his entire title: "His Excellency President for Life, Field Marshal Alhaji Dr Idi Amin Dada, VC, DSO, MC, CBE."

Dissent within Uganda and Amin's attempt to annex the Kagera province of Tanzania in 1978 led to the Uganda-Tanzania War and the fall of his regime. Amin later fled to exile in Libya and then Saudi Arabia where he continued to live until his death on 16 August 2003 at the age of 80. And as the Daily Telegraph, London, stated after he died:

"Throughout his disastrous reign, he encouraged the West to cultivate a dangerous ambivalence towards him. His genial grin, penchant for grandiose self-publicity and ludicrous public statements on international affairs led to his adoption as a comic figure. He was easily parodied... however, this fascination, verging on affection, for the grotesqueness of the individual occluded the singular plight of his nation."

Early life and military career

Amin never wrote an autobiography nor did he authorise any official written account of his life. Therefore, there are discrepancies regarding when and where he was born.

Most biographical sources hold that he was born in either Koboko or Kampala in around 1925. Other unconfirmed sources state Amin's year of birth from as early at 1923 to as late as 1928.

According to Fred Guweddeko, a researcher at Makerere University, Idi Amin was the son of Andreas Nyabire (1889–1976). Nyabire, a member of the Kakwa ethnic group which straddles the Ugandan-Sudanese-Congolese borders, converted from Roman Catholicism to Islam in 1910 and changed his name to Amin Dada. He named his first-born son after himself.

Abandoned by his father at a young age, Idi Amin grew up with his mother's family in a rural farming town in northwestern Uganda. Guweddeko states that Amin's mother was called Assa Aatte (1904–1970). She was a member of the Lugbara ethnic group or tribe. She was also a traditional herbalist who treated members of Buganda royalty, among others.

Amin joined an Islamic school in Bombo in 1941. After a few years, he left school with nothing more than a standard four English-language education and did odd jobs before being recruited into the army by a British colonial army officer. Other reports say his formal education was less than that. They say he had only standard two education, which is two years of primary school.

Colonial British Army

Amin joined the King'a African Rifles (KAR) of the British colonial army in 1946 as an assistant cook.

He claimed he was forced to join the Army during World War II and that he served in the Burma campaign. But records indicate he was first enlisted after the war ended.

He was transferred to Kenya for infantry service as a private in 1947 and served in the 21st KAR infantry battalion in Gilgil, Kenya, until 1949. That year, his unit was deployed to Somalia to fight the Somali Shifta rebels. In 1952, his brigade was deployed against the Mau Mau rebels in Kenya. He was promoted to corporal the same year, then to sergeant in 1953.

In 1959 Amin was made *effendi*, or *efendi*, which means "warrant officer" – *afande* or *afwande* in Kiswahili – the highest rank possible for a black African in the British colonial army of that time. Amin returned to Uganda the same year. In 1961, he was promoted to lieutenant, becoming one of the first two Ugandans to become commissioned officers.

He was then assigned to quell the cattle rustling

between Uganda's Karamojong and Kenya's Turkana nomads.

In 1962, following Uganda's independence from Great Britain, Amin was promoted to captain and then to major in 1963. The following year, he was appointed Deputy Commander of the Army.

Amin was an active athlete during his time in both the British and Ugandan army. At 6 feet 4 inches tall and powerfully built, he was the Ugandan light heavyweight boxing champion from 1951 to 1960, as well as a swimmer.

He was also a formidable rugby forward, although one officer said of him: "Idi Amin is a splendid type and a good (rugby) player, but virtually bone from the neck up, and needs things explained in words of one letter."

In the 1950s, he played for Nile RFC. There is a frequently repeated urban legend that he was selected as a replacement by East Africa for their match against the 1955 British Lions.

However, the story is entirely unfounded. Amin doesn't appear on the team photograph or on the official team list. And replacements were not allowed in international rugby until 13 years after this event is supposed to have taken place.

Army commander

In 1965, Prime Minister Milton Obote and Amin were implicated in a deal to smuggle ivory and gold into Uganda from Zaire, now the Democratic Republic of Congo (DRC).

The deal, as later alleged by General Nicholas Olenga, an associate of the former Congolese leader Patrice Lumumba, was part of an arrangement to help troops opposed to the Congolese government trade ivory and gold for arms supplies secretly smuggled to them by

Amin.

In 1966, the Ugandan parliament demanded an investigation. Partly in response to that, Obote imposed a new constitution abolishing the ceremonial presidency held by Kabaka (King) Edward Mutesa II of Buganda and declared himself executive president. He promoted Amin to colonel and army commander.

Amin led an attack on the Kabaka's palace and forced Mutesa into exile in the United Kingdom where he remained until his death in 1969.

Amin began recruiting into the army and security services members of the Kakwa, Lugabara, Nubian and other ethnic groups from the West Nile area, his home region, bordering Sudan.

The Nubians had been residents in Uganda since the early 20th century, having come from Sudan to serve the colonial army. Many African ethnic groups in northern Uganda inhabit both Uganda and Sudan; allegations persist that Amin's army consisted mainly of Sudanese soldiers. In fact, when Amin claimed parts of Sudan as Ugandan territory, Sudanese President Gaafar Nimeiri said Amin was Sudanese himself.

Seizure of power

Eventually, a rift developed between Amin and Obote, worsened by the support Amin had built within the army by recruiting soldiers from the West Nile region, his involvement in operations to support the rebellion in southern Sudan against the Arab-dominated government in Khartoum in northern Sudan, and an attempt on Obote's life in 1969.

In October 1970, Obote himself took control of the armed forces, reducing Amin from his months-old post of commander of all the armed forces to that of commander of the army.

Having learned that Obote was planning to arrest him for misappropriating army funds, Amin seized power in a military coup on 25 January 1971 while Obote was attending a commonwealth summit meeting in Singapore.

Troops loyal to Amin sealed off Entebbe International Airport, the main artery into Uganda, and took the capital Kampala. Soldiers surrounded Obote's residence and blocked major roads.

A broadcast on Radio Uganda accused Obote's government of corruption and preferential treatment of the Lango region where Obote came from.

Cheering crowds were reported in the streets of Kampala after the radio broadcast.

Amin announced that he was a soldier, not a politician, therefore a man of few words. He also said the military government would remain only as a caretaker until new elections, which would be announced when the situation was normalised. He promised to release all political prisoners.

Amin gave former king and president Mutesa (who had died in exile) a state burial in April 1971, freed many political prisoners, and reiterated his promise to hold free and fair elections to return the country to democratic rule in the shortest period possible.

None of that took place. He remained in power for eight years. No elections were held during his reign of terror. And throughout all those years, he proved to be exactly the opposite of what he said he was. He was not a man of few words.

Establishment of military rule

On 2 February 1971, one week after the coup, Amin declared himself president of Uganda, commander-in-chief of the armed forces, army chief of staff, and chief of air staff.

He announced that he was suspending certain provisions of the constitution and soon instituted an Advisory Defence Council composed of military officers with himself as the chairman.

He placed military tribunals above the system of civil law, appointed soldiers to top government posts and parastal agencies, and informed the newly inducted civilian cabinet ministers that they would be subject to military discipline.

He renamed the presidential lodge in Kampala from Government House to "The Command Post." He disbanded the General Service Unit (GSU), an intelligence agency created by the previous government of Obote, and replaced it with the State Research Bureau (SRB). SRB headquarters at the Kampala suburb of Nakasero became the scene of torture and executions over the next few years. Other agencies used to root out political dissent included the military police and the Public Safety Unit (PSU).

Obote took refuge in Tanzania, having been offered sanctuary there by Tanzanian President Julius Nyerere. He was soon joined by 20,000 Ugandan refugees fleeing Amin. The exiles attempted to regain the country in 1972 through a poorly organised coup attempt.

Persecution of ethnic and other groups

Amin retaliated against the attempted invasion by Ugandan exiles in 1972 by purging the army of Obote supporters, predominantly those from the Acholi and Lango ethnic groups. In July 1971, Lango and Acholi soldiers were massacred in the Jinja and Mbarara Barracks. By early 1972, about 5,000 Acholi and Lango soldiers, and at least twice as many civilians, had disappeared.

The victims soon came to include members of other

ethnic groups, religious leaders, journalists, artists, senior bureaucrats, judges, lawyers, homosexuals, students and intellectuals, criminal suspects, and foreign nationals. In this atmosphere of violence, many other people were killed for criminal motives or simply at will.

The killings, motivated by ethnic, political, and financial factors, continued throughout Amin's eight-year reign of terror.

The exact number of people killed is unknown. The International Commission of Jurists estimated the death toll at no fewer than 80,000 and more likely around 300,000. An estimate compiled by exile organisations with the help of Amnesty International puts the number killed at 500,000. Most sources say he killed at least 300,000.

Among the most prominent people killed were Benedicto Kiwanuka, the former prime minister and later chief justice; Janani Luwum, the Anglican archibishop; Joseph Mubiru, the former governor of the Central bank; Frank Kalimuzo, the vice chancellor of Makerere University; Byron Kawadwa, a prominent playwright; and two of Amin's own cabinet ministers, Erinayo Wilson Oryema and Charles Oboth Ofumbi.

In August 1972, Amin declared what he called an "economic war," a set of policies that included the expropriation of properties owned by Asians and Europeans. Uganda's 80,000 Asians were mostly from the Indian subcontinent and born in the country, their ancestors having come to Uganda when the country was still a British colony. Many owned businesses, including large-scale enterprises which formed the backbone of the Ugandan economy.

On 4 August 1972, Amin issued a decree ordering the expulsion of the 60,000 Asians who were not Ugandan citizens (most of them held British passports). This was later amended to include all 80,000 Asians, except for professionals, such as doctors, lawyers, and teachers.

A plurality of the Asians with British passports, around

30,000, emigrated to Britain. Others went to Australia, Canada, India, Kenya, Pakistan, Sweden, Tanzania, and the United States. Amin expropriated businesses and properties belonging to the Asians and handed them over to his supporters. The businesses were mismanaged, and industries collapsed from lack of maintenance. This proved disastrous for the already declining economy.

In 1977, Henry Kyemba, Amin's health minister and a former official of the first Obote regime, defected and resettled in Britain. Kyemba wrote and published *A State of Blood*, the first insider exposé of Amin's brutal rule.

International relations

Following the expulsion of Ugandan Asians in 1972, most of whom were of Indian descent, India severed diplomatic relations with Uganda. The same year, as part of his "economic war," Amin broke diplomatic ties with Britain and nationalised 85 British-owned businesses, although Britain was the first country to recognise Amin's regime and supported Amin in his coup against President Milton Obote.

Relations with Israel also soured in the same year. Although Israel had previously supplied Uganda with arms and Israeli military and intelligence officials helped Amin to plan and execute the coup against Milton Obote, Amin expelled Israeli military advisers in 1972 and turned to Muammar al-Gaddafi of Libya and to the Soviet Union for support.

He became an outspoken critic of Israel. In return, Gaddafi gave financial aid to Amin.

In the 1974 French-produced documentary film *General Idi Amin Dada: A Self Portrait*, Amin discussed his plans for war against Israel, using paratroops, bombers and suicide squadrons. He later stated that Hitler "was right to burn six million Jews." He also wanted to build a monument to Hitler in the Ugandan capital, Kampala, because of what the German leader did to Jews, but never did.

The Soviet Union became Amin's largest arms supplier. East Germany was involved in the General Service Unit and the State Research Bureau, the two agencies which were most notorious for terror. Later during the Ugandan invasion of Tanzania in 1979, East Germany attempted to remove evidence of its involvement with these agencies.

In 1973, Thomas Patrick Melady, the United States ambassador to Uganda from 1972 to 1973, recommended that the United States reduce its presence in Uganda. Melady described Amin's regime as "racist, erratic and unpredictable, brutal, inept, bellicose, irrational, ridiculous, and militaristic." Accordingly, the United States closed its embassy in Kampala.

In June 1976, Amin allowed an Air France airliner hijacked by two members of the Popular Front for the Liberation of Palestine – External Operations (PFLP-EO) and two members of the German *Revolutionäre Zellen* (Revolutionary Cells) to land at Entebbe Airport. There the hijackers were joined by three more.

Soon after, 156 non-Jewish hostages who did not hold Israeli passports were released and flown to safety, while 83 Jews and Israeli citizens, as well as 20 others who refused to abandon them (among whom were the captain and crew of the hijacked Air France jet), continued to be held hostage.

In the subsequent Israeli rescue operation, codenamed Operation Thunderbolt (popularly known as Operation Entebbe), on the night of July 3–4, 1976, a group of Israeli commandos were flown in all the way from Israel and seized control of Entebbe Airport, freeing nearly all the hostages. Three hostages died during the operation and 10 were wounded; seven hijackers, about 45 Ugandan soldiers, and one Israeli soldier, Yoni Netanyahu (elder

90

brother of future Israeli prime minister, Benjamin Netanyahu), were killed.

A fourth hostage, 75-year-old Dora Bloch, an elderly Jewish Englishwoman who had been taken to Mulago Hospital in Kampala before the rescue operation, was subsequently murdered in reprisal. The incident further soured Uganda's international relations, leading Britain to close its high commission in Uganda.

Uganda under Amin embarked on a large military build-up which raised concerns in Kenya.

Early in June 1975, Kenyan officials impounded a large convoy of Soviet-made arms *en route* to Uganda at the port of Mombasa. Tension between Uganda and Kenya reached its climax in February 1976 when Amin announced that he would investigate the possibility that parts of southern Sudan and western and central Kenya, up to within 20 miles of the Kenyan capital Nairobi, were historically a part of colonial Uganda.

The Kenyan government responded with a stern statement that Kenya would not part with "a single inch of its territory." Amin backed down after the Kenyan army deployed troops and armoured personnel carriers along the Kenyan–Ugandan border.

King of Scotland

Near the end of 1976, Amin officially declared himself "the uncrowned King of Scotland." He lavished his guests and dignitaries with Scottish accordion music, while dressed in Scottish kilts. He also said he was going to liberate Scotland from British tyranny.

He wrote to Queen Elizabeth II: "I would like you to arrange for me to visit Scotland, Ireland and Wales to meet the heads of revolutionary movements fighting against your imperialist oppression," and allegedly sent the Queen a telex that stated: "Dear Liz, if you want to know a real man, come to Kampala."

Amin sometimes argued that he was "the last King of Scotland."

Erratic behaviour, self-bestowed titles and media portrayal

As the years progressed, Amin's behaviour became more erratic, unpredictable, and outspoken. After Great Britain broke off all diplomatic relations with his regime in 1977, Amin declared he had defeated the British and conferred on himself the decoration of CBE (Conqueror of the British Empire).

His full self-bestowed title ultimately became "His Excellency, President for Life, Field Marshal Al Hadji Doctor Idi Amin Dada, VC, DSO, MC, Lord of All the Beasts of the Earth and Fishes of the Seas and Conqueror of the British Empire in Africa in General and Uganda in Particular," in addition to his officially stated claim of being the "uncrowned King of Scotland."

He also claimed he was the "King of Africa" and "professor of geography." These ridiculous claims and others can be heard directly from him on Youtube and elsewhere.

During the Watergate crisis, Amin sent President Richard Nixon a telegram, stating: "I wish you quick recovery from the Watergate fever."

He said about British Prime Minister Edward Heath who smoked a pipe: "His head is full of smoke."

Many people questioned his sanity. And there are those who did not dismiss him lightly, including one British journalist who said Amin was by no means stupid. He knew exactly what he was doing.

One Asian lady who was expelled from Uganda by Idi Amin and who ended up in Britain also stated in an interview on television that Amin was not a fool or the kind of buffoon he appeared to be and knew exactly what to say and when; he knew how to use the media very well.

Amin became the subject of rumours and myths, including a widespread belief that he was a cannibal. Some of the unsubstantiated rumours, such as the mutilation of one of his wives, were spread and popularised by the 1980 film *Rise and Fall of Idi Amin* and alluded to in the film *The Last King of Scotland* in 2006.

During Amin's time in power, popular media outside Uganda often portrayed him as an essentially comic and eccentric figure. In a 1977 assessment typical of the time, a *Time* magazine article described him as a "killer and clown, big-hearted buffoon and strutting martinet."

The foreign media was often criticised by Ugandan exiles and defectors for focusing on Amin's excessive tastes and self-aggrandizing eccentricities, and downplaying or excusing his murderous behaviour.

Other commentators even suggested that Amin had deliberately cultivated his eccentric reputation in the foreign media as an easily parodied buffoon in order to defuse international concern over his administration of Uganda.

Deposition and exile

By 1978, the number of Amin's supporters and close associates had shrunk significantly and he faced increasing dissent from the populace within Uganda as the economy and infrastructure collapsed from years of neglect and abuse.

After the killings of Bishop Luwum and ministers Oryema and Ofumbi in 1977, several of Amin's ministers defected or fled into exile.

In November 1978, after Amin's vice president, General Mustafa Adrisi who also never finished primary school, was injured in a car accident, troops loyal to him mutinied; he was vice president from 1977 to 1978.

Amin sent troops against the mutineers, some of whom had fled across the Tanzanian border.

Amin accused Tanzanian President Julius Nyerere of waging war against Uganda, ordered the invasion of Tanzania, and formally annexed a section of the Kagera Region across the border.

In January 1979, Nyerere mobilised the Tanzania People's Defence Forces (TPDF) and counterattacked, joined by several groups of Ugandan exiles who had united as the Uganda National Liberation Army (UNLA).

Amin's army retreated steadily and, despite military help from Gaddafi, he was forced to flee into exile by helicopter on 11 April 1979 when the capital Kampala was captured by Tanzanian soldiers.

He escaped first to Libya where he stayed until 1980 and ultimately settled in Saudi Arabia where the Saudi royal family allowed him sanctuary and paid him a generous subsidy in return for his staying out of politics.

Amin lived for a number of years on the top two floors of the Novotel Hotel on Palestine Road in Jeddah. Brian Barron, who covered the Uganda–Tanzania war for the BBC as chief Africa correspondent from 1977 to 1981, together with cameraman Mohammed Amin of Visnews in Nairobi, located Amin in 1980 and secured the first interview with him since his deposition. As Barron stated about the 1980 interview in his article, "The Idi Amin I knew," BBC Africa, 16 August 2003:

"The first time I encountered the intimidating presence of the one-time sergeant major in the King's African Rifles was 26 years ago at a military ceremony in West Nile Province, his home tribal district.

We landed on an old British colonial airstrip in one of his Hercules transports, normally used to import scarce luxury goods for the Ugandan dictator and his henchmen.

It was a scorching day but Amin was wearing his field marshal's kit with its specially lengthened tunic - reaching almost to his knees - to accommodate all the medals he had awarded himself.

Glinting in the sun was his Victoria Cross as self-proclaimed Conqueror of the British Empire.

He was an obvious bully but capable of menacing charm. He was by no means stupid though he devoted his energy to preserving his own tyranny as well as liquidating his enemies and those who possessed something he wanted, like an attractive wife.

Grouped around him were his hardcore toadies, headed by a seedy expatriate known universally as Major Bob.

For hours Amin reviewed a military march-past, one of his favourite pastimes.

By early 1979 his grip on power was slipping. A comically absurd series of attacks on Tanzanian territory by his incompetent and often drunk soldiers finally provoked President Julius Nyerere.

The Tanzanian leader mobilised an armoured column and after several months it was closing in on the Ugandan capital, Kampala.

Colonel Muammar Gaddafi of Libya sent his own intervention force to try to bolster Amin but they too proved almost useless and the Ugandan army retreated towards Jinja.

Concrete dungeons

We were the first foreign correspondents to reach abandoned Kampala and, through crowds dancing in the street, we immediately went to the headquarters of his secret police, the State Research Bureau, SRB.

Below ground level the power had failed. We stumbled down the stairs of the empty building into a charnel house. The floor was awash with blood, the bodies of the SRB's last victims lying in the darkness in their concrete dungeons.

Upstairs, the electricity was working. In one vast room we found the SRB's abandoned wiretapping operation still functioning.

Neat rows of Akai tape recorders were patched into Kampala's phone grid - the spools rotating, pencils and pads on the desks for the note-takers who had fled.

Who knows how many phone calls the secret police thugs had intercepted over the years with fatal results?

In another room stuffed with files marked Top Secret, I found one detailing the surveillance of my BBC colleague Philip Short who had been expelled by Amin.

Then we headed for Amin's living quarters in Nile Mansions. The priority was to search the refrigerators because of persistent reports that he sometimes kept the heads of his victims in the freezer.

With relief, we found no evidence to back this up.

Within a few weeks, Idi Amin escaped from Uganda, probably with the help of Colonel Gaddafi.

Tracked down to Jeddah

A year later, in partnership with cameraman Mohammed Amin of Visnews in Nairobi, I mounted a search for the fugitive strongman.

Eventually we located him in the Saudi city of Jeddah.

The Saudis had been staunch allies because Idi was a Muslim convert who ordered mosques built across Uganda when he was in power.

After weeks of negotiation through an intermediary we fixed a meeting at his hideaway in Jeddah.

He stipulated the interview had to be done clandestinely without the knowledge of the Saudi authorities.

Homesick

We rang the bell and the front door was opened by several nervous Saudi government bodyguards.

They would not admit us. Then Idi appeared behind them and loudly told them: 'These visitors are my guests. You all know I am living here at the invitation of the King. Do not interfere.'

Looking stressed but cowed by the mention of the monarchy, the Saudi secret police retreated to the kitchen.

Amin beckoned us to the lounge reverberating to bagpipe music - he was playing a recording of the Edinburgh Tattoo at maximum volume.

After introducing us to two of his sons, both with Scottish clans as their Christian names, Amin gave me a 45 minute interview.

He was relaxed and clearly homesick, promising he would regain control in Uganda. He rejected any responsibility for the years of brutality, for the murder of his opponents, for the scenes of horror we had witnessed at the SRB headquarters.

All had been fabricated by his enemies, he insisted.

What he told us that evening in 1980 was a lie from beginning to end.

Idi Amin was the most flamboyant of a group of African dictators I covered during that turbulent period.

Emperor Bokassa, another army sergeant gone wrong, in Central Africa; the mad, bad General Siad Barre in Somalia; the psychopathic Sergeant Doe ruling Liberia.

Despite Amin's crimes against humanity, he escaped justice for one reason only: the Saudi authorities shielded one of the monsters of our time."

During interviews he gave during his exile in Saudi Arabia, Amin claimed that Uganda needed him. He never expressed remorse for the nature of his regime.

In 1989, he attempted to return to Uganda, apparently to lead an armed group organised by Colonel Juma Oris. He reached Kinshasa, Zaire (now the Democratic Republic of Congo – DRC), before Zairian President Mobutu Sese Seko forced him to return to Saudi Arabia.

Amin's death

On 20 July 2003, one of Amin's wives, Madina, reported that he was in a coma and near death at King Faisal Specialist Hospital in Jeddah, Saudi Arabia, from kidney failure.

She pleaded with the Ugandan President Yoweri Museveni to allow him to return to Uganda for the remainder of his life. Museveni replied that Amin would have to "answer for his sins the moment he was brought back."

Amin died at the hospital in Jeddah, Saudi Arabia, on 16 August 2003 and was buried in Ruwais Cemetery in Jeddah.

Family and associates

A polygamist, Idi Amin married at least six women, three of whom he divorced.

He married his first and second wives, Malyamu and Kay, in 1966. The next year, he married Nora and then Nalongo Madina in 1972.

On 26 March 1974, he announced on Radio Uganda that he had divorced Malyamu, Nora and Kay.

Malyamu was arrested in Tororo on the border with Kenya in April 1974 and was accused of attempting to smuggle a bolt of fabric into Kenya. She later moved to London.

Kay died on 13 August 1974, reportedly from an attempted surgical abortion performed by her lover, Dr.

Mbalu Mukasa, who himself reportedly committed suicide, according to an article in a Ugandan newspaper, *Daily Monitor* and other sources.

Kay's body was found dismembered.

Kay was made pregnant by Dr. Mukasa. Bob Astles, Amin's British adviser, believed that her body was mutilated not on Amin's orders but by Mukasa while attempting to hide it.

In August 1975, during the Organisation of African Unity (OAU) summit meeting in Kampala, Amin married Sarah Kyolaba.

Sarah's boyfriend, whom she had been living with before she met Amin, vanished and was never heard from again.

By 1993, Amin was living with the last nine of his children and a single wife, Mama a Chumaru, the mother of the youngest four of his children. His last known child was a daughter called Iman, born in 1992. According to the *Daily Monitor*, Amin married again a few months before his death in 2003.

Sources differ widely on the number of children Amin fathered; most say that he had 30 to 45. Until 2003, Taban Amin (born 1955), Idi Amin's eldest son, was the leader of the West Nile Bank Front (WNBF), a rebel group opposed to the government of Yoweri Museveni.

In 2005, he was offered amnesty by President Yoweri Museveni, and in 2006, he was appointed deputy director-general of the Internal Security Organisation.

Another of Amin's sons, Haji Ali Amin, ran for election as chairman (i.e. mayor) of Njeru Town Council in 2002 but was not elected.

In early 2007, the award-winning film *The Last King of Scotland* prompted one of his sons, Jaffar Amin (born in 1967), to speak out in his father's defence. Jaffar Amin said he was writing a book to rehabilitate his father's reputation. Jaffar is the tenth of Amin's 40 official children by seven official wives.

On 3 August 2007, Faisal Wangita (born in 1983), one of Amin's sons, was convicted of playing a role in a murder in London. Wangita's mother is Amin's fifth wife, Sarah Kyolaba (born 1955), a former go-go dancer, but known as 'Suicide Sarah', because she was a go-go dancer for the Ugandan Army's Revolutionary Suicide Mechanised Regiment Band.

Among Amin's closest associates was the British-born Bob Astles who is considered by many to have been a malignant influence and by others as having been a moderating presence.

Isaac Malyamungu was an instrumental affiliate and one of the more feared officers in Amin's army.

When Amin died, his death brought back many bad memories. As BBC reporter Paul Martin stated in "My Experience of Idi Amin, " BBC News, 24 August 2003:

"The recent death in exile of Idi Amin - the former Ugandan dictator and self-styled 'Conqueror of the British Empire' - has brought back memories of a bloody era in Uganda's recent history.

He seized power in 1971 and subjected Uganda to a reign of terror, ordering the killing of hundreds of thousands of people and expelling the country's Asian community.

Amin was finally forced to flee Uganda in 1979 and spent the rest of his life in Libya and Saudi Arabia.

I first met the Ugandan dictator in 1978 - the year Amin declared to be 'a year of love, peace and reconciliation' - as a young researcher with BBC Television.

On the manicured lawns of the palatial Nile mansions close to Africa's longest river, Idi Amin was finally giving us our long awaited interview, after keeping us in suspense for days.

Fear

It was a gorgeous, sunny day but we feared it could be our last.

Amin's guards had stopped lolling about and as the interview progressed with tougher and tougher questions, like 'Why do you keep murdering people?,' the Ugandan leader's features grew more angry, and the guards were standing stiffly, clutching their guns firmly, and glancing around as if awaiting orders.

'Tell me,' barked Amin to our reporter David Lomax, 'are you not afraid to be talking to the Conqueror of the British Empire?'

Conqueror of the British Empire was a title Amin had given himself, along with the Victoria Cross and the Military Cross, part of his obsession with showing himself equal or superior to Queen Elizabeth II - who had failed to accept his invitation to visit him in Uganda.

But while all this may have seemed amusing in some ways, we (the small BBC television team) were not amused.

We were, as Amin had suggested we should be, afraid.

A British car salesman in Uganda, Robert Scanlon, had been accused by Amin the year before of being a British spy - he disappeared and I had reported he had been sledge-hammered to death in a secret prison.

So I was just contemplating whether we were going to meet the same fate - the so-called 'hammer treatment,' or perhaps, I wondered, the river treatment - being dropped into the Nile tied to a cement block.

Or even I thought, the helicopter treatment, when people were dropped out from a fatal height.

If David answered: 'Yes, I am afraid,' Amin I feared, would say: 'Well, you've every reason to be afraid.'

And if David said he was not afraid, I could just hear Idi saying: 'Well, I'll make you afraid.'

What David then did, I'm convinced, saved our skins.

He simply fired an innocuous question. Amin's eyes darted to his henchmen, he glowered.

Then to my intense relief, he answered the new question.

Strained humour

During each change of film (every 10 minutes), the reporter would try to keep Amin calm by explaining: 'Well, I'm only asking you these things because that's what our listeners want to hear your responses to.'

By the end of the interview, Amin was back to his benign, childishly humorous persona.

From his huge frame, he shook hands powerfully with each of us and declared: 'It seems to me the people of Great Britain are getting smaller and smaller.'

'Ha, ha, ha Mr President, very funny,' I recall myself saying, embarrassingly sycophantic.

He was now on a roll - and looking at my beard Amin added: 'It also seems me that the people of Great Britain are getting hairier and hairier.'

It had been a tense visit from the start. I had flown in first, clearly, as a low level researcher. I was a sort of expendable human guinea pig, by the reckoning of our editor back in London.

I had been taken to the office of Amin's security chief, who, amazingly, turned out to be an Asian, even though Amin had expelled almost all 50,000 Indians and Pakistanis (the country's main businessmen) in 1972.

The rest of the team arrived and after two days we were summoned to a particular location.

Film surprise

Cameras rolling, we entered a room expecting to be filming Idi Amin.

102

We saw instead two lines of suited gentlemen across a large table.

The jaws of the men on one side dropped open.

They were a team of cabinet ministers from neighbouring Kenya, involved in what was supposed to be top secret talks to re-establish diplomatic relations after several, tense years.

Amin himself walked in, and made a short speech.

The head of the Kenyan delegation then responded, saying it was an honour to have the president come in person.

'As unexpected, he said, 'as the arrival of the international media.'

Round one, it seemed, to Amin.

Next day we had our exclusive and nearly disastrous interview.

Next stop was Idi Amin Dada Sea - as Amin had renamed Africa's largest expanse of water, Lake Victoria.

It was, on its shores at Cape Town Villas, that Amin would often relax as he was served tea and gargantuan meals by another of his security chiefs, Major Bob Astles, who, in reality, had once been a sergeant in the British army, then a road gang leader in Uganda, before Amin's coup.

Astles certainly knew he had to satisfy his master's every need.

We saw him rushing across the lakeside lawn with a tea tray, breathlessly exclaiming 'H. E.' which stood for the colonial title by which Amin was to be addressed: His Excellency.

While Astles was serving his master, I surreptitiously used his phone inside the house and called a private aircraft company in Kenya, giving them a pre-arranged code phrase.

Sure enough, a light plane flew in that evening to a disused airstrip and we literally did a midnight flit.

We had got the last TV interview with Uganda's most

notorious leader before he was overthrown, and, perhaps more importantly, we had just got away in one piece."

Amin's legacy is mixed. In most cases, he is a reviled figure. But there are those who still admire him. They include some black Americans (African Americans) and a significant number of black Africans as well as other blacks elsewhere who feel that he spoke for them and stood up against the white man who had humiliated, exploited and oppressed them for so long. Amin was able to twist the white man's nose to their delight. They felt vindicated in their desire to exact vengeance. Idi Amin did that on their behalf. And there are those who still feel that way.

Yoweri Museveni

Yoweri Kaguta Museveni (born c. 1939) is the longest-ruling Uganda leader and one of the longest-ruling on the entire African continent. He has been president of Uganda since 26 January 1986.

Museveni was involved in the war that deposed Idi Amin and in the rebellion that subsequently led to the end of President Milton Obote's rule in 1985.

With the exception of northern parts of Uganda, Museveni has brought relative peace and stability and economic growth to a country that has endured decades of government mismanagement, brutal dictatorship under Amin and during Obote's second presidency, rebel activity and civil war. His tenure has also witnessed one of the most effective national responses to HIV/AIDS in Africa.

In the mid-to-late 1990s, Museveni was lauded by the West as part of a new generation of African leaders. However, his presidency was marred by invading and occupying Congo during the Second Congo War which resulted in an estimated 5.4 million deaths since 1998, and by other conflicts in the Great Lakes region in which Uganda was involved.

Rebellion in the north of Uganda by the Lord;s Resistance Army (LRA) continues to perpetuate one of the world's worst humanitarian crises.

Recent developments, including the abolition of presidential term limits before the 2006 elections and the harassment of democratic opposition, have attracted concern from domestic commentators and the international community.

Early life and career (1944–1972)

Born in Ntungamo in southwestern Uganda on the border with Rwanda during British colonial rule when Uganda was a protectorate, Museveni is a member of the Banyankole ethnic group. His surname, Museveni, means "Son of a man of the Seventh", in honour of the Seventh Battalion of the King's African Rifles (KAR), the British colonial army in which many Ugandans served during World War II.

Museveni gets his middle name from his father, Amos Kaguta, a cattle herder. Amos Kaguta is also the father of Museveni's brother Caleb Akandwanaho, popularly known in Uganda as Salim Saleh, and sister Violet Kajubiri.

Museveni attended Kyamate Elementary School, Mbarara High School, and Ntare School. It was when he was in high school that he became a born-again Christian.

In 1967, he went to the University of Dar es Salaam in Tanzania. There, he studied economics and political science and became a Marxist, involving himself in radical pan-African politics.

He formed an activist group, the University Students' African Revolutionary Front, and led a student delegation to Mozambique where he received guerrilla training under the Mozambique Liberation Front (FRELIMO) which had liberated the northern part of the country from the Portuguese colonial rule.

One of his professors at the University of Dar es Salaam was Dr. Walter Rodney, author of *How Europe Underdeveloped Africa*. Dr. Rodney wrote the book when he was teaching there and let his students comment on the manuscript before it was published. The book became an internationally acclaimed work.

When he was one of Rodney's students, Museveni wrote a university thesis on the applicability of Frantz Fanon's ideas on revolutionary violence to post-colonial Africa.

In 1970, Museveni joined the intelligence service of Ugandan President Dr. Milton Obote.

When Major-General Idi Amin seized power in a military coup in January 1971, Museveni fled to Tanzania with other exiles, including the deposed president.

The power bases of Amin and Obote were very different, consolidated on ethnic and regional basis. Therefore, the conflict between Obote and Amin also assumed ethnic and regional dimensions fuelled by ethno-regional loyalties and rivalries.

Obote was a member of the Lango ethnic group of the central north. Amin was a Kakwa from the northwestern corner of the country.

During British colonial rule, the largest number of soldiers in the army were members of two tribes, the Lango and the Acholi, from northern Uganda. The two tribes were also allies, in addition to being fellow northerners. Southerners such as the Baganda from the Buganda kingdom and others were involved in other activities including business and were not well-represented in the army.

Therefore when independence came, the Ugandan army was predominantly Acholi and Lango. And that continued to be the case during the presidency of Obote, who was a northerner himself, until Amin overthrew him.

106

After Amin seized power, he embarked on a policy of ethnic cleansing, focusing on the army. He filled the top positions in the government and in the army with members of his tribes, the Kakwa and the Lugbara – he was a product of both, according to his lineage – and eliminated the Lango and the Acholi. It was one of the worst cases of ethnic cleansing in Ugandan history; probably the worst.

FRONASA and the toppling of Amin (1972–80)

The exile forces opposed to Idi Amin were predominantly Lango and Acholi. They invaded Uganda from Tanzania in September 1972 but were repelled, suffering heavy losses. The invasion was not well-organised.

The army of exiles which invaded Uganda included a significant number of people who were members of other tribes as well, such as Museveni, a Munyankole.

The problems for the rebels got even worse when a peace agreement was by Tanzania and Uganda later in the same year, denying the rebels the use of Tanzanian soil for aggression against Uganda.

During that period, Museveni briefly worked as a lecturer at a co-operative college in Moshi in northern Tanzania before breaking away from the mainstream opposition. He formed the Front for National Salvation (FRONASA) in 1973.

In August the same year, he married Janet Kataha, a former secretary and airline stewardess with whom he would have four children.

In October 1978, Amin ordered the invasion of Tanzania in order to claim the Kagera province for Uganda. From 24 to 26 March 1979, Museveni and FRONASA attended a gathering of exiles and rebel groups in the northern Tanzanian town of Moshi. Overcoming ideological differences, for the time being at least, the various groups established the Uganda National Liberation Front (UNLF).

Museveni was appointed to an 11-member Executive Council, chaired by Yusuf Kironde Lule. This was accompanied by a National Consultative Council (NCC) with one member for each of the 28 groups represented at the meeting.

The UNLF joined forces with the Tanzanian army to launch a counter-attack which culminated in the toppling of the Amin regime in April 1979.

Museveni was named the new minister of state for defence in the new UNLF government. He was the youngest minister in Yusuf Lule's administration.

The thousands of troops which Museveni recruited into FRONASA during the war were incorporated into the new national army. They retained their loyalty to Museveni, however, and would be crucial in later rebellions against the second Obote regime.

The NCC selected Godfrey Binaisa as the new chairman of the UNLF after infighting led to the deposition of Yusuf Lule in June 1979.

Machinations to consolidate power continued with Binaisa in a similar manner to his predecessor. In November, Museveni was reshuffled from the ministry of defence to the ministry of regional cooperation, with Binaisa himself taking over the key defence role.

In May 1980, Binaisa himself was placed under house arrest after an attempt to dismiss Oyite Ojok, the army chief of staff, in what was a *de facto* coup led by Paulo Muwanga, Yoweri Museveni, Oyite Ojok and Tito Okello. A presidential commission,with Museveni as vice-chairman, was installed and quickly announced plans for a general election in December.

Now a relatively well-known national figure, Museveni established a new political party, the Uganda Patriotic Movement (UPM), which he would lead in the elections. He would be competing against three other political groupings: the Uganda People's Congress (UPC) led by former president Milton Obote; the Conservative Party (CP), and the Democratic Party (DP).

The main contenders were seen to be the UPC and DP. The official results declared UPC the winner, with Museveni's UPM gaining only one of the 126 available seats.

A number of irregularities compromised the credibility of the poll. In the planning of the election, the leader of the ruling commission, Paulo Muwanga, supported the UPC's view that each candidate should have a separate ballot box. This was fiercely opposed by the other parties which maintained that it would make the poll easier to manipulate.

The configuration of political boundaries may also have helped Obote's Uganda People's congress (UPC). Constituencies in generally pro-UPC northern Uganda contained proportionally less voters than the anti-UPC Buganda, giving more power to Obote's party.

Suspicions of fraud were compounded by Muwanga's announcement on the day of the election that all results should be cleared by him before they were announced publicly.

The losing parties refused to recognise the legitimacy of the new regime, citing widespread electoral irregularities.

The war in the bush (1981–86)

The Ugandan Bush War (often referred to as the war in the bush, and also known as the Luwero War, the Ugandan civil war or the Resistance War) refers to the guerrilla war waged between 1981 and 1986 by the National Resistance Army (NRA) against the government of Milton Obote and later that of Tito Okello.

After the Uganda-Tanzania war, there followed a

period of intense competition and fighting for power among different groups which had helped the Tanzanian army remove Idi Amin from power in 1979.

Following the bitterly disputed elections in which Museveni's UPM party was a minor contender, Museveni alleged electoral fraud and declared an armed rebellion against the UNLA (which was now Uganda's national army) and the government of President Milton Obote.

Museveni and his supporters retreated to the southwestern part of the country and formed the Popular Resistance Army (PRA).

The PRA later merged with former president Lule's group, the Uganda Freedom Fighters (UFF), to form the National Resistance Army (NRA) and its political wing, the National Resistance Movement.

Concurrently, two other rebel groups, the Uganda National Rescue Front (UNRF) and the Former Uganda National Army (FUNA), were formed in West Nile, Amin's home region and stronghold, from the remnants of Amin's supporters and fought the UNLA in that region.

NRA's bush war began with an attack on an army installation in the central Mubende District on 6 February 1981. Museveni, who had guerrilla war experience with FRELIMO in Mozambique, and his own Front for National Salvation (FRONASA) formed in Tanzania to fight Idi Amin, campaigned in the rural areas hostile to Obote's government, especially in central and western Buganda and in the regions of Ankole and Bunyoro in western Uganda.

Most of the battles were conducted by small mobile units which were designated as "A" Coy commanded by Steven Kashaka, "B" Coy under Joram Mugume, and "C" Coy under Pecos Kuteesa.

The commander of these forces was Fred Rwigyema. He was assisted by Salim Saleh, Museveni's half-brother.

There were three small zonal forces – Lutta Unit in the areas of Kapeeka, Kabalega Unit in the areas near

Kiwoko, and Nkrumah Unit in the areas of Ssingo.

Obote's UNLA forces responded in an effort to retaliate against the NRA, resulting in the loss of many civilian lives in the affected areas.

UNLA soldiers consisted of many ethnic Acholi and Lango. And although the Acholi and Lango themselves were survivors of Amin's genocidal purges in northern Uganda, they conducted actions reminiscent of Amin's.

In early 1983, to eliminate rural support for Museveni's guerrillas, the area of Luwero District was targeted for a massive population removal affecting almost 750,000 people. The resultant refugee camps were subject to military control, and in many cases human rights abuses took place. Many civilians outside the camps, in what came to be known as the "Luwero triangle," were blamed for being guerrilla sympathisers and were treated accordingly by Obote's army and government.

Museveni's National Resistance Army (NRA) also committed atrocities including the use of land mines specifically against civilians. Child soldiers were also widely used by the NRA as guerrillas, and also subsequently when the NRA became the regular army.

In the deteriorating military and economic situation, Obote subordinated other matters to a military victory over the NRA. North Korean military advisers were invited to take part in government military operations against the NRA rebels.

But the national army under President Obote was war-weary. And after the army chief of staff, General Oyite Ojok, died in a helicopter crash at the end of 1983, the Uganda National Liberation Army (UNLA) – which kept Obote in power – began to split along ethnic lines.

Acholi soldiers complained that they were given too much frontline action and too few rewards for their services. Obote further alienated much of the Acholi-dominated officer corps, including the military leaders Lieutenant-General Bazilio Olara-Okello and General Tito

Okello, by appointing his fellow ethnic Lango, Brigadier Smith Opon Acak, as chief of staff, and by giving more prominence to the Lango-dominated Special Force Units.

On 27 July 1985, an army brigade of the UNLA commanded by Olara-Okello, and composed mostly of Acholi troops, overthrew Obote and seized power. Obote fled to exile.

Before Oyite Ojok died, the National Resistance Army ((NRA) was nearly defeated, with its leader Museveni living in exile in Sweden.

Following the UNLA infighting and the coup against Obote, the NRA's guerrilla war gained momentum. In December 1985, Tito Okello's government signed a peace deal, the Nairobi Agreement, with the NRA.

However, the ceasefire broke down almost immediately. In January 1986, Museveni's half-brother Salim Saleh led NRA's assault on the capital Kampala which eventually led to the end of Tito Okello's rule. Okello was Uganda's president from 29 July 1985 to 26 January 1986. Yoweri Kaguta Museveni became the new president of Uganda after waging a five-year bush war against Obote.

After Museveni became president, the NRA became the national army and was renamed Uganda People's Defence Force (UPDF).

General Okello fled to southern Sudan with his supporters who were members of his army when he was in power. He returned to Uganda in 1993 under an amnesty offered by President Yoweri Museveni whose seizure of power was the result of the first successful rebellion in post-colonial Africa by the people who were not members of the regular armed forces.

Obote II and the National Resistance Army

Museveni returned with his supporters to their rural

strongholds in the Bantu-dominated south and southwest to form the Popular Resitance Army (PRA). There they planned a rebellion against the second Obote regime, popularly known as "Obote II", and its armed forces, the Uganda National Liberation Army (UNLA).

The National Resistance Movement (NRM) developed a "Ten-point Programme" for an eventual government, covering democracy, security, consolidation of national unity, defending national independence, building an independent, integrated and self-sustaining economy, improvement of social services, elimination of corruption and misuse of power, redressing inequality, cooperation with other African countries and a mixed economy.

By July 1985, Amnesty International estimated that Obote's regime had been responsible for more than 300,000 civilian deaths across Uganda, although the *CIA World Factbook* puts the number at over 100,000.

The human rights organisation had made several representations to the government to improve its appalling human rights record from 1982. Abuses were particularly conspicuous in an area of central Uganda known as the Luwero – or Luweero – Triangle.

Reports from Uganda during that period sparked international criticism of Obote's government and increased support abroad for Museveni's rebel force. Within Uganda, the brutal suppression of the insurgency aligned the Buganda, the most numerous of Uganda's ethnic groups, with the NRA against the UNLA which was seen as being dominated by northerners, especially the Lango and Acholi. Until his death in October 2005, Milton Obote blamed the Luwero abuses on the NRA.

1985 Nairobi Agreement

On 27 July 1985, factionalism within the Uganda People's Congress (UPC) government led to a successful military coup against Obote by his former army commander, Lieutenant-General Tito Okello, an Acholi. Museveni and the NRM/A were angry that the revolution for which they had fought for four years had been "hijacked" by the UNLA which they viewed as having been discredited by gross human rights violations during Obote II.

Despite these reservations, however, the NRM/A eventually agreed to peace talks presided over by a Kenyan delegation headed by President Daniel arap Moi.

The talks, which lasted from 26 August to 17 December 1985, were notoriously acrimonious. The final agreement, signed in Nairobi, called for a ceasefire, demilitarisation of the capital Kampala, integration of the NRA with government forces, and absorption of the NRA leadership into the Military Council. These conditions were never met.

The prospects of a lasting agreement were limited by several factors, including the Kenyan team's lack of an in-depth knowledge of the situation in Uganda and the exclusion of relevant Ugandan and international actors from the talks, *inter alia*. In the end, Museveni and his allies refused to share power with generals they did not respect, not least while the NRA had the capacity to achieve an outright military victory.

The push for Kampala

While supposedly involved in the peace negotiations, Museveni had courted General Mobutu Sese Seko of Zaire (now the Democratic Republic of Congo – DRC) in an attempt to forestall the involvement of Zairean forces in support of Okello's military junta. On 20 January 1986, however, several hundred troops loyal to Idi Amin were accompanied into Ugandan territory by the Zairean military.

114

The forces intervened in the civil conflict following secret training in Zaire and an appeal from Okello ten days previously. Mobutu's support for Okello was a score Museveni would settle years later, ordering Ugandan forces into the conflict in Zaire against Mobutu which would finally topple the Zairean leader in May 1997.

By this stage, however, the NRA had developed an unstoppable momentum. By 22 January 1986, government troops in Kampala under President Tito Okello had begun to quit their posts *en masse* as the NRA rebels gained ground from the south and south-west. On January 25th the Museveni-led faction finally overran the capital. The NRA toppled Okello's government and declared victory the next day.

Museveni was sworn in as president three days later. "This is not a mere change of guard, it is a fundamental change," said Museveni after a ceremony conducted by British-born chief justice Peter Allen.

Speaking to crowds of thousands outside the Ugandan parliament, the new president promised a return to democracy and said: "The people of Africa, the people of Uganda, are entitled to a democratic government. It is not a favour from any regime. The sovereign people must be the public, not the government."

Museveni in power (1986–96)

Political and economic regeneration

The post-Amin regimes in Uganda were characterised by corruption, factionalism and an inability to restore order and acquire popular legitimacy. Museveni needed to avoid repeating these mistakes if his new government was not to meet the same fate: being overthrown by discontented fellow citizens who could mobilise forces against him.

115

The NRM declared a four-year interim government, comprising a broader ethnic base than its predecessors. The representatives of the various factions were nevertheless hand-picked by Museveni.

The sectarian violence which had overshadowed Uganda's recent history was put forward as a justification for restricting the activities of political parties and their ethnically distinct bases.

The non-party system introduced by Museveni did not prohibit political parties but prevented them from fielding candidates directly in elections. The so-called "Movement" system, which Museveni said claimed the loyalty of every Ugandan, would be a cornerstone in politics for nearly twenty years.

A system of Resistance Councils, directly elected at the parish level, was established to manage local affairs including the equitable distribution of fixed-price commodities.

The election of Resistance Councils representatives was the first direct experience many Ugandans had with democracy after many decades of varying levels of authoritarianism. And replication of the structure up to the district level has been credited with helping even people at the local level understand the higher-level political structures.

The new government enjoyed widespread international support. And the economy that had been damaged by the civil war began to recover as Museveni initiated economic policies designed to combat key problems such as hyperinflation and balance of payments. Abandoning his Marxist ideals, Museveni embraced the neoliberal structural adjustment programmes (SAPs) advocated by the World Bank and the International Monetary Fund (IMF). The SAPs caused so much hardship in other African countries including neighbouring Tanzania and in other Third World countries even though they also helped rejuvenate the economies of the those countries in some areas, benefiting only a few people.

Uganda began participating in the IMF Economic Recovery Programme (ERP) in 1987. Its objectives included the restoration of incentives in order to encourage growth, investment, employment and exports; the promotion and diversification of trade with particular emphasis on export promotion; the removal of bureaucratic constraints and divestment from ailing public enterprises so as to enhance sustainable economic growth and development through the private sector; and the liberalisation of trade at all levels.

Regional relations and conflict

After January 1986, Museveni continued in his role as commander-in-chief of the National Resistance Army (NRA).

The Kenyan government of Daniel arap Moi was initially suspicious of the new NRM government's alleged support for Kenyan dissident groups. Tensions culminated in a non-violent military standoff at Busia on the Kenya-Uganda border in late 1987. Any closure of borders with Kenya would have been extremely damaging to landlocked Uganda's economy whose access to the Indian Ocean via the port at Mombasa depends on Kenya.

During their guerrilla war against the government of Milton Obote, the National Resistance Army recruited anyone who was willing to fight, regardless of nationality. Persecution at the hands of Obote's regime encouraged many Rwandan exiles living in Uganda to join the ranks of the NRA.

Several years into the Museveni government, the Ugandan army still had several thousand Rwandans on its payroll.

On the night of 30 September 1990, 4,000 Rwandan members of the NRA left their barracks in secrecy, joining other forces to invade Rwanda from Ugandan territory. It

117

transpired that the Rwandan Patriotic Front (RPF) had a large membership within the NRA using a clandestine cell structure.

The RPF was a movement of Rwandan exiles opposed to the government of Juvénal Habyarimana who were linked to Museveni and the NRM. RPF leaders included Fred Rwigema and Paul Kagame, both Rwandan exiles and founding members of Museveni's National Resistance Movement (NRM).

During the initial stages of the invasion of Rwanda by the RPF, Museveni and Habyarimana were both attending a UN summit in the United States. It has been claimed that the date for the invasion was set to allow Museveni to distance himself from the RPF's actions until it was too late to stop them. The Rwandan Hutu-dominated army of President Habyarimana managed to expel the invaders only after it got reinforcements from Belgium, France and Zaire.

Museveni was blamed for complicity in the September 1990 invasion and/or not having control of his army.

After the invasion was stopped by the Rwandan army and its foreign supporters, the RPF invaders melted away into the Virunga Mountains straddling the Rwandan-Ugandan border.

The Habyarimana government accused Uganda of allowing the RPF to use its territory as a rear base and responded by shelling Ugandan villages on the border. Uganda is widely believed to have returned fire. These exchanges forced more than 60,000 people to flee their homes.

Despite the negotiation of a security pact, in which both countries agreed to cooperate in maintaining security along their common border, a resurgent RPF had occupied much of the northern territory of Rwanda by 1992.

In April 1994, a plane carrying President Habyarimana of Rwanda and President Cyprien Ntaryamira of Burundi was shot down over Kigali airport. This precipitated the

Rwandan genocide in which an estimated 800,000 people perished. Most of them were Tutsi. The Tutsi-dominated Rwandan Patriotic Front overran Kigali and took power with the help of the Ugandan army.

In April 1995, Uganda cut off diplomatic relations with Sudan in protest against Sudan's support for the Lord's Resistance Army (LRA), a rebel group active in northern Uganda. Sudan, in turn, claimed that Uganda was providing support to the Sudan People's Liberation Army (SPLA) in the southern part of the country which was fighting against the Sudanese government based in the north.

Both groups – LRA and SPLA – were suspected of operating across the porous Ugandan-Sudanese border.

Disputes between Uganda and Sudan date back to at least 1988. Ugandan refugees sought shelter in southern Sudan during the Amin and Obote II regimes. However, after the NRM seized power in Uganda in 1986, many of these refugees joined the Ugandan rebel groups including the West Nile Bank Front and later the LRA which were fighting against Museveni's government. For a significant period, Museveni's government viewed Sudan as the most significant threat to Ugandan security.

Internal security and human rights

The NRM came to power promising to restore security and respect for human rights. Indeed, this was part of the NRM's ten-point programme, as Museveni noted in his swearing-in speech:

"The second point on our programme is security of person and property. Every person in Uganda must [have absolute] security to live wherever he wants. Any individual, any group who threatens the security of our people must be smashed without mercy. The people of Uganda should die only from natural causes which are

119

beyond our control, but not from fellow human beings who continue to walk the length and breadth of our land."

Although Museveni now headed a new government in Kampala, the NRM could not project its influence fully across Ugandan territory and found itself fighting a number of insurgencies. From the beginning of Museveni's presidency, he drew strong support from the Bantu-speaking south and southwest where Museveni had his base.

Museveni also managed to get the Karamojong, a group of semi-nomads in the sparsely populated northeast who had never had a significant political voice, to align with him by offering them a stake in the new government.

However, the northern region along the Sudanese border proved more troublesome.

In the West Nile sub-region inhabited by the Kakwa and the Lugbara who had previously supported Amin, the UNRF and FUNA rebel groups fought for years until a combination of military offensives and diplomacy pacified the region. The leader of the UNRF, Moses Ali, gave up his struggle to become Uganda's second deputy prime minister in Museveni's government.

The people from the northern parts of the country viewed the rise of a government led by a person from the south with great trepidation. Rebel groups sprang up among the Lango, Acholi and Teso, although they were overwhelmed by the strength of the NRA except in the far north where the Sudanese border provided a safe haven.

The Acholi rebel group, the Uganda People's Democratic Army (UPDA), failed to dislodge the NRA from Acholiland, leading to the desperate chiliasm – or millenarianism – of the Holy Spirit Movement (HSM).

The Holy Spirit Movement (HSM) was led by Alice Auma, a spirit-medium who claimed to receive direction from the spirit Lakwena. An ethnicAcholi, Alice was purportedly directed to form the HSM by Lakwena in

August 1986.

Technically the Holy Spirit Movement (HSM) was the political wing of Alice's organization, and the Holy Spirit Mobile Force (HSMF), its military wing. But there was no real separation of functions between the two. And names were used interchangeably.

After gathering a small group of followers, Alice convinced the rebel group, the Uganda People's Democratic Army (UPDA) to put some of their troops under her command in November 1986.

In November and December 1986, the Holy Spirit Mobile Force (HSMF) achieved two unexpected victories over government National Resistance Army (NRA) forces. These victories brought widespread popular support, even among other northern ethnic groups besides the Acholi, and attracted new recruits to the HSM.

Much of the popular support was the result of a strict but fair set of guidelines given to the HSM followers which governed the relationship between the HSM rebels and the members of the general population. That created a positive impression compared to the government or other rebel groups which were often seen to be abusing their military strength in their dealings with the civilian population.

The Holy Spirit Movement fought as a regular army - taking and controlling territory, as well as holding pitched battles with NRA forces - but had a number of practices which outsiders found bizarre. Spiritual "controllers" were integrated into each unit. Along with duties such as tending to Alice Auma while she was possessed, they smeared blessed oil on combatants that was supposed to stop bullets if the combatant's soul was pure.

Stones were blessed so they would explode like grenades, and combatants walked into combat in cross-shaped formations while singing hymns.

While the HSM suffered a number of horrific defeats, particularly when defending NRA soldiers had machine guns to fire upon the hymn-singing formations walking towards them, these methods were, according to some accounts, surprisingly effective.

The alliance between the Uganda People's Democratic Army (UPDA) and the Holy Spirit Movement (HSM) quickly fell apart. By early 1987 the UPDA was attempting to capture the civilian resource base of the HSM by terrorising Lakwena's supporters into submission.

Despite continued conflicts with other rebel groups, the HSM began an offensive in August 1987 with the objective of taking the capital Kampala and starting a paradise on earth. By November 1987, it had extended its forces far into regions where it had no popular support. After suffering a series of defeats, the shaken HSM was decisively defeated fifty miles from Kampala in a forest battle in which the government's National Resistance Army (NRA) used overwhelming artillery support.

The Holy Spirit Movement left in its wake a number of smaller rebel groups which mimicked its chiliastic message: the doctrine stating that Jesus will reign on earth for 1,000 years.

Most of these groups soon fell into disarray, banditry, disbanded as members drifted away, or were defeated by government forces or by other rebel groups. However, one of the groups eventually became the Lord's Resistance Army (LRA).

The defeat of both the UPDA and HSM left the rebellion to a group that eventually came to be known by its "Christian" name: the Lord's Resistance Army (LRA) which would turn upon the Acholi themselves.

Led by Joseph Kony, Alice Lakwena's cousin, the LRA continued to operate in Acholiland and beyond for decades and was still terrorising people as recently as 2012.

The National Resistance Army (NRA) subsequently earned a reputation for respecting the rights of civilians, although Museveni later received criticism for using child soldiers. Undisciplined elements within the NRA's soon tarnished a hard-won reputation for fairness. "When Museveni's men first came they acted very well – we welcomed them," said one villager, "but then they started to arrest people and kill them."

In March 1989, Amnesty International published a human rights report on Uganda entitled *Uganda, the Human Rights Record 1986–1989*. It documented gross human rights violations committed by NRA troops.

In one of the most intense phases of the war between October and December 1988, the NRA forcibly cleared approximately 100,000 people from their homes in and around the town of Gulu, the largest in northern Uganda. Soldiers committed hundreds of extrajudicial executions as they forcibly moved people, burning down homes and granaries. However, there were few reports of the systematic torture and killings equivalent to those committed during Amin's and Obote's regimes. In its conclusion, the report offered some hope:

"Any assessment of the NRM government's human rights performance is, perhaps inevitably, less favourable after four years in power than it was in the early months. However, it is not true to say, as some critics and outside observers (claim), that there has been a continuous slide back towards gross human rights abuse, that in some sense Uganda is fated to suffer at the hands of bad government."

A new democratic mandate (1996–2001)

Elections

The first elections under Museveni's government were held on 9 May 1996.

Yoweri Museveni defeated Paul Ssemogerere of the Democratic Party who contested the election as a candidate for the "Inter-party forces coalition," and the upstart candidate, Mohamed Mayanja.

Museveni won with a landslide 75.5 per cent of the vote from a turnout of 72.6 per cent of eligible voters. Although international and domestic observers described the vote as valid, both the losing candidates rejected the results. Museveni was sworn in as president for the second time on 12 May 1996.

The main weapon in Museveni's campaign was the restoration of security and economic normality to much of the country. A memorable electoral image produced by his team depicted a pile of skulls in the Luwero Triangle. This powerful symbolism was not lost on the inhabitants of this region, who had suffered rampant insecurity during the civil war.

The other candidates had difficulty matching Museveni's efficacy in communicating his key message. Museveni seemed to have a remarkable ability to relate political messages by using grass-roots language, especially with people from the south. The metaphor of "carrying a grindstone for leadership", referring to an "authoritative individual, bearing the burden of authority", was just one of many imaginative images he created for his campaign. He would often deliver these in the appropriate local colloquial language, demonstrating respect and attempting to transcend tribalistic politics. Museveni's fluency in English, Luganda, Runyankole and Swahili often helped him forward his message.

Until the prospect of presidential elections, Ssemogerere (Museveni's concurrent political rival) had been a minister in the National Resistance Movement (NRM) government. His decision to challenge the record of Museveni and the NRM, rather than claim a stake in Museveni's "movement", was seen as naive opportunism, and regarded as a political error.

Ssemogerere's alliance with the Uganda People's congress (UPC) was anathema to the Baganda who might otherwise have lent him some support as the leader of the Democratic Party (DP).

Ssemogerere also accused Museveni of being a Rwandan, a statement often repeated by Museveni's opponents because of his birthplace near the Ugandan-Rwandan border and his supposedly Rwandan origins (Museveni claims to be an ethnic Munyankole, kin to the Banyarwanda of Rwanda), and his army being dominated by Rwandans, which included current Rwandan president Paul Kagame.

In 1997 he introduced free primary education.

The second set of elections were held in 2001. President Museveni beat his rival Dr. Kizza Besigye as he sailed through with 69% of the vote. Dr Besigye had been a close confidant of the president and he was his bush war physician. But they had a fallout shortly before the 2001 elections when Dr Besigye decided to run for president. The 2001 election campaigns were a heated affair with president Museveni threatening his rival to put him "six feet under."

The election culminated into a petition filed by Dr Besigye at the Supreme Court of Uganda. The court ruled that the elections were not free and fair but declined to nullify the outcome by a 3:2 majority decision. It was held that the many cases of election malpractice did not however affect the result in a substantial manner. Justices Benjamin Odoki (Chief justice), Alfrerd Karokora, and Joseph Mulenga ruled in favour of the respondents while Justices Aurthur Haggai Oder (RIP) and John Tsekoko ruled in favour of Dr Besigye.

The most recent presidential elections were held in 2006 where again Museveni prevailed over Dr Besigye scoring 59% of the vote. The election petition in this case had more evidence of election malpractice but by a 4:3 decision, the result was upheld. As before, the judges ruled as they ruled in the 2001 petition. The additional two judges were Justice George W. Kanyeihamba ruling in favour of Dr Besigye and Justice Bart Katureebe in favour of President Museveni and the electoral commission. Dr Besigye predicted that that could be the last presidential election petition filed in the then constituted Supreme Court.

International recognition

Museveni has won praise from Western governments for his adherence to IMF structural adjustment programmes (SAPs), for example, privatising state enterprises, cutting government spending and urging African self-reliance.

Museveni was elected chairman of the Organisation of African Unity (OAU) in 1991 and 1992.

He permitted a free atmosphere within which the news media could operate, and private FM radio stations flourished during the late 1990s.

Perhaps President Museveni's most widely noted accomplishment has been his government's successful campaign on how to combat AIDS. During the 1980s, Uganda had one of the highest rates of HIV infection in the world. But now Uganda's rates are comparatively low, and the country stands as a rare success story in the global battle against the virus.

One of the campaigns headed by Museveni to fight against AIDS was the ABC programme. The ABC programme had three main parts: Abstain, Be faithful, or use Condoms if A and B are not practised.

In April 1998, Uganda became the first country to be declared eligible for debt relief under the Heavily Indebted Poor Countries (HIPC) initiative, receiving some US$700 million in aid.

Museveni was also lauded for his affirmative action programme for women in the country. He was served by a female vice-president, Specioza Kazibwe, for nearly 10 years from 1994 to 2003. Dr. Kazibwe was the first woman in Africa to hold that position. Museveni also has done much to encourage women to go to college.

On the other hand, he has resisted calls for greater women's family land rights: the right of women to own a share of their matrimonial homes.

From the mid-1990s, Museveni was seen to exemplify a new breed of African leadership, the antithesis of the "big men" who had dominated politics on the continent since independence. The following excerpt from a *New York Times* article in 1997 is illustrative of the high esteem in which Museveni was held by the Western media, governments and academics:

"These are heady days for the former guerrilla who runs Uganda. He moves with the measured gait and sure gestures of a leader secure in his power and his vision. It is little wonder. To hear some of the diplomats and African experts tell it, President Yoweri K. Museveni started an ideological movement that is reshaping much of Africa, spelling the end of the corrupt, strong-man governments that characterized the cold-war era. These days, political pundits across the continent are calling Mr. Museveni an African Bismarck. Some people now refer to him as Africa's 'other statesman,' second only to the venerated South African President, Nelson Mandela."

In official briefing papers from Madeleine Albright's December 1997 Africa tour as US secretary of state, Museveni was called a "beacon of hope" who runs a "uni-party democracy," although Uganda did not permit multi-party politics.

All those generous statements have since been re-evaluated. In many fundamental respects, Museveni turned out to be not the kind of leader they thought he would be. He disappointed many of his admirers and supporters.

Regional conflict

In Uganda, there were significant numbers of ethnic Rwandan Tutsi immigrants who were a significant part of Museveni's NRA fighters.

The members of the Uganda-based and Tutsi-dominated Rwandan Patriotic Front (RPF) rebel group were close allies of the NRA. And once Museveni had solidified his hold on central power, he lent his support to their cause.

Unsuccessful attacks were launched by the RPF against the Hutu government of Rwanda in the first half of the 1990s from bases in southwestern Uganda. It was not until the Rwandan genocide of 1994 that the RPF took power, and its head, Paul Kagame, a former soldier and intelligence chief in Museveni's army, became president of Rwanda.

Following the Rwandan genocide, the new Rwandan government felt threatened by the presence (across the Rwandan border in Congo, then known as Zaïre) of former Rwandan soldiers and members of the previous Hutu-dominated regime. These soldiers were helped by Mobutu Sese Seko, leading Rwanda (with the help of Museveni) and Laurent Kabila's rebels to overthrow him and take power in Congo.

In August 1998, Rwanda and Uganda invaded Congo again; this time to overthrow Museveni and Kagame's former ally, Kabila. Museveni and a few close military advisers alone made the decision to send the Uganda People's Defence Force (UPDF) into Congo.

A number of highly placed sources indicate that the Ugandan parliament and civilian advisers were not consulted over the matter, as is required by the 1995 constitution.

Museveni apparently persuaded an initially reluctant high command to go along with the venture. "We felt that the Rwandese started the war and it was their duty to go ahead and finish the job, but our president took time and convinced us that we had a stake in what is going on in Congo," one senior officer is reported as saying.

The official reasons Uganda gave for the intervention were to stop a "genocide" against the Banyamulenge in the Democratic Republic of Congo (DRC) in concert with Rwandan forces, and that Kabila had failed to provide security along the border and was allowing the Allied Democratic Forces (ADF) to attack Uganda from rear bases in DRC. The ADF is a rebel group opposed to the Ugandan government. It is based in western Uganda with rear bases in the Democratic Republic of Congo. It began as a minor group in the forested Ruwenzori mountain range along the border in 1996 but expanded its activities over the next several years.

With regard to the invasion of Congo by Uganda and Rwanda, the UPDF were, in reality, not deployed in the border region but more than 600 miles to the west of Uganda's frontier with Congo and in support of the Movement for the Liberation of the Congo (*Mouvement pour la Liberation du Congo* – MLC) rebels seeking to overthrow President Laurent Kabila. As such, they were unable to prevent the ADF from invading the major town of Fort Portal and taking over a prison in western Uganda.

Troops from Rwanda and Uganda plundered Congo's rich mineral deposits and timber. The United States responded to the invasion by suspending all military aid to Uganda, a disappointment to the Clinton administration, which had hoped to make Uganda the centrepiece of the African Crisis Response Initiative.

In 2000, Rwandan and Ugandan troops exchanged fire on three occasions in the Congolese city of Kisangani, leading to tensions and a deterioration in relations between Kagame and Museveni.

The Ugandan government has also been criticised for aggravating the Ituri conflict, a sub-conflict of the second

Congo war.

In December 2005, the International Court of Justice ruled that Uganda must pay compensation to the Democratic Republic of the Congo for human rights violations during the second Congo war.

In the north, Uganda had supported the Sudan People's Liberation Army (SPLA) in the second Sudanese civil war against the Arab-dominated government in Khartoum even before Museveni came to power. The continued support for the SPLA, led by Museveni's old acquaintance John Garang, led Sudan to support the Lord's Resistance Army (LRA) and other anti-Museveni rebel groups in the mid-1990s.

The resulting insecurity and conflicts have caused widespread human displacement, death and destruction in southern Sudan and northern Uganda. Subsequent warming of relations with Sudan led to a pledge to stop supporting hostile proxy forces (from both sides) and the granting of approval to the UPDF to attack the LRA within Sudan itself.

A second term (2001–2006)

2001 elections

In 2001 Museveni won the presidential elections by a substantial majority, with his former friend and personal physician Kizza Besigye as the only real challenger.

In a populist publicity stunt, a pentagenarian Museveni travelled on a *bodaboda* motorcycle taxi to submit his nomination form for the election. *Bodaboda* is a cheap and somewhat dangerous (by western standards) method of transporting passengers around towns and villages in East Africa.

There was much recrimination and bitterness during the 2001 presidential elections campaign, and incidents of violence occurred following the announcement of the results – which were won by Museveni.

Besigye challenged the election results in the Supreme Court of Uganda. Two of the five judges concluded that there were such illegalities in the elections, and that the results should be rejected. The other three judges decided that the illegalities did not affect the result of the election in a substantial manner, but stated that "there was evidence that in a significant number of polling stations there was cheating" and that in some areas of the country, "the principle of free and fair election was compromised." Besigye was briefly detained and questioned by the police, allegedly in connection with the offence of treason. In September 2001, he fled to the USA claiming his life was in danger.

Political pluralism and constitutional change

After the elections, political forces allied to Museveni began a campaign to loosen constitutional limits on the presidential term, allowing him to stand for election again in 2006.

The 1995 Ugandan constitution provided for a two-term limit on the tenure of the president. Given Uganda's history of dictatorial regimes, this check and balance was designed to prevent a dangerous centralisation of power around a long-serving leader. This period witnessed the removal of key and influential Museveni supporters from his administration, including his childhood friend Eriya Kategaya and cabinet minister Jaberi Bidandi Ssali.

Moves to change the constitution and alleged attempts to suppress opposition political forces have attracted criticism from domestic commentators, the international community and Uganda's aid donors. In a press release, the main opposition party, the Forum for Democratic Change (FDC), accused Museveni of engaging in a "life presidency project" and for bribing members of parliament to vote against constitutional amendments, FDC leaders claimed:

"The country is polarized with many Ugandans objecting to [the constitutional amendments]. If Parliament goes ahead and removes term limits this may cause serious unrest, political strife and may lead to turmoil both through the transition period and there after ... We would therefore like to appeal to President Museveni to respect himself, the people who elected him and the Constitution under which he was voted President in 2001 when he promised the country and the world at large to hand over power peacefully and in an orderly manner at the end of his second and last term. Otherwise his insistence to stand again will expose him as a consummate liar and the biggest political fraudster this country has ever known."

As observed by some political commentators, including Wafula Oguttu, Museveni had previously stated that he considered the idea of clinging to office for "15 or more" years ill-advised.

Comments by the Irish anti-poverty campaigner Bob Geldof sparked a protest by Museveni supporters outside the British High Commission in Kampala. "Get a grip Museveni. Your time is up, go away," said the former rock star in March 2005, explaining that moves to change the constitution were compromising Museveni's record against fighting poverty and HIV/AIDS.

In an opinion article in the *Boston Globe* and in a speech delivered at the Wilson Center, former U.S. Ambassador to Uganda Johnnie Carson heaped more criticism on Museveni. Despite recognising the president as a "genuine reformer" whose "leadership [has] led to stability and growth", Carson also said, "we may be looking at another Mugabe and Zimbabwe in the making." "Many observers see Museveni's efforts to amend the constitution as a re-run of a common problem that afflicts many African leaders – an unwillingness to follow constitutional norms and give up power."

In July 2005, Norway became the third European country in as many months to announce symbolic cutbacks in foreign aid to Uganda in response to political leadership in the country. The UK and Ireland made similar moves in May. "Our foreign ministry wanted to highlight two issues: the changing of the constitution to lift term limits, and problems with opening the political space, human rights and corruption", said Norwegian Ambassador Tore Gjos. Of particular significance was the arrest of two opposition MPs from the Forum for Democratic Change (FDC).

Human rights campaigners charged that the arrests were politically motivated. Human Rights Watch stated that "the arrest of these opposition MPs smacks of political opportunism."

A confidential World Bank report leaked in May 2005 suggested that the international lender might cut its support to non-humanitarian programmes in the Uganda. "We regret that we cannot be more positive about the present political situation in Uganda, especially given the country's admirable record through the late 1990s," said the paper. "The Government has largely failed to integrate the country's diverse peoples into a single political process that is viable over the long term...Perhaps most significant, the political trend-lines, as a result of the President's apparent determination to press for a third term, point downward."

Museveni responded to the mounting international pressure by accusing donors of interfering with domestic politics and using aid to manipulate poor countries. "Let the partners give advice and leave it to the country to decide ... [developed] countries must get out of the habit of trying to use aid to dictate the management of our countries." "The problem with those people is not the third term or fighting corruption or multipartism," added

Museveni at a meeting with other African leaders, "the problem is that they want to keep us there without growing."

In July 2005, a constitutional referendum lifted a 19-year restriction on the activities of political parties.

In the non-party "Movement system" (so called "the movement") instituted by Museveni in 1986, parties continued to exist but candidates were required to stand for election as individuals rather than as representatives of any political grouping. This measure was ostensibly designed to reduce ethnic divisions, although many observers have subsequently claimed that the system had become nothing more than a restriction on opposition activity.

Before the vote, the Forum for Democratic Change (FDC) spokesperson stated: "Key sectors of the economy are headed by people from the president's home area... We have got the most sectarian regime in the history of the country in spite the fact that there are no parties."

Many Ugandans saw Museveni's conversion to political pluralism as a concession to donors aimed at softening the blow when he announces he wants to stay on for a third term. Opposition MP Omara Atubo said Museveni's desire for change was merely "a facade behind which he is trying to hide ambitions to rule for life."

Death of an ally

On 30 July 2005, Sudanese Vice-President John Garang was killed when the Ugandan presidential helicopter crashed while he was travelling to Sudan from talks in Uganda.

The incident was acutely embarrassing for the Ugandan government and a personal blow for Museveni. Garang had been a political ally since their days together at the University of Dar es Salaam, Tanzania, when they were students there.

Garang had only been Sudanese vice-president for a matter of weeks before his death which damaged hopes of a regional order based on a Uganda-South Sudan alliance.

Widespread speculation as to the cause of the crash led Museveni, on 10 August 2005, to threaten the closure of media outlets which published "conspiracy theories" about Garang's death. In a statement, Museveni claimed such speculation was a threat to national security. "I will no longer tolerate a newspaper which is like a vulture. Any newspaper that plays around with regional security, I will not tolerate it – I will close it."

The following day, a popular radio station, KFM, had its license withdrawn for broadcasting a debate on Garang's death. Radio presenter Andrew Mwenda was eventually arrested for sedition in connection with comments made on his KFM talk show.

February 2006 elections

On 17 November 2005, Museveni was chosen as NRMs presidential candidate for the February 2006 elections. His candidacy for a further third term sparked criticism, as he had promised in 2001 that he was contesting for the last term.

The arrest of the main opposition leader Kizza Besigye on 14 November 2005 – charged with treason, concealment of treason and rape – sparked demonstrations and riots in Kampala and other towns.

Museveni's bid for a third term, the arrest of Besigye, and the besiegement of the High Court during a hearing of Besigye's case (by a heavily armed Military Intelligence (CMI) group dubbed by the press as "Black Mambas Urban Hit Squad"), led Sweden, the Netherlands and the United Kingdom to withhold economic support to Museveni's government due to concerns about the country's democratic development.

On 2 January 2006, Besigye was released after the High Court ordered his immediate release.

The 23 February 2006 elections were Uganda's first multi-party elections in 25 years and were seen as a test of its democratic credentials. Although Museveni did less well than he did in the previous election, he was elected for another five-year tenure. He won won 59% of the vote against Besigye's 37%.

Besigye, who alleged fraud, rejected the results.

The Supreme Court of Uganda later ruled that the election was marred by intimidation, violence, voter disenfranchisement and other irregularities. However, the Court voted 4-3 to uphold the results of the electoral contest.

The Third Term (2006–2011)

In 2007, Museveni deployed troops to the African Union's peacekeeping operation in Somalia.

Another significant issue in Museveni's third term is his decision to open the Mabira Forest to sugarcane planting. While Museveni argues that new plantations are important for Uganda's economic development, environmental activists worry about the loss of ecosystems and biodiversity that will result from that. These concerns led to a riot in 2007 which claimed two lives.

Also in this term, Museveni held meetings with investors, including Wisdek, to promote Uganda's call centre and outsourcing industry and create employment in the country.

September 2009 riots

In September 2009, Museveni denied Kabaka Muwenda Mutebi, the Baganda king, permission to visit some areas of Kampala. Riots occurred and 40 people were killed.

Fundamentalist Christianity

In 2009, many news sources reported on Jeff Sharlet's investigation regarding ties between Museveni and the American fundamentalist Christian organisation, The Fellowship also known as "The Family." Sharlet reported that Douglas Coe, the leader of The Fellowship, identified Museveni as the organisation's "key man in Africa."

Further international scrutiny accompanied the 2009 Ugandan efforts to institute the death penalty for homosexuality, with leaders from Canada, the UK, the US, and France expressing concerns for human rights.

A British newspaper, *The Guardian*, reported that President Museveni "appeared to add his backing" to the legislative effort by, among other things, claiming "European homosexuals are recruiting in Africa," and saying gay relationships were against God's will.

The 2009 effort for harsher penalties for homosexual behaviour in Uganda further strengthened existing laws criminalising homosexuality. Those convicted may face life imprisonment under the law that already exists.

The Fourth Term (2011–)

Museveni was re-elected on 20 February 2011 with a 68% majority. About 59% of registered voters participated in the election.

The results were disputed by both the European Union and the opposition,"The electoral process was marred with avoidable administrative and logistical failures" according to the European Union election observer team.

Books by Museveni

- Museveni, Yoweri. *Sowing the Mustard Seed: The Struggle for Freedom and Democracy in Uganda*, Macmillan Education, 1997
- Museveni, Yoweri. *What Is Africa's Problem?*, University of Minnesota Press, 2000.

Paul Kagame

Paul Kagame (born 23 October 1957) is the sixth and current president of Rwanda.

He rose to prominence as the leader of the Rwandan Patriotic Front (RPF) whose victory over the incumbent government in July 1994 effectively ended the Rwandan genocide.

Under his leadership, Rwanda has been called Africa's "biggest success story" and Kagame has become a public advocate of new models for foreign aid designed to help recipients become self-reliant. However, Paul Kagame's rule has been criticised for his domestic policies which have been described as authoritarian.

He has also been accused of sanctioning and authorising the assassination of his political opponents including those who live in exile.

Under the leadership of Paul Kagame, Rwanda invaded the Democratic Republic of the Congo (DRC) twice and occupied it for five years. In the course of the war, the Rwandan army financed its invasion through the illegal sale of Congo's natural resources.

The second war in Congo which began in 1998 resulted in the deaths of more than five million people. It was the most devastating conflict in human history since the Second World War. It involved armies from seven African countries and came to be known as Africa's World

War.

Remnants of the rebel groups which were also involved in the conflict continued to wreak havoc especially in eastern Congo after the war ended. The region is still mired in conflict, in varying degrees, because of the rebel groups which still exist there.

Early life

Kagame was born to a Tutsi family in Ruhango, Ruanda-Urundi in October 1957 to Deogratius and Asteria Rutagambwa.

Ruanda-Urundi was one Belgian colony which split into two countries, Rwanda and Burundi, at independence.

In November 1959, an increasingly restive Hutu population revolted against its Tutsi rulers and eventually overthrew Mwami (King) Kigeri V Ndahindurwa in 1961.

During the 1959 revolt and its aftermath, more than 150,000 people were killed in the fighting. Tutsis suffered the most.

Several thousands of Tutsis moved to neighbouring countries including Burundi, Uganda, and Tanganyika which became Tanzania in 1964 after uniting with Zanzibar.

In 1960, Kagame left Rwanda with his family at the age of two and moved to Uganda with many other Tutsis. In 1962, they settled in the Gahunge refugee camp, Toro, in southwestern Uganda, where Kagame spent the rest of his childhood. He attended Ntare Secondary School in Uganda.

Military service

Kagame's military career started when he joined Yoweri Museveni's National Resistance Army (NRA) and spent years fighting as a guerrilla against the government of Uganda President Milton Obote in what is commonly known in Uganda as the bush war.

On 27 July 1985, Obote was ousted in a military coup led by General Tito Okello. In 1986 the NRA succeeded in overthrowing Okello and the NRA leader Museveni became president of Uganda.

In the same year, Kagame was instrumental in forming, together with his close friend Fred Rwigema, the Rwandan Patriotic Front (RPF) which was composed mainly of Rwandan Tutsi soldiers who were members of Museveni's National Resitance Army (NRA). The RPF was also based in Uganda.

In 1986, Kagame became the head of military intelligence in the NRA, and was regarded as one of Museveni's closest allies. He also joined the official Ugandan military.

During 1990, Kagame went to Fort Leavenworth in the state of Kansas where the U.S. Army gave him military training.

When the RPF launched an invasion of Rwanda and his close friend and RPF co-founder Fred Rwigema was killed, the U.S. arranged the return of Kagame to Uganda and thence to take the leadership of the invasion, thus signaling that the U.S. was siding with Uganda and the RPF against the incumbent Rwandan government.

Broadening this connection, the U.S. and U.K. military provided further training and active logistical support to the RPF which it used to take over power in Rwanda after 1994. And after coming to power, Kagame arranged for the RPF to receive further counterinsurgency and combat training from U.S. Special Forces which was put to use in the 1996–1997 Rwandan-backed military campaign to overthrow the government of Mobutu Sese Seko of neighbouring Zaire which was renamed Congo after he was overthrown.

Invasions and assassinations

In October 1990, while Kagame was undergoing military training in the U.S., the RPF invaded Rwanda in the struggle for the interests of Rwanda's Tutsi minority ethnic group. Only two days into the invasion, Rwigema was murdered, making Kagame the military commander of the RPF. Despite initial successes, a force of French, Belgian, Rwandan and Zairean soldiers forced the RPF to retreat. A renewed invasion was attempted in late 1991, but also had limited success.

The invasion increased ethnic tensions throughout the region, including neighbouring Burundi where similar tensions between the Hutu and Tutsi existed as they did in Rwanda. Peace talks between the RPF and the Rwandan government resulted in the Arusha accords in Arusha, Tanzania, including political participation of the RPF in Rwanda. Despite the agreement, ethnic tensions still flared dangerously.

On 6 April 1994, a plane carrying both the Rwandan President Juvénal Habyarimana and the Burundian President Cyprien Ntaryamira was shot down by a surface-to-air missile as it approached Kigali airport. All on board were killed. The deaths immediately sparked the Rwandan genocide in which an estimated 800,000 to 1,000,000 Rwandans, mostly Tutsi, were killed.

Under the Arusha accords, the RPF had a small contingent of troops present in Kigali at the time. The outbreak of genocide ended what vestiges remained of the cease fire. The RPF, under the leadership of Kagame, proceeded to take control of the whole country. Kigali was captured 4 July 1994, bringing the downfall of the government of Jean Kambanda who served as prime minister of Rwanda.

Kambanda was sworn in as prime minister on 9 April

1994 after the President Habyarimana and former Prime Minister Agathe Uwilingiyimana were assassinated.

The opposition Democratic Republican Movement (*Mouvement démocratique républicain* – MDR) had been promised the prime ministerial post in the transitional government established by the Arusha accords but Kambanda leapfrogged several levels in the party's hierarchy to take the job from the initial choice, Faustin Twagiramungu. He remained in the post for the hundred days of the genocide until 19 July 1994. After leaving office, he fled the country.

French indictment

The downing of the plane over Kigali brought in outside powers. Because three French citizens, crew members of the aircraft, died during the crash, an investigation was carried out by French judge Jean-Louis Bruguière who controversially concluded that the shooting of the plane was ordered by Kagame.

In November 2006, Judge Bruguière signed international indictments against nine of President Kagame's senior aides and accused Kagame of ordering the assassination of the two African presidents. Kagame could not be indicted under French law, since as a head of state, he had immunity from prosecution.

The indictments have failed to produce any arrests due to non-cooperation from the Rwandan government which accused the judge of partiality.

The Kagame government countered that the indictment was based upon declarations by fugitives and disgruntled former lower rank RPF members who testified that the RPF was the only organisation with the type of missiles that were used in the assassination. It also pointed out that at the time of the shooting of the plane, the French military was in control of Kigali Airport; although that point, and the possible attempt to imply that the French shot down the plane, is irrelevant as the plane was shot down on approach to the airport and not from the zone controlled by French forces.

The former chief prosecutor for Yugoslavia and Rwanda, Judge Richard Goldstone, argued in an interview that political motivations were at play in the indictment, though this did not negate the potential veracity of the accusations levelled by Judge Bruguière.

Judge Goldstone stated:

"Well I don't think that case has been made at all. It's a very political judgement and I don't believe that it's borne out by the evidence. Certainly the witnesses who spoke to Bruguiere allege that those were statements made by President Kagame himself. Whether he did or not obviously is a matter in dispute, in hot dispute, but the political judgement it seems to me is another matter."

The accusations against Kagame were corroborated by several witnesses including former intelligence RPF members, the most publicly known being Commando Lieutenant Abdul Ruzibiza. Ruzibiza published a book, *Rwanda: L'histoire secrete*, and released testimony pertaining to Kagame and the RPF's involvement in the downing of the plane and in the massacres.

However, Ruzibiza subsequently retracted part of his testimony, especially concerning Kagame senior aide Rose Kabuye after she was arrested in Germany and extradited to France.

The *Association des Avocats de la Defence* released a statement backing Judge Bruguière's allegations. Paul Rusesabagina, a Rwandan of mixed Hutu and Tutsi origin whose feat saving 1,268 civilians has been the basis of the Academy Award nominated film *Hotel Rwanda* (2004), has supported the allegation that Kagame and the RPF were behind the plane downing, and stated :

"It defies logic why the UN Security Council has never mandated an investigation of this airplane missile attack to establish who was responsible, especially since everyone agrees it was the one incident that touched off the mass killings commonly referred to as the 'Rwandan genocide of 1994.'"

In a counterattack, Kagame broke off diplomatic relations with France in November 2006 and ordered the formation of a commission of loyal Rwandans that was officially "charged with assembling proof of the involvement of France in the genocide." The political character of that investigation was further averred when the commission issued its report solely to Kagame in November 2007 and its head, Jean de Dieu Mucyo, stated that the commission would now "wait for President Kagame to declare whether the inquiry was valid."

In a 2007 interview with the BBC, Mr Kagame said he would co-operate with an impartial inquiry. The BBC concluded: "Whether any judge would want to take on such a task is quite another matter."

As of 2009, a report commissioned by the Rwandan government concluded that the RPF and Kagame were not responsible for shooting down the president's plane.

Spanish indictment

In February 2008, Fernando Andreu, a Spanish judge, indicted 40 current or former Rwandan military officers for several counts of genocide and human rights abuses during the Rwandan genocide.

The judge issued international arrest warrants against the 40, including General James Kabarebe whom the judge believed to be the chief of staff of Rwanda's military; General Kayumba Nyamwasa, Rwanda's ex-ambassador to India who later fell out with President Kagame and sought refuge in South Africa where he was almost assassinated by Rwandan agents for criticising Kagame; and Lieutenant-Colonel Rugumuya Gacinya, military attaché at Rwanda's embassy in Washington.

Evidence was presented of crimes allegedly perpetrated by the Rwandan Patriotic Army and by the Rwandan Patriotic Front (RPA/RPF) in Rwanda and in the Democratic Republic of Congo (DRC) especially from 1990 to 2000. This revealed that the RPA/RPF's hierarchical chain of command headed by Kagame is responsible for three major and closely interrelated blocks of crime:

1. Crimes perpetrated against 9 Spanish victims – missionaries and aid workers- observers of the killings of Hutu inhabitants in both countries
2. Crimes against Rwandans and Congolese, against various specific leaders, or systematically carried out as mass murders of civilians
3. Crimes of war pillage- the systematic, large-scale plundering of natural resources, especially strategically valuable minerals.

The Second Congo War

Kagame was part of the cabinet of President Pasteur Bizimungu, a Hutu, who came to power in the aftermath of the genocide. Kagame was made vice president and defence minister. Bizimungu was also a member of the RPF. But as its military leader, Kagame was seen as the power behind the throne and eventually became president when Bizimungu was ousted in March 2000.

In 1998, Rwanda got heavily involved in the second Congo war, supporting a well-armed rebel group in Congo, the Congolese Rally for Democracy which was dominated by Congolese Tutsis known as Banyamulenge or Banyamurenge, Kagame's kinsmen as fellow Tutsis.

Together with uganda, Rwandan forces invaded the mineral-rich north and east of the Democratic Republic of Congo, citing Congolese anti-Tutsi policies and historical Rwandan heritage in the area. The government of Congo soon found itself supported by several other African nations, and mounted a counter attack, with limited success.

An April 2001 United Nations report alleged "mass-scale looting" of Congolese mineral resources. The report claimed that senior members of the Rwandan government had made hundreds of millions of dollars from illegal mineral trading, and that:

"Presidents Kagame and [Uganda's President] Museveni are on the verge of becoming the godfathers of the illegal exploitation of natural resources and the continuation of the conflict in the Democratic Republic of the Congo."

A June 2001 Amnesty International report implicated Rwandan and Rwandan-backed forces (amongst others) in the deliberate killing of thousands of Congolese civilians.

Although the Rwandan and Ugandan governments claimed to have withdrawn their forces from Congo, there were consistent reports of ongoing Rwandan involvement in support of rebel fighters trying to protect local Tutsi minorities against remnants of the Interahamwe, the militia involved in the 1994 Rwanda genocide whose members fled to eastern Congo after the RPF overran Kigali and seized power. However, since September 2007 and in the following years, the Rwandan government strongly denied any involvement in the fighting which was still going on in Congo during that period.

Critics allege that the Rwandan occupation of the eastern Congo was mainly motivated by a desire to exploit Congolese mineral resources. Paul Kagame, in turn, claimed that those criticisms were based on Hutu-extremist propaganda and that Rwanda's sole reason for occupying eastern Congo was to defeat the remnants of the Hutu-extremist militia who fled there from Rwanda after the 1994 genocide.

A 2002 United Nations report elaborated on the allegations of illegal profiteering by Rwandan and Ugandan forces in Congo in the following terms:

"The claims of Rwanda concerning its security have justified the continuing presence of its armed forces, whose real long-term purpose is, to use the term employed by the Congo Desk of the Rwandan Patriotic Army, to "secure property." Rwanda's leaders have succeeded in persuading the international community that their military presence in the eastern Democratic Republic of the Congo protects the country against hostile groups in the Democratic Republic of the Congo, who, they claim, are actively mounting an invasion against them.

The Panel has extensive evidence to the contrary. For example, the Panel is in possession of a letter, dated 26 May 2000, from Jean-Pierre Ondekane, First Vice-President and Chief of the Military High Command for [the Rwandan-backed rebel group] RCD-Goma, urging all army units to maintain good relations 'with our Interahamwe and Mayi-Mayi brothers', and further, 'if necessary to let them exploit the sub-soil for their survival'....

A 30-year-old Interahamwe combatant living in the area of Bukavu described the situation in a taped interview with a United Nations officer in early 2002:

'We haven't fought much with the RPA in the last two years. We think they are tired of this war, like we are. In any case, they aren't here in the Congo to chase us, like they pretend. I have seen the gold and coltan mining they do here, we see how they rob the population. These are the reasons for their being here. The RPA come and shoot in the air and raid the villagers' houses but they don't attack

147

us any more.'"

Presidency

Paul Kagame became President of Rwanda in March 2000 after Bizimungu was ousted. Three and a half years later, on 25 August 2003, he won a landslide victory in the first national elections since his government took power in 1994 winning 95.5% of the votes.

Kagame has been highly critical of the United Nations and its role in the 1994 genocide.

And in March 2004, his public criticism of France for its role in the genocide and its lack of preventative actions caused a diplomatic row. In November 2006, Rwanda severed all diplomatic ties with France and ordered all its diplomatic staff out of Rwanda within 24 hours following Judge Bruguiere issuing warrants accusing nine high-ranking Rwandans of plotting the downing of President Juvenal Habyarimana's airplane in 1994 and also accusing Kagame of ordering the plane shot down.

As president, Kagame has also been critical of the West's lack of development aid in Africa. He believes that Western countries keep African products out of the world marketplace. In contrast, he has praised China, saying in a 2009 interview that "the Chinese bring what Africa needs: investment and money for governments and companies."

He has also expressed positive views on private enterprise and free markets.

Human rights

Human Rights Watch has accused Rwandan police of several instances of extra-judicial killings and deaths in custody. In June 2006, the International Federation of Human Rights and Human Rights Watch described what they called "serious violations of international humanitarian law committed by the Rwanda Patriotic Army."

And according to The Economist, Kagame "allows less political space and press freedom at home than Robert Mugabe does in Zimbabwe," and "[a]nyone who poses the slightest political threat to the regime is dealt with ruthlessly."

Adam Hochschild, in a *New York Times* review of Jjason Stearns' book *Dancing in the Glory of Monsters*, wrote: "[H]ow this media-savvy autocrat has managed to convince so many American journalists, diplomats, and political leaders that he is a great statesman is worth a book in itself."

He has also been accused of authorising the assassination of his political opponents, including his former colleagues and supporters, as well as journalists and others. Even non-Rwandans who criticise him are not safe no matter where they are. He has a long reach.

The United States' government in 2006 described the human rights record of Kagame's government as "mediocre," citing the "disappearances" of political dissidents, as well as arbitrary arrests and acts of violence, torture and murders committed by the police.

American authorities listed human rights problems including the existence of political prisoners and limited freedom of the press, freedom of assembly and freedom of religion.

Reporters Without Borders listed Rwanda in 147th place out of 169 for freedom of the press in 2007 and reported that "Rwandan journalists suffer permanent hostility from their government and surveillance by the security services." It cited cases of journalists being threatened, harassed and arrested for criticising the government.

According to Reporters Without Borders, "President Paul Kagame and his government have never accepted that the press should be guaranteed genuine freedom." In 2011,

Kagame took issue with a British journalist on Twitter after the journalist's tweets asserted that Kagame is "despotic."

Patrice Lumumba

Patrice Émery Lumumba (2 July 1925 – 17 January 1961) was a Congolese independence leader and the first legally elected prime minister of the Republic of Congo after he helped win its independence from Belgium in June 1960.

Only ten weeks later, Lumumba's government was overthrown in a coup. Lumumba was subsequently imprisoned and murdered in circumstances suggesting the support and complicity of the governments of Belgium and the United States.

Early life and career

Lumumba was born in Onalua in the Katakokombe region of Kasai Province of the Belgian Congo. He was a member of the Tetela ethnic group.

Raised in a Catholic family as one of four sons, he was educated at a Protestant primary school, a Catholic missionary school, and finally the government post office training school, passing the one-year course with distinction.

He subsequently worked in the capital Leopoldville (now Kinshasa) and Stanleyville (now Kisangani) as a postal clerk and as a travelling beer salesman.

In 1951, he married Pauline Opangu.

In 1955, Lumumba became regional head of the *Cercles* of Stanleyville and joined the Liberal Party of Belgium where he worked on editing and distributing party literature.

After traveling on a three-week study tour in Belgium, he was arrested in 1955 on charges of embezzlement of post office funds. His two-year sentence was commuted to twelve months after it was confirmed by Belgian lawyer Jules Chrome that Lumumba had returned the funds. He was released in July 1956.

After his release, he helped found the broad-based Congolese National Movement (*Mouvement National Congolais* – MNC) in 1958 and later became its president.

Lumumba and his team represented the MNC at the All-African Peoples' Conference in Accra, Ghana, in December 1958. At this international conference, hosted by influential Pan-Africanist President Kwame Nkrumah of Ghana, Lumumba further solidified his Pan-Africanist beliefs.

Leader of MNC

In late October 1959, Lumumba as leader of the MNC was again arrested for allegedly inciting an anti-colonial riot in Stanleyville where thirty people were killed, for which he was sentenced to six months in prison. The trial's start date of 18 January 1960 was also the first day of a round-table conference in Brussels to finalise the future of the Congo.

Despite Lumumba's imprisonment at the time, the MNC won a convincing majority in the December local elections across the country. As a result of pressure from delegates who were enraged at Lumumba's imprisonment, he was released and allowed to attend the Brussels conference.

The conference culminated on 27 January with a declaration of Congolese independence setting 30 June 1960 as the independence date. National elections were held from 11 – 25 May 1960.

Lumumba and the MNC won the elections and the right to form a government. It was announced on 23 June 1960 that the 34-year-old Lumumba was Congo's first

151

prime minister and Joseph Kasavubu its president. In accordance with the constitution, on 24 June the new government passed a vote of confidence and was ratified by the Congolese Chamber and Senate.

Independence Day was celebrated on June 30th in a ceremony attended by many dignitaries including Belgian King Baudouin and the foreign press.

Lumumba delivered his famous independence speech after being officially excluded from the event, despite being the new prime minister. In his speech, King Baudouin praised developments under colonialism and made reference to the "genius" of his great-granduncle Leopold II of Belgium, glossing over the atrocities which were committed when the Congo Free State was a personal estate of Leopold II.

The King continued:

"Don't compromise the future with hasty reforms, and don't replace the structures that Belgium hands over to you until you are sure you can do better... Don't be afraid to come to us. We will remain by your side, give you advice."

Lumumba responded by reminding the audience that the independence of the Congo was not granted magnanimously by Belgium:

"For this independence of the Congo, even as it is celebrated today with Belgium, a friendly country with whom we deal as equal to equal, no Congolese worthy of the name will ever be able to forget that it was by fighting that it has been won, a day-to-day fight, an ardent and idealistic fight, a fight in which we were spared neither privation nor suffering, and for which we gave our strength and our blood. We are proud of this struggle, of tears, of fire, and of blood, to the depths of our being, for it was a noble and just struggle, and indispensable to put an end to the humiliating slavery which was imposed upon us by force."

A number of observers have said Lumumba's fiery speech sealed his fate.

In contrast to the relatively harmless speech of President Kasavubu, Lumumba's reference to the suffering of the Congolese under Belgian colonialism stirred the crowd while simultaneously humiliating and alienating the King and his entourage.

Some media claimed at the time that he ended his speech by ad-libbing, *Nous ne sommes plus vos macaques* (We are no longer your monkeys!) -- referring to a common slur used against Africans by Belgians and other whites. However, those words are neither in his written text nor in radio tapes of his speech.

Lumumba was later harshly criticised for what many in the Western world – but virtually none in Africa – described as the inappropriate nature of his speech.

Actions as prime minister

A few days after Congo gained its independence, Lumumba made the fateful decision to raise the pay of all government employees except for the army. Many units of the army also had strong objections towards their Belgian officers. General Janssens, the army head, told them their lot would not change after independence. They rebelled in protest.

The rebellions quickly spread throughout the country, leading to a general breakdown in law and order.

Although the trouble was highly localised, the country seemed to be overrun by gangs of soldiers and looters, causing a media sensation, particularly over Europeans fleeing the country.

The mineral-rich province of Katanga declared

independence on 11 July 1960 under the leadership of its premier, Moise Tshombe, with support from the Belgian government and mining companies such as *Union Minière du Haut Katanga.*

Despite the arrival of UN troops, unrest continued. Since the United Nations refused to help suppress the rebellion in Katanga, Lumumba sought Soviet assistance in the form of arms, food, medical supplies, trucks, and planes to help move troops to Katanga. Lumumba's decisive actions alarmed his colleagues and President Kasavubu who preferred a more moderate political approach.

Assassination

"Dead, living, free, or in prison on the orders of the colonialists, it is not I who counts. It is the Congo, it is our people for whom independence has been transformed into a cage where we are regarded from the outside… History will one day have its say, but it will not be the history that Brussels, Paris, Washington, or the United Nations will teach, but that which they will teach in the countries emancipated from colonialism and its puppets... a history of glory and dignity." — Patrice Lumumba, October 1960.

Deposition and arrest

In September, the President Kasavubu dismissed Lumumba from government. Lumumba immediately protested the legality of the president's actions. In retaliation, Lumumba declared Kasavubu deposed and won a vote of confidence in the Senate, while the newly appointed prime minister failed to gain parliament's confidence.

The country was torn by two political groups claiming legal power over the country.

On 14 September 1960, a *coup d'état* organised by Colonel Joseph Mobutu (later renamed Mobutu Sese Seko) and endorsed by the Central Intelligence Agency (CIA) incapacitated both Lumumba and Kasavubu. Lumumba was placed under house arrest at the prime minister's residence, although UN troops were positioned around the house to protect him.

Nevertheless, Lumumba decided to rouse his supporters in Haut-Congo. Smuggled out of his residence at night, he escaped to Stanleyville where he attempted to set up his own government and army.

Pursued by troops loyal to Mobutu he was finally captured in Port Francqui on 1 December 1960 and flown the capital Leopoldville (now Kinshasa) in ropes not handcuffs.

Mobutu said Lumumba would be tried for inciting the army to rebellion and other crimes.

United Nations Secretary General Dag Hammarskjöld made an appeal to Kasavubu asking that Lumumba be treated according to due process of law. The USSR denounced Hammarskjöld and the Western powers as responsible for Lumumba's arrest and demanded his release.

UN response

The UN Security Council was called into session on 7 December 1960 to consider Soviet demands that the UN seek Lumumba's immediate release, the immediate restoration of Lumumba as head of the Congolese government, the disarming of the forces of Mobutu, and the immediate evacuation of Belgians from the Congo. Hammarskjöld, answering Soviet attacks against his Congo operations, said that if the UN forces were withdrawn from the Congo "I fear everything will crumble."

The threat to the UN cause was intensified by the

announcement of the withdrawal of their contingents by Yugoslavia, the United Arab Republic (Egypt), Ceylon, Indonesia, Morocco, and Guinea.

The Soviet pro-Lumumba resolution was defeated on 14 December 1960 by a vote of 8-2. On the same day, a Western resolution that would have given Hammarskjöld increased powers to deal with the Congo situation was vetoed by the Soviet Union.

Final days

Lumumba was sent first on 3 December, to Thysville (now Mbanza-Ngungu) military barracks Camp Hardy, about 100 miles from Leopoldville. However, when security and disciplinary breaches threatened his "safety," it was decided that he should be transferred to the Katanga Province.

The main reason he was sent to his arch-enemy Moise Tshombe in Katanga was to be killed.

Lumumba was forcibly restrained on the flight to Elizabethville (now Lubumbashi), the capital of Katanga Province, on 17 January 1961. On arrival, he was taken to Brouwez House under arrest and was held there bound and gagged while President Tshombe and his cabinet decided what to do with him.

Death by firing squad

Later that night, Lumumba was driven to an isolated spot where three firing squads had been assembled. According to David Akerman, Ludo de Witte and Kris Hollington, the firing squads were commanded by a Belgian, Captain Julien Gat. Another Belgian, Police Commissioner Verscheure, had overall command of the execution site.

The Belgian Commission has found that the execution was carried out by Katanga's authorities. But de Witte found written orders from the Belgian government requesting Lumumba's murder. He also found documents on various arrangements, such as death squads.

It reported that President Tshombe and two other ministers were present with four Belgian officers under the command of Katangan authorities.

Lumumba and two other comrades from the government, Maurice Mpolo and Joseph Okito, were lined up against a tree and shot one at a time.

The execution probably took place on 17 January 1961 between 21:40 and 21:43 (9:40 and 9:23 p.m.) according to the Belgian report. Lumumba's corpse was buried nearby.

No statement was released until three weeks later despite rumours that Lumumba was dead.

Announcement of death

His death was formally announced on Katangese radio when it was alleged that he escaped and was killed by enraged villagers.

On January 18th, panicked by reports that the burial of the three bodies had been observed, members of the execution team went to dig up the bodies and move them to a place near the border with Northern Rhodesia (now Zambia) for reburial.

Belgian Police Commissioner Gerard Soete later admitted in several accounts that he and his brother led the first and second exhumation. Police Commissioner Frans Verscheure also took part.

On the afternoon and evening of January 21, Commissioner Soete and his brother dug up Lumumba's corpse for the second time, cut it up with a hacksaw, and dissolved it in concentrated sulfuric acid. Only some teeth and a fragment of skull and bullets survived the process, kept as souvenirs.

In an interview on Belgian television in a programme

on the assassination of Lumumba in 1999, Soete displayed a bullet and two teeth that he boasted he had saved from Lumumba's body.

De Witte also mentions that Verscheure kept souvenirs from the exhumation: bullets from the skull of Lumumba.

After the announcement of Lumumba's death, street protests were organised in several European countries. In Belgrade, the capital of Yugoslavia, protesters sacked the Belgian embassy and confronted the police. And in London, a crowd marched from Trafalgar Square to the Belgian embassy where a letter of protest was delivered and where protesters clashed with police.

American and Belgian involvement

According to an article, "Patrice Lumumba: 50 Years Later," in *Democracy Now*, 21 January 2011:

"Lumumba's pan-Africanism and his vision of a united Congo gained him many enemies. Both Belgium and the United States actively sought to have him killed. The CIA ordered his assassination but could not complete the job. Instead, the United States and Belgium covertly funneled cash and aid to rival politicians who seized power and arrested Lumumba."

U.S. President Dwight D. Eisenhower had said "something [to CIA chief Allen Dulles] to the effect that Lumumba should be eliminated." This was revealed by a declassified interview with then-US National Security Council minute keeper Robert Johnson released in August 2000 from the Senate Intelligence Committee's enquiry on covert action. The committee later found that while the CIA had conspired to kill Lumumba, it was not directly involved in the actual murder.

Church Committee

In 1975, the Church Committee went on record with the finding that Allen Dulles had ordered Lumumba's assassination as "an urgent and prime objective" (Dulles' own words). Furthermore, declassified CIA cables quoted or mentioned in the Church report and in Kalb (1972) mention two specific CIA plots to murder Lumumba: the poison plot and a shooting plot.

Although some sources claim that CIA plots ended when Lumumba was captured, that is not stated or shown in the CIA records. Rather, those records show two still-partly-censored CIA cables from Elizabethville on days significant in the murder: January 17, the day Lumumba died, and January 18, the day of the first exhumation.

The former, after a long censored section, talks about where they need to go from there. The latter expresses thanks for Lumumba being sent to them and then says that, had Elizabethville base known he was coming, they would have "baked a snake."

Significantly, a CIA officer told another CIA officer later that he had had Lumumba's body in the trunk of his car to try to find a way to dispose of it. This cable goes on to state that the writer's sources (not yet declassified) said that after being taken from the airport Lumumba was imprisoned by "all white guards."

Belgian investigation

The Belgian Commission investigating Lumumba's assassination concluded that (1) Belgium wanted Lumumba arrested, (2) Belgium was not particularly concerned with Lumumba's physical well being, and (3) although informed of the danger to Lumumba's life, Belgium did not take any action to avert his death. But the report also specifically denied that Belgium ordered

Lumumba's assassination.

Under its own 'Good Samaritan' laws, Belgium was legally culpable for failing to prevent the assassination from taking place and was also in breach of its obligation (under U.N. Resolution 290 of 1949) to refrain from acts or threats "aimed at impairing the freedom, independence or integrity of another state."

The report of 2001 by the Belgian Commission mentions that there had been previous U.S. and Belgian plots to kill Lumumba. Among them was a Central Intelligence Agency-sponsored attempt to poison him, which may have come on orders from President Eisenhower. CIA chemist, Dr. Sidney Gottlieb, was a key person in this by devising a poison resembling toothpaste. However, the plan is said to have been scrapped because the local CIA Station Chief, Larry Devlin, supposedly did not approve of it.

Devlin became CIA station chief in Congo in July 1960, a mere 10 days after the country's independence from Belgium and shortly before Lumumba's two months in office as prime minister, his dismissal from power and ultimate execution.

In his memoir, Devlin reveals that late in 1960, he received instructions from an agent ("Joe from Paris") who was relaying instructions from CIA headquarters that he (Devlin) was to effect the assassination of Lumumba. Various poisons, including one secreted in a tube of toothpaste, were proffered.

The directive had come from the CIA Deputy Chief of Plans, Richard (Dick) Bissell, but Devlin wanted to know if it had originated at a higher level and if so, how high. "Joe" had been given to understand that it had come from President Eisenhower but Devlin never knew for sure. Devlin wrote, and said in public speaking engagements, that he felt an assassination would have been "morally wrong" and would likely backfire and work against U.S. interests. He claims he temporized and neglected to act until Lumumba was finally killed by his enemies in Katanga.

But that is not the whole truth, if any of it is true.

Madeleine G. Kalb points out in her book, *Congo Cables*, that records show many communications by Devlin himself during that time urged the elimination of Lumumba. Also, Devlin helped to direct the search to capture Lumumba for his transfer to his enemies in Katanga; was involved in arranging his transfer to Katanga; and the CIA base chief in Elizabethville was in direct touch with the killers the night Lumumba was killed.

Furthermore, a CIA agent had Lumumba's body in the trunk of his car in order to try to get rid of it.

Former CIA agent, John Stockwell, who later wrote a book, *In Search of Enemies: A CIA Story*, and who knew Devlin well, said Devlin knew more than anyone else about Lumumba's assassination.

Devlin simply did not tell the truth about his involvement in Lumumba's assassination. And it was direct involvement.

Belgian apology

In February 2002, the Belgian government apologised to the Congolese people, and admitted a "moral responsibility" and "an irrefutable portion of responsibility in the events that led to the death of Lumumba."

U.S. documents

In July 2006, documents released by the United States government revealed that the CIA had plotted to assassinate Lumumba. In September 1960, Sidney Gottlieb took a vial of poison to Congo with plans to place it on Lumumba's toothbrush. The plot was later abandoned.

This same disclosure showed that U.S. perception at the time was that Lumumba was a communist. Eisenhower's reported call, at a meeting of his national security advisers, for Lumumba's elimination must have been brought on by this perception.

Both Belgium and the United States were clearly influenced in their unfavourable stance towards Lumumba by the Cold War. He seemed to gravitate around the Soviet Union, although this was not because he was a communist but because that was the only place where he could find support in his country's effort to rid itself of colonial rule. The United States was the first country from which Lumumba requested help. He was turned down because America supported Belgium, the colonial power which ruled Congo.

Lumumba, for his part, not only denied being a Communist; he said he found colonialism and communism to be equally deplorable and professed his personal preference for neutrality between the East and the West. He was a staunch Pan-Africanist.

Although he was in office for only two months as prime minister of Congo, he left an indelible mark on Africa and on the minds of many people around the world. He was one of the most inspiring leaders Africa has ever produced. And many people are still angry today because of what the United States and Belgium did to him, to Congo and to Africa as a whole when they killed him. He was a beacon hope.

Legacy

"We must move forward, striking out tirelessly against imperialism. From all over the world we have to learn lessons which events afford. Lumumba's murder should be a lesson for all of us." — Che Guevara, 1964.

"Today, it is impossible to touch down at the (far from modernized) airport of Lubumbashi in the south of the Democratic Republic of Congo without a shiver of recollection of the haunting photograph taken of Lumumba there shortly before his assassination, and after beatings, torture and a long, long flight in custody across the vast country which had so loved him." — Victoria Brittain, *The Guardian*, 2011.

Political legacy of Lumumba

The results of his time in office are both mixed and polarising in their subsequent interpretation. To his critics, Lumumba bequeathed very few positive results from his term in office. Their critiques include his inability to promote development and failure to stave off or quell a civil war that erupted within days of his appointment as prime minister. Instead, he behaved impetuously and followed expedients rather than policies that led to the deaths of hundreds of thousands of people, including himself.

Such criticisms are unwarranted and fail to ask a few fundamental questions:

What time did he have to do anything let alone develop Congo?

What could he have done in two months? He was prime minister for only two months. What could any other leader have done in two months?

How could he have stopped a civil war which erupted with the encouragement of foreign powers, stronger than his government?

How could he have done anything when the president of the country, Joseph Kasavubu, worked with Congo's enemies including the Belgians and the CIA, to frustrate Lumumba in everything he tried to do?

To his supporters, Lumumba was an altruistic man of strong character who pursued his policies regardless of opposing viewpoints. He wanted to build a united Congo and opposed division of the country along ethnic and regional lines.

Like many other African leaders, he championed pan-Africanism and strongly supported the liberation of all the countries on the continent which were still under colonial and white minority rule.

He proclaimed his regime one of "positive neutralism," defined as a return to African values and rejection of any imported ideology, including that of the Soviet Union: "We are not Communists, Catholics, Socialists. We are African nationalists."

2006 Congolese elections

Nevertheless, the image of Patrice Lumumba continues to serve as an inspiration in contemporary Congolese politics.

In the 2006 elections, several parties claimed to be motivated by his ideas. And that included the People's Party for Reconstruction and Democracy (PPRD) of incumbent President Joseph Kabila.

Antoine Gizenga, who served as Lumumba's deputy prime minister for the two months Lumumba was in office, was a 2006 presidential candidate of the Unified Lumumbist Party (*Parti Lumumbiste Unifié* - PALU) and was named prime minister of Congo under President Kabila at the end of the year.

Other political parties which directly use his name include the *Mouvement National Congolais-Lumumba* (MNC-L) and the *Mouvement Lumumbiste* (MLP).

Family and politics

Patrice Lumumba's family is actively involved in contemporary Congolese politics.

Patrice Lumumba was married to Pauline Lumumba

and had five children. François was the eldest followed by Patrice Junior, Julienne, Roland and Guy-Patrice-Lumumba.

François was 10 years old when his father was killed. Before his imprisonment, Lumumba arranged for his wife and children to move into exile in Egypt where François spent his childhood. Later, he went to Hungary for further education. He has a doctorate in political economics.

He returned to Congo in 1992 to oppose Mobutu. He has since then been the leader of the *Mouvement National Congolais-Lumumba* (MNC-L), his father's original political party.

Lumumba's youngest son, Guy-Patrice, born six months after his father's death, was an independent presidential candidate in the 2006 elections but received less than 10% of the vote.

Writings by Lumumba

- *Congo, My Country* (1962) London: Pall Mall Press. Foreword and notes by Colin Legum; translated by Graham Heath.
- *Lumumba Speaks: The Speeches and Writings of Patrice Lumumba, 1958–1961* (1972) Boston: Little, Brown and Company. Editor, Jean Van Lierde; translated by Helen R. Lane.

Mobutu Sese Seko

Mobutu Sese Seko Nkuku Ngbendu wa Za Banga (14 October 1930 – 7 September 1997), commonly known as Mobutu or Mobutu Sese Seko, born Joseph-Désiré Mobutu, was the president of Zaire, formerly known as Congo, from 1965 to 1997.

He was one of the longest-ruling leaders in Africa and would have stayed longer in power had he not been overthrown. He ruled for almost 32. He seized power in

November 1965 and was overthrown in July 1997.

He established an authoritarian regime, amassed vast personal wealth, and attempted to purge the country of all colonial cultural influences while also maintaining an anti-communist stance.

He was one of the most corrupt leaders in the world. He is said to have inspired coinage of the term "kleptocracy" and presided over a regime which was probably the most kleptocratic in Africa.

Early years

Mobutu was a member of the Ngbandi ethnic group indigenous to Équateur Province in northwestern Congo. H was born in Lisala, the capital of Mongala District, in Équateur Province. The country was then known as the Belgian Congo until independence in 1960.

Mobutu's mother, Marie Madeleine Yemo, was a hotel maid who fled to Lisala to escape the harem of a local village chief. There she met and married Albéric Gbemani, a cook for a Belgian judge. Shortly she gave birth to Mobutu. The name "Mobutu" was selected by an uncle. Gbemani died when Mobutu was eight.

The wife of the Belgian judge took a liking to Mobutu and taught him to speak, read and write fluently. Yemo relied on the help of relatives to support her four children and the family moved often.

Mobutu's earliest studies were in Leopoldville, the capital of the Belgian Congo, but his mother eventually sent him to an uncle in Conquilhatville (now Mbandaka) in Équateur where he attended the Christian Brothers School, a Catholic mission boarding school.

A physically imposing figure, Mobutu dominated school sports. He also excelled in academics and ran the class newspaper. He was also known for his pranks and impish sense of humour.

A classmate recalled that when the Belgian priests whose first language was Dutch misspoke in French, Mobutu would leap to his feet in class and point out the mistake.

In 1949 Mobutu stowed away aboard a boat to Leopoldville and met a girl. The priests found him several weeks later and at the end of the school year, he was sent to the *Force Publique* (FP), the Belgian Congolese army. Enlistment, which came with a seven-year commitment, was a punishment for rebellious students.

Mobutu found discipline in army life as well as a father figure in Sergeant Joseph Bobozo. He kept up his studies by borrowing European newspapers from the Belgian officers and books from wherever he could find them, reading them on sentry duty and whenever he had a spare moment.

His personal favourites were the writings of French President Charles de Gaulle, British Prime Minister Winston Churchill and Italian philosopher Niccolò Machiavelli.

After passing a course in accounting, he began to dabble professionally in journalism. Still angry after his clashes with the school priests, he did not wed in a church. His contribution to the wedding festivities was a crate of beer, all his army salary could afford.

As a soldier, Mobutu wrote pseudonymously on contemporary politics for a new magazine, *Actunigalités Africaines*, founded by a Belgian living in Congo.

In 1956, he quit the army and became a full-time journalist, writing for the Léopoldville daily *L'Avenir*. Two years later, he went to Belgium to cover the 1958 Exposition and stayed to receive training in journalism. By this time, he had met many of the young Congolese intellectuals who were challenging colonial rule.

He became friends with Patrice Lumumba and joined Lumumba's *Mouvement National Congolais* (MNC). He eventually became Lumumba's personal aide, though several contemporaries indicate that Belgian intelligence had recruited Mobutu to be an informer. He was also already working for the CIA during that period.

During the 1960 talks in Brussels on Congolese independence, the U.S. Embassy held a reception to gain a better sense of the Congolese delegation. Embassy staff were each assigned a list of delegation members to meet and then discuss their impressions. The ambassador noted, "One name kept coming up. But it wasn't on anyone's list because he wasn't an official delegation member, he was Lumumba's secretary. But everyone agreed that this was an extremely intelligent man, very young, perhaps immature, but a man with great potential."

Congo Crisis

Following the granting of independence on 30 June 1960, a coalition government was formed led by Prime Minister Lumumba and President Joseph Kasavubu. The new nation quickly lurched into what came to be famously known as the Congo crisis as the army mutinied against the Belgian officers who were still in the army. Some of the officers had already left.

Lumumba appointed Mobutu as chief of staff of the *Armee Nationale Congolaise* (ANC), which means Congolese National Army, and in that capacity, Mobutu toured the country convincing soldiers to return to their barracks.

Encouraged by a Belgian government intent on maintaining its access to rich Congolese mines, secessionist violence erupted in Katanga Province in the south. Concerned that the United Nations force sent to help restore order was not helping to crush the secessionists, Lumumba turned to the Soviet Union for assistance. He received massive military aid and about a thousand Soviet technical advisers in six weeks.

The United States government saw Soviet activity as a manoeuvre to spread communist influence in Central Africa.

Riled by the Soviet arrival, Kasavubu dismissed Lumumba. An outraged Lumumba declared Kasavubu deposed. They dismissed each other.

Both Lumumba and Kasavubu then ordered Mobutu to arrest the other. As Army Chief of Staff, Mobutu came under great pressure from multiple sources. The embassies of Western nations which helped pay the soldiers' salaries, as well as Kasavubu and Mobutu's subordinates, favoured getting rid of the Soviet presence.

On 14 September 1960, Mobutu took control of the country in a coup engineered and supported by the CIA. The new regime placed Lumumba under house arrest for the second time and kept Kasavubu as president.

All Soviet advisers were ordered to leave. Next, Mobutu accused Lumumba of pro-communist sympathies, thereby hoping to gain the support of the United States. Lumumba fled to Stanleyville where he set up his own government. The USSR again supplied him with weapons and he was able to defend his position.

Later, in November 1960, he was captured. Mobutu still considered him to be a threat and, working with the Americans and the Belgians, ordered him to be beaten publicly. He then disappeared from the public view. He was finally sent to Elisabethville, capital of Katanga Province, on 17 January 1961 where he was executed on the same day.

Inn 1964, Pierre Mulele, Lumumba's minister of education and heir apparent, launched a pro-Lumumbist rebellion from his home region, Kwilu Province, in western Congo. The rebels quickly occupied two thirds of the country. But the Congolese army, with Western support and help from South African mercenaries, was able to regain control of the country in 1965.

Second coup and consolidation of power

On 25 November 1965, General Mobutu seized power for the second time in a bloodless coup, following another power struggle between Ppresident Kasavubu and Prime Minister Moise Tshombe. According to Mobutu, it had taken "the politicians" five years to "ruin" the country; therefore, said Mobutu, "For five years, there will be no more political party activity in the country."

Under the auspices of a *regime d'exception* (the equivalent of a state of emergency), Mobutu assumed sweeping, almost absolute, powers. Parliament was reduced to a rubber-stamp, before being abolished altogether though it was later revived. The number of provinces was reduced, and their autonomy curtailed, resulting in a highly centralized state.

Initially, Mobutu's government was decidedly apolitical, even anti-political. The word "politician" carried negative connotations and became almost synonymous with someone who was wicked or corrupt.

Even so, 1966 saw the debut of the Corps of Volunteers of the Republic, a vanguard movement designed to mobilise popular support behind Mobutu who was proclaimed the nation's "Second National Hero" after Lumumba.

Ironically, given the role he played in Lumumba's ousting, capture and assassination, Mobutu strove to present himself as a successor to Lumumba's legacy, and one of the key tenets early in his rule was "authentic Congolese nationalism."

1967 marked the debut of the *Mouvement Populaire de la Revolution* (*MPR*) – Popular Movement of the Revolution – which until 1990 was the nation's only legal political party under Mobutu. Membership became obligatory for all citizens.

Among the themes advanced by the MPR in its doctrine, the Manifesto of N'Sele, was nationalism, revolution, and authenticity.

Revolution was described as a "truly national revolution, essentially pragmatic" which called for "the repudiation of both capitalism and communism." One of the MPR's slogans was "Neither left nor right," to which would be added "nor even centre" in later years.

That same year, all trade unions were consolidated into a single union, the National Union of Zairian Workers, and brought under government control. By Mobutu's own admission, the union would serve as an instrument of support for government policy, rather than as a force for confrontation. Independent trade unions were illegal until 1991.

Facing many challenges early in his rule, Mobutu was able to turn most opposition into submission through patronage; those he could not, he dealt with forcefully. In 1966 four cabinet members were arrested on charges of complicity in an attempted coup, tried by a military tribunal, and publicly executed in an open-air spectacle witnessed by over 50,000 people.

Uprisings by former Katangan gendarmeries were crushed, as was an abortive revolt led by white mercenaries in 1967.

By 1970, nearly all potential threats to his authority had been smashed, and for the most part, law and order was brought to nearly all parts of the country.

That year marked the pinnacle of Mobutu's legitimacy and power. King Baudouin of Belgium made a highly successful state visit to Kinshasa. Legislative and presidential elections were also held in 1970.

The electorate was presented a single list of candidates for the legislature, for which 98.33% of voters voted in favour. For the presidential election, Mobutu was the only candidate, and voters were offered two ballot choices: green for hope, and red for chaos: Mobutu won with a vote of 10,131,699 to 157.

The elections were rigged in favour of the ruling party and Mobutu himself. There were no opposition parties which participated in the elections. None existed. They had been banned. And nobody wins over 90% of the vote in a true democracy. There are always people who will oppose you.

As he consolidated power, Mobutu set up several military forces whose sole purpose was to protect him. They included the Special Presidential Division, Civil Guard, and Service for Action and Military Intelligence (SNIP).

Authenticity campaign

Launching on a campaign of pro-Africa cultural awareness, Mobutu renamed the country the Republic of Zaire in October 1971. Africans were ordered to drop their European names for African ones, and priests were warned that they would face five years' imprisonment if they were caught baptising a Zairean child with a European name. Western attire and ties were banned, and men were forced to wear a mao-style tunic known as the abacost.

In 1972, Mobutu renamed himself *Mobutu Sese Seko Nkuku Ngbendu Wa Za Banga* ("The all-powerful warrior who, because of his endurance and inflexible will to win, goes from conquest to conquest, leaving fire in his wake") *Mobutu Sese Seko* for short.

One-man rule

Mobutu consolidated power by publicly executing political rivals, secessionists, coup plotters, and other threats to his rule. To set an example, many were hanged before large audiences. They included former Prime Minister Evariste Kimba who, with three cabinet members

- Jérôme Anany (Defence Minister), Emmanuel Bamba (Finance Minister), and Alexandre Mahamba (Minister of Mines and Energy) - was tried in May 1966 and sent to the gallows on May, 30th before an audience of 50,000 spectators.

The men were executed on charges of being in contact with Colonel Alphonse Bangala and Major Pierre Efomi for the purpose of planning a coup. Mobutu explained the executions as follows: "One had to strike through a spectacular example, and create the conditions of regime discipline. When a chief takes a decision, he decides – period."

In 1968 Pierre Mulele, Lumumba's minister of education and later a rebel leader during the 1964 Simba rebellion, was lured out of exile in Brazzaville, capital of the Republic of Congo which is also known as Congo-Brazzaville, and returned to Congo-Leopoldville.

Born on 11 August 1929, he was member of the Bapende ethnic group in the southwestern part of the country. After a rebel faction he led in his home region of Kwilu Province in 1964 during the Simba rebellion was defeated together with other pro-Lumumbist rebel groups, he fled into exile in Congo-Brazzaville.

In October 1968, President Mobutu lured Mulele out of exile from Brazzaville, the capital of Congo-Brazzaville just across the Congo River from Leopoldville, by promising him amnesty. Mobutu sent his minister of foreign affairs, Justin Bomboko, to convince Mulele to return home. The government of Congo-Brazzaville demanded assurances that Mulele would not be harmed if returned to Congo-Leopoldville. Bomboko gave those assurances and returned with Mulele on a yatch.

Mulele returned to Congo-Leopoldville (renamed Congo-Kinshasa in 1971) believing he would be granted amnesty. Instead, he was publicly tortured and executed. His eyes were pulled from their sockets, his genitals were ripped off, and his limbs were amputated one by one, all

173

while he was alive. What was left was dumped in the Congo River.

The exact date of his torture and murder is not known but it is believed to be between 3 and 9 October 1968.

Besides murder and torture, Mobutu also used another tactic to neutralise the opposition. He bought off political rivals. He used the slogan "Keep your friends close, but your enemies closer still" to describe his tactic of co-opting political opponents through bribery. A favorite Mobutu tactic was to play "musical chairs," rotating members of his government, switching the cabinet roster constantly to ensure that no one would pose a threat to his rule.

Another tactic was to arrest and sometimes torture dissident members of the government, only to later pardon them and reward them with high office. The most famous example of this treatment is Jean Nguza Karl-i-Bond who was fired as foreign minister in 1977, sentenced to death, and tortured. Mobutu then commuted his sentence to life imprisonment, released him after a year, and later appointed him prime minister. Nguza fled the country in 1981 only to return in 1985, first serving as Zaire's ambassador to the U.S. and later as foreign minister.

In 1972 Mobutu tried unsuccessfully to have himself named president for life. In 1983, Mobutu promoted himself to the rank of Field Marshall.

He initially nationalised foreign-owned firms and forced European investors out of the country. In many cases he handed the management of these firms to relatives and close associates who stole the companies' assets. This precipitated such an economic slump that Mobutu was forced by 1977 to try to woo foreign investors back.

Katangan rebels based in Angola invaded Zaire in 1977 in retaliation for Mobutu's support for anti-MPLA rebels. France airlifted 1,500 Moroccan paratroopers into the country and repulsed the rebels, ending the invasion which was named Shaba I.

The rebels attacked Zaire again, in greater numbers, in the Shaba II invasion of 1978. The governments of Belgium and France deployed troops with logistical support from the United States and defeated the rebels again.

Mobutu was re-elected in single-candidate elections in 1977 and 1984. He used the presidency to enrich himself and amassed wealth which in 1984 was estimated to be US $5 billion deposited in foreign banks, mostly in Swiss banks. The amount was almost equivalent to the country's foreign debt at the time and, by 1989, the government was forced to default on international loans from Belgium.

Mobutu also owned a fleet of Mercedes-Benz vehicles wwhich he used to travel between his numerous palaces, while the nation's roads rotted and many of his people starved. During his kleptocratic rule, the infrastructure virtually collapsed and many public service workers went for months without being paid.

Most of the money was siphoned off to Mobutu, his family, and top political and military leaders. Only the Special Presidential Division – on whom his physical safety depended – was paid adequately or regularly.

A popular saying that the civil servants pretended to work while the state pretended to pay them expressed this grim reality.

Another feature of Mobutu's economic mismanagement, directly linked to the way he and his friends siphoned off so much of the country's wealth, was rampant inflation. The rapid decline in the real value of salaries strongly encouraged a culture of corruption and dishonesty among public servants of all kinds.

Mobutu was known to charter a Concorde from Air France for personal use, including shopping trips to Paris for himself and his family. He had an airport constructed in his hometown of Gbadolite in Equateur Province with a runway long enough to accommodate the Concorde's extended take off and landing requirements.

In 1989, Mobutu chartered Concorde aircraft F-BTSD for a 26 June – 5 July trip to give a speech at the United Nations in New York City, 16 July for French bicentennial celebrations in Paris (where he was a guest of President Francois Mitterand), on 19 September for a flight from Paris to Gbadolite, and another nonstop flight from Gbadolite to Marseille, France, with the youth choir of Zaire.

Mobutu's rule earned a reputation as one of the world's foremost examples of kleptocracy and nepotism. His close relatives and fellow Ngbandi tribesmen were awarded with high positions in the military and government. And he groomed his eldest son, Nyiwa, to one day succeed him as president; however, this was thwarted by Nyiwa's death from AIDS in 1994.

He was also the subject of a massive personality cult. The evening news on television was preceded by an image of him descending through clouds from the heavens, portraits of him adorned many public places, government officials wore lapels bearing his portrait, and he held such titles as "Father of the Nation," "Saviour of the People," and "Supreme Combatant."

In the 1996 documentary of the 1974 Foreman-Ali fight in Zaire, dancers receiving the fighters can be heard chanting "Sese Seko, Sese Seko."

At one point, in early 1975, the media was even forbidden from mentioning by name anyone but Mobutu; others were referred to only by the positions they held.

Mobutu was able to successfully capitalise on Cold War tensions and gain significant support from Western countries including the United States and from international organisations such as the International Monetary Fund (IMF).

Foreign policy

Relations with the United States

For the most part, Zaire enjoyed warm relations with the United States. The United States was the third-largest donor of aid to Zaire (after Belgium and France), and Mobutu befriended several American presidents including Richard Nixon, Ronald Reagan, and George H.W. Bush, all Republicans.

But relations did cool significantly in 1974-1975 over Mobutu's increasingly radical rhetoric (which included his scathing denunciations of American foreign policy) and plummeted to an all-time low in the summer of 1975 when Mobutu accused the CIA of plotting to overthrow him. He arrested eleven senior Zairian generals and several civilians, and condemned (in absentia) a former head of the Central Bank.

However, many people viewed these charges with skepticism; in fact, one of Mobutu's staunchest critics, Nzongola-Ntalaja, speculated that Mobutu invented the plot as an excuse to purge the military of talented officers who might otherwise pose a threat to his rule.

In spite of these hindrances, the chilly relationship quickly thawed when both countries found each other supporting the same side during the Angolan civil war.

When Jimmy Carter became president of the United States (1976 – 1980), his administration put some distance between itself and the government in Kinshasa because of Mobutu's poor human rights record. But in spite of all that, Zaire still was the recipient of nearly half of the foreign aid Carter allocated sub-Saharan Africa because of Cold War imperatives.

During the first Shaba invasion launched on 8 March 1977, the United States played a relatively inconsequential role; its belated intervention consisted of little more than the delivery of non-lethal supplies. But during the second Shaba invasion, it played a much more active and decisive role by providing transport and logistical support to the French and Belgian paratroopers that were deployed to help Mobutu against the rebels.

Carter echoed Mobutu's (unsubstantiated) charges of Soviet and Cuban aid to the rebels until it was apparent that no hard evidence existed to verify his claims.

In 1980, the U.S. House of Representatives voted to terminate military aid to Zaire. But the Senate reinstated the funds in response to pressure from Carter and American business interests in Zaire.

Mobutu enjoyed a very warm relationship with the Reagan administration through financial donations. During Reagan's presidency, Mobutu visited the White House three times and criticism of Zaire's human rights record by the United States during Reagan's presidency was effectively muted.

During a state visit by Mobutu in 1983, Reagan praised the Zairian strongman as "a voice of good sense and goodwill."

Mobutu also had a cordial relationship with Reagan's successor, George H. W. Bush. He was the first African head of state to visit Bush at the White House. Even so, Mobutu's relationship with the United States radically changed shortly afterwards with the end of the Cold War. With the Soviet Union gone, there was no longer any reason to support Mobutu as a bulwark against communism. Accordingly, the United States and other Western powers began pressuring Mobutu to democratise his rule.

Regarding the change in U.S. attitude to his regime, Mobutu bitterly remarked: "I am the latest victim of the cold war, no longer needed by the U.S. The lesson is that my support for American policy counts for nothing."

In 1993 during the presidency of Bill Clinton, a

Democrat, Mobutu was denied a visa by the U.S. State Department after he sought to visit Washington, D.C.

Mobutu also had friends in America outside Washington. They were mostly conservatives and Republicans including televangelist Pat Robertson who befriended Mobutu and who promised to try to get the State Department to lift its ban on the African leader.

Relations with Belgium

Relations between Zaire and Belgium wavered between close intimacy and open hostility during Mobutu's reign.

Relations soured early during his rule over disputes involving substantial Belgian commercial and industrial holdings in the country but warmed soon afterwards. Mobutu and his family were received as personal guests of the Belgian monarch in 1968. And a convention for scientific and technical cooperation was signed that year.

During King Baudouin's highly successful visit to Kinshasa in 1970, a treaty of friendship and cooperation between the two countries was signed.

However, Mobutu tore up the treaty in 1974 in protest against Belgium's refusal to ban an anti-Mobutu book written by left-wing lawyer Jules Chomé.

Mobutu's "Zairianization" policy which expropriated foreign-held businesses and transferred their ownership to Zairians added to the strain.

Relations with France

As the second-largest French speaking country in the world after France and the largest one in sub-Saharan Africa, Zaire was of great strategic interest to France.

During Congo's First Republic, France tended to side with the conservative and federalist forces as opposed to unitarists such as Lumumba. Shortly after the Katangan

179

secession was successfully crushed, Zaire (then called the Republic of the Congo), signed a treaty of technical and cultural cooperation with France.

During the presidency of Charles de Gaulle, relations with the two countries gradually grew stronger and closer. In 1971, then-Finance Minister Valéry Giscard d'Estaing paid a visit to Zaire; later, after he became president, he developed a close personal relationship with President Mobutu. and became one of the regime's closest foreign allies.

During the Shaba invasions, French leaders sided firmly with Mobutu. France airlifted 1,500 Moroccan troops to Zaire and the rebels were repulsed.

A year later during the second Shaba invasion, France sent its own paratroopers, the 2nd Foreign Parachute Regiment of the French Foreign Legion, to help Mobutu. Belgium also sent assistance to Zaire to help keep Mobutu in power.

Relations with the Soviet Union

Mobutu's relationship with the Soviet Union was frosty and tense. A staunch anticommunist, he was not anxious to recognise the Soviets. The Soviet Union had supported Lumumba, Mobutu's democratically elected predecessor, and the Simba rebels and Mobutu never forgot that.

However, to project a non-aligned image, he did renew ties with the Soviet Union in 1967. The first Soviet ambassador arrived and presented his credentials in 1968. Mobutu did, however, join the United States and other Western powers in condemning the Soviet invasion of Czechoslovakia that year.

He viewed the Soviet presence in Congo as advantageous for two reasons: it allowed him to maintain an image of non-alignment, and it provided a convenient scapegoat for problems at home. For example, in 1970, he expelled four Soviet diplomats for carrying out "subversive activities," and in 1971, twenty Soviet officials were declared *persona non grata* for allegedly instigating student demonstrations at Lovanium University.

Moscow was the only major world capital Mobutu never visited, although he did accept an invitation to do so in 1974. For reasons unknown, he cancelled the visit at the last minute and toured the People's Republic of China and North Korea, instead.

Relations cooled further in 1975, when the two countries found themselves on opposing sides in the Angolan civil war. This had a dramatic effect on Zairian foreign policy for the next decade. Bereft of his claim to African leadership (Mobutu was one of the few leaders who denied the MPLA government of Angola recognition), Mobutu turned increasingly to the United States and its allies, adopting pro-American stances on such issues as the Soviet invasion of Afghanistan, and Israel's position in international organisations.

Relations with the People's Republic of China

Initially, Zaire's relationship with the People's Republic of China was no better than its relationship with the Soviet Union. Memories of Chinese aid to Mulele and other Maoist rebels in Kwilu Province during the ill-fated Simba rebellion remained fresh in Mobutu's mind. He also opposed seating China at the United Nations.

However, by 1972, he began to see the Chinese in a different light as a counterbalance to both the Soviet Union as well as his intimate ties with the United States, Israel, and South Africa.

In November 1972, Mobutu extended the Chinese (as well as East Germany and North Korea) diplomatic recognition. The following year, Mobutu paid a visit to Beijing where he met personally with Chairman Mao and received promises of $100 million in technical aid.

181

In 1974, Mobutu made a surprise visit to both China and North Korea during the time he was originally scheduled to visit the Soviet Union.

Upon returning home, both his politics and rhetoric became markedly more radical; it was around this time that Mobutu began criticising Belgium and the United States (the latter for not doing enough, in Mobutu's opinion, to combat white minority rule in southern Africa), introduced the "obligatory civic work" programme called *salongo*, and initiated "radicalisation" (an extension of 1973's "Zairianization" policy). Mobutu even borrowed a title - the Helmsman - from Mao.

Incidentally, from late 1974 to early 1975 was when his personality cult reached its peak.

China and Zaire shared a common goal in Central Africa, namely doing everything in their power to halt Soviet gains in the area. Accordingly, both Zaire and China covertly funneled aid to the FNLA (and later, UNITA) in order to prevent the MPLA, who were supported and augmented by Cuban forces, from coming to power.

The Cubans, who exercised considerable influence in Africa in support of leftist and anti-imperialist forces, were heavily sponsored by the Soviet Union during the period.

In addition to inviting Holden Roberto and his guerrillas to Beijing for training, China provided weapons and money to the rebels. Zaire itself launched an ill-fated, pre-emptive invasion of Angola in a bid to install a pro-Kinshasa government but was repulsed by Cuban troops.

The expedition was a fiasco with far-reaching repercussions, most notably the Shaba I and Shaba II invasions, both of which China opposed. China sent military aid to Zaire during both invasions and accused the Soviet Union and Cuba of working to de-stabilise Central Africa. The Soviets and the Cubans were alleged to have supported the Shaban rebels, although this was and remains pure speculation.

Coalition government

In May 1990, as a result of the end of the Cold War and because of a change in the international political climate, as well as economic problems and domestic unrest, Mobutu agreed to end the ban on other political parties and appointed a transitional government that would lead to promised elections. But he retained substantial powers.

Following riots in Kinshasa by unpaid soldiers, Mobutu brought opposition figures into a coalition government but still connived to retain control of the security services and important ministries.

Factional divisions led to the creation of two governments in 1993, one pro and one anti-Mobutu.

The anti-Mobutu government was headed by Laurent Monsengwo and Étienne Tshisekedi of the Union for Democracy and Social Progress.

The economic situation was still dreadful and, in 1994, the two groups joined as the High Council of Republic - Parliament of Transition (HCR-PT).

Mobutu appointed Kengo Wa Dondo, an advocate of austerity and free-market reforms, as prime minister. Mobutu was becoming increasingly physically frail and during one of his absences for medical treatment in Europe, Tutsis captured much of eastern Zaire.

Overthrow

Mobutu was overthrown in the first Congo war by Laurent-Désiré Kabila who was supported by the governments of Rwanda, Burundi and Uganda.

Ethnic Tutsis in Zaire, known as Banyamulenge, had long opposed Mobutu because of his support for Rwandan Hutu extremists responsible for the Rwandan genocide in

1994.

Even before then, he was anti-Tutsi. He did not recognise them as citizens of Zaire in spite of the fact that the Banyamulenge (Zairian or Congolese Tutsis) had lived in the country for more than 200 years after immigrating from Rwanda.

When his government issued an order in November 1996 forcing Tutsis to leave Zaire on penalty of death, they erupted in rebellion. From eastern Zaire, with the support of President Yoweri Museveni of Uganda and the Tutsi Rwandan Defence minister Paul Kagame, they launched an offensive to overthrow Mobutu and joined forces with other people in eastern Congo who were opposed to him as they marched west towards the capital Kinshasa.

Ailing with cancer, Mobutu was unable to coordinate the resistance which crumbled as the rebels advanced towards the capital, with the Zairian army being more used to suppressing civilians than defending a large country.

On 16 May 1997, following failed peace talks, the Tutsi rebels and the Alliance of Democratic Forces for the Liberation of Congo-Zaire (*Alliance des Forces Democratiques pour la Liberation du Congo-Zaire –* AFDL) captured Kinshasa under the leadership of Laurent Kabila. Zaire was renamed the Democratic Republic of Congo.

Burial of Juvénal Habyarimana

Mobutu had the remains of assassinated Rwandan President Juvénal Habyarimana stored in a mausoleum in Gbadolite.

On 12 May 1997, as Laurent Kabila's rebels were advancing on Gbadolite. Mobutu had Habyarimana's remains flown by cargo plane from his mausoleum to

Kinshasa where they waited on the tarmac of Kinshasa International Airport for three days. On May 16th, the day before Mobutu fled Zaire (and the country was renamed the Democratic Republic of the Congo), Habyarimana's remains were burned under the supervision of an Indian Hindu leader.

Exile and death

Mobutu went into temporary exile in Togo but lived mostly in Morocco. He died on 7 September 1997 in Rabat, Morocco, from prostate cancer. He was 66; almost 67. He was buried in Rabat in the Christian cemetery known as Pax.

In December 2007, the National Assembly of the Democratic Republic of Congo recommended returning his remains to the Congo to be interred in a mausoleum.

On the very same day he was exiled, Laurent-Désiré Kabila became the new president of Congo.

Kabila was killed in 2001 under circumstances still not clear. He was succeeded by his son, Joseph Kabila who was still the president of the Democratic Republic of Congo in 2012.

Joseph Kabila won another term in December 2011 in an election which local and international observers concluded was rigged against his strongest opponent, veteran politician Étienne Tshisekedi who refused to accept the results and declared himself president and the true winner of the electoral contest.

Legacy

According to Transparency International, Mobutu embezzled more than $5 billion USD from his country, ranking him as the third-most corrupt leader in the past two decades and the most corrupt African leader during the same period.

His legacy includes an extremely poor record on human rights, total mismanagement of the economy and institutionalised corruption.

Also during his reign, Zaire's capital Kinshasa had the largest CIA station in Africa.

Family

Mobutu was married twice. His first wife, Marie-Antoinette Mobutu, died of heart failure on 22 October 1977 in Genolier, Switzerland. She was 36.

On 1 May 1980, he married his mistress, Bobi Ladawa, on the eve of a visit by Pope John Paul II, thus legitimising his relationship in the eyes of the church. He was a Catholic.

Four of his sons from his first marriage died. Nyiwa died on 16 September 1994; Konga died in 1995; Kongulu died on 24 September 1998; and Manda died on 27 November 2004.

A son from his second marriage, François Joseph Nzanga Mobutu Ngbangawe, was a candidate in the 2006 presidential elections and served in the government of the Democratic Republic of the Congo as minister of state for agriculture among other posts.

A daughter, Yakpwa (nicknamed Yaki), was briefly married to a Belgian man named Pierre Janssen who later wrote a book which described Mobutu's lifestyle in vivid detail.

Altogether, Mobutu had seventeen children.

Leopold Sedar Senghor

Léopold Sédar Senghor (9 October 1906 – 20 December 2001) was a Senegalese poet, politician, and cultural theorist who for two decades served as the first president of Senegal (1960–1980).

Senghor was the first African elected as a member of *L'Académie française*, the pre-eminent French learned body on matters pertaining to the French language. The Académie was officially established in 1635 by Cardinal Richelieu, the chief minister to King Louis XIII.

Before independence, Senghor founded the political party called the Senegalese Democratic Bloc.

He is regarded by many as one of the most important African intellectuals of the 20th century.

Early life and education: 1906-1928

Léopold Sédar Senghor was born on 9 October 1906 in the small coastal city of Joal, about one hundred kilometres south of the nation's capital Dakar.

Basile Diogenes Senghor, Leopold's father, was a businessman. He was a member of the Serer ethnic group. It is one of the minority groups in Senegal.

Gnilane Ndiémé Bakhou, Léopold's mother, who was the third wife of his father, was a Muslim of Fula origin. She was a member of the Tabor tribe. She gave birth to six children, including two sons.

At the age of eight Senghor began his studies in Senegal in the Ngasobil boarding school. It was a Catholic school run by the Fathers of the Holy Spirit.

In 1922 he entered a seminary in Dakar. After being told the religious life was not for him, he attended a secular institution. By then, he was already passionate about French literature. He won distinctions in French, Latin, Greek and Algebra. With his Baccalaureate completed, he was awarded a scholarship to continue his studies in France.

"Sixteen years of wandering": 1928-1944

In 1928 Senghor sailed from Senegal for France, beginning in his words, "sixteen years of wandering." Starting his post-secondary studies at the Sorbonne, he quit and went on to Louis-Le-Grand to finish his prep course for entrance to the *École Normale Supérieure*, a *grande école*. Paul Cary, Henri Queffélec, Robert Verdier and Georges Pompidou were also studying at this elite institution. After failing the entrance exam, Senghor prepared for his grammar *Agrégation*. He was granted his *agrégation* in 1935 after a failed first attempt.

Academic career

He graduated from the University of Paris where he received the *Agrégation* in French Grammar. Subsequently, he was designated professor at the universities of Tours and Paris where he taught from 1935-1945.

Senghor decided to start his teaching years at the Lycée René-Descartes in Tours. He also taught at the Lycée Marcelin Berthelot in Saint-Maur-des-Fosses near Paris. He also studied linguistics taught by Lilias Homburger at the *École pratique des hautes études*. He studied with prominent social scientists such as Marcel Cohen, Marcel Mauss and Paul Rivet, director of the *Institut d'ethnologie de Paris*.

Senghor, along with other intellectuals of the African diaspora who had come to study in the colonial capital, coined the term and conceived the notion of "négritude", which was a response to the racism still prevalent in France. It turned the racial slur *nègre* into a positively connoted celebration of African culture and character. The idea of *négritude* informed not only Senghor's cultural criticism and literary work but also became a guiding principle for his political thought in his career as a statesman.

In 1939, Senghor was enrolled as a French army officer within the 59th Colonial Infantry division. A year later, during the German invasion of France in 1940, he was taken prisoner by the Germans in la Charité-sur-Loire. He was interned in different camps, and finally at Front Stalag 230, in Poitiers. Front Stalag 230 was reserved for colonial troops captured during the war.

German soldiers wanted to execute him and the others the same day they were captured, but they escaped this fate by yelling *Vive la France, vive l'Afrique noire!* ("Long live France, long live Black Africa!"). A French officer told the soldiers that executing the African prisoners would dishonour the Aryan race and the German army.

Senghor spent two years in different prison camps where he spent most of his time writing poems. He was released in 1942 for medical reasons.

He resumed his teaching career while remaining involved in the resistance during the Nazi occupation.

Political career: 1945-1982

Colonial France

Once the war was over, Senghor was selected as dean of the Linguistics Department with the *École Nationale de la France d'Outre-Mer*, a position he would hold until Senegal's independence in 1960.

While travelling on a research trip for his poetry, he met the local socialist leader, Lamine Guèye, who suggested that Senghor run for election as a member of the *Assemblée nationale française*. Senghor accepted and became *député* for the riding of Sénégal-Mauritanie, when colonies were granted the right to be represented by elected individuals.

They took different positions when the train conductors on the line Dakar-Niger went on strike. Guèye voted against the strike, arguing the movement would paralyse the colony, while Senghor supported the workers, which gained him great support among Senegalese.

Marriage and family

In 1946, Senghor married the daughter of the late colonial leader Félix Éboué, who had been governor of Chad until 1944. They had two sons: Francis (1947-) and Guy (1948–1983).

They later divorced. In 1957 Senghor married Colette Hubert, a French national from Normandy. They had a son, Philippe Maguilien (1960–1981).

Political changes

In 1947, Senghor left the African Division of the French Section of the Workers International (SFIO) which had given enormous financial support to the social movement. With Mamadou Dia, he founded the *Bloc démocratique sénégalais* (1948). They won the legislative elections of 1951. Guèye lost his seat.

Re-elected deputy in 1951 as an independent overseas member, Senghor was appointed state secretary to the Council's president in Edgar Faure's government from 1 March 1955 to 1 February 1956.

He became mayor of the city of Thiès, Senegal, in November 1956 and then advisory minister in theMichel Debre's government from 23 July 1959 to 19 May 1961. He was also a member of the commission responsible for drafting the Fifth Republic's constitution, general councillor for Senegal, member of the *Grand Conseil de l'Afrique Occidentale Francaise*, and member for the parliamentary assembly of the European Council

In 1964, Senghor published the first volume of a series of five, titled *Liberté*. The book contains a variety of speeches, essays and prefaces.

Senegal

Senghor supported federalism for newly independent African states, a type of "French Commonwealth". Since federalism was not favoured by the African countries, he decided to form, along with Modibo Keita, the Mali Federation with former French Sudan (present day Mali). Senghor was president of the Federal Assembly until the collapse of the federation in 1960.

Afterwards, Senghor became the first president of the Republic of Senegal, elected on 5 September 1960.

He is also the author of the Senegalese national anthem.

The prime minister, Mamadou Dia, was in charge of executing Senegal's long-term development plan, while Senghor was in charge of foreign relations. The two men quickly disagreed. In December 1962, Mamadou Dia was arrested under suspicion of fomenting a *coup d'état*. He was held in prison for twelve years. Following this, Senghor created a presidential regime.

On 22 March 1967, Senghor survived an assassination attempt. The suspect, Moustapha Lô, pointed his pistol towards the president after he had participated in the sermon of Tabaski at the Dakar Grand Mosque. But the gun did not fire. Lô was sentenced to death for treason. He was executed by firing squad on 15 June 1967, even though it remained unclear if he had actually wanted to kill Senghor.

Senghor resigned his position before the end of his fifth term in December 1980. Abdou Diouf replaced him as president.

During Senghor's presidency, Senegal had a multi-party system (limited to three: socialist, communist, and liberal).

Even after the end of colonial rule, the value of the Senegalese currency continued to be fixed by France; the official language was still French; and Senghor ruled the country while relying heavily on French advisors. He was known to be a Francophile and even spent the rest of his life in France with his French wife.

Francophonie

Senghor strongly supported the creation of *la Francophonie*, an international organisation of politics and governments with French as the mother or customary language and where a significant proportion of the people are Francophones – French speakers – or where there is a notable affiliation with the French language or culture. He was elected vice-president of the High Council of the Francophonie.

In 1982, he was one of the founders of an organisation intended to forge strong ties between France and developing countries. The main objective of this association was ostensibly to bring attention to the problems of developing countries. However, the real objective was to safeguard and promote French interests in the Third World, something Senghor himself obviously knew. But as a Francophile, it was an objective he undoubtedly supported.

Académie française: 1983-2001

Senghor was the first African to sit at the *l'Académie française*. The entrance ceremony in his honor took place on 29 March 1984 in presence of then-French President Francois Mitterrand. This was considered as a further step towards greater openness in the Académie after the previous election of a woman, Marguerite Yourcenar.

In 1993, Senghor's last and fifth book of the *Liberté* series was published: *Liberté 5: le dialogue des cultures.*

"Je ne suis pas sûr de mourir. Et si c'était ça l'enfer?" ("I'm not sure that I will die. What if that were hell?") said Senghor, post-retirement, in 1996.

Death

He spent the last years of his life with his wife in Verson near the city of Caen in Normandy, where he died on 20 December 2001.

His funeral was held on 29 December 2001 in Senegal's capital Dakar. Officials attending the ceremony included Raymond Forni, president of the *Assemblée nationale* (French National Assembly), and Charles Josselin, state secretary for France's minister of foreign affairs, in charge of the Francophonie.

French President Jacques Chirac, who did not attend the funeral, said: "Poetry has lost one of its masters, Senegal a statesman, Africa a visionary and France a friend."

French Prime Minister Lionel Jospin also did not attend the funeral.

Their failure to attend Senghor's funeral made waves as it was deemed a lack of acknowledgement for what the politician had been in his life.

The analogy was made with the Senegalese Tirailleurs (black Senegalese soldiers in the colonial army) who, after having contributed to the liberation of France, had to wait more than forty years to receive an equal pension (in terms of buying power) to their French counterparts.

Érik Orsenna (the pen-name of Érik Arnoult), a French scholar, politician and novelist and close collaborator of French President François Mitterrand, upon hearing about the failure of the two French leaders to attend Senghor's funeral, wrote in the French newspaper *Le Monde* an editorial entitled: "J'ai honte" (I am ashamed).

Legacy

Although a socialist, Senghor avoided the Marxist and anti-Western ideology that had become popular in post-colonial Africa, favouring instead the maintenance of close ties with France and the rest of the Western world. This is seen by many observers as a contributing factor to Senegal's political stability. Senegal remains one of the few African countries never to have had a coup and always to have had a peaceful transfer of power.

Senghor's tenure as president was characterized by the development of African socialism which was created as an indigenous alternative to Marxism, drawing heavily from the *négritude* philosophy. In developing this, he was assisted by Ousmane Tanor Dieng, one of his advisers.

Senghor voluntarily stepped down from the presidency on 31 December 1980 in favour of his prime minister, Abdou Diouf.

Seat number 16 of the Académie was vacant after the Senegalese poet's death. He was ultimately replaced by another former president, Valéry Giscard d'Estaing.

Honours

Senghor received several honours in the course of his life.

He was made Grand-Croix of the Légion d'honneur, Grand-Croix of the l'Ordre national du Mérite, commander of arts and letters. He also received academic palms and the Grand-Croix of the l'Ordre du lion du Sénégal.

His war exploits earned him the medal of Reconnaissance franco-alliée 1939-1945 and the combattant cross 1939-1945.

He was named honorary doctor of thirty-seven universities.

The French Language International University in Alexandria was officially opened in 1990 and was named after him.

In 1994 he was awarded the Lifetime Achievement Award by the African Studies Association. However, there was controversy about whether he met the standard of contributing "a lifetime record of outstanding scholarship in African studies and service to the Africanist community."

Nigerian Professor Michael Mbabuike (August 1943 – December 2006), president of the New York African Studies Association (NYASA), said that the award also honors those who have worked "to make the world a better place for mankind."

Senegal's Dakar international airport was renamed *Aéroport International Léopold Sédar Senghor* on his 90th birthday on 9 October 1996.

The Passerelle Solférino, a footbridge over the River Seine in the VIIe arrondissement of Paris served by the Metro station Assemblée Nationale, was renamed Passerelle Léopold-Sédar-Senghor on the centenary of his birth in 2006.

Poetry

Senghor's poetry was widely acclaimed, and in 1978 he was awarded the Prix mondial Cino Del Duca.

His poem *A l'appel de la race de Saba* published in 1936 was inspired by the entry of Italian troops in Addis Ababa.

In 1948, Senghor compiled and edited a volume of Francophone poetry called *Anthologie de la nouvelle poésie nègre et malgache* for which Jean-Paul Sartre wrote an introduction entitled "Orphée Noir" (Black Orpheus).

For his epitaph was a poem he had written, namely:

Quand je serai mort, mes amis, couchez-moi sous Joal-l'Ombreuse.
Sur la colline au bord du Mamanguedy, près l'oreille du sanctuaire des Serpents.
Mais entre le Lion couchez-moi et l'aïeule Tening-Ndyae.
Quand je serai mort mes amis, couchez-moi sous Joal-la-Portugaise.
Des pierres du Fort vous ferez ma tombe, et les canons garderont le silence.
Deux lauriers roses-blanc et rose-embaumeront la Signare.

When I'm dead, my friends, place me below Shadowy Joal,
On the hill, by the bank of the Mamanguedy, near the ear of Serpents' Sanctuary.
But place me between the Lion and ancestral Tening-Ndyae.
When I'm dead, my friends, place me beneath Portuguese Joal.
Of stones from the Fort build my tomb, and cannons will keep quiet.
Two laurier roses -- white and pink -- will perfume the Signare.

Négritude

With Aimé Césaire and Léon Damas, Senghor created the concept of *Négritude*, an important intellectual movement that sought to assert and to valorise what they believed to be distinctive African characteristics, values, and aesthetics.

This was a reaction against the too strong dominance of French culture in the colonies and against the perception that Africa did not have culture developed

196

enough to stand alongside that of Europe.

Building upon historical research identifying ancient Egypt with black Africa, Senghor argued that sub-Saharan Africa and Europe are in fact part of the same cultural continuum, reaching from Egypt to classical Greece, through Rome to the European colonial powers of the modern age.

Négritude was by no means – as it has in many quarters been perceived – an anti-white racism but rather emphasised the importance of dialogue and exchange among different cultures – European, African, Arab, Asian, and so on.

A related concept later developed in Mobutu's Zaire is that of *authenticité* or Authenticity.

Works of Senghor

- *Prière aux masques* (Circa 1935 - Published in collected works during the 1940s).
- *Chants d'ombre* (1945)
- *Hosties noires* (1948)
- *Anthologie de la nouvelle poésie nègre et malgache* (1948)
- *La Belle Histoire de Leuk-le-Lièvre* (1953)
- *Éthiopiques* (1956)
- *Nocturnes* (1961). (English tr. by Clive Wake and John Reed, *Nocturnes*, London: Heinemann Educational, 1969. African Writers Series 71)
- *Nation et voie africaine du socialisme (1961)*
- *Pierre Teilhard de Chardin et la politique africaine (1962)*
- *Lettres de d'hivernage* (1973)
- *Élégies majeures* (1979)
- *La poésie de l'action: conversation avec Mohamed Aziza* (1980)
- *Ce que je crois* (1988)

Modibo Keita

Modibo Keita (Bamako, 4 June 1915 - Bamako, 16 May 1977) was the first president of Mali (1960–1968). He also served as prime minister of the Mali Federation when Leopold Sedar Senghor was president of that union – of Mali and Senegal.

Like Senghor, Keita also espoused a form of African socialism.

But their versions of socialism came nowhere close to President Julius Nyerere's brand of African socialism in terms of authenticity as products of African heritage. Among all African leaders, it was Nyerere who came to be acknowledged as the most articulate exponent and theorist of African socialism called *ujamaa* (family-hood). He could even legitimately be called "the father of African socialism."

His country Tanzania underwent the most radical transformation in the economic arena – more than any other country on the entire African continent. The establishment of *ujamaa* villages was the most extensive exercise in social engineering ever attempted anywhere in Africa.

Youth

Modibo Keita was born in Bamako-Coura, a neighborhood of Bamako, which was at the time the capital of French Sudan (renamed Mali). His family were Malian and practising Muslims.

He was educated in Bamako, the capital of Mali, and at the *École normale supérieure William Ponty* in Dakar where he was top of his class. Beginning in 1936, he worked as a teacher in Bamako, Sikasso and Timbuktu.

Entering politics

Modibo Keïta was involved in various associations. In 1937, he was the coordinator of an art and theatre group. Along with Ouezzin Coulibaly, he helped found the Union of French West African Teachers.

Keïta also joined the Communist Study Groups (in French *Groupes d'Etudes Communistes* – GEC) cell in Bamako. Founded in 1943 under the influence of the French communist Party, GEC was a communist group in colonial French West Africa and French Equatorial Africa. It had branches in the capital cities of the West African territories and was primarily based amongst intellectuals.

In 1943, Keita founded the *L'oeil de Kénédougou*, a magazine critical of colonial rule. This led to his imprisonment for three weeks in 1946 at the *Prison de la Santé* in Paris.

In 1945 Keïta was a candidate for the Constituent Assembly of the French Fourth Republic. He was supported by GEC and the Sudanese Democratic Party. Later the same year, he and Mamadou Konaté founded the *Bloc soudanais* which developed into the Sudanese Union.

Political life

In October 1946, the African Democratic Rally (*Rassemblement Démocratique Africain* – RDA) was created in Bamako at a conference of delegates from the African French colonies.

The coalition was led by Félix Houphouët-Boigny. Modibo Keïta became RDA secretary-general in French Sudan and head of the Soundanese affiliate: the US-RDA.

The Sudanese Union-African Democratic Rally (US-RDA *Union Soudanaise-Rassemblement Démocratique Africain*), a Malian political party, was formed in 1945 by

Mamdou Konaté and Modibo Keita and was named Sudanese Bloc (*Bloc Soudanais*).

In 1948, Modibo Keita was elected general councilor of French Sudan. And in 1956, he was elected mayor of Bamako and became a member of *Assemblée nationale* (the French National Assembly).

He twice served as secretary of state in the governments of Maurice Jean Marie Bourgès-Maunoury (who was French prime minister from June to November 1957) and Félix Gaillard d'Aimé who succeeded Maurice Bourgès-Maunoury and served as prime minister from 1957 to 1958.

Modibo Keïta was elected constituent assembly president of the Mali Federation on 20 July 1960. Senegal left the federation on 20 August 1960.

President of Mali

After the collapse of the federation, the US-RDA proclaimed the Soudanese Republic's complete independence as the Republic of Mali. Keita became its first president.

As a socialist, he led his country towards socialisation of the economy, starting with agriculture and trade. In October 1960, he created the SOMIEX (Malian Import and Export Company) which had a monopoly over the exports and imports including their distribution in the country.

But the establishment of the Malian franc in 1962, and the difficulties of provisioning, resulted in a severe inflation and dissatisfaction with Keita's economic policies especially among businessmen and even among peasants.

Although Keita was initially viewed by the United States as a socialist, he made it clear that he sought good relations with Washington.

In September 1961, he travelled to the United States

200

with Indonesian Prime Minister Surkano as representatives of the Non-Aligned Movement and met with President John F. Kennedy.

Modibo Keïta also imprisoned political oppoenents. One of the most prominent opponents he imprisoned was Fily Dabo Sissoko.

Also a highly influential writer and an exponent of Negritude, Sissoko was one of the most influential political leaders of pre-independence Mali. Unlike Keita, he was a conservative. He was the most prominent conservative politician in Mali opposed to Keita's socialist policies. He died in prison in the town of Kidal in northeastern Mali on 30 June 1964.

From 1967, President Modibo Keita started the "revolution active" and suspended the constitution by creating the National Committee for the Defence of the Revolution (CNDR). The exactions of the "milice populaire" (the US-RDA militia) and the devaluation of the Malian franc in 1967 led to general unrest in the country, creating conditions for military intervention.

On 19 November 1968, Lieutenant Moussa Traoré overthrew Modibo Keïta and sent him to prison in the northern Malian town of Kidal.

After being transferred back to the capital Bamako in February 1977 in what was claimed to be an action by the government towards national reconciliation in preparation for his release, Modibo Keïta died, still a prisoner, on 16 May 1977.

His reputation was rehabilitated in 1992 following the ouster of Moussa Traoré in a military coup and subsequent elections of President Alpha Oumar Konaré. A monument for Modibo Keïta was dedicated in Bamako on 6 June 1999.

As a Pan-Africanist

Modibo Keïta devoted his entire life to African unity. He first played a prominent role in the creation of the Mali Federation with Léopold Sédar Senghor.

After the federation collapsed, he moved away from Senghor and, together with Guinean President Ahmed Sekou Toure and Ghanaian President Kwame Nkrumah, formed the Union of the States of Western Africa which was simply known as the Ghana-Guinea-Mali union. Modibo Keita also played a prominent role in formation of the Organisation of African Unity (OAU).

In 1963, he invited the king of Morocco and the president of Algeria to Bamako in an attempt to end the Sand War, a frontier conflict between the two countries. Along with Emperor Haile Selassie of Ethiopia, Keïta was successful in negotiating the Bamako Accords which brought an end to the conflict. As a result, he won the Lenin Peace Prize that year.

From 1963 to 1966, he normalised relations with the countries of Senegal, Upper Volta and Ivory Coast.

He was also a strong advocate of the Non-Aligned Movement and defended nationalist movements such as the Algerian National Liberation Front (FLN).

In literature

Malian author Massa Makan Diabaté satirises Keïta's presidency in his novel *The Butcher of Kouta* which features a socialist, dictatorial president named "Bagabaga Daba" (literally, "ant with a big mouth") who is later overthrown in a military coup.

Ahmed Sékou Touré

Ahmed Sékou Touré – or Ahmed Seku Ture – (9 January 1922 – 26 March 1984) was president of Guinea from 1958 until his death in 1984.

He was the most prominent leader in his country's struggle for independence from France.

He was also one of the most prominent Pan-Africanist leaders together with Kwame Nkrumah, Julius Nyerere, and Modibo Keita who strongly supported African liberation and continental unity.

Former Algerian President Ahmed Ben Bella said in an interview in Geneva, Switzerland, in 1995 that there were six African leaders in the Organisation of African Unity (OAU) who worked together secretly. They were Kwame Nkrumah, Ahmed Sekou Toure, Gamal Abdel Nasser, Ahmed Ben Bella, Julius Nyerere, and Modibo Keita, and were known as the Group of Six.

Early life

Sékou Touré was born into a poor Mandinka family in Faranah, French Guinea. He was the great-grandson of Samore Toure, a prominent leader in Guinea who resisted French rule from 1882 until his capture in 1898.

Sékou Touré's, early life was characterised by challenging authority. He rebelled against authority even in primary school demanding student rights and was looked upon by other pupils as their leader.

He was expelled from primary school and later began working for the postal services – *Postes, télégraphes et téléphones* (PTT). He also became involved in labour union activities when he was a postal employee.

During his youth and after becoming president, Touré studied the works of communist philosophers, especially those of Karl Marx and Vladmir Lenin.

Politics

His involvement in political activities began when he worked for the postal services. He was one of the founders of Guinea's postal workers' union in 1945 and became its secretary-general in the same year.

In 1952, he became the leader of the Guinean Democratic Party (*Parti Démocratique de Guinée-Rassemblement Démocratique Africain*) which was the Guinean branch of the RDA (*African Democratic Rally*, French: *Rassemblement Démocratique Africain*), an umbrella organisation which had branches in all the African French colonies agitating for independence.

In 1956 he organised the *Union Générale des Travailleurs d'Afrique Noire*, a trade union for French West Africa. In the same year, he was elected Guinea's deputy to the French National Assembly and mayor of Conakry, the capital of Guinea, and continued to agitate for independence.

He also served for some time as a representative of African groups in France where he worked to negotiate for the independence of France's African colonies.

A constitutional referendum was held in Guinea on 28 September 1958 as part of a wider referendum across all French colonies (and France itself) on whether to adopt the new French constitution. If the constitution was accepted, the colonies would become part of the new French Community; if rejected, the territory would be granted independence.

Alongside Niger, Guinea was one of only two territories where the major political party campaigned for a "no" vote. But Guinea was the only colony which rejected the constitution and opted for independence.

The results showed that more than 95% of voters voted

against the constitution, with a turnout of 85.5%.

The Democratic Party of Guinea which had won all but four seats in the Territorial Assembly elections the previous year under the leadership of Sékou Touré pushed for a rejection of the constitution.

On 19 October 1958 the Democratic Party of Guinea severed ties with the rest of the RDA. The other RDA members supported a closer union with France, while Sekou Toure wanted total independence.

Following the referendum, Guinea declared independence on 2 October 1958.

The French government was furious and tried to punish Guinea for rejecting close association with France. Guineans did not want to expel the French but rejected membership in the French Union.

Under Sekou Toure's leadership, not only was Guinea the only country among the French African colonies to vote for immediate independence rather than continued association with France; it was also the only French colony which left the French Community; the French Community replaced the French Union in 1958.

In retaliation, The French withdrew totally from the country and halted any development assistance. They pulled out of Guinea abruptly, taking files, destroying infrastructure, and breaking political and economic ties.

As a result of that, the Guinean government turned to the Communist bloc for aid, a move which the French government used in pressuring Western countries not to accept the Guinean independence.

The rest of Francophone Africa won independence in 1960.

As President of Guinea

Sekou Touré was a strong leader. In 1960, he declared the Democratic Party of Guinea (PDG) to be the only legal party, though the country had effectively been a one-party state since independence.

During his presidency, he pursued socialist policies, centralised economic planning, and nationalised foreign-owned companies.

Most of his political opponents – opposed to one-party rule and socialism – were arrested and jailed or exiled. His rejection of close association with France and nationalisation of major means of production including land angered many powerful forces including traditional landlords; so did his failure to provide economic opportunities through free market forces and his refusal to allow democracy.

While still revered in much of Africa and in the rest of the Pan-African including the diaspora, Sekou Toure was not popular among many Guineans. Many of them were critical of his policies.

Opposition to single party rule grew slowly, and by the late 1960s, many of his opponents ended up in prison or in detention camps. Guinea's secret police made things even worse. Sekou Toure's opponents often had two choices – say nothing or flee abroad.

From 1965 to 1975, Sekou Toure, ended all his relations with France. He argued that Africans had lost a lot during colonial rule and that Africa ought to cut off ties with the former colonial powers.

Throughout his dispute with France, Guinea maintained good relations with several socialist countries. However, Touré's attitude toward France was not generally well received, and some African countries ended diplomatic relations with Guinea over the incident. In spite of that, Touré's move won the support of many anti-colonialist and Pan-Africanist groups and leaders.

It was only in 1978, as Guinea's ties with the Soviet Union soured, that a French president visited Guinea for the first time. It was a sign of reconciliation. The visit was made by Valéry Giscard d'Estaing who served as president from 1974 to 1981.

Touré's primary allies in West Africa were Kwame Nkrumah, overthrown in February 1966; and Modibo Keita, who was also overthrown as we learned earlier.

After Nkrumah was overthrown, Touré offered him asylum and made him co-president of Guinea.

As a leader of the Pan-Africanist movement, Sekou Toure consistently spoke out against colonialism and imperialism and befriended leaders from the African diaspora such as Malcolm X and Stokely Carmichael. Carmichael moved to Guinea in 1967 and spent the rest of his life there. He also changed his name to Kwame Ture in honour of Kwame Nkrumah and Sekou Toure.

Kwame Ture supported Nkrumah in forming the All-African People's Revolutionary Party (A-APRP). Nkrumah formed the party in Conakry, Guinea, in 1968. The party promoted Pan-Africanism and continental unification under a socialist government.

Guinea's relations with the United States fluctuated during Sekou Touré's presidency. For example, he was not impressed by President Eisenhower because of his policies towards Africa. But he liked John F. Kennedy and considered him to be a friend of Africa. He was impressed by Kennedy's interest in African development and commitment to civil rights in the United States.

In 1962, Touré blamed Guinean labour unrest on interference by the Soviet Union and relations between the two countries deteriorated.

Also, relations with the United States soured after Kennedy's assassination. When a Guinean delegation was imprisoned in Ghana after the ouster of President Kwame Nkrumah in a coup engineered and masterminded by the CIA, Sekou Touré blamed Washington for that. He also believed that the CIA was plotting to overthrow him just as they overthrew his ideological compatriot, Kwame Nkrumah, in a coup which angered many Africans.

Over time, Sekou Touré's increasing paranoia led him

to arrest large numbers of suspected political opponents and imprison them in camps such as the notorious Camp Boiro National Guard Barracks. About 50,000 people are believed to have been killed in detention camps during his reign. And tens of thousands of Guinean dissidents sought refuge in exile.

Once Guinea's rapprochement with France began in the late 1970s, some of his supporters, Marxists, began to oppose his government's increasing move towards capitalist liberalisation. In 1978, he formally renounced Marxism and re-established trade with the West.

Elections for an expanded National Assembly were held in 1980. Sekou Touré was elected unopposed to a fourth seven-year term as president on 9 May 1982. Also a new constitution was adopted that month.

During the summer, Sekou Touré visited the United States as part of an economic policy reversal that found Guinea seeking Western investment to develop its huge mineral reserves. Measures announced in 1983 brought further economic liberalisation including the relegation of produce marketing to private traders.

Sekou Touré died on 26 March 1984 while undergoing cardiac treatment at the Cleveland Clinic in Cleveland, Ohio. He had been rushed to the United States after being stricken in Saudi Arabia the previous day.

Prime Minister Louis Lansana Béavogui became acting president, pending elections that were to be held within 45 days. However, on 3 April, just as the political bureau of the ruling Guinea Democratic Party (PDG) was about to name its choice as Sekou Touré's successor, the armed forces seized power, denouncing the last years of Touré's rule as a "bloody and ruthless dictatorship."

The constitution was suspended, the National Assembly dissolved, and the PDG abolished.

The leader of the coup, Colonel Lansana Conté, assumed the presidency on 5 April, heading the Military Committee for National Recovery (*Comité Militaire de*

Redressement National—CMRN). About 1,000 political prisoners were freed.

In 1985, Conté took advantage of an alleged coup attempt to execute several of Sekou Touré's close associates including Ismael Touré, Seydou Keita, Siaka Touré, former commander of Camp Boiro, and Moussa Diakité.

Works by Sekou Touré (partial list)

- Ahmed Sékou Touré. 8 novembre 1964 (Conakry): Parti démocratique de Guinée, (1965)
- Ahmed Sékou Touré. A propos du Sahara Occidental: intervention du président Ahmed Sékou Touré devant le 17e sommet de l'OUA, Freetown, le 3 juillet 1980. (S.l.: s.n., 1980)
- Ahmed Sékou Touré. Address of President Ahmed Sékou Touré, President of the Republic of Guinee (sic): suggestions submitted during the West Africa consultative regional meeting held at Conakry, during 19 and 20 November 1971. (Cairo : Permanent Secretariat of the Afro-Asian Peoples' Solidarity Organization, 1971)
- Ahmed Sékou Touré. Afrika and imperialism. Newark, N.J. : Jihad Pub. Co., 1973.
- Ahmed Sékou Touré. (Conférences, discours et rapports .). Conakry : Impr. du Gouvernement, (1958-
- Ahmed Sékou Touré. Congres général de l'U.G.T.A.N. (Union général des travailleurs de l'Afrique noire): Conakry, 15-18 janvier 1959: rapport d'orientation et de doctrine. (Paris): Présence africaine, c1959.
- Ahmed Sékou Touré. Discours de Monsieur Sékou Touré, Président du Conseil de Gouvernement des 28 juillet et 25 aout 1958, de Monsieur Diallo Saifoulaye, Président de L'Assemblée territoriale et du Général de Gaulle, Président du Gouvernement de la Républ (Conakry): Guinée Française, (1958)

- Ahmed Sékou Touré. Doctrine and methods of the Democratic Party of Guinea (Conakry 1963).
- Ahmed Sékou Touré. Expérience guinéenne et unité africaine. Paris, Présence africaine(1959)
- Ahmed Sékou Touré. Guinée-Festival / commentaire et montage, Wolibo Dukuré dit Grand-pére. Conakry: Commission Culturelle du Comité Central, 1983.
- Ahmed Sékou Touré. Guinée, prélude à l'indépendance (Avant-propos de Jacques Rabemananjara) Paris, Présence africaine (1958)
- Ahmed Sékou Touré. Hommage a la révolution Cubaine; Message du camarade Ahmed Sekou Toure au peuple Cubain a l'occasion du 20e anniversaire de l'attaque de la Caserne de Moncada (Juillet 1973). Conakry: Bureau de Presse de la Presidence de la Republique, (1975).
- Ahmed Sékou Touré. International policy and diplomatic action of the Democratic Party of Guinea; extracts from the report on doctrine and orientation submitted to the 3d National Conference of the P.D.G. (Cairo, Société Orientale de Publicité-Press, 1962)
- Ahmed Sékou Touré. Opening speech of the Summit of Heads of State and Government by President Ahmed Sékou Touré, chairman of the Summit (November 20, 1980). (S.l.: s.n., 1980)
- Ahmed Sékou Touré. Poemes militants. (Conakry, Guinea): Parti démocratique de Guinée, 1972
- Ahmed Sékou Touré. Political leader considered as the representative of a culture. (Newark, N. J.: Jihad Productions, 19--)
- Ahmed Sékou Touré. Pour l'amitié algéro-guinéenne. (Conakry, Guinea: Parti démocratique de Guinée, 1972)
- Ahmed Sékou Touré. Rapport de doctrine et de politique générale. Conakry: Imprimerie Nationale, 1959.
- Ahmed Sékou Touré. Strategy and tactics of the revolution. Conakry, Guinea: Press Office, 1978.
- Ahmed Sékou Touré. Unité nationale. Conakry, République de Guinée (B.P. 1005, Conakry, République de Guinée):

Bureau de presse de la Présidence de la République, 1977.

William Tubman

William Vacanarat Shadrach Tubman (29 November 1895 – 23 July 1971) was the 19th president of Liberia from 1944 until his death in 1971.

He is regarded as the "father of modern Liberia."

His presidency was marked by the influx of foreign investment into his country and its modernization. During his tenure, Liberia experienced a period of prosperity. He also led a policy of national unity in order to reduce the social and political differences between his fellow Americo-Liberians and indigenous Liberians who are members of different ethnic groups or tribes. However, as he continued to rule Liberia, he became increasingly dictatorial.

Youth and early political career

Tubman was born in Harper, Liberia. His father, the Reverend Alexander Tubman, was a stonemason, general in the Liberian army and a former Speaker of the Liberian House of Representatives as well as a Methodist preacher.

Alexander Tubman's parents, Sylvia and William Shadrach Tubman, were part of a group of 69 slaves freed and sent to Liberia by Emily Tubman, a philanthropic widow living in Augusta, Georgia, in 1844.

Emily Tubman had been instrumental in the manumission and repatriation of African slaves in the antebellum South. They took the name Tubman after arriving in the country, naming their community Tubman Hill.

Willliam Tubman's mother, Elizabeth Rebecca Barnes Tubman, came from Atlanta, Georgia.

His father required him and his other four children to attend daily family prayer services and sleep on the floor because, he thought, beds were too soft and therefore "degrading to character development."

Willliam Tubman, who was the second son, went to primary school in Harper, then the Methodist Cape Palmas Seminary, and finally Harper County High School.

He participated in several military operations from 1910 and 1917, rising from a private to become an officer.

He first planned to be a preacher and was named, at age 19, a Methodist lay pastor.

After studying law under various private tutors, he passed the bar examination and became a lawyer in 1917.Subsequently, he served as a recorder in the Maryland County Monthly and Probate Court, as a tax collector, teacher, and even a colonel in a militia.

Tubman was a member of the True Whig Party (TWP) which was the dominant political party in Liberia since 1878.

In 1923, when he was 28 years old, he was elected to the Senate of Liberia from Maryland County, holding the record as the youngest senator in the history of Liberia. Labeling himself the "Convivial Cannibal from the Downcoast Hinterlands," he fought for the rights of indigenous Liberians who were dominated by Americo-Liberians. But he did not go do enough to champion their cause. He was an Americo-Liberian himself, thus an integral part of the dominant minority group of settlers from America who ruled Liberia.

He was re-elected in 1929 and served as the legal adviser to then-vice president Allen Yancy while at the same time serving in the senate.

He resigned from the senate in 1931 to defend Liberia before the League of Nations amidst allegations that the Liberian government dominated by Americo-Liberians was using the native people as slaves within Liberia and in Panama where they were sent to work virtually as slaves while the Liberian government was being paid for their labour.

Tubman was reelected to the national legislature in 1934 but resigned in 1937 when President Edwin Barclay appointed him associate justice of the Supreme Court of Liberia, a post he held until 1943. An official biography speculates that Tubman's elevation to the Liberian Supreme Court was intended to remove him from actively seeking the presidency.

The new president of Liberia

In December 1942, Liberia was faced with the question of the succession: who would succeed President Edwin Barclay. Six candidates sought the presidency, including two favourites: Tubman and Foreign Minister Clarence L. Simpson.

Without much opposition from Simpson, Tubman was elected president on 4 May 1943 at the age of 48 and was inaugurated on 3 January 1944.

Throughout its history, Liberia maintained close ties to the United States. The United States also established a military base in Liberia. Liberia also supported the United States against Germany and Japan during World War II. Severing diplomatic relations with Germany and expelling all German citizens from Liberia was a difficult decision for Liberia to make for several reasons: German merchants in Liberia ran the Liberian economy; (2) Germany was Liberia's major trading partner; and (3), most of the doctors in Liberia were Germans.

Despite the fact that Liberia found itself between a rock and a hard place, it agreed to expel all German residents and declare the full "might" of the Liberian economy against Nazi Germany and the Axis. It was really no more than a symbolic gesture since the Liberian economy was very small; it still is.

In foreign policy, Tubman aligned himself with the United States (in June, 1944 he and Edwin Barclay traveled to the White House to be guests of President Franklin D. Roosevelt – the first African heads of state to do so) while strengthening ties among fellow Africans by participating in the Asian-African Conference of 1955 and the First Conference of Independent African States in Accra, Ghana, organised by Kwame Nkrumah in 1958. In 1959, Tubman organized the Second Conference of African States.

In 1961, following a Pan-African conference held in Monrovia, Tubman helped in founding the Monrovia Group, a moderate association of African leaders who worked for gradual unification of Africa, unlike the milintant Casablanca Group.

The "father of modern Liberia"

The moderniser of Liberia

Upon Tubman's succession to the Supreme Court, infrastructure in Liberia was virtually non-existent. Tubman explained this situation by the fact that Liberia never received "benefits of colonization".

To remedy the situation, he adopted a new economic policy known as open-door policy. Working to facilitate and encourage foreign businesses to locate in Liberia, the policy was very successful and, between 1944 and 1970, the value of foreign investments, mainly American, increased two hundredfold. From 1950-1960, Liberia experienced an average annual growth of 11.5%.

Liberia'e economic success allowed Tubman to begin modernisation: the streets of the capital Monrovia were paved, a sanitation system was created, hospitals were built, and a literacy programme was launched in 1948. Tubman built several thousand kilometres of roads and established a railway line to connect the iron mines to the coast. During this period, he transformed the port of Monrovia into a free port.

Economic prosperity

In early 1960, Liberia began to experience its first real era of prosperity, thanks in part to Tubman's modernisation of infrastructure.

Regarded as a pro-Western, stabilising influence in West Africa, Tubman was courted by many Western politicians, especially American. Also Tubman had a long-term relationship with Amy Ashwood Garvey, a Pan-Africanist from Jamaica and the first wife of Marcus Garvey.

A gunman attempted to assassinate Tubman in 1955 at the behest of his political opponents, after which he cracked down brutally on any known opposition politicians.

Legacy

Tubman's term is best known for the policies of national unification – bringing the maritime provinces and the hinterland as well as the indigenous people and the Americo-Liberians together – and open door in the economic realm.

He tried to reconcile the interests of the native tribes with those of the Americo-Liberian elite, and increased foreign investment in Liberia to stimulate economic growth.

These policies led to the crowning achievement of the Liberian economy during the 1950s when the country had the second-largest rate of economic growth in the world.

At his death in 1971 in a London clinic, Liberia had the largest mercantile fleet in the world and the world's largest rubber industry. Liberia was also the third-largest exporter of iron ore in the world and had attracted more than US$1 billion in foreign investment.

Tubman was succeeded by his long-time vice president William Tolbert.

The economic prosperity of Liberia during that time fuelled political opposition and finally led to the overthrow of Americo-Liberian rule – the True Whig oligarchy – in 1980 by soldiers of indigenous origin led by Samuel Doe.

Ellen Johnson Sirleaf

Ellen Johnson Sirleaf was the 24th president of Liberia. She served as minister of finance under President William Tolbert from 1979 until the 1980 military coup after which she left Liberia and held senior positions at various financial institutions.

She placed a very distant second in the 1997 presidential election which Charles Taylor won. The people voted for him because they were afraid he would plunge the country back into war if he was not elected.

Mrs. Sirleaf was elected president in 2005 and took office on 16 January 2006. She was the first elected female head of state in Africa.

Family background

Although Ellen Johnson Sirleaf is not Americo-Liberian by ancestry, she is considered to be culturally Americo-Liberian by some observers or she is assumed to be Americo-Liberian. But she does not identify herself as one.

Her ethnic background is half-Gola from her father's side, one-fourth German (grandfather), and one-fourth Kru (grandmother) from her mother's side.

216

Sirleaf's father, Jahmale Carney Johnson, was born into a region known for its rural poverty. He was the son of a minor Gola chief named Jahmale and one of his wives, Jenneh, in Julijuah, Bomi County. Her father was sent to the nation's capital Monrovia where his last name was changed to Johnson because of his father's loyalty to President Hilary R.W. Johnson, Liberia's first Liberian-born president.

He grew up in Monrovia where he was raised by an Americo-Liberian family with the surname McGritty. Sirleaf's father later became the first Liberian from an indigenous ethnic group to sit in the country's national legislature.

Sirleaf's mother was also born into poverty in Greenville, Liberia. Her grandmother, Juah Sarwee, sent Sirleaf's mother to Monrovia when Sirleaf's German grandfather had to flee the country after Liberia declared war on Germany during World War I. A member of a prominent Americo-Liberian family, Cecilia Dunbar, adopted and raised Sirleaf's mother.

Early life and career

Sirleaf was born on 29 October 1938 in Monrovia and studied economics and accountancy from 1948 to 1955 at the College of West Africa in the nation's capital.

She married James Sirleaf when she was 17 years old and went with him to the United States in 1961 to continue her studies. She earned an accounting degree at the University of Wisconsin-Madison and a degree in economics from the University of Colorado-Boulder. She later studied economics and public policy at Harvard's John F. Kennedy School of Government from 1969 to 1971 and earned a master's degree in public administration. She then returned to Liberia to work in the government of President William Tolbert.

She served as assistant minister of finance from 1972 to 1973 but resigned from Tolbert's government after getting into a disagreement over spending. She later served as minister of finance from 1979 to April 1980 during the last year of Tolbert's – and Americo-Liberian – rule. Master Sergeant Samuel K. Doe, a member of the Krahn ethnic group, seized power on 12 April 1980 in a military coup in which President Tolbert was assassinated. And all but four members of his cabinet were executed by firing squad.

The new military rulers formed the People's Redemption Council to rule the country and led a purge against the former government. Ellen Johnson Sirleaf initially accepted a post in the new government as president of the Liberian Bank for Development and Investment but fled the country in November 1980 after publicly criticising Samuel Doe and the People's Redemption Council for their poor management of the country.

Sirleaf first moved to Washington, D.C. to work for the World Bank before moving to Nairobi in 1981 to serve as vice president of the African Regional Office of Citibank. She resigned from Citibank in 1985 following her involvement in the 1985 election in Liberia and went to work for Equator Bank, a subsidiary of HSBC (Hong Kong and Shanghai Banking Corporation).

In 1992, Sirleaf was appointed as the assistant administrator of the United Nations Development Programme's (UNDP's) Regional Bureau for Africa. She resigned from that position in 1997 to run for president of Liberia.

During her time at the UN, she was one of the seven internationally eminent persons designated in 1999 by the Organisation of African Unity (OAU) to investigate the Rwandan genocide. She was also one of the five Commission Chairs for the Inter-Congolese Dialogue and one of the two international experts selected by UNIFEM to investigate and report on the effect of conflict on women and women's roles in peace building.

Mrs. Sirleaf was also the first chairperson of the Open Society Initiative for West Africa (OSIWA) and a visiting professor of governance at the Ghana Institute of Management and Public Administration (GIMPA).

Political career

1985 general election

While working at Citibank, Sirleaf returned to Liberia

in 1985 to run for vice president on the ticket of the Liberian Action Party in the 1985 elections. But she was placed under house arrest in August of that year and soon after was sentenced to ten years in prison for sedition because of her speech in which she was said to have insulted the members of Samuel K. Doe's regime.

Following international calls for her release, Doe pardoned and released her in September. Due to government pressure, she was removed from the presidential ticket and instead ran for a senate seat in Montserrado County.

Although the elections – which Doe and his National Democratic Party (NDP) won, getting large majorities in both houses – were widely condemned as neither free nor fair, Sirleaf was declared the winner of her senate race. But she refused to accept the seat in protest of the election fraud.

After an attempted coup against Samuel Doe by Thomas Quinwonkpa on 12 November 1985, Sirleaf was arrested and imprisoned again on November 13th. Despite continuing to refuse to accept her seat in the senate, she was released in July 1986 and secretly fled to the United States later that year.

1997 presidential campaign

At the outbreak of the first Liberian civil war in 1989, Sirleaf first supported Charles Taylor's rebellion against Samuel Doe, helping to raise funds for his cause. However, she later went on to oppose him.

By 1996, the presence of ECOWAS peace keepers led to the cessation of hostilities, resulting in the 1997 general election. Sirleaf returned to Liberia to run for president. She ran on the Unity Party ticket and won 10% of the vote; Charles Taylor won 75% in the highly controversial election. Sirleaf left the country soon after and again went into exile in Abidjan, Ivory Coast.

2005 presidential campaign

After the end of the second Liberian civil war and the establishment of a transitional government, Sirleaf was proposed as a possible candidate for leadership of the government. Ultimately, Gyude Bryant, a political neutral, was chosen to leade the transitional government. Sirleaf became head of the Governance Reform Commission.

Sirleaf once again stood for president as the candidate of the Unity Party in the 2005 general election. She placed second in the first round of voting behind footballer George Weah.

In the subsequent run-off election, Sirleaf earned 59% of the vote to 40% for Weah, though Weah disputed the results.

The announcement of the new leader was postponed until further investigations were carried out.

On 23 November 2005, Sirleaf was declared the winner and confirmed as the country's next president.

Her inauguration, attended by many foreign dignitaries including United States Secretary of State Condoleeza Rice and First Lady Laura Bush, took place on 16 January 2006.

2011 presidential campaign

In January 2010, Sirleaf announced that she would run for a second term in the 2011 presidential election when she spoke to a joint session of the Liberian legislature. She was renominated as the Unity Party's presidential candidate at the party's national convention on 31 October 2010. That same day, Vice President Joseph Boakai was nominated by Sirleaf and confirmed by the delegates as

Sirleaf's running mate.

The awarding of the Nobel Peace Prize to Sirleaf four days before the election sparked criticism from opposition parties, with Congress for Democratic Change candidate Winston Tubman calling the award "undeserved" and "a political interference in our country's politics."

Sirleaf called the timing of the award a coincidence and avoided mentioning the award during the final days of campaigning.

Sirleaf garnered 43.9% of the vote in the first round, more than any other candidate but short of the 50% needed to avoid a run-off. Tubman came in second with 32.7%, pitting him against Sirleaf in the second round.

Tubman called for a boycott of the run-off, claiming that the results of the first round had been fraudulent. Sirleaf denied the allegations, and international observers reported that the first round election had been free, fair and transparent.

As a result of the boycott, Sirleaf won the second round with 90.7% of the vote, though voter turnout significantly declined from the first round.

Following the election, Sirleaf announced the creation of a "national peace and reconciliation initiative" led by Nobel Peace Prize laureate Leymah Gbowee to address the country's divisions and begin "a national dialogue that would bring us together."

Presidency

Domestic policy

A fire broke out at the Executive Mansion on 26 July 2006, seriously damaging the structure. An independent panel formed to investigate the incident ruled out arson and attributed the fire to an electrical malfunction.

Sirleaf's government called funding for the repair of

the mansion a low priority in the face of more pressing needs. Sirleaf transferred her office to the nearby Foreign Ministry building and chose to live at her personal home in Monrovia.

On 26 July 2007, Sirleaf celebrated Liberia's 160th Independence Day under the theme "Liberia at 160: Reclaiming the future."

She took an unprecedented and symbolic move by asking 25-year old Liberian activist Kimmie Weeks to serve as National Orator for the celebrations when Weeks called for the government to put priority on education and health care. A few days later, President Sirleaf issued an Executive Order making education free and compulsory for all elementary school aged children.

In October 2010, Sirleaf signed into law a Freedom of Information bill, the first legislation of its kind in West Africa. In recognition of this, she became the first sitting head of state to receive the Friend of the Media in Africa Award from The African Editor's Union.

On 1 April 2011, Sirleaf told reporters that she planned to charge an opposition candidate with sedition for organising a rally protesting corruption in the government. Her press secretary later clarified that the remark had been an April Fool's prank.

Debt relief

From the beginning of her presidency, Sirleaf vowed to make reduction of the national debt, which stood at approximately $4.9 billion in 2006, a top priority for her administration.

The United States became the first country to grant debt relief to Liberia, waiving the full $391 million owed to it by Liberia in early 2007.

In September of that year, the G-8 headed by German Chancellor Angela Merkel provided $324.5 million to paying off 60% of Liberia's debt to the International

Monetary Fund (IMF), crediting their decision with the macroeconomic policies pursued by the Sirleaf administration.

In April 2009, the government successfully wrote off an additional $1.2 billion in foreign commercial debt in a deal that saw the government buy back the debt at a 97% discounted rate through financing provided by the International Development Association (IDA), Germany, Norway, the United States and the United Kingdom. The discounted rate was the largest ever for a developing country.

The country was deemed eligible to participate in the Heavily Indebted Poor countries (HIPC) initiative in 2008. In June 2010, the country reached the completion point of the HIPC initiative, qualifying it for relief from its entire external debt. That same month, the World Bank and IMF agreed to fund $1.5 billion in writing off Liberia's multilateral debt.

On 16 September, the Paris Club agreed to cancel $1.26 billion, with independent bilateral creditors canceling an additional $107 million, essentially writing off Liberia's remaining external debt.

Sirleaf vowed to prevent unsustainable borrowing in the future by restricting annual borrowing to 3% of GDP and limiting expenditure of all borrowed funds to one-off infrastructure projects.

Truth and Reconciliation Commission

In 2006, Sirleaf established a Truth and Reconciliation (TRC) with a mandate to "promote national peace, security, unity and reconciliation" by investigating more than 20 years of civil conflict in the country.

In their final report issued in June 2009, the TRC included Sirleaf on a list of 50 names of people that should be "specifically barred from holding public offices; elected or appointed for a period of thirty (30) years" for "being associated with former warring factions." The proposed ban stemmed from her financial support of former President Taylor in the first months of the first Liberian civil car.

On 26 July 2009, Sirleaf apologised to Liberia for supporting Charles Taylor, adding that "when the true nature of Mr. Taylor's intentions became known, there was no more impassioned critic or strong opponent to him in a democratic process" than she.

On 28 August, the Legislature announced they must "consult our constituents for about a year" before deciding whether or not to implement the commission's recommendations.

During an appearance at the council on Foreign Relations in 2010, Sirleaf argued that the implementation of the TRC's recommended ban would unconstitutionally violate her right to due process.

In October 2010, the chairman of Sirleaf's Unity Party, Varney Sherman, argued that implementation of the recommendation would be unconstitutional, as Article 21(a) of the Constitution prohibits *ex post facto* laws, and Sirleaf had broken no law by financially supporting Taylor that imposed a ban from public office as a penalty.

In January 2011, the Supreme Court ruled in *Williams v. Tah*, a case brought by another person recommended for being banned from public office in the TRC report, that the TRC's recommendation was an unconstitutional violation of the listed individuals' right to procedural due process, and that it would be unconstitutional for the government to implement the proposed bans.

Foreign policy

Upon her election to office, Sirleaf made her first foreign trip as president to neighbouring Ivory Coast (Cote d'Ivoire) and met with Ivorian President Laurent Gbagbo in an attempt to repair relations between the two countries following Ivory Coast's support of the Movement for Democracy in Liberia during the second Liberian civil war.

And during the 20110 – 2011 Ivorian crisis, Sirleaf, as chairperson of the Mano River Union, supported ECOWAS's recognition of Gbago's opponent, Alassane Ouattara, as the winner of the disputed presidential election but rejected calls for a military solution to the crisis.

Sirleaf has forged close relations with the United States, Liberia's traditional ally and mother country; it was the United States which founded Liberia as a nation.

Following the establishment of the United States Africa Command (USAFRICOM or AFRICOM) – one of nine Unified Combatant Commands of the United States Armed Forces – by the United States military, Sirleaf offered to allow the US to have AFRICOM headquarters in Liberia, the only African leader to do so. The command was eventually headquarted in Stuttgart, Germany.

On 15 March 2006, President Sirleaf addressed a joint session of the United States Congress, asking for American support to help her country "become a brilliant beacon, an example to Africa and the world of what love of liberty can achieve."

Sirleaf has also strengthened relations with the People's Republic of China, reaffirming Liberia's commitment to the One-China policy. In return, China has contributed to Liberia's reconstruction, building several transmitters to extend the Liberia Broadcasting System (LBS) nationwide and constructing a new campus for the University of Liberia.

Sirleaf is a member of the Council of Women World Leaders, an international network of current and former female presidents and prime ministers whose mission is to mobilise the highest-level female leaders globally for collective action on issues of critical importance to women and equitable development.

During the 2011 Libyan civil war, Sirleaf added her voice to a chorus of calls from the international community for Libyan leader Muammar al-Gaddafi to stop using violence and political repression. However, she criticized the international military intervention in Libya, declaring that "violence does not help the process whichever way it comes."

Her government later severed diplomatic ties with Libya, stating that "The Government took the decision after a careful review of the situation in Libya and determined that the Government of Colonel Gaddafi has lost the legitimacy to govern Libya."

Administration and Cabinet

Following her election in 2005, Sirleaf pledged to promote national reconciliation by bringing in opposition leaders into her administration.

Opposition politicians who joined her initial administration included Minister of Transport Jeremiah Sulunteh, Minister of Education Joseph Korto, and Ambassador to the United Nations Nathaniel Barnes.

Sirleaf also appointed several women to high-level posts in her administration, with female ministers initially leading the ministries of finance, law, commerce and industry, gender and development, and youth and sports. Sirleaf said that while she had planned on appointing an all-female cabinet, she had been unable to find qualified female candidates for every position.

Upon her inauguration, Sirleaf promised that she would impose a "zero tolerance" policy on corruption within the government. In spite of that pledge, critics have argued that corruption remains rampant within Sirleaf's administration.

Information Minister Lawrence Bropleh was sacked in

2008 over allegations that he had stolen more than $200,000 in state funds, while Internal Affairs Minister Ambullai Johnson, Sirleaf's brother, was dismissed in 2010 after the disappearance of funds for county development.

Sirleaf herself has acknowledged that corruption in her government remains a serious problem, noting that her zero tolerance policy was hampered by the need to pass major economic reforms through the legislature, a goal that would have been impeded by significant anti-corruption legislation and prosecutions.

However, Sirleaf has rejected claims that she has failed to fight corruption, pointing to the establishment of the Liberian Anti-Corruption Commission and the restructuring of the General Auditing Commission.

Sirleaf dismissed her entire cabinet from office on 3 November 2010, promising to reassemble the cabinet in a short of time. She argued that the move was taken to give her administration a "clean slate" in preparation for the final year of her term, though critics argued that the move was aimed to bolster her chances at re-election by confronting corruption in her administration. By early December 2010, Sirleaf had reconstituted her entire cabinet, replacing seven of her nineteen ministers.

Judicial appointments

Upon the inauguration of Sirleaf, the entire Supreme Court bench, which had been selected as part of the transitional government in 2003, stepped down, leaving Sirleaf to fill all five seats on the Court.

Sirleaf nominated Johnnie Lewis, a Yale Law School graduate and former circuit court judge, to be the chief justice. Lewis and three of Sirleaf's associate justice nominees, J. Emmanuel Wureh, Francis Korkpor and Gladys Johnson, were confirmed by the senate on 2 March

2006.

Sirleaf's nomination of Kabineh Ja'neh, a former leader in the rebel LURD movement, as associate justice drew criticism from the opposition Congress for Democratic change due to concerns over Ja'neh's human rights record during the civil war, and Ja'neh was not confirmed until 9 May.

Following the death of Justice Wureh in July 2006, Sirleaf nominated Christiana Tah, a deputy minister at the justice ministry, to fill his seat. However, the senate later rejected Tah's nomination, leading Sirleaf to nominate her minister of youth and sports, Jamesetta Howard Wolokollie, who was confirmed.

Justice Johnson retired from the Court on 26 March 2011 after reaching the constitutionally mandated retirement age of seventy.

International image

Forbes magazine named Sirleaf as the 51st most powerful woman in the world in 2006.

In 2010, *Newsweek* listed her as one of the ten best leaders in the world, while *Time* counted her among the top ten female leaders. That same year, *The Economist* called her "arguably the best president the country has ever had."

Personal life

In 1956, Sirleaf married James Sirleaf, whom she later divorced. Sirleaf is the mother of four sons and has eight grandchildren. Her great nephew, Emmanuel Sumana Elsar Sr., was her political advisor during the 2005 presidential elections against George Weah.

Felix Houphouet-Boigny

Félix Houphouët-Boigny was the first of the Ivory Coast. Originally a village chief, he worked as a doctor, an administrator of a plantation, and a union leader before being elected to the French parliament and serving in a number of ministerial positions in the French government. From the 1940s until his death, he played a leading role in his country's politics.

Under Houphouët-Boigny's politically moderate leadership, the Ivory Coast prospered economically. This success, uncommon in poverty-ridden West Africa, came to be known as the "Ivorian miracle" and was attributed to a combination of sound planning, the maintenance of strong ties with the West (particularly France), and development of the country's significant coffee and cocoa industries. However, the agricultural sector suffered in 1980 after a sharp drop in the prices of coffee and cocoa.

Throughout his presidency, Houphouët-Boigny had close ties with France – a relationship known as Francafrique – and built a close friendship with Jacques Foccart, the chief adviser on African policy in the de Gaulle and Pompidou governments.

He also helped the conspirators who overthrew Ghana's first president, Dr. Kwame Nkrumah in 1966. He also helped facilitate a military coup against Benin's military head of state, Mathieu Kérékou, in 1977, and was suspected of involvement in the 1987 coup that removed Thomas Sankara from power in Burkina Faso. Sankara was killed in the coup. A former Liberian warlord, Prince Yormie Johnson, told Liberia's Truth and Reconciliation Commission (TRC) that Sankara's ouster and assassination was engineered by Charles Taylor who led the biggest and most powerful rebel force in Liberia.

President Felix Houphouët-Boigny maintained an

ardently anticommunist foreign policy which resulted in, among other things, severing diplomatic relations with the Soviet Union in 1969 (after first establishing ties in 1967). Relations between the two countries were re-established in February 1986. He also refused to recognise the People's Republic of China (PRC) until 1983 and provided assistance to UNITA, an American-backed rebel movement in Angola that was also anti-communist.

Houphouët-Boigny moved the country's capital from Abidjan to his birthplace and hometown of Yamoussoukro and built the world's largest church there, the Basilica of Our Lady of Peace of Yamoussoukro, at a cost of US$300 million.

At the time of his death on 7 December 1993 at the age of 88, he was the longest-serving leader in Africa's history and the third longest-serving leader in the world after Fidel Castro of Cuba and Kim Il-sung of North Korea.

After his death, conditions in the Ivory Coast quickly deteriorated. From 1994 until 2002, there was political and civil unrest including a military coup in 1999 and other military interventions, a currency devaluation, an economic recession and, beginning in 2002, a civil war.

Early life

Birth, childhood and education

According to his official biography, Houphouët-Boigny was probably born on 18 October 1905, in Yamoussoukro, Ivory Coast (Côte d'Ivoire), to a family of chiefs of the Baoule ethnic group. Unofficial accounts, however, place his birth date up to seven years earlier.

Born into the animist Akouès tribe, he was given the name Dia Houphouët: his first name *Dia* means "prophet" or "magician" and his surname came from his father, N'Doli Houphouët.

Dia Houphouët was the great-nephew of Queen Yamousso and the village chief, Kouassi N'Go. When N'Go was murdered in 1910, Dia was called on to succeed him as chief. Due to his young age, his stepfather Gbro Diby ruled as regent, Dia's father having already died.

Houphouët-Boigny was descended from tribal chiefs through his mother, Kimou N'Drive (also known as N'Dri Kan), who died in 1936.

Doubts remain as to the identity of his father, N'Doli. Officially a native of the N'Zipri of Didiévi tribe, N'Doli Houphouët died shortly after the birth of his son Augustin, although no reliable information regarding his death exists. This uncertainty has given rise to rumours, including a widespread one, that his father was a Sudaense-born Muslim named Cissé.

Houphouët-Boigny had two elder sisters, Faitai (1898?-1998) and Adjoua (d. 1987), as well as younger brother Augustin (d. 1939).

Recognising his place in the hierarchy, the colonial administration sent Houphouët to school at the military post in Bonzi, not far from his village, despite strenuous objections from relatives, especially his grandaunt Yamousso. In 1915, he was transferred to the *école primaire supérieure* (secondary) at Bingerville in spite of his family's reluctance. The same year, at Bingerville, he converted to Christianity; he considered it a modern religion and an obstacle to the spread of Islam. He chose to be christened Félix.

First in his class, he was accepted into the *École William Ponty* (a government teachers' college in what is now Senegal) in 1919 and earned a teaching degree.

In 1921, he attended the *École de médecine de l'AOF* (French West Africa School of Medicine) in Senegal where he came first in his class in 1925 and qualified as a medical assistant. However, he never completed his studies in medicine and could only aspire to a career as a *médecin africain*, a poorly paid doctor.

Medical career

On 26 October 1925, Houphouët began his career as a doctor's aide at a hospital in Abidjan where he founded an association of indigenous medical personnel. This undertaking proved short-lived as the colonial administration viewed it unsympathetically, considering it a trade union. As a consequence, they decided to move Houphouët to a particularly insanitary hospital in Guiglo on 27 April 1927._ After he proved his considerable talents, however, he was promoted on 17 September 1929 to a post in Abengourou which until then had been reserved for Europeans.

At Abengourou, Houphouët witnessed the mistreatment of indigenous cocoa farmers by the colonists. In 1932, he decided to act, leading a movement of farmers against the influential white landowners and for the economic policies of the colonial government who favoured the farmers.

On 22 December 1932, he published an article under a pseudonym titled *On nous a trop volés* (*They have stolen too much from us*), which appeared in the *Trait d'union*, an Ivorian socialist newspaper.

The following year, Houphouët was summoned by his tribe to assume the responsibilities of village chief, but preferring to pursue his medical career, he deferred in favour of his younger brother Augustin. However, wishing to live closer to his village, he obtained a transfer to Dimbokro on 3 February 1934 and then to Toumodi on 28 June 1936.

While Houphouët had displayed professional qualities, his attitude had chafed those around him. As a result, in September 1938, his clinical director demanded that he choose between his job as a doctor and his involvement in local politics. The choice was quickly made for him: his brother died in 1939 and Houphouët became *chef de*

233

canton, an office created by the colonial administration to collect the tax-quota. *Chef de canton* was the highest position attainable by Africans in the French system of colonial administration before World War I. Because of that, he ended his medical career the following year.

First marriage

In 1930, Houphouët married Kady Racine Sow (1913–2006) in Abengourou despite the fact that he was a practising Catholic and she was the daughter of a wealthy Muslim from Senegal. The families of the two eventually overcame their opposition and accepted the interfaith union, the first ever celebrated in the Ivory Coast. The couple had five children: Felix (who died in infancy), Augustine, Francis, Guillaume and Marie, all raised as Catholics.

Chef de canton and union leader

By becoming *chef de canton*, Houphouët assumed responsibility for the administration of Akouè, a canton which comprised 36 villages. He also took charge of the family plantation – at the time one of the most important in the country – and worked to diversify its rubber, cocoa and coffee crops. He soon became one of Africa's richest farmers.

On 3 September 1944, he established, in cooperation with the colonial administration, the African Agricultural Union (*Syndicat agricole africain*, SAA). Under his presidency, the SAA brought together African farmers who were dissatisfied with their working conditions and worked to protect their interests against those of European planters.

Anti-colonialist and anti-racist, the organisation demanded better working conditions, higher wages, and the abolition of unfree labour, a form of slavery. The union quickly received the support of nearly 20,000 plantation workers, together with that of the left-wing French administrators placed in office by the Provisional Government. The Provisional Government of the French Republic (*gouvernement provisoire de la République française* or GPRF) was an interim government which governed France from 1944 to 1946, following the fall of Vichy France and before the Fourth French Republic.

The success of the African Agricultural Union (*Syndicat agricole africain*, SAA) irritated the French colonialists so much that they took legal action against Houphouët, accusing him of being anti-French for never seeking French citizenship. However, Houphouët befriended the Inspector Minister of the Colonies who ordered the charges dropped. The colonial settlers were more successful in obtaining the replacement of the sympathetic Governor André Latrille with the hostile Governor Henri de Maudui.

Houphouët entered electoral politics in August 1945 when elections for the Abidjan city council were held for the first time. The French electoral rules established a common roll: half of the elected would have to be French citizens (who were mostly Europeans) and the other half non-citizens. Houphouët reacted by creating a multi-ethnic all-African roll with both non-citizens and citizens (mostly Senegalese with French citizenship). As a result, most of the African contenders withdrew and a large number of the French protested by abstaining, thus assuring a decisive victory for his African Bloc.

In October 1945, Houphouët moved onto the national political scene; the French government decided to represent its colonies in the *assemblée constituante* (*Constituent Assembly*) and gave the Ivory Coast and Upper Volta two representatives in parliament combined. One of these would represent the French citizens and the other would represent the indigenous population. But the suffrage was limited to less than 1% of the population.

In an attempt to block Houphouët, the governor, de Mauduit, supported a rival candidature and provided him the full backing of the administration. But in spite of that, and thanks to the SAA's strong organisation, Houphouët, running for the indigenous seat, easily came first with a 1,000-vote majority. He failed, however, to obtain an absolute majority due to the large number of candidates running.

Houphouët emerged victorious again in the second round of elections held on 4 November 1945 in which he narrowly defeated an Upper Volta candidate with 12,980 votes out of a total of 31,081. At this point, he decided to add "Boigny" to his surname, meaning "irresistible force" in the Baoulé language and symbolising his role as a leader.

French political career

Member of Parliament

In taking his seat in the National Assembly in the *Palais Bourbon* (a palace located on the left bank of the Seine. Paris, and the seat of the French National Assembly) alongside compatriots Daniel Ouezzin Coulibaly and Philippe Zinda Kaboré, Houphouët-Boigny had to first decide with which group to side. He chose the Mouvements Unis de la Résistance (MUR – Unified Movements of the Resistance), a small party composed of Communist sympathizers but not formal members of the Communist party.

He was appointed a member of the *Commission des territoires d'outre-mer* (Commission of Overseas Territories). During this time, he worked to implement the wishes of the SAA, in particular proposing a bill to abolish forced labour – the single most unpopular feature of French rule. The Assembly adopted this bill, known as *Loi*

Houphouët-Boigny, on 11 April 1946, greatly enhancing the author's prestige not only in his country but in other French African colonies as well as in France.

On 3 April 1946, Houphouët-Boigny proposed to unify labour regulations in the territories of Africa; this would eventually be completed in 1952. Finally, on 27 September 1946, he filed a report on the public health system of overseas territories, calling for its reformation. Durirng his parliamentary tenure, he also supported the idea of a union of French territories. Such a union would, in his view, create a policy that was *"métropolitaine et démocratique"* (metropolitan and democratic), unlike the other: *"coloniale et réactionnaire"* (colonial and reactionary).

The first constitution proposed by the Constituent Assembly was rejected by the voters and new elections were held in 1946 for a second constituent assembly. For these elections Houphouët-Boigny organised the *Democratic Party of Côte d'Ivoire* (PDCI) on 9 April 1946 with the help of the *Groupes d'Etudes Communistes* (*Communist Study Groups*) which was a communist group in colonial French West Africa and French Equatorial Africa founded in 1943 under the influence of the French Communist Party.

The structure of the *Democratic Party of Côte d'Ivoire* (PDCI) closely followed that of the SAA. And it immediately became the first successful independent African party. Houphouët-Boigny easily swept the elections with 21,099 out of 37,888 votes, his opponents obtaining only a few hundred votes each. In this he was helped by the recall of Governor Latrille whose predecessor had been fired by the Overseas Minister Marius Moutet for his opposition to the abolition of the *Indigénat* – or the Code de l'indigenat – which was a set of laws creating an inferior legal status for the natives of the French colonies from 1887 until 1944–1947. A similar strategy was employed by other European colonial

237

powers, especially the British, under the concept of indirect rule which was first introduced in Northern Nigeria by Frederick Lugard, later known as Lord Lugard; a policy he enunciated in his work, *The Dual Mandate in British Tropical Africa* which discusses indirect rule, first published in 1922.

With his return to the assembly, Houphouët-Boigny was appointed to the *Commission du règlement et du suffrage universel* (Commission for Regulation of Universal Suffrage). As secretary of the commission from 1947 to 1948, he proposed on 18 February 1947 to reform French West Africa (AOF), French Equatorial Africa (AEF) and the French territories' federal council to better represent the African peoples. He also called for the creation of local assemblies in Africa so that Africans could learn how to be autonomous.

Foundation of the RDA and Communist alliance

During the second Constituent Assembly, African representatives witnessed a strong reaction against the colonial liberalism that had been embedded in the rejected constitution drafted by the previous assembly. The new text, approved by the voters on 13 October 1946, reduced the African representatives from 30 to 24. It also reduced the number of those entitled to vote. And a large number of colonial topics – or areas of policy – were left in which the executive could govern by decree. Also, supervision over the colonial administration remained weak.

Reacting to what they felt was a betrayal of the MRP's and the Socialists' promises, the African deputies concluded they needed to build a permanent coalition independent from the French parties. Houphouët-Boigny was the first to propose this to his African colleagues and obtained their full support for a founding congress to be held in October in Bamako, French Soudan later renamed Mali.

The French government did all it could to sabotage the congress, and in particular the Socialist Overseas Minister was successful in persuading the African Socialists, who were originally among the promoters, from attending. This ultimately backfired, radicalising those who convened when they founded the African Democratic Rally (RDA) as an inter-territorial political movement. The pro-Communist Gabriel d'Arboussier, a Senegalese, dominated the congress.

The new movement's goal was to free "Africa from the colonial yoke by the affirmation of her personality and by the association, freely agreed to, of a union of nations". Its first president was Houphouët-Boigny. Gabriel d'Arboussier became its secretary-general. The PDCI became the Ivoirian branch of the RDA.

Too small to form their own parliamentary group, the African deputies were compelled to join one of the larger parties in order to sit together in the Palais Bourbon. [Thus, the RDA soon joined the French Communist Party (PCF) as the only openly anti-colonialist political faction and soon organised strikes and boycotts of European imports.

Houphouët-Boigny justified the alliance with the communists because it seemed, at the time, to be the only way for his voice to be heard: "Even before the creation of RDA, the alliance had served our cause: in March 1946. The abolition of compulsory labour was adopted unanimously, without a vote, thanks to our tactical alliance."

As the Cold War set in, the alliance with the Communists became increasingly damaging for the RDA. The French colonial administration showed itself increasingly hostile toward the RDA and its president, whom the administration called a "Stalinist". Tensions reached their height at the beginning of 1950 when, following an outbreak of anti-colonial violence, almost the entire PDCI leadership was arrested.

239

Houphouët-Boigny managed to slip away shortly before police arrived at his house. Although he would have been saved by his parliamentary immunity, his missed arrest was popularly attributed to his influence and his prestige.

In the ensuing chaos, riots broke out in the Ivory Coast, the most significant of which was a clash with the police at Dimbokro in which 13 Africans were killed and 50 wounded. According to official figures, by 1951 a total of 52 Africans had been killed, several hundred wounded and around 3,000 arrested (numbers which, according to journalist Ronald Segal in *African Profiles*, are certainly underestimated).

In order to defuse the crisis, Prime Minister René Pléven entrusted the France's Minister for Overseas Territories, Francois Mitterrand, with the task of detaching the RDA from the PCF, and in fact an official alliance between the RDA and Mitterrand's party, the UDSR, was established in 1952.

Knowing he was at an impasse, Houphouët-Boigny agreed in October 1950 to break the Communist alliance. Asked in an undated interview why he worked with the communists, Houphouët-Boigny replied: "I, a bourgeois landowner, I would preach the class struggle? That is why we aligned ourselves with the Communist Party, without joining it."

Rehabilitation and entry into government

In the 1951 elections, the number of seats was reduced from three to two; while Houphouët-Boigny still won a seat, the other RDA candidate, Ouezzin Coulibaly, did not. All in all, the RDA only garnered 67,200 of 109,759 votes in that election, and the party opposing won one seat.

On 8 August 1951, Boigny, speaking at René Pleven's inauguration as president of the board, denied being the leader of a communist group; he was not believed until the

RDA's 1952 affiliation with UDSR. On the 24th of that same month, Boigny delivered a statement in the Assembly contesting the result of the elections which he said were tainted by fraud. He also denounced what he saw as the exploitation of overseas deputies as "voting machines" who, as political pawns, supported the colonial government's every action.

Thereafter, Houphouët-Boigny and the RDA were briefly unsuccessful before their success was renewed in 1956. During that year's elections, the party won 502,711 of 579,550 votes cast.

From then on, Houphouët-Boigny's relationship with the communists was forgotten. He was embraced as a moderate and became a member of the Committees on Universal Suffrage (distinct from the aforementioned committee *regulating* said suffrage), Constitutional Laws, Rules and Petitions.

On 1 February 1956, he was appointed Minister Discharging the Duties of the Presidency of the Council in the government of Guy Mollet, a post he held until 13 June 1957. This marked the first time an African was given a leading position in the French colonies' government. His main achievement in this role was the creation of an organisation of Saharan regions that would help ensure sustainability for the French Union and counter Morrocan territorial claims in the Sahara.

On 6 November 1957, Houphouët-Boigny became Minister of Public Health and Population in the Gaillard administration and attempted to reform the public health code. He had previously served as Minister of State under Maurice Jean Marie Bourgès-Maunoury (13 June – 6 November 1957).

Following his ministerial service under Gaillard, he was again appointed Minister of State and served from 14 May 1958 to 20 May 1959. In this capacity, he participated in the development of France's African policy, notably in the cultural domain. At his behest, the Bureau of French Overseas Students and the University of Dakar were created.

On 4 October 1958, Houphouët-Boigny was one of the signatories, along with de Gaulle, of the Constitution of the Fifth Republic. The last post he held in France was Minister-Counsellor in the Michel Debré government from 23 July 1959 to 19 May 1961.

Leading up to independence

Until the mid-1950s, French colonies in west and central Africa belonged two federations: French Equatorial Africa (AEF) and French West Africa (AOF).

The Ivory Coast was part of the French West Africa federation, financing roughly two thirds of its budget. Wishing to liberate the country from the guardianship of the AOF, Houphouët-Boigny championed the cause of an Africa made up of nations which would generate wealth rather than share poverty and misery.

He participated actively in the drafting and adoption of the framework of the *Loi-cadre Defferre*, a French legal reform which, in addition to granting autonomy to African colonies, would break the ties that bound the different territories together, giving them more autonomy through local legislatures or assemblies.

But the *Loi-cadre Defferre* was not unanimously accepted by Houphouët-Boigny's compatriots in Africa. Léopold Sédar Senghor, the leader of Senegal, was the first to speak out against this attempted "Balkanisation" of Africa, arguing that the colonial territories "do not correspond to any reality: be it geographical, economic, ethnic, or linguistic".

Senghor argued that maintaining the AOF would give the territories stronger political credibility and would allow them to develop harmoniously as well as emerge as a genuine people. This view was shared by most members of the African Democratic Rally who backed Ahmed

242

Sékou Touré and Modibo Keita, placing Houphouët-Boigny in the minority at the 1957 congress in Bamako.

Following the adoption of the *Loi Cadre* reform on 23 June 1956, a territorial election was held in the Ivory Coast on 3 March 1957 in which the PDCI – transformed under Houphouët-Boigny's firm control into a political machine – won many seats. Houphouët-Boigny, who was already serving as a minister in France, as president of the Territorial Assembly and as mayor of Abidjan, chose Auguste Denise to serve as vice president of the Government Council of the Ivory Coast, even though Houphouët-Boigny remained, the only interlocutor in the colony for France.

Houphouët-Boigny's popularity and influence in France's African colonies had become so pervasive that one French magazine claimed that by 1956, the politician's photograph "was in all the huts, on the lapels of coats, on the corsages of African women and even on the handlebars of bicycles."

On 7 April 1957, the prime minister of Ghana, Kwame Nkrumah, on a visit to the Ivory Coast, called on all colonies in Africa to declare their independence. Houphouët-Boigny, in response to Nkrumah, said:

"Your experience is rather impressive ... But due to the human relationships between the French and the Africans, and because in the 20th century people have become interdependent, we considered that it would perhaps be more interesting to try a new and different experience than yours and unique in itself, one of a Franco-African community based on equality and fraternity."

Unlike many African leaders who immediately demanded independence, Houphouët-Boigny wished for a careful transition within the "*ensemble français*" because, according to him, political independence without economic independence was worthless. He also invited

Nkrumah to meet with him again in 10 years to see which one of the two had chosen the best approach toward independence.

On 28 September 1958, Charles de Gaulle proposed a constitutional referendum on the Franco-African community: the territories were given the choice of either supporting the constitution or proclaiming their independence and being cut off from France. For Houphouët-Boigny, the choice was simple: "Whatever happens, Côte d'Ivoire will enter directly into the Franco-African community. The other territories are free to group between themselves before joining."

Only Guinea chose independence; its leader, Ahmed Sékou Touré, opposed Houphouët-Boigny, stating that his preference was "freedom in poverty over wealth in slavery".

The referendum produced the French Community, an institution meant to be an association of free republics which had jurisdiction over foreign policy, defence, currency, common ethnic and financial policy, and strategic raw materials.

Houphouët-Boigny was determined to stop the hegemony of Senegal in West Africa and a political confrontation ensued between Ivorian and Senegalese leaders. Houphouët-Boigny refused to participate in the Inter-African conference in Dakar on 31 December 1958 which was intended to lay the foundation for the Federation of Francophone African States.

Although the federation was never realised, Senegal and Mali (known at the time as French Sudan) formed their own political union, the Mali Federation.

After de Gaulle allowed the Mali Federation to gain independence in 1959, Houphouët-Boigny tried to sabotage the federation's efforts to wield political control. In cooperation with France, he managed to convince Upper Volta, Dahomey, and Niger to withdraw from the Mali Federation before it collapsed in August 1960.

Two months after the 1958 referendum, seven member states of French West Africa, including the Ivory Coast, became autonomous republics within the French Community. Houphouët-Boigny had won his first victory against those supporting federalism. This victory established the conditions that made the future "Ivorian miracle" possible. Between 1957 and 1959, revenues grew by 158%, reaching 21,723,000,000 CFA francs and the Ivory Coast became the most prosperous country in West Africa, drawing workers from as far as Nigeria.

President of the Ivory Coast (Côte d'Ivoire)

Early years and second marriage

Houphouët-Boigny officially became the head of the government of the Ivory Coast on 1 May 1959.

Although he faced no opposition from rival parties and the PDCI became the *de facto* party of the state in 1957, he was confronted by opposition from his own government. Radical nationalists led by Jjean-Baptiste Mockey openly opposed the government's Francophile policies. In an attempt to solve this problem, Houphouët-Boigny decided to exile Mockey in September 1959, claiming that Mockey had attempted to assassinate him using voodoo in what Houphouët-Boigny called the *"complot du chat noir"* (black cat conspiracy).

Houphouët-Boigny began drafting a new constitution for the Ivory Coast after the country's independence from France on 7 August 1960. It drew heavily from the United States constitution in establishing a powerful executive branch, and from the French constitution which limited the power of the legislature. He transformed the National Assembly into a mere recording house for bills and budget proposals.

On 27 November 1960, Houphouët-Boigny was

elected unopposed as president of the Ivory Coast, while a single list of PDCI candidates was elected to the National Assembly.

1963 was marked by a series of alleged plots that played a decisive role in ultimately consolidating power in the hands of Houphouët-Boigny. There is no clear consensus on the unfolding of the 1963 events; in fact, there may have been no plot at all and the entire series of events may have been part of a plan by Houphouët-Boigny to consolidate his hold on power.

Between 120 and 200 secret trials were held in Yamoussoukro in which key political figures – including Mockey and the president of the Supreme Court Ernest Boka – were implicated. There was discontent in the army, as the generals grew restive following the arrest of Defense Minister Jjjean Konan Banny, and the president had to intervene personally to pacify them.

For the next 27 years, almost all power in the Ivory Coast was centered in Houphouët-Boigny. From 1965 to 1985, he was reelected unopposed to five successive five-year terms as president. Also every five years, a single list of PDCI candidates was returned to the National Assembly. For all intents and purposes, all of them were appointed by the president since, in his capacity as leader of the PDCI, he approved all candidates.

The media were tightly controlled and served mainly as outlets for government propaganda.

Nevertheless, Houphouët-Boigny's regime was somewhat less harsh than those of other authoritarian African leaders. Once he had consolidated his power, he freed political prisoners in 1967. Under his "unique brand of paternalistic authoritarianism", Houphouët-Boigny subdued dissent by offering government positions instead of detaining or imprisoning his critics. As a result, according to Robert Mundt, author of *Côte d'Ivoire: Continuity and Change in a Semi-Democracy*, he was never seriously challenged after 1963.

In order to foil any plans for a *coup d'etat*, the president took control of the military and the police, reducing their numbers from 5,300 to 3,500. Defence was entrusted to the French armed forces which, in accordance with the treaty on defence cooperation of 24 April 1961, were stationed at Port-Bouët – a commune in the nation's capital Abidjan – and could intervene at Houphouët-Boigny's request or when they considered French interests to be threatened. They subsequently intervened during attempts by the Sanwi monarchists to secede in 1959 and 1969, and again in 1970 when an unauthorised political group, the Eburnian Movement, was formed and Houphouët-Boigny accused its leader Kragbé Gnagbé of wishing to secede.

Houphouët-Boigny married the much younger Marie-Thérèse Houphouët-Boigny in 1962, having divorced his first wife in 1952. The couple had no children of their own but adopted two: five-year-old Hélène in 1960, the granddaughter of King Baoulé Anoungbré, and Olivier Antoine in 1981.

The marriage was not without scandal: in 1958, Marie-Thérèse went on a romantic escapade in Italy, while in 1961, Houphouët-Boigny fathered a child (Florence, d. 2007) out of wedlock with his mistress Henriette Duvignac.

Leadership in Africa

Following the example of de Gaulle who refused proposals for an integrated Europe, Houphouët-Boigny opposed Nkrumah's proposed United States of Africa which called into question Ivory Coast's recently acquired national sovereignty. However, Houphouët-Boigny was not against African unity which developed on a case by case basis.

On 29 May 1959, in cooperation with Hamani Diori of Niger, Maurice Yaméogo of Upper Volta, and Hubert

Maga of Dahomey, Houphouët-Boigny created the *Conseil de l'Entente* (Council of Accord or Council of Understanding), a regional organisation founded in order to counter the Mali Federation. The council was designed with three major functions: to allow shared management of certain public services, such as the port of Abidjan or the Abidjan–Niger railway line; to provide a solidarity fund accessible to member countries, 90% of which was provided by the Ivory Coast; and to provide funding for various development projects through low-interest loans to member states (70% of the loans were supplied by the Ivory Coast).

In 1966, Houphouët-Boigny even offered to grant dual citizenship to nationals from the member countries of the *Conseil de l'Entente* but the proposition was quickly abandoned following popular protests especially in the Ivory Coast.

The ambitious Ivorian leader had even greater plans for French-speaking Africa: he intended to rally the different nations behind a large organisation whose objective was the mutual assistance of its member states. The project became a reality on 7 September 1961 with the signing of a charter giving birth to the *l'Union africaine et malgache* (UAM – African and Malagasy Union) comprising 12 French-speaking countries including Léopold Sédar Senghor's Senegal.

Agreements were signed in various sectors, such as economic, military and telecommunications, which strengthened solidarity among Francophone states. However, the creation of the Organisation of African Unity (OAU) in May 1963 affected his plans: supporters of Pan-Africanism demanded the dissolution of all regional groupings such as the UAM. Houphouët-Boigny reluctantly ceded, and transformed the UAM into the *Organisation africaine et malgache de coopération économique et culturelle* (African and Malagasy Organization of economic and cultural cooperation).

Considering the OAU a dead-end organisation, especially because Paris was opposed to the group, Houphouët-Boigny decided to create in 1965 *l'Organisation commune africaine et malgache* (OCAM – African and Malagasy Organisation), an organisation of former French African colonies in competition with the OAU.

The organisation had 16 member-countries whose aim was to neutralise revolutionary goals in Africa, such as Nkrumah's quest for immediate continental unification, formation of an African high command to help liberate countries still under white minority rule, and support for African liberation movements whose military campaigns Houphouët-Boigny considered to be counter-productive. He never supported any of the liberation movements even in terms of financial contributions but instead had good relations with apartheid South Africa the same way Malawi's president, Dr. Hastings Kamuzu Banda, did. However, over the years, the organisation became too subservient to France, resulting in the departure of half of its members.

In the mid-1970s, during times of economic prosperity, Houphouët-Boigny and Senghor put aside their differences and joined forces to thwart Nigeria which, in an attempt to establish itself as the dominant power in West Africa, had been the driving force behind the creation of the Economic Community of West African States (ECOWAS). The two leaders countered the ECOWAS by creating the Economic Community of West Africa (ECWA) which superseded the old trade partnerships in the French-speaking regions in the western part of the continent. However, after assurances from Nigeria that ECOWAS would function in the same manner as the earlier Francophone organisations, Houphouët-Boigny and Senghor decided to merge their organisation with ECOWAS in May 1975.

Françafrique

Throughout his presidency, Houphouët-Boigny surrounded himself with French advisers such as Guy Nairay, chief of staff from 1960 to 1993, and Alain Belkiri, secretary-general of the Ivorian government, whose influence extended to all areas. This type of diplomacy, which he called *Françafrique*, allowed him to maintain very close ties with the former colonial power, making the Ivory Coast France's primary African ally.

Whenever one country – Ivory Coast or France – would enter an agreement with an African nation, the other would unconditionally give its support. Through this arrangement, Houphouët-Boigny built a close friendship with Jacques Foccart, the chief adviser on African policy in the de Gaulle and Pompidou governments.

Destabilisation of revolutionary regimes

By claiming independence for Guinea through the 28 September 1958 French constitutional referendum, Ahmed Sékou Touré had not only defied de Gaulle but also his fellow African, Houphouët-Boigny.

Houphouët-Boigny distanced himself from Guinean officials in Conakry and the Guinean Democratic Party was excluded from the RDA. Tensions between Houphouët-Boigny and Touré also began to rise due to the conspiracies of the French intelligence agency SDECE against the Sékou Touré regime.

In January 1960, Houphouët-Boigny delivered small arms to former Guinean rebels in Man, Ivory Coast, and incited his council in 1965 to agree to taking part in an attempt to overthrow Sékou Touré. In 1967, he promoted the creation of the *Front national de libération de la Guinée* (FNLG – *National Front for the Liberation of Guinea*), a reserve of men ready to plot the downfall of

Sékou Touré.

Houphouët-Boigny's relationship with Kkwame Nkrumah, the leader of neighbouring Ghana, deteriorated considerably following Guinea's independence because of Nkrumah's financial and political support for Sékou Touré. After Sékou Touré convinced Nkrumah to support the secessionist Sanwi, a traditional kingdom in the southeastern part of the Ivory Coast, Houphouët-Boigny began a campaign to discredit the Ghanaian regime. He accused Nkrumah of trying to destabilise the Ivory Coast in 1963 and called for the Francophone states to boycott the Organisation of African Unity (OAU) conference scheduled to take place in Ghana's capital Accra. The Sanwi kingdom was established in 1740 by Anyi migrants, an Akan people, from what is now Ghana.

Nkrumah was ousted from power on 24 February 1966 in a military coup engineered and masterminded by the CIA. Houphouët-Boigny allowed the conspirators to use the Ivory Coast as a base to coordinate the arrival and departure of their missions.

Also in collaboration with Foccart, Houphouët-Boigny took part in the attempted coup of 16 January 1977 led by famed French mercenary Bob Denard against the revolutionary regime of Mathieu Kérékou in Dahomey, later renamed Benin. Houphouët-Boigny also supported Jonas Savimbi and UNITA against the MPLA during the Angolan civil war.

In spite of his reputation as a destabaliser of regimes, Houphouët-Boigny granted refuge to Jean-Bedel Bokassa after the exiled dictator of the Central African Republic was overthrown by French paratroopers in September 1979. The move was met with international criticism and, having become a political and financial burden on Houphouët-Boigny, Bokassa was expelled from the Ivory Coast in 1983.

Alignment with France

Houphouët-Boigny was a participant in the November 1960 Congo crisis in which the UN and world powers were heavily involved, a crisis that eventually led to the assassination of Prime Minister Patrice Lumumba. The Ivorian leader supported President Joseph Kasavubu, an opponent of Lumumba, and followed France in supporting the controversial leader of Katanga Province, Moise Tshombe who was disliked by much of Africa. Tshombe was passionately defended by Houphouët-Boigny and was even invited into OCAM in May 1965.

After the ouster of Kasavubu by General Joseph Mobutu in November 1965, the Ivorian president supported, in 1967, a plan proposed by the French secret service which aimed at bringing the deposed Congolese leader back into power. But the plan failed. In response, Houphouët-Boigny decided to boycott the fourth annual summit of the OAU held in September 1967 in the Zairean (Congolese) capital Kinshasa.

Houphouët-Boigny was also a major supporter of secessionist Biafra and recognised it as an independent state after the Eastern Region of Nigeria seceded from the federation on 30 May 1967.

Considering Nigeria a potential danger to French-influenced African states, Foccart sent Houphouët-Boigny and Lieutenant-Colonel Raymond Bichelot on a mission back in 1963 to monitor political developments in the country. The opportunity to weaken the former British federation presented itself in May 1967 when Biafra, led by Lieutenant-Colonel Chukwuemeka Odumegwu Ojukwu, seceded from Nigeria.

French-aligned African countries supported the secessionists who were provided with mercenaries and weapons by Jean Mauricheau-Beaupré.

By the end of the 1960s, French-supported countries

suddenly and openly distanced themselves from France and Ivory Coast's position on the civil war. Isolated on the international scene, both countries decided to suspend their assistance to Ojukwu who eventually went into exile in the Ivory Coast.

At the request of Paris, Houphouet-Boigny began forging relations with South Africa in October 1970, justifying his attitude by stating that "[t]he problems of racial discrimination, so painful, so distressing, so revolting to our dignity as Negros, must not be resolved, we believe, by force." He even proposed to the OAU in June 1971 that they follow his lead. In spite of receiving some support, his proposal was rejected. This refusal did not, however, prevent him from continuing his attempts to approach the apartheid regime.

His attempts bore fruit in October of that year when a semi-official meeting between a delegation of high-level Ivorian officials and South African Prime Minister John Vorster was held in Pretoria, the administrative capital of South Africa. Moreover, mindful of the communist influence in Africa, he met Vorster in Geneva in 1977 after the Soviet Union and Cuba tried to spread their influence in Angola and Ethiopia. Relations with South Africa continued on an official basis until the end of his presidency.

Houphouët-Boigny and Thomas Sankara, the leader of Burkina Faso, had a highly turbulent relationship. Tensions reached their climax in 1985 when Côte d'Ivoire Burkinabés accused the authorities of being involved in a conspiracy to forcibly recruit young students in order to send them for military training in camps in Libya. Houphouët-Boigny responded by inviting the dissident Jean-Claude Kamboulé to take refuge in Côte d'Ivoire so that he could organise opposition to the Sankara regime.

Sankara was overthrown and assassinated in a military coup on 15 October 1987. The coup may have had French involvement since the Sankara regime had fallen into disfavour in France. Houphouët-Boigny was also suspected of involvement in the coup and in November 1987, the Ivorian ruling party, PDCI, asked the government to ban the sale of *Jeune Afrique* in the country following the magazine's allegations that Houphouët-Boigny had participated in the coup which led to Sankara's assassination.

The Ivorian president would have greatly benefited from the divisions in the Burkina Faso government; so he contacted Blaise Compaoré, the second-most powerful man in the regime after his so-called friend Thomas Sankara whom he eventually betrayed and killed.

It is believed that Houphouët-Boigny and Compaoré worked together with French President Francois Mitterrand, Laurent Dona Fologo, Robert Guéï and Pierre Ouédraogo to overthrow Sankara. Liberian rebel leader Charles Taylor was also reportedly involved in Sankara's ouster and assassination, according to another former Liberian rebel leader, Prince Yormie Johnson, in his testimony before Liberia's Truth and Reconciliation Commission (TRC).

Besides supporting policies pursued by France, Houphouët-Boigny also influenced their actions in Africa. He pushed France to support and provide arms to warlord Charles Taylor's rebels during the first Liberian civil war in hopes of receiving some of Liberia's assets and resources after the war.

Opposition to the Soviet Union and China

From the time of Côte d'Ivoire's independence, Houphouët-Boigny considered the Soviet Union (USSR) and the People's Republic of China (PRC) to be "malevolent" influences on developing countries.

He did not establish diplomatic relations with Moscow until 1967 and then severed them in 1969 following allegations of direct Soviet support to a 1968 student protest at the National University of the Ivory Coast. The two countries did not restore ties until February 1986, by which time Houphouët-Boigny had embraced a more active foreign policy reflecting his quest for greater international recognition.

Houphouët-Boigny was even more outspoken in his criticism of the People's Republic of China (PRC). He voiced fears of an "invasion" by the Chinese and subsequent colonisation of Africa by the communist power.

He was especially concerned that Africans would see the problems of development in China as analogous to those of Africa and see China's solutions as appropriate to the problems of African countries, especially those of sub-Saharan Africa. And because of that, the Ivory Coast was one of the last countries to normalise relations with China, doing so on 3 March 1983.

Under the principle demanded by Beijing for "one China," the recognition of the People's Republic of China by the Ivory Coast effectively disestablished diplomatic relations between Abidjan and Taiwan which mainland China has always considered to be its own despite Taiwan's claim to independence and sovereign status.

Economic policies in the 1960s and 1970s

Houphouët-Boigny adopted a system of economic liberalism in the Ivory Coast in order to obtain the trust and confidence of foreign investors, most notably the French.

The advantages granted by the investment laws he established in 1959 allowed foreign business to repatriate up to 90% of their profits to their country of origin (the remaining 10% was reinvested in the Ivory Coast). He also developed an agenda for modernising the country's infrastructure, for example, building an American-style business district in Abidjan where five-star hotels and resorts welcomed tourists and businessmen.

The Ivory Coast experienced economic growth of 11–12% from 1960 to 1965. The country's gross domestic product (GDP) grew twelve-fold between 1960 and 1978, from 145 to 1,750 billion CFA francs, while the trade balance continued to record a surplus.

The origin of this economic success stemmed from the president's decision to focus on the primary sector of the economy rather than the secondary sector. As a result, the agricultural sector experienced significant development: between 1960 and 1970, cocoa cultivators tripled their production to 312,000 tonnes and coffee production rose by nearly 50%, from 185,500 to 275,000 tonnes. As a result of this economic prosperity, the Ivory Coast saw an influx of immigrants from other West African countries. The foreign workforce – mostly Burkinabés (from Burkina Faso, formerly Upper Volta) – who worked mostly on cocoa and coffee plantations, represented more than a quarter of the Ivorian population by 1980.

Both Ivorians and foreigners began referring to Houphouët-Boigny as the "Sage of Africa" for performing what became known as the "Ivorian miracle" of economic prosperity. He was also respectfully nicknamed "The Old One" (*Le Vieux*).

However, the economic system developed in cooperation with France was far from perfect. As Houphouët-Boigny described it, the economy of the Ivory Coast experienced "growth without development." The growth of the economy depended on capital, initiatives and a financial framework from investors abroad; it had not become independent or self-sustaining.

Crisis in the Ivory Coast

Economy on the brink of collapse

Beginning in 1978, the Ivorian economy experienced a serious decline due to the sharp downturn in international market prices of coffee and cocoa. The decline was perceived as fleeting, since its impact on planters was buffered by the Caistab, the agricultural marketing board, which ensured them a livable income.

The following year, in order to contain a sudden drop in the prices of exported goods, Houphouët-Boigny raised prices to resist international tariffs on raw materials. However, by applying only this solution, the Ivory Coast lost more than 700 billion CFA francs between 1980 and 1982. From 1983 to 1984, the country fell victim to a drought that ravaged nearly 400,000 hectares of forest and 250,000 hectares of coffee and cocoa plants.

To address this problem, Houphouët-Boigny travelled to London to negotiate an agreement on coffee and cocoa prices with traders and industrialists; by 1984, the agreement had fallen apart and the Ivory Coast suffered a major financial crisis.

Even offshore oil drilling and petrochemical industries, developed to supply the Caistab, were affected by the 1986 worldwide economic recession. The Ivory Coast, which had bought planters' harvests for double the market price, fell into heavy debt. By May 1987, the foreign debt had reached US$10 billion, prompting Houphouët-Boigny to suspend payments of the debt. Refusing to sell off its cocoa supply, the country shut down its exports in July and forced world rates to increase. However, this "embargo" failed.

In November 1989, Houphouët-Boigny liquidated his enormous stock of cocoa to big businesses to jump-start the economy. Gravely ill at this time, he named a Prime Minister (the post was unoccupied since 1960), Alassane Ouattara, who established a series of belt-tightening economic measures to bring the country out of debt.

Social tensions

The general atmosphere of enrichment and satisfaction during the period of economic growth in the Ivory Coast made it possible for Houphouët-Boigny to maintain and control internal political tensions; his easy-going dictatorship, where political prisoners were almost nonexistent, was well-accepted by the population. However, the economic crisis that began in the 1980s caused a sharp decline in living conditions for the middle class and underprivileged urban populations.

According to the World Bank, the population living below the poverty threshold went from 11% in 1985 to 31% by 1993. Despite the implementation of certain measures, such as the reduction of the number of young French workers (who worked abroad while serving in the military) from 3,000 to 2,000 in 1986, allowing many jobs to go to young Ivorian graduates, the government failed to control the rising rates of unemployment and bankruptcy in many companies.

Strong social agitations shook the country, creating insecurity. The army mutinied in 1990 and 1992, and on 2 March 1990, protesters organized mass demonstrations in the streets of Abidjan with slogans such as "thief Houphouët" and "corrupt Houphouët". These popular demonstrations prompted the president to launch a system of democratisation on 31 May, in which he authorised political pluralism and trade unions.

Opposition

Laurent Gbagbo gained recognition as one of the main

instigators of the student demonstrations during the protests against Houphouët-Boigny's government on 9 February 1982 which led to the closing of the universities and other educational institutions. Shortly thereafter, his wife and he formed what would become the Ivorian Popular Front (FPI). Gbagbo went into exile in France later that year, where he promoted the FPI and its political platforms.

Although the FPI was ideologically similar to the Unified Socialist Party, the French socialist government tried to ignore Gbagbo's party to please Houphouët-Boigny. After a lengthy appeal process, Gbagbo obtained status as a political refugee in France in 1985. However, the French government attempted to pressure him into returning to the Ivory Coast, as Houphouët-Boigny had begun to worry about Gbagbo's developing a network of contacts, and believed "his stirring opponent would be less of a threat in Abidjan than in Paris."

In 1988, Gbagbo returned to the Ivory Coast after Houphouët-Boigny implicitly granted him forgiveness by declaring that "the tree did not get angry at the bird". In 1990, Houphouët-Boigny legalised opposition parties.

On 28 October 1988, a presidential election was held, which for the first time featured a candidate other than Houphouët-Boigny: Gbagbo. He highlighted the President's age, suggesting that he was too old for a seventh five-year term. Houphouët-Boigny countered by broadcasting television footage of his youth and was re-elected to a seventh term with 2,445,365 votes to 548,441.

Displays of wealth

During his presidency, Houphouët-Boigny benefited greatly from the country's wealth. By the time of his death in 1993, his personal wealth was estimated to be between US$7 and $11 billion.

With regards to his large fortune, Houphouët-Boigny

said in 1983, "People are surprised that I like gold. It's just that I was born in it."

The Ivorian leader acquired a dozen properties in the metropolitan area of Paris (including Hotel Masseran on Masseran Street in the 7th arrondissement of Paris), a property in Castel Gandolfo in Italy, and a house in Chêne-Bourg, Switzerland. He owned real estate companies such as Grand Air SI, SI Picallpoc and Interfalco and had many shares in prestigious jewelry and watchmaking companies inccluding Piaget SA and Harry Winston. He placed his fortune in Switzerland, once asking if "there is any serious man on Earth not stocking parts of his fortune in Switzerland."

In 1983, Houphouët-Boigny moved the capital from Abidjan to Yamoussoukro There, at the expense of the state, he built many buildings such as the Institute Polytechnique and an international airport. The most luxurious project was the Basilica of Our Lady of Peace which is currently the largest church in the world, with an area of 30,000 square metres (320,000 sq ft) and a height of 158 metres (518 ft).

Financed by Houphouët-Boigny himself, construction of the Basilica of Our Lady of Peace was carried out by Lebanese architect Pierre Fakhoury at a total cost of about US$150–200 million. Houphouët-Boigny offered it to Pope John Paul II as a "personal gift"; the latter, after having unsuccessfully requested it to be shorter than St. Peter's in Rome, consecrated it all the same on 10 September 1990.

Due to a collapse of the national economy coupled with lavish amounts spent on its construction, the Basilica was criticised: it was called "the basilica in the bush" by several western news agencies.

Death and legacy

Succession and death

The political, social, and economic crises also touched the issue of who would succeed Houphouët-Boigny as head of state. After severing ties with his former political heir Philippe Grégoire Yacé in 1980, who, as president of the National Assembly, was entitled to exercise the full functions of president of the republic if the head of state was incapacitated or absent,_ Houphouët-Boigny delayed as much as he could in officially designating a successor. A founding member of the ruling Democratic Party of Cote d'Ivoire which was founded in 1946, Yacé died at his home in Abidjan on 29 November 1998 after a long illness. He was 78.

President Houphouët-Boigny's health became increasingly fragile, with Prime Minister Alassane Ouattara administering the country from 1990 onwards, while the president was hospitalised in France.

There was a struggle for power which ended when Houphouët-Boigny rejected Ouattara in favour of Henri Konan Bédié, the president of the National Assembly, and a member of the Baoule tribe like Houphouët-Boigny himself. Ouattara was a northerner.

In December 1993, Houphouët-Boigny, terminally ill with prostate cancer, was urgently flown back to the Ivory Coast so he could die there. He was kept on life support to ensure that the last dispositions concerning his succession were defined. After his family consented, Houphouët-Boigny was disconnected from life support at 6:35 a.m. GMT on 7 December 1993. At the time of his death, he was the longest-serving leader in Africa and the third longest-serving in the world after Fidel Castro of Cuba and Kim Il Sung of North Korea.

Houphouët-Boigny left no written will or legacy report for the Ivory Coast upon his death in 1993. His recognised heirs, especially Helena, led a battle against the government to recover part of the vast fortune Houphouët-Boigny had left, which she claimed was "private" and did not belong to the state.

Funeral

Following Houphouët-Boigny's death, the country's stability was maintained, as seen by his impressive funeral on 7 February 1994. The funeral for this "doyen of francophone Africa" was held in the Basilica of Our Lady of Peace in Yamoussoukro, with 7,000 guests inside the building and tens of thousands outside.

The two-month delay before Houphouët-Boigny's funeral, common among members of the Baoule ethnic group, allowed for many ceremonies preceding his burial. The president's funeral featured many traditional African funerary customs including a large chorus dressed in bright batik dresses singing "laagoh budji gnia" (which in the Baoule language means "Lord, it is you who has made all things") and village chiefs displaying strips of kente and korhogo cloth.

Baoulés are traditionally buried with objects they enjoyed while alive; Houpouët-Boigny's family, however, did not state what, if anything, they would bury with him.

Over 140 countries and international organisations sent delegates to the funeral. However, according to *The New York Times*, many Ivorians were disappointed by the poor attendance of several key allies, most notably the United States.

The small United States delegation was led by Secretary of Energy Hazel R. O'Leary and Assistant Secretary of State for African Affairs George Moose, both African Americans, in President Bill Clinton's administration. In contrast, Houphouët-Boigny's close personal ties with France were reflected in the large French delegation which included President Francois Mitterand; Prime Minister Édouard Balladur; the presidents of the National Assembly and of the Senate Philippe Séguin and René Monory; former President Valery Giscard d'Estaing; former Prime Minister – and later President – Jacques René Chirac; his friend Jacques Foccart; and six other former prime ministers.

According to *The New York Times*, "Houphouët-Boigny's death is not only the end of a political era here, but perhaps as well the end of the close French-African relationship that he came to symbolize."

Félix Houphouët-Boigny Peace Prize

To establish his legacy as a man of peace, Houphouët-Boigny created an award in 1989, sponsored by UNESCO and funded entirely by extra-budgetary resources provided by the Félix-Houphouët-Boigny Foundation, to honour those who search for peace.

The prize is "named after President Félix Houphouët-Boigny, the doyen of African Heads of State and a tireless advocate of peace, concord, fellowship and dialogue to solve all conflicts both within and between States". It is awarded annually along with a check for €122,000, by an international jury composed of 11 persons from five continents.

The prize was first awarded in 1991 to Nelson Mandela, president of the African National Congress, and Frederik Willem de Klerk, president of the Republic of South Africa, and has been awarded each year since, with the exception of 2001 and 2004.

Kwame Nkrumah

Kwame Nkrumah (21 September 1909 - 27 April 1972)

was the leader of Ghana and, before then, the Gold Coast, from 1952 to 1966. He was the first prime minister and first president of Ghana. He is also remembered as the most vocal exponent of African unity under one government.

Early life and education

Nkrumah was born in the village of Nkroful in Nzima in the southwestern part of what was then the Gold Coast near the border with the Ivory Coast, prompting some of detractors to say he was actually born in the Ivory Coast and was not really Ghanaian.

His recorded birth date is 21 September 1909. But he did not know his exact date of birth and may have been born in 1912. As one of his sons who is also his last-born child, Sekou Nkrumah, stated in an article, "My Father's Legacy," *Ghanaian Times*, September 14, 2011:

"The only certain facts about Nkrumah's birth appear to be that he was born in the village of Nkroful in Nzima around mid¬day on a Saturday in mid-September.

Nzima lies in the extreme South¬west of Ghana and covers an area of about a thousand square miles stretching from the river Ankobra on the east to the river Tano and its lagoon on the west.

Nzima was known to Europeans for many years as Apollonia because it was on the feast day of St. Apollo that the white man first set foot in Nzima land.

In the outlying areas of the then Gold Coast, nobody bothered to record the dates of births, marriages and deaths, as is the custom of the Western world. Such happenings were remarkable only because they provided a cause for celebration. By tribal custom it was enough for a mother to assess the age of her child by calculating the number of national festivals that had been celebrated since its birth.

The national festival of Nzima is called Kundum. According to Nkrumah's mother's calculations, forty-five Kundums have taken place since he was born, which makes the year of his birth 1912.

On the other hand, the priest who later baptized him into the Roman Catholic Church recorded his birth date as September 21, 1909.

In Nkrumah's autobiography he writes: '...Although this was a mere guess on his part, I have always used this date on official documents, not so much because I believed in its accuracy, but in so far as officialdom was concerned, it was the line of least resistance. It was not until recently that I came to realise how near the mark this guess must have been.'

Nkrumah goes on to recapture a short holiday spent in Nzima where he had the opportunity to revisit some of his childhood haunts, and to recapture the past. As he sat with some friends on the sea shore at Half Assini their eyes were drawn to the rusty brink of the Bakana, a cargo boat owned by the British and African steam Navigation Company which had been wrecked in 1913 and had come to rest on the sea shore.

The Bakana had been a landmark to Nkrumah for so long that he had never realised how significant a part it could play in throwing light on his age. One of his friends then asked what had happened and whether he could remember it. Although Nkrumah was certainly not older than three or four years at the time, he could well remember being told the story of this disaster.

His mother confirmed the fact that he was a small boy at that time the event occurred some little time after she had brought him from Nkroful to live with his father at Half Assini. Assuming, therefore, that the year of Nkrumah birth was 1909, the Saturday nearest to the middle of September in that year was the 18th. It seems likely, therefore, that he was born on Saturday, September

18, 1909."

Nkrumah studied at Achimota College, renamed Achomota School, in Accra The renowned Ghanaian scholar, Dr. Kwegyir Aggrey, was appointed by the British governor of the Gold Coast as the First Vice Principal of Achimota College.

Nkrumah graduated from Achimota in 1930. He then studies at a Roman Catholic seminary and taught at a Catholic school in Axim.

In 1935, he left Ghana for the United States to pursue high education. He earned a B.A. from Lincoln University, Pennsylvania, in 1939. He also earned a bachelor's degree in theology in 1942.

Nkrumah also earned a master of science in education from the University of Pennsylvania in 1942, and a master of arts in philosophy the following year from the same school.

While lecturing in political science at Lincoln University, he was elected president of the African Students Organisation of America and Canada. As an undergraduate at Lincoln, he participated in at least one student theatre production and published an essay on European colonial rule in Africa in the student newspaper, *The Lincolnian.*

During his time in the United States, Nkrumah preached at black churches in Philadelphia and New York, as he states in his autobiography, *Ghana: The Autobiography of Kwame Nkrumah.*

Nkrumah was influenced by the teaching of Marcus Garvey and in 1943 met and began a lengthy correspondence with a Trinidadian Pan-Africanist and Marxist, C.L.R. James, Russian expatriate Rava Dunayevskaya, and Chinese-American Grace Lee Boggs, all of whom were members of a US based Trotskyist intellectual fraternity. Nkrumah later credited C.L.R. James with teaching him "how an underground movement worked."

After living in the United States for 10 years, Nkrumah left and arrived in London in May 1945 and briefly studied at the London School of Economics (LSE) where he intended to earn a PhD in philosophy specialising in positivism. After meeting with George Padmore, to whom he was introduced by C.L.R. James by correspondence, Nkrumah helped organise the Fifth Pan-African Congress in Manchester, England, that year. He and his friend Jomo Kenyatta – who also helped organise the conference – served as secretaries for the conference.

Nkrumah also founded the West African National Secretariat in London to work for the decolonisation of Africa and served as vice-president of the West African Students' Union (WASU).

Return to the Gold Coast

In the autumn of 1947, Nkrumah was invited to serve as the general-secretary to the United Gold Coast Convention (UGCC), a conservative political party under the leadership of Joseph B. Danquah. The party sought independence but took a gradualist approach. Nkrumah accepted the position and sailed for the Gold Coast.

After brief stops in Sierra Leone, Liberia and the Ivory Coast, Nkrumah arrived in the Gold Coast in December 1947.

On the same ship was his friend Ako Adjei, a founding member of the UGCC who later served under Nkrumah as a cabinet member after Nkrumah became prime minister and then president of Ghana.

In February 1948, the police fired on African ex-servicemen protesting the rising cost of living. The shooting spurred riots in Accra, Kumasi and elsewhere in the Gold Coast. The British colonial government suspected the UGCC was behind the protests and arrested

Nkrumah and other party leaders.

Realising their mistake, the British soon released the UGCC leaders. After his imprisonment, Nkrumah emerged as the leader of the youth movement in 1948.

After he came out of prison, Nkrumah travelled around the country, many times hitchhiking, to mobilise the people in the struggle for independence. He proclaimed that the Gold Coast needed "self-government now" and built a large power base among the youth and other Ghanaians.

Cocoa farmers rallied to his cause because they disagreed with British policy to contain swollen shoot disease which was destroying cocoa. He also invited women to participate in the political process at a time when women's suffrage was new to Africa.

The trade unions also allied with his movement and, by 1949, he organised these groups into a new political party, the Convention People's Party (CPP), whose slogan was "Independence Now" through positive action. As Nkrumah stated:

"What is Positive Action? By Positive Action we mean the adoption of all legitimate and constitutional means by which we can cripple the forces of imperialism in this country.

The Weapons of Positive Action are: (1) Legitimate political agitation (2) Newspaper and educational campaigns and (3) as a last resort, the constitutional application of strikes, boycotts and non-co-operation based on the principle of absolute non-violence."

The British convened a selected commission of middle-class Africans to draft a new constitution that would give Ghana more self-government. Under the new constitution, only those with sufficient wage and property would be allowed to vote.

Nkrumah organized a "People's Assembly" with CPP

party members, youth, trade unionists, farmers, and veterans. They called for universal franchise without property qualifications, a separate house of chiefs, and self-governing status under the Statue of Westminster 1931. These amendments, known as the Constitutional Proposals of October 1949, were rejected by the colonial administration.

When the colonial administration rejected the People's Assembly's recommendations, Nkrumah organised a "positive Action" campaign in January 1950 whose tactics included civil disobedience, non-cooperation, boycotts, and strikes. The colonial administration arrested Nkrumah and many CPP supporters. Nkrumah was sentenced to three years in prison.

The colonial rulers wanted to silence Nkrumah and neutralise the struggle for independence but the strategy backfired.

Facing international protests and internal resistance, the British decided to leave the Gold Coast.

Britain organised the first general election to be held under universal franchise on 5–10 February 1951. Though in jail, Nkrumah's CPP was elected by a landslide taking 34 out of 38 seats in the Legislative Assembly.

Nkrumah was released from prison on February 12th and summoned by the British Governor Charles Arden-Clarke and asked to form a government on the following day, February 13th.

The new Legislative Assembly met on 20 February, with Nkrumah as Leader of Government Business, and Emmanuel Charles Quist as President of the Assembly.

A year later, the constitution was amended to provide for a prime minister on 10 March 1952, and Nkrumah was elected to that post by a secret ballot in the Assembly, 45 to 31, with eight abstentions on 21 March. He presented his "Motion of Destiny" to the Assembly, requesting independence within the British Commonwealth "as soon as the necessary constitutional arrangements are made" on

10 July 1953, and the Legislative Assembly approved it.

Independence

As a leader of this government, Nkrumah faced many challenges: first, to learn to govern; second, to unify the four territories of the Gold Coast; third, to win his nation's complete independence from the United Kingdom. Nkrumah was successful at all three goals. Within six years of his release from prison, he was the leader of an independent nation.

At 12 a.m. on 6 March 1957, Nkrumah declared Ghana independent. He was hailed as the *Osagyefo*, which means "redeemer" in the Twi language.

On 6 March 1960, Nkrumah announced plans for a new constitution which would make Ghana a republic. The draft included a provision to surrender Ghanaian sovereignty to a Union of African States. On 19, 23, and 27 April 1960 ,a presidential election and plebiscite on the constitution were held. The constitution was ratified and Nkrumah was elected president, defeating J.B. Danquah, the United Party (UP) candidate, 1,016,076 to 124,623.

In 1961, Nkrumah laid the first stones in the foundation of the Kwame Nkrumah Ideological Institute at Winneba established to train Ghanaian civil servants as well as promote Pan-Africanism.

In 1964, all students entering college in Ghana were required to attend a two-week "ideological orientation" at the Institute. Nkrumah remarked that "trainees should be made to realise the party's ideology is religion and should be practiced faithfully and fervently."

Ghana was a founding member of the Organisation of African Unity (OAU) in Addis Ababa, Ethiopia, in May 1963. The OAU had 32 original members, all independent African states. It was also in the same year that Nkrumah was awarded the Lenin Peace Prize by the Soviet Union.

The Gold Coast had been among the wealthiest and most socially advanced areas in Africa, with schools, railways, hospitals, social security and an advanced economy. Under Nkrumah's leadership, Ghana adopted some socialist policies and practices. Nkrumah created a welfare system, started various community programmes, and established schools.

It was also during Nkrumah's presidency when Ghana embarked on a programme of rapid industrialisation, based on central planning, and the country achieved remarkable success within only a few years Nkrumah was in power before he was overthrown in a military coup.

Politics

Nkrumah generally articulated a non-aligned Marxist perspective on economics and believed that capitalism was wrong and destructive for Africa.

Nkrumah was clear on distancing himself from the African socialism espoused by many of his contemporaries and argued that there is only one form of socialism, and that is scientific socialism. He maintained that socialism was the only system that would best accommodate the changes that capitalism had brought about in Africa, while still respecting African values. He specifically addresses these issues and his politics in a 1967 essay entitled "African Socialism Revisited":

"We know that the traditional African society was founded on principles of egalitarianism. In its actual workings, however, it had various shortcomings. Its humanist impulse, nevertheless, is something that continues to urge us towards our all-African socialist reconstruction.

We postulate each man to be an end in himself, not merely a means; and we accept the necessity of

271

guaranteeing each man equal opportunities for his development. The implications of this for socio-political practice have to be worked out scientifically, and the necessary social and economic policies pursued with resolution.

Any meaningful humanism must begin from egalitarianism and must lead to objectively chosen policies for safeguarding and sustaining egalitarianism. Hence, socialism. Hence, also, scientific socialism."

Nkrumah was also perhaps best known politically for his strong commitment to and promotion of Pan-Africanism. He was inspired by the writings of black intellectuals like Mrcus Garvey, W.E.B. DuBois and George Padmore and his relationships with them.

Nkrumah's biggest success in that area was perhaps his significant influence in the founding of the Organisation of African Unity (OAU). He also wrote a book, *Africa Must Unite*, whose publication in May 1963 was timed to coincide with the first conference which led to establishment of the Organisation of African Unity.

Economics

Nkrumah attempted to rapidly industrialise Ghana's economy. He reasoned that if Ghana escaped the colonial trade system by reducing dependence on foreign capital, technology, and material goods, it could become truly independent. However, overspending on capital projects caused the country to be driven deeply into debt—estimated as much as $1 billion USD by the time he was ousted in 1966.

Decline and fall

The year 1954 was a pivotal point during Nkrumah's

era. In that year's independence elections, he tallied some of the independence election vote. However, that same year saw the world price of cocoa rise from £150 to £450 per ton. Rather than allowing cocoa farmers to maintain the windfall, Nkrumah appropriated the increased revenue through levies and then invested the capital in various national development projects. The policy alienated one of the major constituencies that helped him come to power.

In 1958 Nkrumah introduced legislation to restrict various freedoms in Ghana. After the Gold Miners' Strike of 1955, Nkrumah introduced the Trade Union Act which made strikes illegal.

When he suspected opponents in parliament of plotting against him, he introduced the Preventive Detention Act which empowered his government to arrest and detain anyone charged with treason without due process of law. Prisoners were often held without trial and their only legal method of recourse was personal appeal to Nkrumah himself.

When the railway workers went on strike in 1961, Nkrumah ordered strike leaders and opposition politicians arrested under the Trade Union Act of 1958.

While Nkrumah himself had organised strikes just a few years before, he now opposed such industrial democracy because it interfered with rapid industrial development. He told the unions that their days as advocates for the safety and just compensation of miners were over, and that their new job was to work with the management to mobilise human resources. Wages must give way to patriotic duty because the good of the nation superseded the good of individual workers, Nkrumah's government contended.

The Detention Act led to widespread disaffection with Nkrumah's leadership. Some of his associates used the law to arrest innocent people to acquire their political offices and business assets. Advisers close to Nkrumah became reluctant to question policies for fear that they might be seen as opponents. Even when clinics ran out of medicine, no one notified him. Some people believed that he no longer cared.

The police came to resent their role in society, especially after most of their power was neutralised and Nkrumah's personal guard – the National Security Service and presidential Guard regiments – assumed most of the responsibilities which had earlier been handled by them.

Nkrumah also disappeared from public view out of justifiable fear of assassination following many attempts on his life.

In 1964, he proposed a constitutional amendment to make the Convention People's Party (CPP) the only legal party and himself life president of both the nation and the ruling party. The amendment passed with more than 99 percent of the vote. It really didn't make any difference because Ghana had effectively been a one-party state since independence. The amendment only transformed Nkrumah's presidency into a *de facto* legal dictatorship.

Nkrumah's advocacy of industrial development at any cost, with help of his longtime friend and minister of finance, Komla Agbeli Gbedemah, led to the construction of a hydroelectric power plant, the Akosombo Dam on the Volta River in eastern Ghana; coincidentally Gbedemah's home region mostly inhabited by the Ewe, one of Ghana's and West Africa's largest ethnic groups of which Gbedemah himself was a member.

 Kaiser Aluminum agreed to build the dam for Ghana but restricted what could be produced using the power generated.

Nkrumah borrowed money to build the dam and drove Ghana into debt. To finance the debt, he raised taxes on the cocoa farmers in the south. This accentuated regional differences and jealousy. The dam was completed and opened by Nkrumah amidst world publicity on 22 January 1966. Nkrumah appeared to be at the zenith of his power, but, unbeknownst to him, the end of his regime was only days away.

Nkrumah wanted Ghana to have modern armed forces. So he acquired aircraft and ships and introduced conscription.

He also gave military support to those fighting Ian Smith's regime in Rhodesia, now Zimbabwe. One of the main reasons Akwasi A. Afrifa gave – in his book *The Ghana Coup* – to explain why they overthrew Nkrumah was that he was getting ready to send Ghanain soldiers to Rhodesia to help the African freedom fighters remove Smith from power and end white minority rule.

In February 1966, while Nkrumah was on a state visit to North Vietnam and China, his government was overthrown in a military coup led by Emmanuel Kwasi Kotoka. He and his colleagues formed the National Liberation Council (NLC) to rule the country. Several commentators including former CIA agent John Stockwell contend that the coup was supported by the CIA.

Exile, death and tributes

Nkrumah never returned to Ghana but continued to push for his vision of African unity. He lived in exile in Conakary, Guinea, as the guest of President Ahmed Sekou Toure who made him honorary co-president of the country. He read, wrote, corresponded, gardened, and entertained guests.

Despite retirement from public office, he was still afraid of Western intelligence agencies. When his cook died, he feared that someone would poison him and began hoarding food in his room.

He suspected that foreign agents were going through his mail and lived in constant fear of abduction and assassination. In failing health, he flew to Bucharest, Romania, for medical treatment in August 1971. He died of skin cancer on 27 April 1972. He was 62.

Nkrumah was buried in a tomb in the village of his birth, Nkroful, in southwestern Ghana. While the tomb remains in Nkroful, his remains were transferred to a large national memorial tomb and park in the nation's capital Accra.

During his lifetime, Nkrumah was awarded honorary doctorates by Lincoln University, Moscow State University, Cairo University in Cairo, Egypt; Jagiellonian University in Krakow, Poland; Humboldt University in former East Berlin in East Germany, and by other universities.

In 2000, he was voted Africa's man of the millennium by listeners to the BBC World Service.

Works by Kwame Nkrumah

"Negro History: European Government in Africa," *The Lincolnian*, 12 April 1938, p. 2 (Lincoln University, Pennsylvania) - see Special Collections and Archives, Lincoln University.

- *Ghana: The Autobiography of Kwame Nkrumah* (1957)
- *Africa Must Unite* (1963)
- *African Personality* (1963)
- *Neo-Colonialism: The Last Stage of Imperialism* (1965)
- *Axioms of Kwame Nkrumah* (1967)
- *African Socialism Revisited* (1967)
- *Voice From Conakry* (1967)
- *Dark Days in Ghana* (1968)
- *Handbook of Revolutionary Warfare* (1968)
- *Consciencism: Philosophy and Ideology for De-Colonisation* (1970)
- *Class Struggle in Africa* (1970)
- *The Struggle Continues* (1973)
- *I Speak of Freedom* (1973)
- *Revolutionary Path* (1973)

Jerry Rawlings

Jerry John Rawlings (born Jeremiah Rawlings John on 22 June 1947 in Accra, the Gold Coast) is a former head of state of Ghana.

He ruled Ghana as a military dictator in 1979 and from 1981 to 1992 and then as the first elected president of the Fourth Republic from 1993 to 2001.

He initially took power in a coup d'état but in the 1990s following sustained political and economic pressure from international institutions and governments began a process of economic and then political liberalisation. He founded the National Democratic Congress (NDC) which won the 1992 general election. He took office in 1993 and was re-elected in 1997.

Rawlings appeared on the Ghanaian political scene on 15 May 1979 when he led a group of junior officers in the Ghana Air Force in a coup attempt against the regime of Fred Akuffo which resulted in his arrest and imprisonment. He was court-martialled in public and sentenced to death.

On 4 June 1979, soldiers overthrew Akuffo and released Rawlings and his colleagues from prison just weeks before general elections were scheduled.

The leader of the coup which brought Rawlings to power was his secondary school friend, Major Kojo Boakye-Djan, also known as Kwadwo Boakye Djan. They met at Achimota School. Boakye Djan is the one who planned the coup. In 2003, he explained that the main purpose of the coup was to save Jerry Rawlings who had been sentenced to death for his abortive coup attempt the previous month. According to an article, "Why I Saved Rawlings," published on modernghana.com on 21 January 2003 and attributed to the *New African* as the source:

"Major Kojo Boakye Djan, spokesman for the erstwhile Armed Forces Revolutionary Council (AFRC), has said that the reason for staging the June Four 1979 uprising was because of his school-day friendship with Jerry John Rawlings, the former president, and also the fact that he did not want Rawlings to die.

Boakye Djan indicated that a group made up of soldiers in the Ghana Armed Forces known as the Free Africa Movement (FAM) which he headed, had planned to seize the reins of political power in 1984 when they had wanted to resort to an uprising in an emergency. The FAM was founded in 1970, the very year that Boakye Djan was enlisted in the Ghana Army after he had worked as a journalist.

Speaking to the *New African* magazine, a UK publication recently, Major Boakye Djan who is now living in exile in the United Kingdom claimed that he warned Flight Lieutenant Jerry John Rawlings not to attempt the May 15 uprising, as he would fail, but he did not listen.

15 May Fiasco

'On May 10, 1979,' Djan said 'I was sleeping when Rawlings came in and said: 'JC, let's go for a drink'. So we went to the Continental Hotel (now Golden Tulip) in Accra. After a few drinks, according to Boakye Djan, Rawlings suddenly said; 'JC, we are ready to take over'. I queried 'you and who?' Then Rawlings replied and said 'I have got a lot of the boys?' 'Which boys?,' I nearly shouted the words out.

According to Boakye Djan, he told Rawlings that if he tried the May 15 uprising, he would be setting himself for use as canon fodder.

He said he told him that his plan won't work – and that the military generals won't forgive him.

Rawlings, according to Boakye Djan, replied: 'Oh, JC,

278

you temporise too much; you risk being seen as a coward.'

'I said you never associate me with cowardice. I have come a long way because I don't believe in uneducated bravado. We shall see.' So, I left him at the hotel.

Justification For June 4

Rawlings went on to stage his coup with about 15 men and was arrested. 'Now, with Rawlings in the noose, we had plenty of factors to justify action, though this was not 1984 but 1979. So, we decided to move. We knew that the ground FAM project, conceived in 1970, had been derailed; in fact, hijacked by one man and his rash actions.'

The tribunal that was trying Rawlings and his 15 men was meant to convict him and his 'boys' for committing treason which is punishable by death in Ghana.

The *New African* reports that with their friend staring death in the face, Boakye Djan and the Free Africa Movement had to do something to save J.J. Rawlings from the gallows.

Boakye Djan continued that when the trial of Rawlings began, the FAM met in a crisis session and decided that instead of waiting to strike in 1984, they should bring their planned resort to an uprising in an emergency, right then. This mean that Boakye Djan and his group were going to plan a deliberate attack to overthrow a regime and then punish the senior military officers.

According to Boakye Djan who joined the Ghana Armed Forces after graduating from the University of Ghana, Legon, and practising as a journalist, he told his group that their deliberate attack planned for 1984 had been reduced to a hasty attack, thanks to Rawlings' foolish action.

He explained that even though they had not planned to move at that stage, the exigency of the situation forced them to launch the June Four uprising, led by him.

'The options were clear' according to Boakye Djan. We

had to release Rawlings before he was executed and also to ensure the self-preservation of the movement (FAM) because its activities were becoming known.

'If we had allowed Rawlings to be tried and found guilty, we would be the next target.'

Boakye Djan claimed that there was no way he, in particular, was going to survive.

Need to punish officers

One objective of the FAM which gave birth to June 4 was the desire to deal with senior officers who had committed treasonable subversion and whom the FAM suspected to be corrupt and were trying to manipulate the 1979 general elections to protect themselves.

One other reason for staging June Four, according to Boakye Djan, was the fact that he and Rawlings had become inseparable friends.

Boakye Djan traced his relationship with Rawlings to their student days at Achimota School in Accra.

According to him, it was his belief in ancestral worship or African Traditional Religion (ATR) that endeared him to Rawlings even though the latter was a Catholic.

Ancestral worship involves the process of libation to invoke elements in the sky that symbolise the Supreme Being (God).

Because Boakye Djan believed in ancestral worship, he failed to attend the school's morning devotion which attracted the attention of the British headmaster, Mr Alan Rudwick. This nearly resulted in his dismissal.

Whilst Djan was in Sixth Form, Rawlings was in Form Four. They had first met in 1962 through a most bizarre event. Djan had been hauled in before the school authorities (then predominantly British) to answer why he was not attending morning prayers.

'At the time,' Djan remembers, 'Achimota was obsessed with rituals. Students had to fill an elaborate admission form which covered almost every area of their lives. On my form, I had written 'ancestral worshipper' in the box for religion. But it didn't apparently register with the school authorities until I began to absent myself from morning prayers.'

One day, the British headmaster, Rudwick, saw Djan in the reading room at prayer time. 'What do you think you are doing, young man? Why aren't you at morning prayers,' he asked.

'Sir,' Djan replied. 'But I have already informed the school that I am an ancestral worshipper. It's on my admission form.'

'Ancestral what?' Rudwick nearly spat out the words. 'You come from a Catholic School, Opoku Ware (in Kumasi), and you tell me you are an ancestral worshipper?'

'Yes, sir,' Djan said. 'I was supposed to be a Catholic, but I change my mind on the way.'

Later at a meeting with the school authorities in the house of the headmaster, Boakye Djan was able to acquit himself so well that instead of being sacked, the school authorities allowed him to stay out of the morning devotion by pinning a note on the notice board: It read: 'Citizen Boakye Djan is an ancestral worshipper; therefore, during early morning prayers, he is allowed to go to the library or the reading room to do his own thing.'

Soon, the news spread. One evening, after dinner, as Djan was coming out of the dinning hall, Rawlings accosted him. 'Citizen,' he told Djan, 'we all dig (like) what you are doing. You've stood up to those bastards.'

At this juncture, according to Boakye Djan, he asked Rawlings whether he believed in Catholicism 'No' said Rawlings flatly, 'but I cannot help it.'

'I told him: 'Then go and fight for your corner, your beliefs and stop fooling about:' said Boakye Djan.

'To be fair,' Djan says, 'Rawlings was one of the few people who came to me, in the night, to congratulate me.

Until then, I had seen him walk around like everybody else.'

Streetwise

'He was one of the crowd.

At the time, I was regarded as a kind of pariah. So, nobody wanted to openly identify with me.

Even, Rawlings did not like to discuss the issue with one in daylight hours.

He came to me after dinner. From that day, any time Rawlings saw me, he would greet me with the black power salute, the clenched fist.'

Boakye Djan was the best man at Rawlings' wedding.

Major Boakye Djan recalls that at Rawlings' wedding to Konadu, he (Djan) and Rawlings wore a tunic. They did not wear anything fanciful. They wore radical things and 'looking back, it was good.'

'Our friendship grew by leaps and bounds' he said.

The only snag was that there was a time-bomb ticking under Rawlings' feet all the time, said Boakye Djan.

'Current Affairs was Rawlings' weakest subject,' Djan reveals.

'He never passed it on his own merit.'

'Sadly, promotion in the army was tied to passing all the papers. Technically, he had passed all the other subjects like Flying, Map Reading, etc, but because Flt Lt Jerry John Rawlings had not passed Current Affairs, his promotion was held up for years.

Things were getting pretty desperate for him, so we had to beef up his marks in Current Affairs in order for him to pass his promotion examination. This is what saved his career.

'But by 1979, Rawlings was back in dire straits. This is because of his inability to pass his promotion exams. He was, therefore, put on notice to be demobilised; in civilian language, this means to be sacked from the Ghana Armed

Forces (GAF) in July 1979.

'In military terms, he was on short service. So, he was desperate,' said Boakye Djan.

'In addition, funds that he had failed to return to official coffers after his course in Pakistan had been cancelled; was also being deducted from his pay at source.

So, Jerry Rawlings was in serious financial problems as well.'"

After overthrowing the government, Rawlings and his colleagues formed the Armed Forces Revolutionary Council (AFRC) and conducted what it termed 'a housecleaning exercise' where large sums of stolen government money were retrieved into government coffers and inflation was stabilised.

An election held that year was won by Dr. Hilla Limann of the People's National Party (PNP). However, on 31 December 1981, Rawlings and the AFRC overthrew Dr. Limann's government, citing economic mismanagement. Rawlings then installed the Provisional National Defence Council (PNDC) government with himself as chairman.

Rawlings retired from the Armed Forces and set up the National Democratic Congress. This party, with Rawlings as its candidate, won 58.3% of the votes (the largest percentage won by a presidential candidate in Ghana's political history) in the 1992 elections.

The opposition New Patriotic Party (NPP) claimed that the election was stolen, although international observers judged the elections "largely free and fair."

In 1996, Rawlings won the general elections by 57 percent and elections were judged largely free and fair by international observers.

After two terms in office, barred by the constitution from standing in any election, Rawlings endorsed his vice-president John Evans Atta Mills as the presidential candidate of their party in 2000. But the NDC lost the

283

elections to the NPP candidate John Agyekum Kufuor.
Once again, elections were judged to be free and fair.

Rawlings is married to Nana Konadu Agyeman. The
couple has four children: three girls and a boy.

Jerry Rawlings is the joint recipient of the 1993 World
Hunger Award which he used as seed capital in
establishing the University of Development Studies
(UDS) in the north of Ghana.

Background

J.J. Rawlings was born 22 June 1947 to Victoria
Agbotui from Keta in the Volta Region in eastern Ghana
and to James Ramsey John, a Scottish chemist working in
the then Gold Coast. His mother was a member of the Ewe
tribe dominant in eastern Ghana.

He married Nana Konadu Agyeman in 1977.

He enlisted as a flight cadet in the Ghana Air Force in
August 1967 and was subsequently selected for officer
cadet training at the Ghana Military Academy and
Training School, Teshie, in Accra.

Military career

In March, 1968, Jerry Rawlings was posted to Takoradi
in the Western Region to continue his studies. He
graduated in January 1969 and was commissioned a pilot
officer, winning the coveted "Speed Bird Trophy" as the
best cadet in flying and airmanship. He earned the rank of
flight lieutenant in April 1978.

On 28 May 1979, Rawlings, together with six others
who were arrested earlier, appeared before a General
Court Martiall in Accra, charged with leading a mutiny of
junior officers and enlisted men of the Ghanaian Armed
Forces on 15 May 1979.

There was a strong public reaction, especially after

Rawlings' statement had been read in court, explaining the social injustices that had prompted him to act. The ranks of the Armed Forces, in particular, expressed deep sympathy with his stated aims.

While awaiting his next appearance before the court, Rawlings was sprung from custody on 4 June 1979 by a group of soldiers led by Kojo Boakye-Djan.

With the support of both the military and civilians, he led the uprising that ousted the Supreme Military Council from office and brought the Armed Forces Revolutionary Council (AFRC) to power.

On the night of June 4th, lives were lost on both sides. However, the uprising was not as bloody as critics claim because the majority of the soldiers decided not to fight each other on the orders of the top brass.

As one of his first acts in power, Rawlings signed orders for the execution of three former military heads of state: Akwasi Afrifa, Ignatius Acheampong, and Fred Akuffo. Five other generals – Joy Amedume, Yaw Boakye, Roger Felli, Kotei, and Utuka – were also put to death.

Rawlings has never denied responsibility for this. The country was in a state of vengeful anarchy and both civilians and lower ranks in the army were calling for the 'blood' of the Supreme Military Council (SMC) and other officers they felt had caused misery and perpetrated injustices against the people of Ghana.

The AFRC, under the chairmanship of Rawlings, carried out a much wider "house-cleaning exercise" aimed at purging the armed forces and society at large of corruption and graft as well as restoring a sense of moral responsibility and accountability in public life. Meanwhile, following a programme already set in motion before the June 4 uprising, the ruling military government organised free general elections.

On 24 September 1979, the AFRC handed over power to a civilian government led by the People's National Party (PNP) under President Hilla Limann.

The killings of Supreme Court Justices Kwadjo Agyei Agyepong, Frederick Sarkodie, and Cecilia Koranteng Addo, and of military officers Major Sam Acquah and Major Dasana Nantogmah, was another painful incident in Ghana's history.

Limann's administration was cut short on 31 December 1981 when Rawlings overthrew him in another coup.

A Provisional National Defence Council (PNDC) composed of both civilian and military members was established, with Rawlings as chairman, to rule the country.

The coming of the PNDC was widely praised by Ghanaians who were disappointed with Limann's corrupt government. The PNDC began the process of decentralisation which helped lay the foundation for democracy in Ghana.

Primary health care was another goal the PNDC pursued, focusing on disease prevention.

Democratic president

In J.J Rawlings' first official speech subsequent to the removal of the Limann government, he announced the creation of the National Commission on Democracy (NCD) which would begin the decentralisation of government and the dissemination of people-power. Opposition to the PNDC, with pressure from the United States through the CIA, began demanding a return to multi-party democracy, although a referendum showed mixed feelings by the Ghanaian citizenry on this.

The National Commission on Democracy was put into high gear to begin the process to return the country to multi-party elections. The NCD was empowered to hold regional debates and formulate some suggestions for a transition to multi-party democracy. Although opposition groups complained that the NCD was too closely associated with the PNDC, the commission continued its work through 1991.

In March of that year, the NCD released a report recommending the election of an executive president, the establishment of a national assembly, and the creation of a prime minister post. The PNDC accepted the report. And the following year, the report was approved in a national referendum.

Political parties were legalised – with the provision that none could use names that had been used before – and a timetable was set for presidential and parliamentary elections.

Rawlings retired from the Ghanaian Armed Forces on 14 September 1992.

When presidential elections were held in 1992, Rawlings stood as the candidate for the National Democratic Congress (NDC), the successor party to the PNDC. Although his opponents were given access to television and newspaper coverage, and limits to freedom of the press had been lifted, no single candidate could match the popularity of the sitting head of state.

Election returns on 3 November 1992 showed that Rawlings had won 58.3 percent of the vote, a landslide victory. Foreign observers declared the voting to be free and fair.

Almost immediately, the leaders of the country's opposition parties claimed that the presidential election was not fair and that widespread abuses had occurred. The leaders encouraged their followers to boycott subsequent parliamentary elections. As a result of the boycott, the NDC won 189 of 200 seats in the new parliament. Rawlings was therefore accorded a four-year term backed by an elected assembly of supporters for his platform. Answering questions about polling place irregularities, he promised to initiate a new voter registration programme to be completed in time for elections in four years.

In 1993, President Rawlings headed the Ghana

delegation which participated in the first Tokyo International Conference on African Development.

Rawlings and the NDC were elected in 1992 and 1996. Per constitutional mandate, Rawlings's term of office ended in 2001; he retired in 2001 and was succeeded by John Kufuor, his main opponent in the 1996 elections. Kufuor succeeded in defeating Rawlings's vice-president John Atta-Mills in the 2000 election.

In 2004, Mills conceded to Kufuor in spite of complaints by Jerry Rawlings and other NDC officials that the election was rigged. That was Kufuor's second and last four-year term in office as president.

Post-presidency activities

Rawlings later played a key role as a check on the NPP government.

He has also given lectures in universities around the world including one at Oxford University entitled "Security and Democracy in Africa." And he continued to criticise even his own party which won the presidential election in 2008.

In trying to stop Rawlings' NDC from coming back to power, the then ruling NPP government had fought the election by trying to say that Rawlings would control Mills. However Mills proved to be rather independent, which frustrated Rawlings.

Sylvanus Olympio

Sylvanus Epiphanio Olympio (6 September 1902 - 13 January 1963) was the prime minister and then president of Togo from 1958 until his assassination in 1963.

Political career

Olympio served as prime minister from 1958 to 1961. He then served as the first president of Togo between 1961 and 1963, winning an election that barred Nicolas Grunitzky's party. Coincidentally, Grunitsky was his brother-in-law.

Opposition leaders including majr ones such as Grunitzky, Anani Santos, and Antoine Meatchi were either jailed in Mango prison sought exile in Ghana and Dahomey (later renamed Benin).

Using the "Ablode Sodja" militia, Olympio squashed political dissent. But he also had a reputation as a very effective leader.

During his presidency, Olympio pursued a pro-Western foreign policy. At one point, he visited the United States and had a friendly meeting with President John F. Kennedy.

Togo maintained friendly relations with most of its neighbours. But relations with Ghana and its leader Kwame Nkrumah were consistently poor.

Assassination

Olympio was assassinated in a military coup on 13 January 1963. The coup, reportedly led by Étienne Eyadéma, a sergeant, is considered to be the first coup d'état in Africa and sent shock waves through the continent. Grunitzky became the new president.

Eyadéma overthrew Grunitzky in 1967 and remained in power until his death in 2005.

He also claimed to have personally fired the shot which killed Olympio in 1963. But according to other sources, the head of the group of soldiers who overthrew and killed Olympio was Sergeant Emmanuel Bodjollé. Eyadema was not even a sergeant at the time. And according to *Time* magazine in its article "Death at the Gate," 25 January 1963:

"For Sylvanus Olympio, 60, President of Togo, the nightmare began shortly after midnight. Disturbed by strange sounds in his comfortable house in the capital city of Lomé, Olympio grabbed a pistol and went to the head of the stairs. There, to his consternation, was a crowd of mutinous soldiers crowding the floor below. Barefoot, clad in shorts and a sports shirt, Olympio leaped through a window onto the soft, sandy earth of his garden.

He made it to the U.S. embassy compound next door. In the graveled courtyard, Olympio found a parked Plymouth sedan belonging to the embassy, and crawled in. There, in the early morning sunlight, he was spotted huddled beneath the steering wheel by one of the mutineers. Crying 'All right, you have me!,' Olympio surrendered and, prodded by rifle butts, was hustled down the driveway, past a mango tree and through the green gate. There he balked. Sergeant Etienne Eyadema, commander of the rebel detachment, later declared: 'He could not stay there. There would have been demonstrations. He would not move. I shot him.'

At 7 that morning, U.S. Ambassador Leon Poullada drove up to the embassy building, found President Olympio lying in a pool of blood just outside the compound. There were red finger smears on the gate, as if he had struggled to rise. As embassy aides carried the corpse into the courtyard, fat lizards scuttled away across the gravel and lounging Togolese soldiers watched silently from a nearby street corner.

"Blow to Progress."

Thus last week died the man who was ruler of a postage-stamp-sized republic (75 by 340 miles) on the sweltering West African coast. Chief architect of Togo's 1960 independence from French control, London-educated Olympio practiced stern austerity at home, rejected demagoguery, and sided openly with the West. President Kennedy, whom Olympio visited in Washington last March, mourned his death as 'a blow to the progress of stable government in Africa.'

Suspicion immediately focused on Ghana's strongman Kwame Nkrumah, who has conducted a bitter feud with Olympio over control of the powerful, 700,000-member Ewe (pronounced Evvy) tribe, which was split between both countries by European boundary-setters. Twice before, assassins had tried to kill Olympio; each time Ghana's agents were accused. But this time it was Olympio's own zealous economies that brought disaster.

"Bon. Ça Va."

As part of his economic austerity program, Olympio had stubbornly refused to expand Togo's flyspeck army beyond its standing strength of 250 men – exactly one company. This angered both the 'army' and the demobilized, hard-eyed Togolese veterans of French colonial wars, who had fought from Indo-China to Algeria but could find no place in their homeland's armed forces. Recently, a tough ex-sergeant, Emmanuel Bodjolle, 35, jobless and with a family to support, organized a conspiracy with 30 other noncoms. Last week, after Olympio tore up a final plea to take into the service at least 60 of the most qualified veterans, Bodjolle snapped: 'Bon. Ça va.' That midnight his battle-tough insurgents struck, easily occupying the capital.

Olympio's successor is Nicolas Grunitzky, 49, his brother-in-law, who was swept out of office as territorial premier for the French when Olympio took over five years ago. Grunitzky's first act was to announce that Togo would align itself with the Afro-Malagasy Union, the pro-French association of West Africa states. Then he declared free elections would soon follow. But, as so often happens in such circumstances, he decided it would be best to dissolve Parliament and rule alone until things settled down."

Aftermath

Sylvanus Olympio was succeeded by Emmanuel Bodjollé, head of an "Insurrection Committee" that ruled for only two days after which Nicolas Grunitzky was put in charge.

Years later, his son, Gilchrist Olympio, became one of the most prominent opposition leaders in Togo.

Thomas Sankara

Thomas Isidore Noël Sankara (December 21, 1949 – October 15, 1987) was president of Burkina Faso from 1983 to 1987. Viewed as a charismatic and an iconic figure of revolution, he is commonly referred to as "Africa's Che Guevara."

Sankara seized power in a 1983 popularly supported coup at the age of 33, with the goal of eliminating corruption and the dominance of the former French colonial power.

He immediately launched one of the most ambitious programmes for social and economic change ever attempted on the African continent, probably surpassed only by Tanzania's policy of Ujamaa and the country's

Arusha Declaration.

Trinidadian Pan-Africanist and renowned scholar C.L.R. James described Tanzania's Arusha Declaration as "the highest stage of resistance ever reached by revolting Blacks." He also commended Nyerere's ideas especially in the field of education and self-reliance as the most significant socialist thought since Lenin. He also said about the Arusha Declaration: "Its depth, range and the repercussions which flow from it, go far beyond the Africa which gave it birth."

Sankara may not have articulated his ideas to such depths and in a comprehensive manner the way Nyerere did. But he did chart out a course for self-reliance and development starting at the grassroots level few African leaders have.

And to symbolise this new autonomy and rebirth, he even changed the name of his country from Upper Volta to Burkina Faso which means the "land of upright men.," a description whose essence very much reflected what Tanzania also tried to do with the Arusha Declaration: to create a new man in terms of thought, spirit, and commitment.

Sankara's foreign policies were centred around anti-imperialism, with his government eschewing all foreign aid, pushing for odious debt reduction, nationalising all land and mineral wealth, and averting the power and influence of the International Monetary fund (IMF) and the World Bank.

His domestic policies were focused on preventing famine with agrarian self-sufficiency and land reform, giving education high priority with a nation-wide literacy campaign, and promoting public health by vaccinating 2.5 million children against meningitis, yellow fever and measles.

Other components of his national agenda included planting over ten million trees to halt the growing desertification of the Sahel which was creeping on the country, doubling wheat production by redistributing land from feudal landlords to peasants, suspending rural poll taxes and domestic rents, and establishing an ambitious road and rail construction programme to "tie the nation together."

Moreover, his commitment to women's rights led him to outlaw female genital mutilation, forced marriages and polygamy, while appointing females to high government positions and encouraging them to work outside the home and stay in school even if pregnant.

In order to achieve this radical transformation of society, he increasingly exerted authoritarian control over the nation, eventually banning unions and a free press which he believed could stand in the way of his plans and be manipulated by powerful outside influences.

To counter opposition in towns and workplaces around the country, he also tried corrupt officials, counter-revolutionaries and "lazy workers" in people's revolutionary tribunals. Additionally, as an admirer of Fudel Castro's Cuban Revolution, Sankara set up Cuban-style committees for the Defence of the Revolution (CDRs).

His revolutionary programmes for African self-reliance as a defiant alternative to the neo-liberal development strategies imposed by the West made him an icon to many of Africa's poor.

Sankara remained popular with most of his country's impoverished citizens. However, his policies alienated and antagonised the vested interests of an array of groups which included the small but powerful Burkinabé middle class, the tribal leaders whom he stripped of the long-held traditional right to forced labour and tribute payments, and the foreign financial interests in France and their ally the Ivory Coast. As a result, he was overthrown and assassinated on 15 October 1987 in a military coup led by his "friend," Blaise Compaore, who was supported by France. A week before his execution, he declared: "While revolutionaries as individuals can be murdered, you cannot kill ideas."

Early life

Thomas Sankara was the son of Marguerite Sankara (died 6 March 2000) and Sambo Joseph Sankara (1919 – 4 August 2006), a gendarme. Born into a Roman Catholic, "Thom'Sank" was a Silmi-Mossi, an ethnic group that originated with marriage between Mossi men and women of the pastoralist Fulani people.

The Silmi-Mossi are among the least advantaged people in the Mossi caste system.

Thomas Sankara attended primary school in Gaoua and high school in Bobo-Dioulasso, the country's second-largest city after the capital Ouagadougou.

His father fought in the French army during World War II and was detained by the Nazis. Thomas Sankara's family wanted him to become a Catholic priest. And fittingly for a country with a large Muslim population, he was also familiar with the Qur'ān.

Military career

After basic military training in secondary school in 1966, Sankara began his military career at the age of 19, and a year later was sent to Madagascar for officer training at Antsirabe where he witnessed popular uprisings in 1971 and 1972 against the government of Philibert Tsiranana and first read the works of Karl Marx and Vladimir Lenin, profoundly influencing his political views for the rest of his life.

He returned to Upper Volta in 1972 and in 1974 he fought in a border war between Upper Volta and Mali. He earned fame for his heroic performance in the border war with Mali but years later renounced the war as "useless and unjut," a reflection of his growing political consciousness.

He also became a popular figure in the capital of Ouagadougou. The fact that he was a decent guitarist (he played in a band named "Tout-à-Coup Jazz") and rode a motorcycle may have contributed to his charismatic public images.

In 1976, he became commander of the Commando Training Centre in Pô, a city in southern Burkina Faso which is also the capital of Nahouri province whose main ethnic group is the Gurunsi.

In the same year he met Blaise Compaoré in Morocco. During the presidency of Colonel Saye Zerbo, a group of young officers formed a secret organisation, the "Communist Officers' Group" (*Regroupement des officiers communistes*, or ROC), whose best-known members were Henri Zongo, Jean-Baptiste Boukary Lingani, Compaoré and Thomas Sankara.

Government posts

Sankara was appointed secretary of state for information in the military government in September 1981, going to his first cabinet meeting on a bicycle. But he resigned on 21 April 1982 in opposition to what he saw as the regime's anti-labour drift, declaring "Misfortune to those who gag the people!" (*"Malheur à ceux qui baillonnent le peuple!"*)

After another coup (7 November 1982) brought to power Major-Doctor Jean-Baptiste Ouédraogo, Sankara became prime minister in January 1983 but was dismissed (May 17) and placed under house arrest after a visit by the French president's son and African affairs adviser Jean-Christophe Mitterrand. Henri Zongo and Jean-Baptiste Boukary Lingani were also placed under arrest; this caused a popular uprising.

President

"Our revolution in Burkina Faso draws on the totality of man's experiences since the first breath of humanity. We wish to be the heirs of all the revolutions of the world, of all the liberation struggles of the peoples of the Third World. We draw the lessons of the American revolution. The French revolution taught us the rights of man. The great October revolution brought victory to the proletariat and made possible the realization of the Paris Commune's dreams of justice." — Thomas Sankara, October 1984.

A military coup organised by Blaise Compaoré made Sankara President on 4 August 1983 at the age of 33. The rebellion by a military unit under Compaoré started in Pô and led to Thomas Sankara's release from prison and ascension to the presidency.

The *coup d'état* was supported by Libya which was, at the time, on the verge of war with France in Chad.

Sankara saw himself as a revolutionary and was inspired by the examples of Fidel Castro, Che Guevara and Ghana's military ruler Jerry Rawlings. As President, he promoted the "Democratic and Popular Revolution" (*Révolution démocratique et populaire*, or RDP). The ideology of the revolution was defined by Sankara as anti-imperialist in a speech, the *Discours d'orientation politique* (DOP) on 2 October 1983. The speech was written by his close associate Valère Somé. Sankara's policy was oriented towards fighting corruption, promoting reforestation. averting famine, and making education and health main priorities.

Abolition of chiefs' privileges

The government suppressed many of the powers held by

tribal chiefs such as their right to receive tribute payment and obligatory labour. The CDRs (*Comités de Défense de la Révolution*) were formed as popular mass organisations and were armed. Sankara's government also initiated a form of military conscription with the SERNAPO (*Service National et Populaire*). Both were a counterweight to the power of the army.

In 1984, on the first anniversary of his rise to power, Thomas Sankara renamed the country Burkina Faso, meaning "the land of upright people" in Mòoré (the Mossi language) and Djula, the two major languages of the country. He also gave it a new flag and wrote a new national anthem, *Une Seule Nuit* (also known as *L'Hymne de la victoire* or *Ditanyè*), which replaced the *Hymne Nationale Voltaïque* or national anthem of Upper Volta.

Women's rights and AIDS

"The revolution and women's liberation go together. We do not talk of women's emancipation as an act of charity or because of a surge of human compassion. It is a basic necessity for the triumph of the revolution. Women hold up the other half of the sky." — Thomas Sankara

Improving women's status was one of Sankara's explicit goals and his government included a large number of women, an unprecedented policy priority in West Africa. His government banned female genital mutilation, forced marriages and polygamy; while appointing females to high government positions and encouraging them to work outside the home and stay in school even if pregnant. Sankara also promoted contraception and encouraged husbands to go to market and prepare meals to experience for themselves the conditions faced by women. Furthermore, Sankara was the first African leader to appoint women to major cabinet positions and to recruit them actively for the military.

298

Sankara's administration was also the first African government to publicly recognise the AIDS epidemic as a major threat to Africa.

Second Agacher strip war

In 1985, Burkina Faso organised a general population census. During the census, some Fula camps in Mali were visited by mistake by Burkinabé census agents. The Malian government claimed that the act was a violation of its sovereignty on the Agacher strip.

Following efforts by Mali asking African leaders to pressure Sankara, tensions erupted on Christmas Day 1985 in a war that lasted five days and killed about 100 people (most victims were civilians killed by a bomb dropped on the marketplace in Ouahigonya by a Malian MiG plane). The conflict is known as the "Christmas war" in Burkina Faso.

Personal image and popularity

Sankara had an array of original initiatives that contributed to his popularity and brought some international media attention to the Burkinabé revolution:

Solidarity

He sold off the government fleet of Mercedes cars and made the Renault 5 (the cheapest car sold in Burkina Faso at that time) the official service car of the ministers.

He reduced the salaries of all public servants, including his own, and forbade the use of government chauffeurs and first-class airline tickets.

He redistributed land from the feudal landlords and gave it directly to the peasants. Wheat production rose in just three years from 1700 kilogrammes per hectare to

3800 kilogrammes per hectare, making the country self-sufficient in food.

He opposed foreign aid, saying that "he who feeds you, controls you."

He spoke eloquently in forums like the Organisation of African Unity (OAU) against continued neo-colonialist penetration of Africa through Western trade and finance.

He called for a united front of African nations to repudiate their foreign debt. He argued that the poor and exploited did not have an obligation to repay money to the rich and exploiting.

In Ouagadougou, Sankara converted the army's provisioning store into a state-owned supermarket open to everyone (the first supermarket in the country).

He forced civil servants to pay one month's salary to public projects.

He refused to use the air conditioning in his office on the grounds that such luxury was not available to anyone but a handful of Burkinabes.

As President, he lowered his salary to only $450 a month and limited his possessions to a car, four bikes, three guitars, a fridge and a broken freezer.

Style

A motorcyclist himself, he formed an all-women motorcycle personal guard.

He required public servants to wear a traditional tunic woven from Burkinabe cotton and sewn by Burkinabe craftsmen.

He was known for jogging unaccompanied through Ougadougou in his track suit and posing in his tailored military fatigues, with his mother-of-pearl pistol.

When asked why he didn't want his portrait hung in public places, as was the norm for other African leaders, Sankara replied "There are seven million Thomas Sankaras."

An accomplished guitarist, he wrote the new national anthem himself.

"Thomas knew how to show his people that they could become dignified and proud through will power, courage, honesty and work. What remains above all of my husband is his integrity." — Mariam Sankara, Thomas' widow.

"Africa's Che Guevara"

"Che Guevara taught us we could dare to have confidence in ourselves, confidence in our abilities. He instilled in us the conviction that struggle is our only recourse. He was a citizen of the free world that together we are in the process of building. That is why we say that Che Guevara is also African and Burkinabè." — Thomas Sankara.

Sankara, who is often referred to as "Africa's Che Guevara", emulated Guevara (1928–1967) in both style and substance. Stylistically, Sankara emulated Guevara by preferring to wear a starred beret and military fatigues, living ascetically with few possessions, and getting a small salary after he came to power.

Both men also considered themselves allies of Fidel Castro (Sankara was visited by Castro in 1987), spoke fluent French, are well known for having ridden motorcycles, and are often cited as effectively utilising their charisma to motivate their followers.

Substantively, Guevara and Sankara were both Marxist revolutionaries who believed in armed revolution against imperialism and monopoly capitalism, denounced neo-colonialism before the United Nations, carried out agrarian land reform and literacy campaigns as key parts of their agenda, and utilised revolutionary tribunals and CDR's against counter-revolutionaries.

Both men were also murdered in their late thirties (Guevara when he was 39, Sankara 38) by opponents, with

Sankara coincidentally giving a speech marking and honouring the 20th anniversary of Che Guevara's 9 October 1967 execution one week before his own assassination on 15 October 1987.

Assassination

"Sankara's assassins were guided by imperialism which could not allow a man with the ideas and actions of Sankara to lead a country on a continent so exploited for hundreds of years by international imperialism, colonialism and neo-colonial governments that do their bidding. Sankara's political ideas will endure like those of Patrice Lumumba of Congo and Amilcar Cabral of Guinea-Bissau, also assassinated by traitors at the behest of the empire." — Ulises Estrada, a key organiser of Che Guevara's 1966-67 guerrilla mission to Bolivia.

On 15 October 1987, Sankara was killed by an armed gang with twelve other officials in a *coup d'état* organised by his former colleague, Blaise Compaoré.

Deterioration in relations with neighbouring countries was one of the reasons given to "justify" the coup and apparently even Sankara's assassination, with Compaoré stating that Sankara jeopardised foreign relations with the former colonial power, France, neighbouring Ivory Coast and other countries in the region, obviously including Mali, a country which fought a five-day war with Burkina Faso when Sankara was president.

Prince Yormie Johnson, a former Liberian warlord once an ally of Liberia's main rebel leader Charles Taylor, told Liberia's Truth and Reconciliation Commission (TRC) that the military coup in Burkina Faso which led to Sankara's assassination was engineered by Charles Taylor.

After the coup and although Sankara was known to be dead, some CDRs mounted an armed resistance to the army for several days.

Sankara's body was dismembered and was quickly buried in an unmarked grave, while his widow and two children fled the nation.

Compaoré immediately reversed nationalisation, overturned nearly all of Sankara's policies, returned the country back under the IMF fold, and ultimately spurned most of Sankara's legacy.

A week before his death, Sankara gave what would become his own epitaph, remarking that "while revolutionaries as individuals can be murdered, you cannot kill ideas."

Legacy

"Africa and the world are yet to recover from Sankara's assassination, just as we have yet to recover from the loss of Patrice Lumumba Kkwame Nkrumah, Eduardo Mondlane, Amilcar Cabral, Steve Biko, Samora Machel, and most recently John Garang, to name only a few. While malevolent forces have not used the same methods to eliminate each of these great pan-Africanists, they have been guided by the same motive: to keep Africa in chains."— Antonio de Figueiredo, February 2008.

Twenty years later, on 15 October 2007, Thomas Sankara was commemorated around the world in ceremonies that took place in Burkina Faso, Mali, Senegal, Niger, Tanzania, Burundi, France, Canada, and the United States.

List of works

Thomas Sankara Speaks: The Burkina Faso Revolution, 1983-87, by Thomas Sankara, Pathfinder Press, 1988
We Are the Heirs of the World's Revolutions: Speeches

from the Burkina Faso Revolution 1983-87, by Thomas Sankara, Pathfinder Press, 2007

Women's Liberation and the African Freedom Struggle, by Thomas Sankara, Pathfinder Press, 1990.

Nnamdi Azikiwe

Benjamin Nnamdi Azikiwe (November 16, 1904 – May 11, 1996), usually referred to as Nnamdi Azikiwe and popularly known as "Zik," was one of the leading figures of modern Nigerian nationalism who became the first president of Nigeria when Nigeria won independence from the United Kingdom on 1 October 1960.

Early life

Azikiwe was born on 16 November 1904 in Zungeru, Northern Nigeria. His parents were Igbo, one of the three largest ethnic groups, or "nations within a nation," in Nigeria; the other two being Hausa-Fualni in the north, and the Yoruba in the southwest.

Nnamdi Azikiwe's father was Obed-Edom Chukwuemeka Azikiwe (1879–1958), a clerk in the British colonial government. His mother was Rachel Ogbenyeanu Azikiwe.

Nnamdi means "My father is alive" in the Igbo language.

After studying at Hope Wadell Training Institution, Calabar, in Eastern Nigeria, Azikiwe went to the United States for further education.

He attended Howard University in Washington, D.C., and later went to Lincoln University, Pennsylvania, and graduated in 1930. He obtained a master's degree in 1933 from the University of Pennsylvania and worked as an instructor at Lincoln before returning to Nigeria.

Kwame Nkrumah also went to Lincoln University and

to the University of Pennsylvania but after Azikiwe did. In fact, when Nkrumah left Ghana in 1935 to go to the United States, Azikiwe had already returned to Africa.

Newspaper career

After teaching at Lincoln University, Azikiwe became, in November 1934, the editor of the *African Morning Post*, a daily newspaper in Accra, Ghana. In that position he promoted a pro-African nationalist agenda which angered the colonialists. Yuri Smertin, in his work, *Kwame Nkrumah* (Moscow, 1977), described Azikiwe's writings in the *African Morning Post* in the following terms:

"In his passionately denunciatory articles and public statements he censured the existing colonial order: the restrictions on the Africans' right to express their opinions, and racial discrimination. He also criticised those Africans who belonged to the 'elite' of colonial society and favoured retaining the existing order, as they regarded it as the basis of their well being."

As a result of publishing an article on 15 May 1936 titled "Has the African a God?" written by I.T.A. Wallace-Johnson of Sierra Leone, Azikiwe was brought to trial on charges of sedition. Although he was found guilty of the charges and sentenced to six months in prison, he was acquitted on appeal.

He returned to Lagos, Nigeria, in 1937 and founded the *West African Pilot* which he used as a vehicle to foster Nigerian nationalism. He founded the Zik Group of Newspapers, publishing multiple newspapers in cities across the country. And he became active in the Nigerian Youth Movement (NYM), the first genuinely nationalist organisation in Nigeria.

However, in 1941 he backed Samuel Akinsanya to be

305

the NYM candidate for a vacant seat in the Legislative Council, but the executive selected Ernest Ikoli instead. Azikiwe and Akinsanya both resigned from the NYM among accusations of discrimination against non-Lagos members, taking most non-Yoruba members with them.

Political career

After a successful journalism enterprise, Azikiwe entered into politics, co-founding the National Council of Nigeria and the Cameroons (NCNC) alongside Herbert Macaulay in 1944. He became the secretary-general of the NCNC in 1946 and was elected to Legislative Council of Nigeria the following year.

In 1951, he became the leader of the Opposition to the government of Obafemi Awolowo in the Western Region's House of Assembly.

In 1952, he moved to the Eastern Region, the homeland of his people, the Igbo, and was elected to the position of chief minister. He became premier of the Eastern Region (Eastern Nigeria) in 1954.

On 16 November 1960, he became the governor-general of Nigeria and on the same day became the first Nigerian named to the Queen's Privy Council. With the proclamation of a republic in 1963, he became the first president of Nigeria. Abubakar Tafawa Balewa became the first prime minister when the country won independence on 1 October 1960.

On 15 January 1966, soldiers overthrew the government. About a year-and-a-half later, on 30 May 1967, the Eastern Region seceded from the federation and declared independence as the Republic of Biafra. Azikiwe, an Easterner himself, became a spokesman for the nascent republic and an adviser to its leader Chukwuemeka Odumegwu Ojukwu.

After the war, Zik served as Chancellor of Lagos

University from 1972 to 1976. In 1978, he joined the Nigerian People's Party (NPP), making unsuccessful bids for the presidency in 1979 and in 1983. He left politics involuntarily after a military coup on 31 December 1983 led by Major-General Muhammadu Buhari overthrew the democratically elected government of President Shehu Shagari.

Azikiwe died on 11 May 1996 at the University of Nigeria Teaching Hospital in Enugu, Enugu State, eastern Nigeria, after a protracted illness. He was 91.

His time in politics spanned most of his adult life and he was referred to by admirers as "The Great Zik of Africa." His motto in politics was "talk I listen, you listen I talk."

The writings of Azikiwe spawned a philosophy of African liberation, Zikism, which identifies five concepts for Africa's movement towards freedom: spiritual balance, social regeneration, economic determination, mental emancipation, and political resurgence.

Places named after Azikiwe include the Nnamdi Azikiwe International Airport in Nigeri'a federal capital, Abuja; the Nnamdi Azikiwe Stadium in Enugu, the Nnamdi Azikiwe University in Awka, Anambra State in eastern Nigeria; Nnamdi Azikiwe Press Centre, Dodan Barracks, Obalende, Ikoyi, Lagos. His portrait adorns Nigeria's five hundred naira currency note.

Prime Minister Abubakar Tafawa Balewa once said: "Nigeria can never adequately reward Dr. Azikiwe" for his nationalism.

Achievements

Azikiwe was inducted into the prestigious Agbalanze society as Nnayelugo in 1946, a customary recognition for men of significant accomplishment. Then, in 1962, he became a second-rank red cap nobleman (Ndichie Okwa), as Oziziani Obi. In 1970, he was installed as Owelle-

Osowa-Anya, making him a first-rank red cap nobleman (Ndichie Ume).

In 1960, Queen Elizabeth II awarded him the title of Privy Councilor to the Queen of England.

He was conferred with the highest national honour of Grand Commander of the Federal Republic (GCFR) by the Federal Republic of Nigeria in 1980.

He had fourteen honorary degrees from Nigerian, American and Liberian universities. The schools include Lincoln University, Storer College, Howard University, Michigan State University, University of Nigeria-Nsukka, University of Lagos, Ahmadu Bello University, University of Ibadan, Nnamdi Azikiwe University-Awka, and the University of Liberia.

Sports

Azikiwe was actively involved in sports at every stage of his life and was successful in a lot of events that he participated in. They include Welterweight Boxing Champion, Storer College (1925–27); High Jump champion, Howard University Inter-Scholastic Games (1926); Gold Medalist in Cross Country, Storer College (1927); Back-stroke Swimming Champion and No. 3 swimmer in Freestyle Relay team, Howard University (1928); Captain, Lincoln University Soccer Team (1930); Winner Two Miles Run, Central Inter-Collegiate Athletic Association Championships at Hampton Institute Virginia (1931); Bronze Medalist, Richmond Cross Country Marathon (1931); Gold Medalist in the 1,000 yard run, One Mile Run and Three Mile Run, Catedonian Games in Brooklyn, NY (1932); Silver Trophy winner in the Half Mile race, and Silver Cup winner in the One Mile Race, Democratic Field Day Championships, New Haven, Connecticut (1933); Runner-up (with G.K. Dorgu) at the Lagos Tennis Men's Double Championships (Division B

1938); anchor man for the ZAC team which won the 50 yards Freestyle Relay at the Lagos Swimming Championships (1939).

He won letters in athletics (Lincoln University) and cross country (Storer College and Lincoln University), swimming (Howard University), and football (soccer) (Lincoln University); entered to compete in the Half-Mile Race and One-Mile run at the British Empire Games to represent Nigeria but was rejected by the A.A.A. of Great Britain on technical grounds (he dropped his Christian name, "Benjamin"); and founded (with M.R.B. Ottun) the Zik's Athletic Club to promote athletics, boxing, cricket, football, swimming and tennis in Nigeria.

Politics

During his lifetime, he held several political posts, especially in Nigeria. They include Executive Committee Member of Mambili Party, Accra (1935–37); General Secretary of National Council of Nigeria and the Cameroons - NCNC (1944–45); President of the NCNC (1946–60); Vice-President of the Nigerian National Democratic Party (1947–60); Member for Lagos in the Legislative Council of Nigeria (1947–51); Member for Lagos and Leader of the Opposition in the Western House of Assembly (1952–53) Member for Onitsha in the Eastern House of Assembly (1954–60); Minister of Internal Affairs (Jan.–September 1954); Minister of Internal Affairs, Eastern Region (1954); Member of His Excellency Privy Council, Eastern Nigeria (1954–59); Primer of Eastern Nigeria (1954–59); President of the Senate of the Federation (Jan.-November 1960); Governor-General and Commander-in-Chief of Nigeria (1960–63); President of the Republic of Nigeria (1963–1966); and Chairman and Presidential candidate of the Nigeria People's Party (1978–83).

Professional world

He made a name for himself in the professional world. He was a Third-class Clerk, Treasury Department, Lagos (1921–1924); Recruit, Gold Coast Police Force (Jul.-September 1924); Solicitor Clerk to the late Mr. Justice Graham Paul at Calabar (Jan.-Aug. 1925); Instructor in Political Science, Lincoln University (1931–34); University Correspondent for the Baltimore Afro-American (1928–34); General and Sports Correspondent for the Philadelphia Tribune (1928–34); Editor-in Chief of the West African Pilot (1937–45); Correspondent for the Associated Negro Press (1944–47); Correspondent for Reuters (1944–46); Managing Director of Zik's Press Limited printers and publishers of the *West African Pilot* (Lagos), *Eastern Guardian* (Port Harcourt), *Nigerian Spokesman* (Onitsha), *Southern Nigeria Defender* (Ibadan), *Daily Comet* (Kano), and *Eastern Sentinel* (Enugu); Managing Director of Comet Press Limited (1945–53); Chairman of West African Pilot Limited and the Associated Newspapers of Nigeria Limited and six other limited liability companies (1952–53); Chairman, Nigerian Real Estate Corporation Limited (1952–53); etc.

Societies and organisations

He was a member of many organisations and societies, including Anti-Slavery Society for the protection of Human Rights; Phi Beta Sigma fraternity (Alpha Chapter and Mu Chapter); West African Students Union; Onitsha Improvement Union; Zik's Athletic Club; Ekine Sekiapu Society of Buguma, Kalabari; St. John's Lodge of England; Royal Economic Society; Royal Anthropological Institute; British Association for the Advancement of Science; American Society of International Law;

American Anthropological Association; American Political Science Society; American Ethnological Society; Amateur Athletic Association of Nigeria; Nigerian Swimming Association, Nigerian Boxing Board of Control; Nigerian Cricket Association; Ibo State Union; and Nigerian Table Tennis Association; Nigeria Olympic Committee and British Empire and Commonwealth Games Association.

Works

Zik (1961)
My Odyssey: An Autobiography (1971)
Renascent Africa (1973)
Liberia in World Politics (1931)

Abubakar Tafawa Balewa

Alhaji Sir Abubakar Tafawa Balewa (December 1912 – January 15, 1966) was the only prime minister of Nigeria. First trained as a teacher, he became a vocal leader for Northern Nigerian interests as one of the few educated northerners. He was also one of the leaders who strongly supported the formation of the Organisation of African Unity (OAU) in his capacity as the head of Nigerian federal government when the OAU was founded in May 1963 in Addis Ababa, Ethiopia.

Early life and career

Abubakar Balewa was born in Bauchi in Northern Nigeria. Bauchi is now a state. It was until 1976 a province in the then North-Eastern state of Nigeria. During the colonial era up to independence, it formed part of the Bauchi-Plateau of the then Northern Region until the 1967 when 12 states were created for the whole country, the North-Eastern state – comprising the

311

provinces of Bauchi, Borno, and Adamawa – being one of them.

The Abubakar Tafawa Balewa is located in the capital city Bauchi.

The son of a Bageri Muslim district head in the Bauchi divisional district of Lere, Abubakar Tafawa Balewa started early education at the Koranic school in Bauchi and, like most of his contemporaries, studied at Katsina College where he earned a teaching certificate.

He returned to Bauchi to teach at Bauchi Middle School.

In 1944, along with a few teachers from Northern Nigeria, he was chosen to study for a year at the University of London's Institute of Education. Upon returning to Nigeria, he became an inspector of schools for the colonial administration and later entered politics.

He was elected in 1946 to the colony's Northern House of Assembly and to the federal Legislative Assembly in 1947. As a legislator, he was a vocal advocate for the rights of Northern Nigeria and, together with Alhaji Ahmadu Bello who held the hereditary title of *Sardauna* of Sokoto, founded the Northern People's Congress (NPC), one of the three major political parties in Nigeria. The other two were the National Council of Nigeria and the Cameroons (NCNC) renamed in 1959 the National Council of Nigerian Citizens, dominant in Eastern Nigeria; and the Action Group with its stronghold in Western Nigeria.

From self-government to independence

Balewa administration

Balewa entered the federal government in 1952 as minister of works and later served as minister of transport. In 1957, he was elected chief minister, forming a coalition government between the NPC and the NCNC. He retained the post as prime minister when Nigeria won independence in 1960 and was re-elected in 1964.

Before Nigeria's independence, a constitutional conference in 1954 had adopted a regional political framework for the country, with all regions given a considerable amount of political freedom but short of autonomy.

The three regions then were composed of diverse ethnic and cultural groups. The regional premiers or prime ministers and some prominent leaders of the regions later took on a policy of guiding their regions against political encroachment from other regional leaders. Later on, this political environment influenced the Balewa administration. His term in office was turbulent, with regional factionalism constantly threatening his government.

However, as prime minister of the Nigerian federation, he played important roles in the country and on the continent. He was an important leader in the formation of the Organization of African Unity (OAU) and in creating a cooperative relationship between Nigeria and the former French colonies in Africa.

He was also instrumental in negotiations between Moise Tshombe, the leader of secesionist Katanga Province in Congo, and the leaders of Congo's central government during the Congo crisis of 1960–1964.

Balewa also led a vocal protest against the Sharpeville massacre of 1960 in South Africa and joined Commonwealth leaders such as Nkrumah and Nyerere who wanted South Africa to leave the Commonwealth in 1961. Nyerere stated in August 1960 that his country Tanganyika would not join the Commonwealth if apartheid South Africa remained a member.

However, a treason charge and conviction against one of the main leaders of the Western Region of Nigeria, Chief Obafemi Awolowo, led to protests and condemnation of Balewa and the federal government from many of his supporters. The 1965 election in the Western Region later produced violent protests. Rioting and violence were soon synchronous with what was perceived as inordinate political encroachment and an over-exuberant election outcome for Awolowo's Western opponents.

From 1960 to 1961, Balewa also served as Nigeria's minister of foreign affairs while retaining his post as federal prime minister. He relinquished his post as foreign affairs minister in favour of Jaja Wachuku who served in that position 1961 to 1965. And it is Jaja Wachuku who is acknowledged as Nigeria's first minister of foreign affairs.

Honours

In January 1960, Balewa was knighted by Elizabeth II as a Knight Commander of the Order of the British Empire. He was also awarded an honorary doctorate by the University of Sheffield, UK, in May 1960.

Overthrow

Balewa was overthrown and assassinated in a military coup on 15 January 1966. The coup was carried out mianly by Igbo junior officers of Igbo. Other leaders who were executed included Balewa's mentor and old political colleague, Ahmadu Bello who was during that time – since independence – the premier of Northern Nigeria. The premier of the Western Region, Samuel Akintola, was also killed in the coup.

Balewa's body was discovered by a roadside near the federal capital, Lagos, in Western Nigeria, six days after he was overthrown and executed. He was buried in Bauchi, his homeland.

The university in Baruchi, Abubakar Tafawa Balewa

University, is named in his honour not only as federal prime minister and the first one to hold that position at independence, but also as the most prominent person who came from Baruchi.

Odumegwu Ojukwu

Chukwuemeka Odumegwu-Ojukwu (born 4 November 1933) is most remembered as the leader of secessionist Biafra. He is also the one who announced on 30 May 1967 the establishment of Biafra as an independent state in the southeastern part of Nigeria which was formerly the Eastern Region. The secession triggered the Nigerian civil war (July 1967 – January 1970).

Early life and education

Chukwuemeka Odumegwu-Ojukwu was born on 4 November 1933 in the town of Zungeru, Northern Nigeria, to Louis Phillippe Odumegwu Ojukwu, a businessman from Nnewi in southeastern Nigeria. His father was in the transport business who benefited from the economic boom during World War II. He became a millionaire. He died in 1966 and was one of the richest men in Nigeria.

Emeka, as he was fondly called, first went to school in Lagos in southwestern Nigeria. In 1944, the young Ojukwu was briefly jailed for attacking a white British colonial teacher who was humiliating a black woman at King's College in Lagos, an event which generated widespread coverage in local newspapers.

At 13, his father sent him to study in Britain, first at Epsom College in Surrey. He later earned a masters degree in history at Lincoln College, Oxford University. Thereafter, he returned to colonial Nigeria. That was in 1956.

Early career and the coups

He joined the civil service in Eastern Nigeria as an administrative officer at Udi in present-day Enugu State. In 1957, within months of working with the colonial civil service, he left and joined the military as one of the first and few university graduates to join the army; the other ones were O. Olutoye who joined the army in 1956; E. A. Ifeajuna and C. O. Rotimi, in 1960; and A. Ademoyega in 1962.

Ojukwu's background and good education guaranteed his promotion. The Nigerian army had 250 officers. Only 15 were Nigerians. The first Nigerian to be commissioned as an officer, Lieutenant L. V. Ugboma, left the army in 1948. Ojukwu rose fast and becoming quartermaster-general.

After serving in the United Nations' peacekeeping force in Congo under Major-General Johnson Thomas Umunnakwe Aguiyi-Ironsi, Ojuwkwu was promoted to Lieutenant-Colonel in 1964 and posted to Kano, Northern Nigeria, where he became in charge of the 5th Battalion of the Nigerian Army.

He was in Kano when Major Patrick Chukwuma Kaduna Nzeogwu on 15 January 1966 executed and announced the bloody military coup in Kaduna, also in Northern Nigeria.

It is to Ojukwu's credit that the coup lost much steam in the North where it had succeeded. Ojukwu supported the forces loyal to the Supreme Commander of the Nigerian Armed Forces, Major-General Aguiyi-Ironisi. Major Nzeogwu was in control of Kaduna but the coup had flopped in other parts of the country. He surrendered.

General Aguiyi-Ironsi took over the leadership of the country and became Nigeria's first military head of state. On 17 January 17 1966, he appointed military governors for the four regions; another region, the Mid-West, was created in 1963, carved out of the Western Region, to satisfy local demands and defuse tensions which could have led to major conflict had the people not been given their own region.

Lt. Col. Odumegwu-Ojukwu was appointed military governor of the Eastern Region; Lt.-Cols Hassan Usman Katsina (North), Francis Adekunle Fajuyi (West), and David Akpode Ejoor (Mid-West).

Together, they formed the Supreme Military Council to rule Nigeria. Brigadier B.A.O Ogundipe was appointed chief of staff, Supreme Headquarters; Lt. Col. Yakubu Gowon, chief of staff, Army HQ; Commodore J. E. A. Wey, head of the Nigerian Navy; and Lt. Col. George T. Kurubo, head of the Air Force.

By 29 May 1966, things quickly fell apart. Massacres took place in Northern Nigeria in which Nigerians of southeastern origin, most of them Igbo, were targeted and killed. This caused problems for Ojukwu as the military governor of Eastern Nigeria. He did everything in his power to prevent reprisals and even encouraged people to return to the North, as assurances for their safety had been given by his supposed colleagues in Northern Nigeria and even in the Western Region where Igbos and other Easterners were also not safe.

On 29 July 1966, a group of army officers of Northern origin, notably Majors Murtala Ramat Rufai Muhammed, Theophilus Yakubu Danjuma, and Martin Adamu, led the majority of the soldiers of Northern origin in a mutiny which was later acknowledged as a counter-coup. The supreme commander, General Aguiyi-Ironsi, and his host Colonel Fajuyi, the military governor of Western Nigeria, were abducted and killed in Ibadan, capital of the Western Region.

Ojukwu insisted that the military hierarchy must be preserved; in which case, Brigadier Ogundipe – not Colonel Gowon – would take over the leadership of the

317

army and of the country. But Ogundipe no longer had the stomach to deal with the army. He was easily convinced to step aside and was posted to the Nigerian High Commission in London. Gowon became Nigeria's military head of state. Ojukwu refused to accept that. But he had no choice. He had to deal with Gowon as the New Nigerian leader.

Biafra

As the Nigerian civil war went on, many attempts, including intervention by other African leaders, were made to end the conflict. The military governors of Nigeria ended up in Aburi, Ghana, in January 1967 for a peace conference hosted by Ghana's military head of state, General Joseph Ankrah.

They signed the Aburi Accords which stipulated, among other things, that the regions should move further apart and that soldiers in the army should be stationed in their regions of origin to avoid conflict. Ojukwu tried to implement the agreement but Gowon reneged on his promise to do so.

On 30 May 1967, Colonel Odumegwu-Ojukwu declared Eastern Nigeria a sovereign state to be known as Biafra:

"Having mandated me to proclaim on your behalf, and in your name, that Eastern Nigeria be a sovereign independent Republic, now, therefore I, Lieutenant Colonel Chukwuemeka Odumegwu-Ojukwu, Military Governor of Eastern Nigeria, by virtue of the authority, and pursuant to the principles recited above, do hereby solemnly proclaim that the territory and region known as and called Eastern Nigeria together with her continental shelf and territorial waters, shall, henceforth, be an independent sovereign state of the name and title of The

Republic of Biafra."

On 6 July 1967, Gowon declared war and attacked Biafra. For 30 bloody months, the war raged on. Ojukwu, knew that the odds against the new republic were overwhelming.

Most European states recognised the illegitimacy of the Nigerian military rule and banned all supplies of arms. In contrast, the British government substantially increased its supplies to the Nigerian federal military government and even sent army and air force advisors.

After three years of fighting and starvation, a hole did appear in the Biafran front lines and this was exploited by the Nigerian military. As it became obvious that all was lost, Ojukwu was convinced to leave the country to avoid capture and possible assassination.

On 9 January 1970, Ojukwu handed over power to his second-in-command, Chief of General Staff Major-General Philip Effiong. He left on January 11th for the Ivory Coast where President Felix Houphöuet-Biogny – who had recognised Biafra on 14 May 1968 – granted him political asylum.

After Biafra

After 13 years in exile, the Nigerian federal government under President Shehu Aliyu Usman Shagari granted an official pardon to Odumegwu-Ojukwu and opened the road for his return in 1982.

The people of Nnewi gave him the title of Ikemba which means "power of the people." And Igbos in general called him Dikedioramma which means "beloved hero."

He also unsuccessfully ran for president of Nigeria but remained a hero to many of his people, the Igbo.

He died on 26 November 2011 at a hospital in London, England. He was 78. His death was attributed to complications from a stroke for which he had been hospitalised since December 2010.

According to a report by The Associated Press (AP) from Lagos, Nigeria, "Breakaway Biafra Leader Dies at 78," reproduced by CBS News, 26 November 2011:

"Ojukwu spent 13 years in exile, coming home after he was unconditionally pardoned in 1982. He returned to politics, but lost a race for a senate seat. Authorities sent him to a maximum-security prison for a year when Nigeria suffered yet another of the military coups that punctuated life after independence.

He later wrote his memoirs and lived the quiet life of an elder statesman until he unsuccessfully challenged incumbent Olusegun Obasanjo for the presidency in 2003. Obasanjo served as a colonel in the Biafran war and gave the final statement on rebel-controlled radio announcing the conflict's end.

Despite the long and costly civil war, Nigeria remains torn by internal conflict. Tens of thousands have died in riots pitting Christians against Muslims in a country of more than 160 million people. Militant groups attack foreign oil firms in the oil-rich Niger Delta while criminal gangs kidnap the middle class. Poverty continues to grind the country.

The Igbos, meanwhile, continue to suffer political isolation in the country. While an Igbo man recently became one of the country's top military officers, others say they've been locked out of higher office over lingering mistrust from the war.

Some in the former breakaway region still hold out hope for their own voice, even their own country despite the cataclysmic losses.

As did Ojukwu himself.

'Biafra,' Ojukwu told journalists in 2006, 'is always an alternative.'"

And as Robert D. McFadden stated in his report,

"Odumegwu Ojukwu, Breakaway Biafra Leader, Dies at 78," in *The New York Times*, 26 November 2011:

"Odumegwu Ojukwu, an Oxford-educated Nigerian colonel who proclaimed the Republic of Biafra in 1967 and led his Ibo people into a secessionist war that cost more than a million lives, many of them starved children whose skeletal images shocked the world, has died at a hospital in London. He was 78.

International news reports quoted Maja Umeh, a spokesman for the All Progressive Grand Alliance Party in Nigeria, as confirming Mr. Ojukwu's death. The Associated Press said he died on Saturday, but Bloomberg News said the death occurred on Friday. The cause was not cited. Mr. Ojukwu had a stroke at his home in Enugu, Nigeria, in December 2010, and had since been under treatment in London.

Mr. Ojukwu was an unlikely militarist and a reluctant rebel: the sports-car-driving son of one of Nigeria's richest men, an urbane student of history and Shakespeare who read voraciously, wrote poetry, played tennis and, with his wealth and connections, might have been a business mogul or a worldly *rouge-et-noir* playboy.

But he spurned his father's offer of a business partnership, joined Nigeria's civil service and then its army in the turbulent last years of British colonial rule. And as maps of Africa were redrawn by forces of national and tribal self-determination, he became military governor of the Ibo homeland, one of three tribal regions, at a historic juncture.

At 33, he found himself at the vortex of simmering ethnic rivalries among Nigeria's Hausas in the north, Yorubas in the southwest and Ibos in the southeast. The largely Christian Ibos were envied as one of Africa's best-educated and most industrious peoples, possessed of much of Nigeria's oil wealth. Tensions finally exploded into assassinations, coups and a massacre of 30,000 Ibos by

321

Hausas and federal troops.

While he denounced the massacre and cited other Ibo grievances, Colonel Ojukwu for months resisted rising Ibo pressure for secession. He proposed a weak federation to separate Nigeria's three tribal regions politically. But Col. Yakubu Gowon, leader of the military government in Lagos, rejected the idea. A clash over federal taxation of the Ibo region's oil and coal industries precipitated the final break.

'Long live the Republic of Biafra,' Colonel Ojukwu proclaimed on May 30, 1967.

Five weeks later, civil war began when Nigerian military forces invaded the breakaway province. It was a lopsided war, with other nations supporting federal forces seeking to unify the country and Biafra standing virtually alone. Nigeria was Africa's most populous nation, with 57 million people, of which 8 million to 10 million were Ibos.

Poorly equipped and outnumbered four to one, Biafra's 25,000-member army held its own for months, supported by a citizenry that donated food, clothing and supplies. Colonel Ojukwu ran Biafra as a wartime democracy, fought alongside his troops and was said to be revered by his people.

He gave orders in a slow, deliberate baritone: native Igbo with an Oxford accent. Fond of Sibelius, he chose "Finlandia" as Biafra's national anthem. And he read Shakespeare. 'Hamlet was my favorite,' he told a *New York Times* correspondent. 'I wonder what the psychiatrists will make of that.'

Over a battle map he looked like a brooding Othello, with solemn eyes and a luxuriantly bearded countenance. He slept irregularly, sometimes working nonstop for days, taking a meal now and then, rarely touching alcohol but chain-smoking English cigarettes.

Tanzania, Zambia, the Ivory Coast and Gabon recognized Biafra, and France and other nations provided covert aid. But the Soviet Union, Egypt and even Britain, after a period of neutrality, supplied weapons and advisers to Nigeria. The United States, officially neutral, provided diplomatic and relief coordination aid. But after 15 months of war, Biafra's 29,000 square miles had been reduced to 5,000, and deaths had soared.

As crops burned and refugees streamed away from advancing federal forces, much of the population was cut off from food supplies. As the 30-month civil war moved onto the world stage as one of the first televised wars, millions around the globe were stunned by pictures of Biafran babies with distended bellies and skeletal children who were succumbing to famine by the thousands daily in the war's final stages.

Colonel Ojukwu appealed to the world to save his people. International relief agencies responded, and scores of cargo planes ferried food in to the encircled Biafrans, but airlifts were woefully inadequate. Deaths from starvation were estimated at more than 6,000 a day, and postwar studies suggested that a third of Biafra's surviving preschoolers — nearly 500,000 — were malnourished at war's end.

In January 1970, secessionist resistance was crushed and its leader, by then a general, fled into exile in Ivory Coast and London. Granted a presidential pardon after 13 years, he returned to Nigeria in 1982 and was welcomed by enormous crowds. He became a Lagos businessman and ran unsuccessfully for president several times, but remained a hero in the eyes of many of his countrymen.

The legacies of the war were terrible. Deaths from fighting, disease and starvation were estimated by international relief agencies at one million to three million. Besides widespread destruction of hospitals, schools, homes and businesses, Ibos faced discrimination in employment, housing and political rights. Nigeria reabsorbed Biafra, however, and the region was rebuilt over 20 years as its oil-based economy prospered anew.

Chukwuemeka Odumegwu Ojukwu (pronounced chukwoo-MA-ka oh-doo-MAG-woo oh-JU-kwoo) was born on Nov. 4, 1933, in Zungeru, Nigeria. From modest beginnings, his father, Sir Louis Phillipe Odumegwu Ojukwu, had made fortunes in transportation and real estate, and was Nigeria's wealthiest entrepreneur when he died in 1966.

The boy nicknamed Emeka attended Kings College in Lagos, Nigeria's most prestigious secondary school; Epsom College, a boys' prep school in Surrey, and Lincoln College, Oxford, where he graduated with honors in history in 1955. Classmates said he was popular, dressed stylishly, drove a bright red MG sports car and loved discussions of Machiavelli, Hobbes, Louis XIV and Shakespeare.

He had three wives. His first, Njideka, a law student he met at Oxford and wed in 1962, died in 2010. His second, Stella Onyeador, died in 2009. He married Bianca Odinaka Onoh, a former beauty queen and businesswoman 34 years his junior, in 1994. Returning to Nigeria in 1956, he rejected his father's business overtures, worked on development in remote villages, and in 1957 joined the army. He called himself an amateur soldier, but rose rapidly in the ranks after Nigeria gained independence in 1960. In 1966, he became military governor of the Ibo region, and declared Biafran independence after repression enveloped his people.

He sometimes compared Biafrans to Israelis. 'The Israelis are hard-working, enterprising people,' he told a visitor to his besieged field headquarters in 1969. 'So are we. They've suffered from pogroms. So have we. In many ways, we share the same promise and the same problems.'"

In literature

Frederick Forsyth, sometimes cynically referred to as a

friend of General Ojukwu, was a journalist at the time of the Nigerian civil war. He was the first journalist to write of the events direct from the Niger Delta, publishing the facts of the events in his illuminating book The Biafra Story: *The making of an African Legend.*

Forsyth later wrote a biography about Ojukwu entitled Emeka. It was published in 1982.

Ojukwu also gave some inspiration to the creation of the anonymous General character in Forsyth's novel *The Dogs of War* published in 1974.

In his collection *Wampeters, Foma & Granfalloons,* Kurt Vonnegut tells of his meeting Ojukwu and refers to him as "The Nigerian George Washington."

Yakubu Gowon

General Yakubu "Jack" Dan-Yumma Gowon (born 19 October 1934) was the head of the Nigerian federal military government from 1966 to 1975.

He came to power after a military coup and was overthrown in another.

During his rule, the Nigerian government stopped the Eastern Region from seceding from the Nigerian federation during the Nigerian civil war which was fought from 6 July 1967 to 15 January 1970.

Early life

Yakubu Gowon was a member of the Ngas tribe, also known as Angas, in what is now the Plateau State in a region known as the Middle Belt.

The term "Middle Belt" refers to the region of central Nigeria populated largely by minority ethnic groups. It has the largest number of minority ethnic groups in the country. They are mostly Christians and members of traditional religions with few Muslim converts. It stretches longitudinally across the country and is the fault line between Muslim north and Christian south.

Gowon's parents, Nde Yohanna and Matwok Kurnyang, left for Wusasa, Zaria, in Northern Nigeria, as Church Missionary Society (CMS) missionaries in the early days of his life.

Yakubu Gowon was the fifth of eleven children. He grew up in Zaria and had his early life and education there. He was a avery good athlete in school. He was the school football (soccer) goalkeeper, pole vaulter, and long distance runner. He broke the school mile record in his first year. He was also the boxing captain.

Early career and political ascent

Yakubu Gowon joined the Nigerian army in 1954. He was commissioned as a second-lieutenant on 19 October 1955, his 21st birthday.

He also attended the Royal Military Academy, Sandhurst, from 1955 to 1956; the Joint Staff College, Camberley, in 1962, and the Joint Staff College, Latimer, in 1965, all in the UK.

He saw action in Congo as part of the United Nations peace-keeping force in 1960 – 1961 and in 1963. He was a battalion commander by 1966. He was a lieutenant-colonel during that time.

Until that year, Gowon remained strictly a career soldier with no involvement in politics. Suddenly, he was thrust into leadership by the events which unfolded after the military coup in January 1966. His background as a northerner who was not a member of the largest ethnic groups in the north – Hausa and Fulani – and who was not a Muslim (he was a Christian) made him a safe choice to lead the country plagued by ethnic animosities, especially after the tragic events of that year.

In January 1966, he became Nigeria's youngest military

chief of staff at the age of 32 after a military coup by a group of mostly Igbo junior officers led by Major Chukwuma Kaduna Nzeogwu. Several high-ranking Northern army officers were killed during the coup, besides a number of civilian leaders including federal prime minister, Abubakar Tafawa Balewa, and the premiers of the Northern and Western regions.

Gowon, who was then a lieutenant-colonel, returned from his course at the Joint Staff College, Latimer, two days before the coup, a late arrival that possibly saved him from being on the hit list of the soldiers who overthrew the government.

The failure by Major-General Johnson Aguiyi Ironsi – he was the military head of state and Gowon, the chief of staff – to meet Northern demands for the prosecution of the coup plotters further inflamed anger in the North and among northerners elsewhere in the country. There was significant support for the coup in the Eastern Region and among some Yorubas in the Western Region.

Then came Decree Number 34 by the ruling Supreme Military Council (SMC) which was rightly or wrongly described as Ironsi's decree although he did not make that decision alone but with the support of the other members of the SMC. The decree proposed the abolition of the federal system of government in favour of a unitary state, a form of government which had long been advocated by the parties in the South: the National Council of Nigeria Citizens (NCNC) dominant in the Eastern Region and the Action Group dominant in the West.

The decree was wrongly interpreted by Northerners as a Southern (Eastern, Midwestern and Western Regions) attempt to takeover all levers of power in the country including the North.

The North lagged far behind the Western and Eastern regions in terms of education and development because of its conservatism and refusal to accept European education early while concentrating on Islamic teachings of the

Koran. In remarkable contrast, Igbos enthusiastically accepted western education first provided by the missionaries, as did Yorubas in the Western Region. As a result of that, it was Igbos and Yorubas who were already in the federal civil service in large numbers by the time the country won independence in 1960.

On 29 July 1966, while Ironsi was staying at the house of the governor of the Western Region in Ibadan, northern troops led by Major Theophilus Danjuma and Captain Martin Adamu stormed the building, seized Ironsi and his host, Lieutenant Colonel Adenkule Fajuyi (governor of the West), had the two men stripped naked, flogged, beaten and tortured, and finally shot.

Other northern troops led by Lieutenant-Colonel Murtala Mohammed, the real leader of the counter-coup and who later succeeded Yakubu Gowon as head of state, seized the Ikeja airport in Lagos, the federal capital. Several Igbo and Eastern minority army officers were killed during the counter-coup.

The original intention of Murtala Mohammed and his fellow coup-plotters seems to have been to engineer the secession of the Northern region from Nigeria. But they were subsequently dissuaded from doing so.

The young officers then decided to name Lieutenant-Colonel Yakubu Gowon, who apparently had not been involved in the tragic events of 1966 until then, as Nigerian head of state. After he assumed control, he reversed Ironsi's decision to abolish the federal system.

The buildup to the Biafran War

The July counter-coup helped fuel massacres of the Igbo and other Eastern Nigerians throughout Northern Nigeria. Hundreds of Igbo army officers were murdered during the revolt. And in the North, as commanding officers either lost control of their troops or actively egged them on to violence against Igbo civilians, it did not take long for Northerners from all walks of life to participate in the pogroms. Tens of thousands of Igbos were killed throughout the North.

The massacres and persecution precipitated the flight of more than a million Igbos to their ancestral homeland in Eastern Nigeria.

Lieutenant-Colonel Ojukwu, the military governor of the Eastern Region who did not allow attempts by Northern soldiers stationed in his region to replicate the massacres of Igbo officers, argued that if Igbo lives could not be preserved by the Nigerian state, then the Igbo reserved the right to establish a state of their own where they would be safe.

There arose tensions between the Eastern Region and the Northern-controlled federal government led by Gowon, a Northerner himself.

On 4–5 January 1967, in line with Ojukwu's demand to meet for talks only on neutral ground, a summit attended by Gowon, Ojukwu and other members of Nigeria's ruling Supreme Military Council (SMC) was held at Aburi in Ghana in an attempt to resolve all outstanding conflicts and establish Nigeria as a confederation of existing regions instead of being a federation.

The outcome of the summit was the Aburi Accord. But it was never implemented. Gowon's government was worried that it would lose revenues from oil in the Eastern Region if the regions became autonomous, each controlling resources on its soil.

In a move to neutralise Ojukwu's government in the East, Gowon announced on 5 May 1967 the division of the three Nigerian regions (North, East and West) into 12 states: North-Western State, North-Eastern State, Kano State, North-Central State, Benue-Plateau State, Kwara State, Western State, Lagos State, Mid-Western State, and, from Ojukwu's Eastern Region – Rivers State, South-Eastern State, and East-Central State.

The non-Igbo South-Eastern and Rivers states which had the oil reserves and access to the sea were carved out to isolate the Igbo areas as East-Central State.

Division of the regions was not a part of the Aburi agreement. Therefore what Gowon did was in violation of the Aburi Accord and helped cause the Nigeria civil war by forcing the East to secede.

One controversial aspect of the division of the three regions was Gowon's decision to annex Port Harcourt, a large city in the Niger Delta sitting on some of Nigeria's largest oil reserves, and make it a part of the new Rivers State, emasculating the migrant Igbo population of traders there. The flight of many of them back to their villages in the Igbo heartland in Eastern Nigeria where they felt safer was alleged to be a contradiction of Gowon's "no victor, no vanquished" policy when, at the end of the war, the properties they left behind were reclaimed by the Rivers State indigenes.

Members of minority groups in the Eastern Region were not enthusiastic about secession, as it would mean living in what they felt would be an Igbo-dominated nation. Some non-Igbos living in the Eastern Region either refused to support the Biafran struggle or actively supported the federal side by enlisting in the Nigerian army and providing it with intelligence about Biafran military activities.

However, some did play active roles in the Biafran government. There were even those who had prominent positions. Lt. Col (later Major-General) Philip Effiong served as Biafra's Chief of Defence Staff. N.U. Akpan served as Secretary to the Biafran Government. And others including Chiefs Bassey and Graham-Douglas served in other significant roles.

Gowon as war leader

On 30 May 1967, Ojukwu responded to Gowon's announcement of the division of the regions into 12 states by declaring the formal secession of the Eastern Region which was now to be known as the Republic of Biafra. The secession ignited a civil war which lasted for about 30 months. More than 100,000 soldiers died in the war. More than one million Igbos died, mostly from starvation as a result of a blockade imposed on Biafra by the Nigerian federal government.

Starvation was effectively used as a weapon by the federal government. Chief Anthony Enahoro, Nigeria's commissioner of information, and thus the country's minister of information, stated at a press conference in July 1968 that starvation was a legitimate weapon of war and that the federal government had every intention of using it against the rebels.

Chief Obafemi Awolowo, vice chairman of Nigeria's ruling council, hence the country's vice president under Gowon, was just as blunt when he stated: "All is fair in war and starvation is one of the weapons of war. I don't see why we should feed our enemies fat in order for them to fight us harder."

The war saw a massive expansion of the Nigerian army in size and a steep increase in its doctrinal and technical sophistication, while the Nigerian Air Force was essentially born in the course of the conflict.

However, significant controversy has surrounded the air operations of the Nigerian forces, as several residents of Biafra, including Red Cross workers, foreign missionaries and journalists, accused the Nigerian Air Force of specifically targeting civilian populations, relief centres and marketplaces.

Gowon steadfastly denied those claims, along with

claims that his army committed atrocities such as rape, wholesale executions of civilian populations and extensive looting in occupied areas. However, one of his wartime commanders, Colonel Benjamin Adenkule who during the war was famously known as The Black Scorpion and who was the most popular army officer during that conflict, seems to give some credence to those claims in his book, while excusing them as unfortunate by-products of war. The Third Marine Commando Division he led was the youngest in the war and gained more territory than the other two divisions fighting from the north of Biafra. It virtually won the war against Biafra. And Adenkule made it clear he was bent on total destruction. As he stated in during the war:

"I want see no Red Cross, no caritas, no World Council of Churches, no pope, no missionaey and no United Nations delegation. I want to prevent even one Igbo from having even one piece to eat before their capitulation. We shoot at everything that moves and when our troops march into the centre of Igbo territory, we shoot at everything even at things that don't move."

The end of the war came on 13 January 1970, with Colonel Olusegun Obasanjo's acceptance of the surrender of Biafran forces. Obasanjo announced that on the next day on the former rebel radio station: Radio Biafra Enugu. Gowon subsequently declared in his speech, "No victor, no vanquished." He also offered an amnesty to the secessionists who fought in the war and launched a programme of "Reconciliation, Reconstruction and Rehabilitation" to rebuild the infrastructure and the economy which had suffered extensive damage during the war.

Unfortunately, many of the promises made by Gowon and his colleagues in the federal government were never fulfilled; the programmes were not implemented the way they should have been, if at all. In addition to that, Gowon's policy of giving 20 pounds (pounds means currency in this context, as in British pound) to everyone who had a bank account in Nigeria before the war, regardless of how much money had been in their account, was criticised by foreign and local aid workers, as this led to an unprecedented scale of begging, looting and robbery in the former Biafran areas after the war.

Gowon's career after the Biafran War

The postwar years saw Nigeria enjoying a meteoric, oil-fueled, economic upturn in the course of which the scope of activity of the Nigerian federal government grew to an unprecedented scale because of increased earnings from oil revenues. Unfortunately, this period also saw a rapid increase in corruption, mostly bribery, of and by federal government officials; and although the head of state himself, General Gowon, was never found complicit in the corrupt practices, he was often accused of turning a blind eye to the activities of his staff and cronies.

Indigenisation Decree

Another decision made by Gowon at the height of the oil boom was to have what some considered to be negative repercussions for the Nigerian economy in later years, although its immediate effects were scarcely noticeable. That was his indigenisation decree of 1972 which declared many sectors of the Nigerian economy off-limits to all foreign investment; only limited participation by foreigners was allowed in other areas.

The decree provided windfall gains to many well-connected Nigerians but proved to be highly detrimental to non-oil sectors of the Nigerian economy.

Overthrow

On 1 October 1974, in violation of his earlier promises, Gowon declared that Nigeria would not be ready for civilian rule by 1976. He also said the handover date would be postponed indefinitely.

Furthermore, because of the growth in the bureaucracy, there were allegations of an increase in corruption.

Increased wealth in the country resulted in fake import licenses being issued. There were stories of tons of stones and sand being imported into the country and of General Gowon himself saying to a foreign reporter:

"The only problem Nigeria has is how to spend the money she has."

All that caused a lot of anger within the army. On 25 July 1975, while Gowon was attending the OAU summit in Kampala, Uganda, a group of army officers led by Colonel Joe Nanven Garba overthrew the government. The coup plotters appointed Brigadier Murtala Muhammad as head of the new government, and Brigadier Olusegun Obasanjo as his deputy.

Garba was a close ally of Gowon. The coup was led by junior military officers who were also unhappy at the lack of progress General Gowon had made in moving the country towards democratic rule. Garba's role as an insider, someone who was close to Gowon, is credited with ensuring that the coup was bloodless.

Garba and Gowon later reconciled to the extent that Gowon attended Garba's funeral in Langtang in Plateau State in 2002.

Later life

Gowon subsequently went into exile in the United Kingdom where he earned a Ph.D. In political science from the University of Warwick. He lived in north London-Hertfordshire and very much became part of the community in his area where he served a term as a church warden in the local church.

In February 1976, Gowon was implicated in the military coup led by Lieutenant-Colonel Buka Suka Dimka which resulted in the death of Murtala Mohammed who had been promoted from brigadier to general after he became military head of state.

According to Dimka's "confession," he met with Gowon in London and obtained support from him for the coup. In addition, Dimka mentioned before his execution that the purpose of the coup was to re-install Gowon as head of state. As a result of the coup tribunal findings, Gowon was declared wanted by the Nigerian government, was stripped of his rank in absentia and had his pension cut off.

Although he was implicated in the abortive coup, he escaped justice because he was living in exile in London. The British Government refused to extradite him.

He was finally pardoned – along with Ojukwu – when Shehu Shagari was president.

He returned to Nigeria in the 1980s. In the 1990s, he formed a non-denominational religious group, Nigeria Prays. He also went to play a role as an "elder statesman."

Kenneth Kaunda

Kenneth David Kaunda, known as KK, (born 28 April 1924) served as the first president of Zambia from 1964 to 1991.

Early life

Kaunda was the youngest of eight children. He was born at Lubwa Mission in Chinsali in the Northern Province of Northern Rhodesia, now Zambia.

His father was the Reverend David Kaunda, an ordained minster of the United Free Church of Scotland. who was also a teacher.

David Kaunda was born in Nyasaland which was renamed Malawi after independence. He moved to Chinsali to work at Lubwa Mission. The mission was near Chinsali.

Kenneth Kaunda attended Munali Training Centre in the capital Lusaka_ (August 1941–1943). He taught at Lubwa Primary School and served as headmaster of the school from 1943 to 1945.

He also once worked at Salisbury and Bindura Mine.

In early 1948, he became a teacher in Mufulira for the United Missions to the Copperbelt (UMCB). He also served as an assistant at an African Welfare Centre and as a boarding master of a mine school in the same town.

He was also for a time an assistance secretary of the Nchanga Branch of the African National Congress (ANC), a political party led by Harry Nkumbula. The ANC in Northern Rhodesia was different from South Africa's ANC, although both were political parties fighting for the rights of Africans.

Independence struggle

In April 1949 Kaunda returned to Lubwa to become a part-time teacher but resigned in 1951. In that year he became organising secretary of the African National Congress in the Northern Province. During that period, what is now Luapula Province was a part of the Northern

Province.

On 11 November 1953, he moved to Lusaka to take up the post of secretary general of the ANC under the leadership of Harry Nkumbula.

African leaders in Northern Rhodesia were opposed to formation of the Federation of Rhodesia and Nyasaland, as were those in Nyasaland and Southern Rhodesia. But even with their combined efforts, Kaunda and Nkumbula failed to mobilise Africans against the federation which was established to consolidate white minority rule over the black African majority. Their compatriots in Nyasaland and Southern Rhodesia also failed to stop the establishment of the federation.

In 1955 Kaunda and Nkumbula were imprisoned for two months with hard labour for distributing "subversive" literature. Such imprisonment and other forms of harassment were normal rites of passage for African nationalist leaders. The experience of imprisonment had a radicalising impact on Kaunda.

The two leaders drifted apart as Nkumbula became increasingly influenced by white liberals and was seen as being willing to compromise on the issue of black majority rule, waiting until the majority was 'ready' before the franchise was extended to them.. This was, however, to be determined by existing property and literacy qualifications, dropping race altogether.

Nkumbula's allegedly autocratic leadership of the ANC eventually resulted in a split. Kaunda broke from the ANC and formed the Zambian African National Congress (ZANC) in October 1958. ZANC was banned in March 1959.

In June 1959, Kaunda was sentenced to nine months' imprisonment, which he spent first in Lusaka, then in Salisbury, Southern Rhodesia. Salisbury was renamed Harare, and Southern Rhodesia was renamed Zimbabwe after the country won independence in April 1980.

When Kaunda was in prison, Mainza Chona and other

337

nationalists broke away from the ANC and, in October 1959, Chona became the first president of the United National Independence Party (UNIP), the successor to ZANC. However, Chona did not see himself as the party's main founder. When Kaunda was released from prison in January 1960 he was elected President of UNIP.

In July 1961 Kaunda organised a civil disobedience campaign in Northern Province, the so called Cha-cha-cha campaign, to carry on the struggle for independence. During the 1962 elections, he ran as a UNIP candidate. The elections led to the formation of a UNIP–ANC coalition government in which Kaunda served as minister of local government and social welfare.

In January 1964, UNIP won the general election under a new constitution, defeating the ANC led by Harry Nkumbula. Kaunda was appointed prime minister.

On 24 October 1964, Kaunda became the first president of independent Zambia. Reuben Kamanga was appointed vice president.

Born on 26 August 1929, Reuben Kamanga was one of the stalwarts of the independence struggle. Before independence, he served as the deputy president of the United National Independence Party (UNIP) and as minister of labour and mines.

After independence, he served for three years as vice president. He was demoted in 1967 to serve as minister of foreign affairs. In 1969, he became minister of rural development. He retired from politics in 1991 and died at his home on 20 September 1996 almost one month before his 67th birthday.

Presidency

In the year of independence, Kenneth Kaunda had to deal with the Lumpa Church led by Alice Lenshina in Chinsali, his home district in the Northern Province.

An independent Christian church, the Lumpa Church was established in 1953 by "Alice" Lenshina Mulenga in the village of Kasoma. The church promoted a blend of Christian and traditional religious values and practices, including a belief in the role of women as spiritual mediums

The Lumpa Church tried to take up a neutral position in the political conflict between UNIP and the ANC but was then accused by UNIP of collaborating with the white minority governments.

Conflicts arose between UNIP youth and Lumpa members, especially in Chinsali District where the headquarters of the church were. Kaunda, as prime minister of an African majority government sent two battalions of the Northern Rhodesian Regiment to deal with the crisis.

Fighting led to the deaths of about 1500 villagers and the flight to Katanga Province in neighbouring Congo of tens of thousands of followers of Lenshina. Kaunda banned the Lumpa Church in August 1964 and proclaimed a state of emergency to neutralise the group.

Educational policies

At the time of its independence, Zambia had just 109 university graduates. Less than 0.5% of the population was estimated to have completed primary education. The nation's educational system was one of the most poorly developed in all of Britain's former colonies. Because of this, Zambia had to invest heavily in education at all levels.

Kaunda formulated a policy under which all children, irrespective of their parents' ability to pay, were given free exercise books, pens and pencils. The parents' main responsibility was to buy uniforms, pay a token "school fee" and ensure that the children attended school.

This approach meant that the best pupils had the

opportunity to get education from from primary school all the way to university. Not every child could go to secondary school but those who did had the chance to go to university. And those who did not were still able to get good secondary school education.

The University of Zambia was opened in Lusaka in 1966 after Zambians all over the country had been encouraged to donate whatever they could afford towards its construction. Kaunda was appointed chancellor and officiated at the first graduation ceremony in 1969.

The main campus was located on the Great East Road, while the medical campus was located at Ridgeway near the University Teaching Hospital.

In 1979, another campus was established at the Zambia Institute of Technology in Kitwe. In 1988 the Kitwe campus was upgraded and renamed Copperbelt University , offering business industrial and environmental studies.

Other tertiary-level institutions established during Kaunda's era were vocationally focused and fell under the aegis of the department of technical education and vocational training. They include the Evelyn Hone College of Applied Arts and Commerce and the Natural Resources Development College (both in Lusaka), the Northern Technical College at Ndola, the Livingstone Trades Training Institute in Livingstone, and teacher-training colleges.

Economic policies

At independence, Kaunda took over a country whose economy was completely under the control of foreigners. For example, the British South Africa (BSAC founded by British imperialist Cecil Rhodes) retained commercial assets and mineral rights it claimed it acquired from a concession signed with the Litunga (King) of Bulozi in 1890 (the Lochner Concession). Only by threatening to expropriate it, on the eve of independence, did Kaunda manage to get the BSAC to assign its mineral rights to the incoming Zambian government.

During the days of the federation (of Rhodesia and Nyasaland), Northern Rhodesia's copper revenues were siphoned off by white Southern Rhodesians, since they were the dominant group in the polity. Salisbury in Southern Rhodesia was also the capital of the federation. In their view, Southern Rhodesia was well-suited to providing managerial and administrative skills, Northern Rhodesia would provide the copper revenues, and Nyasaland would provide the labour. Also, most of the white settlers in the federation, who were mostly British, lived in Southern Rhodesia.

When Zambia won independence, Salisbury was much more developed than Lusaka, the capital of Zambia.

Zambia instituted a programme of five-year national development plans under the direction of the National Commission for Development Planning. There was the Transitional Development Plan followed by the First National Development Plan (1966–71). The two plans, which provided for major investment in infrastructure and manufacturing, were largely implemented and were generally successful. But that was not the case with subsequent plans.

A major switch in the structure of Zambia's economy came with the Mulungushi Reforms of April 1968. The government declared its intention to acquire an equity holding (usually 51% or more) in a number of key foreign-owned firms to be controlled by the Industrial Development Corporation (INDECO).

By January 1970, Zambia had acquired majority holding in the Zambian operations of the two major foreign mining corporations, the Anglo American Corporation and the Rhodesia Selection Trust (RST). The two became the Nchanga Consolidated Copper Mines (NCCM) and Roan Consolidated Mines (RCM),

341

respectively.

Kaunda announced the creation of a new parastatal body, the Mining Development Corporation (MINDECO). The Finance and Development Corporation (FINDECO) allowed the Zambian government to gain control of insurance companies and building societies. The foreign-owned banks, such as Barclays, Standard Chartered and Grindlays, successfully resisted takeover.

In 1971, INDECO, MINDECO, and FINDECO were brought together under an omnibus parastatal, the Zambia Industrial and Mining Corporation (ZIMCO), to create one of the largest companies in sub-Saharan Africa, with Kaunda as chairman of the board.

The management contracts under which day-to-day operations of the mines had been carried out by Anglo American and RST were ended in 1973.

In 1982 NCCM and RCM were merged into the giant Zambia Consolidated Copper Mines Ltd. (ZCCM).

Unfortunately, these programmes of nationalisation, even assuming they could have worked, were ill-timed. Events that were beyond their control would wreck the country's plans for national development.

In 1973 the massive increase in the price of oil was followed by a slump in copper prices in 1975 and a diminution of export earnings.

In 1973 the price of copper accounted for 95% of all export earnings; this halved in value on the world market in 1975. By 1976 Zambia had a balance-of-payments crisis and rapidly became massively indebted to the International Monetary Fund (IMF). The Third National Development Plan (1978–83) had to be abandoned as crisis management replaced long-term planning.

By the mid-1980s, Zambia was one of the most indebted nations in the world, relative to its gross domestic product (GDP).

The IMF was insisting that the Zambian government should introduce programmes aimed at stabilising the economy and restructuring it to reduce dependence on copper. The proposed measures included: the ending of price controls; devaluation of the kwacha (Zambia's currency); cut-backs in government expenditure; cancellation of subsidies on food and fertiliser; and increased prices for farm produce.

Kaunda's removal of food subsidies caused massive increases in the prices of basic foodstuffs; the country's urban population rioted in protest. In desperation, Kaunda broke with the IMF in May 1987 and introduced a New Economic Recovery Programme in 1988. However, this did not help him and he eventually moved toward a new understanding with the IMF in 1989.

In 1990, with the collapse of the Soviet Union and Eastern Europe, whose socialist policies were similar to Kaunda's philosophy of humanism, Kaunda was forced to make a major policy shift. He announced his government's intention to partially privatise the parastatals. However, these changes came too late to prevent his fall from power which was largely the result of the economic troubles.

One-party state and African socialism

In 1964, there was the Lumpa uprising in Northern Zambia, four months before independence.

Although the uprising was inspired by religious ideals of the Lumpa church, it also had political implications. The church was what could be deemed the "eradication movement" in African religion. It began with the ideals of Alice Mulenga Lubusha who rechristened herself Alice Lenshina or essentially "Alice Regina and strongly opposed polygamy and sorcery.

By 1958, the organisation adopted the controversial rejection of all earthly authority. It began having its own courts and refused to pay taxes or be registered with the state. This led to a confrontation soon after Northern Rhodesia became independent and was renamed Zambia.

The violent confrontation with the government led to the deaths of approximately 700 members of the Lumpa church and the arrest of Alice Lenshina. Some reports say more than 1,000 people died in the conflict.

Alice was released in 1975. But she was imprisoned two years later for trying to revive the movement's strength.

The Catholic Lay movement Legion of Mary adopted some of their hymns and thus converted some of the former members, although the Lumpa Church itself is said to survive in a diminished and largely underground form.

During the 1964 Lumpa uprising, Kaunda declared a state of emergency which gave Kaunda a lot of power.

The Lumpa Church was a major source of opposition because it refused to allow church members to participate in politics which went against the 100% participation wanted by UNIP. This created a lot of animosity between the two groups and violence that began on a small scale escalated into a small civil war.

The crisis was brought about by a combination of complacency on the part of the colonial administration and UNIP intransigence. Kaunda tried to mediate the differences between the church, local authorities and UNIP party members but was eventually unable to control party cadres in the Northern Province.

And after violence erupted during the 1968 elections, Kaunda banned all parties except UNIP. In 1972, he made Zambia a one-party state. Some people say he did that probably because he was worried by Simon Kapwepwe's decision to leave UNIP and found a rival party, the United Progressive Party (UPP), which Kaunda immediately banned. Kapwepwe was his childhood friend who later became Zambia's vice president under him.

After Kaunda declared his intention to make Zambia a one-party state, he appointed the Chona Commission under the chairmanship of Mainza Chona in February 1972 to make recommendations for the constitution of a 'one-party participatory democracy' (i.e. a one-party state).

The Commission's terms of reference did not permit it to discuss the pros and cons of Kaunda's decision. The sole surviving opposition party, Harry Nkumbula's African National Congress (ANC), boycotted the commission and unsuccessfully challenged the constitutional change in the courts.

The Chona report was based on four months of public hearings and was submitted in October 1972. It was widely regarded as a 'liberal' document. Finally, Kaunda neutralised Nkumbula by getting him to wind-up the ANC, join UNIP and sign a document called the Choma Declaration on 27 June 1973. The ANC ceased to exist after the dissolution of parliament in October 1973. Allegedly Kaunda "bought off" Nkumbula by offering him an emerald mine.

With no more opposition against him, Kaunda enunciated a nationalist-socialist ideology called Zambian Humanism. This was based on a combination of mid-twentieth-century ideas of central planning/state control and what he considered basic African values: mutual aid, trust and loyalty to the community.

Similar forms of African socialism were introduced inter alia in Ghana by Kwame Nkrumah ("Consciencism") and Tanzania by Julius Nyerere ("Ujamaa"), while in Zaire, Mobutu Sese Seko was at a loss until he hit on the ideal ideology – 'Mobutuism'.

To elaborate his ideology, Kaunda published several books: *Humanism in Zambia and a Guide to its Implementation, Parts 1, 2 and 3*. Other publications on Zambian Humanism are: *Fundamentals of Zambian Humanism* by Timothy Kandeke; *Zambian Humanism: Religion and Social Morality* by S. J. Cleve Dillion-Malone, and *Zambian Humanism: Some Major Spiritual and Economic Challenges* by Justin B. Zulu.

Freedom fighters

Although it was Kaunda's nationalisation of the copper mining industry in the late 1960s which led to increased economic problems, matters were made worse by his economic and logistical support for the freedom fighters in the region: South Africa, the Portuguese colonies of Angola and Mozambique, and the British colony of Rhodesia which is now Zimbabwe.

Kaunda tried to solve the conflict in southern Africa between the white minority governments of Rhodesia, South Africa and Angola and Mozambique and the African freedom fighters by mediation and boycotts. But the white rulers were uncompromising, forcing Africans to take up arms.

On 25–26 August 1976, Kaunda met with South African Prime Minister B.J. Vorster at Victoria Falls and again on 30 April 1982 with Prime Minister P.W. Botha on the Botswana border to discuss the political situation in South West Africa and South Africa. However, he did not manage to get serious concessions from the South African government.

Kaunda was criticised in the African press for talking to representatives of the apartheid regime.

Foreign policy

Early in his presidency, Kaunda was an outspoken supporter of the anti-apartheid movement and opposed Ian Smith's white minority rule in Rhodesia. He allowed several African liberation movements such as ZAPU and ZANU of Rhodesia and the African National Congress (ANC) of South Africa to have offices and military training camps in Zambia.

Former ANC president Oliver Tambo spent a significant part of his 30-year exile living and working in

Zambia. Joshua Nkomo, the leader of ZAPU, also had a home and a military base in Zambia.

In retaliation the white minority governments of Rhodesia and South Africa carried out espionage and frequently executed bombing attacks in Zambia.

Herbert Chitepo, a prominent ZANU leader who had moved from Dar es Salaam, Tanzania, to Zambia, was killed with a car bomb in Lusaka in 1975.

The struggle in both Rhodesia and South Africa and its offshoot wars in Namibia, Angola and Mozambique placed a huge economic burden on Zambia as these were the country's main trading partners. In response to that, Kaunda agreed with President Nyerere of Tanzania to build a railway linking the two countries to end Zambia's dependence on the white-ruled countries of southern Africa as an outlet to the sea and as her main trading partners.

The Tanzania-Zambia Railway known as TAZARA was built linking Kapiri Mposhi on the Zambian Copperbelt with Tanzania's port of Dar es Salaam on the coast of the Indian Ocean. Completed in 1975, it was the only route for Zambia's bulk trade which did not have to go through white-controlled territories.

This precarious situation lasted for more than 20 years until the end of apartheid in South Africa.

When Nelson Mandela was released from prison on 11 February 1990, the first country he visited was Zambia on February 27[th.]

During the Cold War, Kaunda was a strong supporter of the Non-Aligned Movement (NAM). He hosted a NAM summit in Lusaka in 1970 and served as the movement's chairman from 1970 to 1973.

He maintained a close friendship with Yugoslavia's long-time leader Josip Broz Tito and is remembered by many former citizens of Yugoslavia for weeping openly over his casket in 1980. He even had a house built in Lusaka for Tito's visits to the country.

Kaunda had frequent but cordial differences with US President Ronald Reagan whom he met 1983 and Margaret Thatcher mainly over what he saw as the West's blind eye to apartheid.

He always maintained warm relations with the People's Republic of China who had provided assistance on many projects in Zambia including the TAZARA Railway.

In the late 1980s prior to the first Gulf War, Kaunda developed a friendship with Saddam Hussein with whom he struck various agreements to supply oil to Zambia. He named streets in Saddam's honour (Saddam Hussein Blvd., now Los Angeles Blvd.).

During the events that led to the Gulf War, Saddam became increasingly isolated and had only a few friends like Kaunda.

In August 1989, Farzad Bazoft was arrested in Iraq for alleged espionage. He was accompanied by a British nurse, Daphne Parish, who was arrested as well. Bazoft was an Iranian-born British freelance journalist who was about to expose Saddam Hussein's gassing of the Kurds. He was later tried, sentenced to death and executed.

Parish was sentenced to 15 years in prison. But in 1990 just as the Gulf War was about to break out, Kaunda successfully managed to negotiate with Saddam Hussein the release of Parish.

Kaunda served as chairman of the Organisation of African Unity (OAU) from 1970 to 1973.

UNIP and Kaunda's autocracy during the Second Republic

After promulgation of the Second Republic following Mainza Chona's recommendations for the constitution of a "one-party participatory democracy," Kaunda's leadership took on more autocratic characteristics.

He personally appointed the Central Committee of UNIP, although the process was given a veneer of legitimacy by being "approved" by a National Congress of the party. In theory, Kaunda's nominations could be discarded by Congress, but in practice they were always accepted without modification.

The argument used was that "the President knows the people who can work well with him, so if we modify the nominations we will end up with a less effective team." In turn, the Central Committee nominated a sole candidate for the post of president of the party. Of course, since the members of the Central Committee had been nominated by him, Kaunda was always the sole presidential candidate.

After that charade, the rest of the Zambian population was given the opportunity to express approval or disapproval of the sole candidate's nomination by voting either "Yes" or "No". Since the presidential "election" was always accompanied by parliamentary elections, there was great pressure placed on parliamentary candidates to "campaign" for the president's "Yes" vote, in addition to their own campaigns.

Parastatal companies (which were controlled through ZIMCO – Zambia Industrial and Mining Corporation) were also under pressure to "campaign" for Kaunda by buying advertising space in the two national newspapers, *Times of Zambia* and *Zambia Daily Mail*, exhorting the electorate to give the president a "massive 'Yes' vote".

The parliamentary elections were also controlled by Kaunda: the names of candidates had to be submitted to UNIP's Central Committee, which then selected three people to stand for any particular constituency. Anyone could be vetoed without the Central Committee giving any reason, since UNIP was supreme and its decisions were unchallengeable. Using these methods, Kaunda kept any enemies at bay by ensuring that they never got into political power.

This was the tactic he used when he neutralised Nkumbula and Kapwepwe's challenges to his sole candidacy for the 1978 UNIP elections.

On that occasion, the UNIP's constitution was "amended" overnight to bring in rules that invalidated the two challengers' nominations. Kapwepwe was told he could not stand because only people who had been members for five years could be nominated to the presidency; he had only rejoined UNIP three years before.

Nkumbula was outmaneuvered by introducing a new rule that said each candidate needed the signatures of 200 delegates from *each* province to back his candidacy.

Less creative tactics were used on a third candidate called Chiluwe; he was just beaten up by the UNIP Youth Wing to within an inch of his life. This meant that he was in no state to submit his nomination.

Fall from power

Eventually, economic troubles and increasing international pressure to bring more democracy to Africa forced Kaunda to change the rules which helped to keep him in power.

People who had been afraid to criticise him were now emboldened to challenge his competence. His close friend Julius Nyerere had stepped down from the presidency in Tanzania in 1985 and was quietly encouraging Kaunda to follow suit.

Pressure for a return to multiparty politics increased and Kaunda voluntarily yielded and called for multiparty elections in 1991 in which the Movement for Multiparty Democracy (MMD) won.

Kaunda left office with the inauguration of MMD leader Frederick Chiluba as president on 2 November 1991.

He was the second mainland African head of state to allow free multiparty elections and to have relinquished power when he lost; the first, Mathieu Kérékou of Benin, had done so in March of that year.

Post-presidency

President Chiluba later attempted to deport Kaunda to Malawi on the grounds that he was a Malawian because his parents came from there.

The MMD-dominated government under the leadership of Chiluba had the constitution amended, barring citizens with foreign parentage from standing for the presidency, to prevent Kaunda from contesting the next elections in 1996, and Kaunda retired from politics after he was accused of involvement in a failed coup attempt in 1997.

In March 1999, Kaunda was declared stateless by the Ndola High Court in a judgement delivered by Mr. Justice Chalendo Sakala. A full transcript of the judgment was published in the *Times of Zambia* edition of 1 April 1999. Kaunda successfully challenged the decision in the Supreme Court of Zambia which declared him to be a Zambian citizen in the year 2000.

After retiring from politics, he got involved in various charitable organisations. His most notable contribution was in the fight against the spread of HIV/AIDS.

One of Kaunda's children, Masuzyo, died of AIDS in 1986.

From 2002 to 2004, Kaunda was an African President-in-Residence at the African Presidential Archives and Research Center at Boston University in Boston, Massachusetts, in the United States.

On 19 October 2007, he was the recipient of the 2007 Ubuntu Award.

Kamuzu Banda

Hastings Kamuzu Banda (February 1898 – 25 November 1997) was the leader of Malawi and, before then, of

Nyasaland from 1961 to 1994. Malawi was known as Nyasaland before independence.

After getting much of his education overseas, in the United States and Great Britain, Banda returned to his home country to campaign for independence.

In 1963, he became prime minister of Nyasaland and led his country to independence as Malawi a year later.

Two years later, Malawi became a republic and Banda, president.

He consolidated power and later declared Malawi a one-party state under the Malawi Congress Party (MCP). In 1970, the MCP made him the party's president for life. In 1971, he became Malawi's life president.

As a leader of the pro-Western bloc in Africa, he was supported by the West during the cold War. He generally supported women's rights, improved the country's infrastructure, and maintained a good educational system, achievements which were in sharp contrast with what took place in many other African countries. However, he presided over one of the most repressive and most brutal regimes in Africa.

He was also ostracised by much of Africa for maintaining full diplomatic relations with apartheid South Africa, a regime that was pariah on the continent.

By 1993, Dr. Banda was under strong international pressure to democratise the country. His government also faced widespread protests across Malawi because of his dictatorial rule.

A referendum ended his one-party rule and a special assembly stripped him of his title as life president. He ran for president in the democratic elections which followed but was defeated, bringing to an end one of the oldest dictatorships in Africa during the post-colonial era.

Dr. Banda died in South Africa in 1997.

His legacy remains controversial, with some hailing him as a national and an African hero, while others denounce him as a tyrant and a traitor to the Pan-African cause.

Early life

Kamuzu Banda was born on a farm near what is now the town of Kasungu in the central part of what was then known as British Central Africa, later renamed Nyasaland. His father was Mphonongo Banda; and his mother, Akupingamnyama Phiri.

His date of birth is unknown, as it took place at a time when there was no birth registration. A biographer, Philip Short, gives February 1898 as the most likely date. His official birthday was 14 May 1906. This is the date which is documented in some of his biographical accounts.

Other reports say he was born in 1896. In fact, when he died, there were reports from different sources that he was 101 years old; which, if true, means he was indeed born in 1896.

The name Kamuzu means "a little root." He was given this name because he was conceived after his mother had been given root herbs by a medicine man to cure infertility. His last name, Banda means "a small hut."

He took the European name, Hastings, after being baptised into the Church of Scotland. He named himself after John Hastings, a Scottish missionary working near his village whom he admired. The prefix Doctor was earned through his education.

However, there are some disputes about his name as well. According to one Malawian, Felix Ngasama, in his article, Malawi's Kamuzu Banda Must Have Laughed All The Way to his Grave," in *All Voices*, 2 March 2009:

"After Banda's death, a man claiming to be Banda's family member, Elia Katola Phiri dismissed the year 1906 as Banda's year of birth saying that the age distortion was created by Banda's uncle Hanock Msokera Phiri.

Mr Katola Phiri went on to spin the yarn and say that Hastings Kamuzu Banda was in fact born Kamnkhwala Banda at Mphonongo village in Kasungu in 1896. Katola said that in 1910, Kamnkhwala was baptized as Akim Kamnkhwala Mtunthama Banda. He also contradicted with the official history saying that Banda left Malawi (Nyasaland) for Zimbabwe (Southern Rhodesia) at the age 21 and not 13 as widely claimed.

While Katola did not mention Banda's parents, some websites such as *Wikipedia*, claim that they were Mr Mphonongo Banda and his wife Akupingamnyama Phiri.

Katola Phiri said that Banda changed his name from Akim Kamnkhwala Mtunthama Banda to Hastings Kamuzu Banda while he was abroad but *Wikipedia* says he took the Christian name Hastings after being baptized into the Church of Scotland in around 1905 while he was still in Malawi. We were told Banda was born at Chiwengo village but now we are told he was in fact born at Mphonongo village...

There are (also) doubts whether Banda was really a Malawian as he claimed. If he left Malawi at the age of 13 or 21 why was he totally out of practice in Chichewa his mother tongue that he needed an interpreter, John Tembo, when he came back? Are the people that he claimed to be his relatives in Kasungu really his blood relatives? This can be proven scientifically through DNA tests.

If a group of eminent and concerned Malawians can embark on this mission and prove beyond reasonable doubt that it is a just and honourable cause, they can obtain legal powers to carry out DNA tests between Banda and his so called sister the late Chatinkha Banda."

According to *Wikipedia*, around 1915–16, Banda left home on foot with Hanock Msokera Phiri, an uncle who had been a teacher at the nearby Livingstonia mission school, for Hartley, Southern Rhodesia (now Chegutu, Zimbabwe). In 1917, he left on foot for Johannesburg,

South Africa.

He had various jobs at the Witwatersrand Deep Mine on the Transvaal Reef for several years. During this time, he met Bishop W. T. Vernon of the African Methodist Church (AME) who offered to pay his tuition fee at a Methodist school in the United States if he could pay his own passage. In 1925, he left for New York.

Life abroad (1925–1958)

United States

Banda studied in the high school section of Wilberforce Institute, an African American AME college now known as Central State University in Wilberforce, Ohio, and graduated in 1928. With his financial support now ended, Banda earned some money on speaking engagements arranged by the renowned Ghanaian educator, Kweyir Aggrey, whom he had met in South Africa.

Speaking at a Kiwanis club meeting, he met a Dr. Herald who helped him to get enrolled as a premedical student at Indiana University in Bloomington, Indiana, where he lodged with Mrs. W.N. Culmer. While at Bloomington, he wrote several essays about his native Chewa tribe for the folklorist Stith Thompson who introduced him to Edward Sapir, an anthropologist at the University of Chicago to which he transferred after studying for four semesters at the University of Indiana.

When he was at the University of Chicago, he collaborated with the anthropologist and linguist Mark Hanna Watkins, providing information on Chewa culture. In Chicago, he lodged with an African-American, Mrs. Corinna Saunders.

He majored in history, graduating with a B. Phil. in 1931. During this time, he got financial support from a

Mrs. Smith, whose husband, Douglas Smith, had made fortunes from patent medicines and Pepsodent toothpaste; and also from a member of the Eastman Kodak board. He then, still with financial support from these and other benefactors (including Dr. Walter B. Stephenson of the Delta Electric Company), studied medicine at Meharry Medical College in Nashville, Tennessee, from which he graduated in 1937.

United Kingdom

After finishing his studies in the United States, he went to Scotland where he attended and graduated from the School of Medicine of the Royal College of Physicians and Surgeons of the University of Edinburgh in 1941.

His studies there were funded by stipends of 300 pounds per year from the British colonial government of Nyasaland (in order to facilitate his return there as a doctor) and from the Scottish Presbyterian Kirk; it was said neither of these benefactors was aware of the other. However, there are conflicting accounts about that. He may still have been funded by Mrs. Smith.

When he enrolled for courses in tropical diseases in Liverpool, England, the Nyasaland government terminated his stipend. He was forced to leave Liverpool when he refused on conscientious grounds to be conscripted as an army doctor.

He obtained the qualifications LRCP and LRCS (Edinburgh) and LRFPS (Glasgow) in Scotland. He also became an elder of the Church of Scotland.

Between 1942 and 1945, he worked as a doctor in North Shields near Newcastle upon Tyne in northeast England. He was a tenant of Mrs. Amy Walton at this time in Alma Place in North Shields and sent a Christmas card to her every year right up to her death in the late 1960s.

In 1948, he worked as a doctor in Renfrew, a town located 6 miles west of Glasgow, Scotland. A resident,

Bill Johnston, remembers the time when, as a lad, Dr. Banda came to his home to see his father who had a nasty boil on the back of his neck. His father was a respected church elder in the town.

Dr. Banda took a small bottle from his case, asked for some boiling water and poured some into the bottle. Emptying the water out, he quickly placed the open end on Bill's father's boil where of course it stuck as the steam condensed. With a cry of anguish, his father leapt to his feet and chased the doctor round and round the kitchen table with the bottle fastened to his neck. Bill was dumbfounded at hearing his father use language that he had never heard before.

Banda originally worked at a mission for coloured seamen before moving to general practice in the London suburb of Harlesden. At this time, he lodged in a hotel in Paddington run by Mrs Janet Evans. Reportedly, he avoided returning to Nyasaland for fear that his new-found financial resources would be consumed by his extended family back home.

In 1946, at the behest of Chief Mwase of Kasungu, whom he had met in England in 1939, and other politically active Malawians, he represented the Nyasaland African Congress (NAC) at the fifth Pan African Congress in Manchester. Others who attended the conference included Kwame Nkrumah and Jomo Kenyatta. Banda got to know them well during their stay in England and they all became friends.

From this time, he took an increasingly active interest in his native land, advising the Nyasaland African Congress and giving it some financial support. With help from sympathetic British, he also lobbied in London on their behalf.

Federation of Rhodesia and Nyasaland
and move to Ghana

Banda was adamantly opposed to the efforts of Sir Roy Welensky, the prime minister of Southern Rhodesia, to form a federation between Southern and Northern Rhodesia with Nyasaland, a move which he feared would result in further deprivation of rights for the Nyasaland blacks. The "stupid" federation, as he famously called it, was formed on 1 August 1953. It was also known as the Central African Federation (CAF).

It was rumoured with some excitement that he would return to Nyasaland in 1951. Instead, he moved to the Gold Coast (now Ghana) where his friend Nkrumah had become a leader.

He may have gone there partly because of a scandal involving his receptionist in Harlesden, Mrs. Merene French, who became pregnant with his child. Banda was cited as co-respondent in the divorce of Major French and was accused of committing adultery with Mrs. French. She followed Banda to Ghana but he wanted nothing more to do with her or their child. She died penniless in 1976.

It was a tragic affair. As Richard Pendelbury stated in his article, "The Despot and his Sunburn Mistress," in *The Daily Mail*, London, 20 December 1997:

"When the aged Dr Hastings Banda, first President of Malawi and one of Africa's most ruthless and durable dictators, died, Peter French was moved to search out a bundle of papers from his attic and study their contents for the first time in 20 years.

Among the workaday paraphernalia of his late mother Merene French's effects, the Suffolk tool-hire manager found a crumpled blue airmail envelope. Inside was a letter from 40 years ago. It was addressed to Merene and began: 'Dearest Sweet.' The note wasn't from William

French, Peter's father. Rather it was signed: 'With sweetest love, Hastings.' For Peter French, the letter has awakened memories and emotions that have lain dormant for many decades.

They encompass an extraordinary, untold story. How, in austere post-war London, a white British wife and mother dumped her emotionally sterile husband to embark on a 16-year love affair with a charismatic black GP (General Practitioner) whom she helped become a driving force in the anti-colonial movement.

By the time Banda died, at the age of 99, he had become synonymous with the worst excesses of Third World despotism.

Swiftly dispensing with democracy after Malawi gained independence from Britain, the doctor established a regime in which, it is estimated, hundreds of thousands of supposed critics or opponents were imprisoned, tortured or simply murdered.

'Food for the crocs' as he flippantly put it.

On his death Banda was also facing charges of massive corruption brought after he stepped down from power in his 90s and democracy was restored.

His former mistress Merene French has faded from history. But 50 years ago her son Peter was the juvenile observer to a menage of bedroom hopping, interracial adultery and the End of Empire. It has left him with a unique perspective on Banda, a father figure for much of his childhood.

QUITE why Merene Robbins married Peter's father William is a mystery, certainly to their only child. In almost everything except their innate intelligence, they were hopelessly different.

Merene was a tall, attractive and sensual character, the youngest of 11 children of a Devon cattle dealer.

She was nursing in London when she met her husband.

A short, bespectacled figure, French was the son of a church elder who became a padre at a seaman's mission.

Brought up in a pit village, he'd won a place at the local grammar school and from there, thanks to his excellence at languages and grinding application, progressed to Leeds University, teacher training college and a post as a London schoolmaster.

Yet while he was an inspirational teacher, according to his son, he had an almost complete inability to communicate out side the classroom.

As if to compensate for his silences, William French recorded the minutiae of his daily life in a journal. While he mostly concerned himself with the weather and expenditure, his later jottings contain more scandalous material.

The Frenches had been married some ten years when Merene met Dr Banda.

Their romance began, like many, during World War II, when Merene's husband was away.

No doubt thanks to his linguistic ability and lack of the more physical martial qualities, William French had been drafted into Army intelligence.

The role suited his recessive character perfectly.

Peter had been born in 1940.

When the London Blitz started, Merene took her baby to stay with friends in Greenock, near Glasgow.

But when her husband's mother fell ill, the dutiful daughter-in-law moved to North Shields to lend her support. The old woman's GP was Dr Banda.

But how did the son of pagan native Africans find himself practising medicine among the Tyneside poor in the Forties?

Banda's achievement was remarkable. Educated at a Church of Scotland missionary school, he began his odyssey from Nyasaland in south-east Africa to the practice in Northumberland Square by walking 1,000 miles through the bush to South Africa.

His parents thought he'd been eaten by lions. But Banda was heading for Johannesburg, working as he went.

360

While sweeping the floors of a hospital he decided he would become a doctor.

He studied at night school and by saving enough money as an interpreter at a mine, he could afford passage to the U.S. On arrival he applied himself again, becoming the only non-white student at the University of Chicago.

After studying medicine at a black university in the South, he moved to Scotland, where he gained his Royal College of Physicians licence at Edinburgh in the early years of the war. Once qualified, he practised as a GP in Liverpool before moving to North-East England.

How quickly the middle-aged doctor's friendship with Merene deepened after their meeting in 1944 is not clear. But even before Banda arrived on the scene, the Frenches did not practise a conventional marriage.

'My father put my mother on a pedestal,' says their son Peter. 'He liked other men to admire her and I believe it was an open marriage. He didn't mind her seeing other men and if she wanted Hastings Banda to make her happy then so be it.

But he never thought it would end in divorce.' The affidavit William French signed when he finally petitioned for divorce on the grounds of his wife's adultery deserves to be reprinted almost verbatim.

'My wife and I were very happy together until I was discharged from the Army on October 12, 1945,' it began. 'Just prior to being discharged, my wife had met in North Shields, where she was staying with my mother and my young son, a Dr Hastings Kumuzu Banda, who is an East African, and she had become friendly with him.

'I had no objections as I thought it was purely a platonic friendship.

'My wife told me that Dr Banda was buying a practice in Harlesden, which was near our home, and she suggested that we could put him up at our flat while he was settling in the practice and getting a home together.

'Not suspecting that there was anything between Dr

Banda and my wife I consented, and so when I came out of the Army in October 1945 and returned to our flat in Harlesden, Dr Banda was already there.

'After a few weeks I began to notice that my wife appeared to be fonder of Dr Banda than a platonic relationship would have permitted, so I spoke to her about it and she did admit to me she was in love with him.

'I thought it was only an infatuation on her part and I frankly did not feel that Dr Banda had any feelings of affection towards my wife, so I didn't speak to him about it. I reasoned he would soon be leaving our flat and that if I were right in my feelings of infatuation the trouble would pass without having to embarrass him by taxing him with it.

'I had a number of discussions with my wife about this and eventually, in July 1946, my wife told me that she really was in love with Dr Banda and that she would not sleep with me anymore. She took off her wedding ring and refused to wear it any longer.'

SEVERAL months passed and still French refrained from confronting Banda, who continued to live as a 'paying guest' in the house.

'My wife moved into a separate bedroom and, although I was not sure, I felt in my own mind that on occasions she would sleep with Dr Banda,' French said in the affidavit.

'I firmly believed that if I took drastic steps it would drive her still further into the arms of Dr Banda, whereas if I was patient I could still win her back to my child and myself. So far as my child is concerned, she was still a good mother, but I wanted a home with my wife and child.

'I also realised that living in the same house I could easily have ascertained whether she was sleeping with Dr Banda, but didn't take steps to that end because I felt that I did know for certain that she was committing adultery it would so change the situation, especially in my mind, that there would be an immediate end to all hopes of a reconciliation. While I didn't know for certain, I could still try to win her back.'

Then came the most unlikely episode, in which William's weakness and cuckoldry were rubberstamped, his humiliation complete.

Dr Banda bought a large Victorian house in Brondesbury Park, North-West London, and he suggested that the Frenches should move in, too, with Merene as housekeeper.

'My wife was very keen on the idea but I didn't like it,' William French recalled. 'But the more I argued the more my wife insisted upon going and, although I realise now that it was a mistake and that I should have made a break, I felt my only hope was to go with her.'

So the doctor, his mistress, her husband and child set up home together, this time with Banda as master of the house.

'We all had separate bedrooms, but I still knew that my wife was sleeping with Dr Banda,' said Mr French.

At the age of six Peter was sent away to prep school in Hertfordshire because his father 'didn't want him to be brought up in that atmosphere'.

Mr French made one last pathetic attempt to persuade his wife away from Banda and, having failed, gave up and moved out in early 1949.

'He went during term time and we never really said goodbye,' says Peter. 'So when I came back it was just Mum, the doctor and me.'

Peter French has fond memories of Banda, although the African was hardly more paternal than his real father. 'He was a strict Victorian figure, very much the head of the household,' says Peter.

'ALTHOUGH he acted as my father, there weren't any hugs or kisses from him and he was as aloof as most people who've got their country's destiny in mind.'

The potentially scandalous domestic situation never seemed to become a public issue. Nor did the matter of race. Certainly Peter can't recall suffering as a result.

'By the age of 12 or so I realised what was happening between my mother and the doctor,' he recalls.

'Their shared bedroom was only across the landing from mine and I grew to understand what adults did in bed.

'But the doctor never came to my school and it wasn't so unusual after the war for children's fathers to be absent. And there weren't any children in the street at home, so I never had any taunts. In any case, it was a time before race was really an issue.'

However, certain proprieties had to be observed. 'When we were alone together at home my mother called him Hastings.

But when others were present she called him Doctor, as if theirs was purely a business relationship. I always called him Doctor.'

Banda was a good doctor and a popular figure in the district, particularly among his less wealthy patients who often bartered services rather than cash for his consultations.

In Harlesden, at least, he's remembered fondly.

Money was never a problem in the Banda household, as it had been when William French was in charge. Banda's 'family' had the first car in the street. The three would motor out to the country each Sunday. Peter was given train sets and other exotic (for the time) gifts for birthdays and Christmas.

'I was a spoiled child,' he admits.

'Perhaps it was the doctor's way of buying my approval.'

Merene provided the support that a GP cum statesman-in-waiting requires. 'She did everything for him,' says her son. 'She cooked, cleaned, ran the surgery, paid the bills, helped with patients and taught him the necessary social graces.'

BUT she was also closely involved in his political activities. The home in Brondesbury Park became a focal point for Nyasaland nationalism. Peter remembers tribal chiefs arriving from Africa and being taken by Banda, accompanied by his stepson, to a shop in Edgware Road to buy hats and coats more suitable for a British winter.

Merene even helped draw up the draft Nyasaland (later Malawi) constitution on the dinner table and was present when similar discussions with leaders from the Gold Coast (now Ghana) took place (one of them was Kwame Nkrumah).

On another occasion the former Labour Chancellor Sir Stafford Cripps and his wife came for lunch.

Lady Cripps gave Peter [pounds sterling]5, he remembers.

It was inevitable that Banda would eventually return to Africa.

In July 1953 he did so, selling his practice in London and settling in the Gold Coast. Six months later, Merene followed him, leaving her son behind.

The eccentric William French said in his subsequent affidavit:

'When my wife went to Africa with Dr Banda, I finally realised that all hope of winning her back had gone and I was considerably upset.'

Not as heartbroken as Peter, then aged 13. He says it was a 'tragic time' in his life. He remembers seeing his mother off on the Southampton-bound platform of Waterloo station. 'I was in floods of tears.'

For a while, during his holidays from a Merchant Navy college, he lived with his mother's sister. Then he had to move into his father's cramped East End flat, where he slept on a camp bed, far removed from the luxuries of the Banda home.

'It was a terrible time in my life,' he says. 'My father was quite unsuited to bringing up a child.'

Peter didn't see his mother for the next five years and received a letter only every three months or so.

How could Merene French have abandoned her only

child in such a way? Peter says: 'She felt she had to go with Dr Banda. That meant leaving the country, and she couldn't take me with her. Mum and the doctor planned to marry. I have no doubt that's what my mother thought at least. And I have no doubt, too, that he used her.'

Indeed, Merene had been useful as an aide de camp to Banda in London. Now, in the colonial Gold Coast, she was useful again, a striking white woman who 'created wow', according to her son, among the Africans, in the bush town where Banda settled, and the leaders in Accra who were about to take power from the British.

Following independence, she took an active if behind-the-scenes role, being particularly close to several key members of the first black administration.

She was known as A'Dench, an African approximation of Auntie French.

But by this time Banda's mission (and a spat with the Ghanaian government) had taken him back to his native Nyasaland, thousands of miles to the south-east, leaving his mistress in Ghana.

On his arrival in Nyasaland in July 1958 he fired off a letter to Merene in which there's strong evidence that an intimacy still existed.

'Dearest Sweet,' Banda began.

'Well, I have been to my birth place.

They arranged a mass meeting there to welcome me home last Sunday. I wish you had been there.' It ended: 'With sweetest love, Hastings.'

But the affair was on the wane.

Could a white woman really be a suitable first lady of a black African state?

'I have no doubt she expected to follow him, but it never happened,' says Peter, who flew out to see his mother in late 1958. He stayed with her for six weeks and Dr Banda was hardly mentioned.

Political unrest was already fermenting in the young country and Merene, perhaps having accepted that her

366

relationship with Banda was over, returned to Britain in 1960.

Initially she settled in London and worked in a public health laboratory.

In 1962, as Banda prepared to take power in an independent Malawi, the distance between the former lovers and Merene's attempts to close the gap are clear in a letter from Banda.

'DEAR Merene,' he wrote, 'Thank you very much for your letter. Actually, I never received any of the letters you mention. This is the first letter I have had from you for a very long time. Enclosed is a cheque for [pounds sterling]100. I hope it will help with warm clothes. How is Peter?' It ends formally: 'Kindest regards and remember me to Madge. Sincerely yours, Hastings.'

In the final years of her life, Merene French never spoke of her former lover, hardly acknowledging even his occasional appearances on television, dressed in homburg hat, dark suit and clutching his trademark gilded fly swat.

Did she dream of a seat alongside his throne?

Banda brought a degree of prosperity to Malawi. But what did Merene make of his one-party totalitarianism, increasing recourse to the torture, imprisonment and murder of critics? Or his pragmatic links with the apartheid regime in South Africa?

How different from the ideals propounded in her sitting room in London.

Surprisingly perhaps, Peter French has survived his childhood traumas and dislocation. Indeed, he's been happily married for more than 30 years, and he and his wife, Susan, have seen three sons through university. 'I wanted to provide them with the family stability that I never had,' he says.

When his mother died in 1976, Peter sent a letter to the Life President, His Excellency Hastings Banda, informing him of the fact. He received no reply."

Call to return home

Several influential leaders of the Nyasaland African Congress (NAC) including Henry Chipembere, Kanyama Chiume, Dunduzu Chisiza and T.D.T. Banda (no relation) pleaded with him to return to Nyasaland to take up leadership of their cause.

A delegation sent to London met with Dr. Banda at the Port of Liverpool where he was making arrangements to return to Ghana. He agreed to return but asked for some time to sort out a few private matters, probably seeking to clear his political name after the Mrs. French debacle.

The delegation returned without him and proceeded to make arrangements for his imminent return.

After two false starts, including a fracas between the police and African crowds threatening to storm a British Overseas Airways Corporation (BOAC) airplane rumoured to be carrying Dr. Banda at Chileka Airport, Banda finally made a showing on 6 July 1958 after an absence of about 42 years. He was acclaimed as the leader of the Nyasaland African Congress (NAC) at Nkata Bay in August the same year.

Return to his homeland

He soon began touring the country, speaking against the Central African Federation and urging its citizens to join the Nyasaland African Congress. He spoke to them in English because he was said to have forgotten his native language, Chichewa. He used an interpreter whenever he spoke, a role performed by John Msonthi and later by john Tembo who remained close to him for most of his career.

He was received enthusiastically wherever he spoke, and opposition to colonialism among the people of Nyasaland became increasingly common.

By February 1959, the situation had become serious enough that Rhodesian troops – from Southern Rhodesia – were flown in to help keep order, and a state of emergency was declared.

On 3 March 1959, Banda, along with hundreds of other Africans, was arrested during "Operation Sunrise." He was imprisoned in Gwelu Prison in Gwelo (now Gweru) in Southern Rhodesia, and leadership of the Malawi Congress Party (the Nyasaland African Congress under a new name) was temporarily assumed by Orton Chirwa who was released from prison in August 1959.

Chirwa was one of the architects of what came to be the new nation of Malawi but who was written out of history when Banda came to power. In fact, it was he who founded the Malawi Congress Party which led the country to independence. As Richard Carver stated in an obituary, "Orton Chirwa," in *The Independent*, London, UK, 22 October 1992:

"Orton Edgar Ching'oli Chirwa, lawyer and politician, born 30 January 1919, called to the Bar London 1958, Malawi Minister of Justice and Attorney General 1964, advocate and law lecturer Tanzania 1964-81, died in Zomba Malawi, 20 October 1992.

It was a small mercy that Orton Chirwa was allowed a final meeting with his wife Vera just a month before his death on Tuesday. The two were held in solitary confinement in separate wings of Zomba prison in southern Malawi. They had been imprisoned for nearly 11 years - Africa's longest serving prisoners of conscience.

That meeting was their first in eight years and only took place because a delegation of British lawyers was visiting. The lawyers said afterwards that Orton was virtually deaf and blind with untreated cataracts.

Orton Chirwa was Malawi's first black barrister. A founder of the Nyasaland African Congress, he was one of a group of young nationalist leaders who in 1958 took the fateful decision to invite Dr Hastings Kamuzu Banda, then living in Ghana, to return to Malawi. Chirwa and his colleagues felt that the experience and gravitas of an old man - Banda was already about 60 - would impress their African constituency.

In later years Banda would boast how he had single-handedly smashed the 'stupid' Central African Federation. Orton Chirwa and others of his generation were written out of history.

In 1959 the Federal Government banned the NAC and arrested many of its leaders, including Banda. As the senior leader at liberty Orton Chirwa set up the Malawi Congress Party and became its first president. The following year, after Banda's release, he stood down and handed him the leadership.

At independence in 1964 Orton Chirwa became Attorney General, but fell out with Banda over the slow pace of African advancement in the civil service. Banda sacked Chirwa and three other ministers, driving them into exile.

Chirwa settled in Tanzania, where he taught and practised law. His new political party, the Malawi Freedom Movement, appears to have had little active support inside Malawi which was now a one-party state with Banda president for life.

On Christmas Eve 1981, Orton, Vera and their son Fumbani were visiting Zambia when they were abducted by Malawian security officials. What exactly happened that night remains a mystery. The Chirwas maintained that they were visiting a sick relative. Perhaps they were tricked into going to the border area. The lurid official description of the now elderly Orton 'infiltrating' the country with two members of his family was clearly nonsense.

Two years later Orton and Vera were put on trial for treason. Malawi's legal system had changed since he was Attorney General. The Chirwas were tried before a 'traditional' court, with judges directly answerable to Banda. There was no defence counsel and they were not allowed to call witnesses. The procedural irregularities were bizarre: thus the police officer in charge of the investigation doubled as an 'independent' handwriting expert.

They were found guilty - of course - and sentenced to death. In 1984, after many appeals from governments and colleagues from their student days in London, Banda commuted their sentences to life imprisonment.

Life imprisonment proved to be a further sentence of death. The Chirwas were denied contact with each other and the outside world. Last year Orton tried to smuggle letters out to Tanzania. They were intercepted and he was punished with two days' squatting in handcuffs and leg-irons, without lavatory facilities.

When Malawian scholars are allowed to write their country's history, Orton Chirwa's role can be judged fairly. Meanwhile he remains a potent symbol of the struggle for human dignity and freedom of conscience."

Release from prison and path to independence

Even before Dr. Banda returned to Nyasaland, the mood in Great Britain had long been moving towards decolonisation but mainly because of political agitation in the colonies.

Banda was released from prison in April 1960 and was almost immediately invited to London for talks aimed at moving the country towards independence within a few years.

Elections were held in August 1961. While Banda was technically nominated as minister of land, natural resources and local government under the British governor, he became *de facto* prime minister of Nyasaland, a title that was formally given to him on 1 February 1963.

He and his fellow MCP ministers quickly expanded secondary education, reformed the so-called Native Courts, ended certain colonial agricultural tariffs and made other reforms.

R. A. Butler, the British Secretary of State for Home Department and Central African Affairs, essentially agreed to end the Federation which was formally dissolved on 31 December 1963.

It is said it was Banda himself who chose the name "Malawi" for the former Nyasaland.

On 6 July 1964, exactly six years after Banda's return to the country, Nyasaland became the independent Commonwealth of Malawi.

President of Malawi

1964 cabinet crisis

Barely a month after independence, Malawi suffered a cabinet crisis. Dr. Banda had already been accused of autocratic tendencies and several cabinet members presented him with proposals designed to limit his powers. He responded by dismissing four of the ministers. Other ministers resigned in sympathy. The dissidents fled the country and sought refuge in Tanzania and Zambia.

New constitution and consolidation of power

Malawi adopted a new constitution on 6 July 1966 in which the country was declared a republic. Banda was elected the country's first president for a five-year term; he was the only candidate.

The new constitution granted Banda wide executive and legislative powers and formally made the MCP the only legal party. However, the country had already been a de facto one-party state since independence.

In 1970, a congress of the ruling party, the Malawi Congress Party (MCP) declared Banda its president for life.

In 1971, the legislature declared Banda president for life. His official title was His Excellency, the Life President of the Republic of Malaŵi, Ngwazi Dr. Hastings Kamuzu Banda. The title *Ngwazi* means "chief of chiefs" (more literally, "great lion," or, some would say, "conqueror") in Chicheŵa.

Banda was mostly viewed externally as a benign, albeit eccentric, leader, an image fostered by his English-style three-piece suits, matching handkerchiefs and fly-whisk. He also spoke no Chichewa, and relied on a translator, John Msonthi.

In June 1967, he was awarded an honorary doctorate by the University of Massachuisetts with the encomium, "...pediatrician to his infant nation."

Within Malawi, views on him ranged from cult-like devotion to fear. While he portrayed himself as a caring headmaster to his people, his government was rigidly aauthoritarian even by African standards of the time. Although the constitution guaranteed civil rights and liberties, they meant almost nothing in practice and Malawi was essentially a police state.

Mail was opened and often edited. Telephones were tapped, and calls were known to be cut off if anyone said a critical word about the government. Overt opposition was not tolerated. Banda actively encouraged the people to report those who criticised him even if they were relatives. Opponents were often arrested, exiled (like Knyama Chiume) or died suspiciously (like Dick Metenje or Dr. Attati Mpakati).

Attati Mpakati, who died 24 March 1983 in Harare, Zimbabwe, was a dissident and leader of the Socialist League of Malawi (LESOMA) from 1975 until his death. He was killed by a letter bomb while in exile in Zimbabwe. It is widely suspected that the parcel was sent by the agents of President Banda. He had survived a similar attack in 1979 which President Banda admitted ordering.

The Mwanza Four incident

In 1983, three ministers – Dick Matenje, Twaibu Sangala, Aaron Gadama – and Member of Parliament David Chiwanga died mysteriously in what was labelled officially as a "traffic accident." Banda had invited an "internal debate on pending multiparty democracy" in Malawi. Unwittingly, during a "cabinet meeting," the three ministers had voiced support for the multiparty idea, effectively challenging Dr. Banda's claim to life presidency.

Angered, Banda promptly "dissolved cabinet" and announced parliament would meet immediately. At the end of that sitting of parliament, everyone in the chambers was effectively stripped of their political status. The three men were then rounded up at the Zomba Parliament buildings for questioning. Chiwanga happened to see them being tortured in a back room and had to be silenced too.

The four men were later bundled in Matenje's Peugeot 604 and driven to Thambani in Mwanza District [west of Blantyre] where the "accident" was staged—allegedly the car had "overturned while the men had been attempting to escape into neighbouring Mozambique". Later, it was found out they had perished from tent pins hammered into their heads. Dr. Banda ordered that the caskets not be opened for a last viewing and a night burial.

Life in Banda's Malawi

Party membership passcards

All adult citizens were required to be members of the

MCP. Party cards had to be carried at all times and presented at random police inspections. The cards were sold, often by Banda's Malawi Young Pioneers (MYP). In some cases, these youths even sold cards to unborn children.

Malawi Young Pioneers

The Malawi Young Pioneers were the notorious paramilitary wing of the MCP that were used to intimidate and harass the public. The Pioneers bore arms, conducted espionage and intelligence operations and were trusted bodyguards for Banda. They enforced the laws of Malawi and helped build a culture of fear.

Cult of personality

Banda was the subject of a very pervasive cult of personality. Every business building was required to have an official picture of him hanging on the wall, and no poster, clock or picture could be higher than his portrait. Before every movie, a video of Banda waving to the people was shown while the anthem played.

When Banda visited a city, a contingent of women were expected to greet him at the airport and dance for him. A special cloth, bearing the president's picture, was the required attire for these performances.

Churches had to be government sanctioned.

Censorship

All movies shown in theatres were first viewed by the Malawi Censorship Board and edited for content. Videotapes had to be sent to the Censorship Board to be viewed. Once edited, the movie was given a sticker stating that it was now suitable for viewing and sent back to the owner.

Items to be sold in book shops were also edited. Pages, or parts of pages, were cut out of magazines like *Newsweek* and *Time*.

The press and radio were tightly controlled, and mainly served as outlets for government propaganda. Television was banned.

Knowledge of pre-Banda history was discouraged, and many books on these subjects were burned.

Banda also allegedly persecuted some of the northern tribes, particularly the Tumbuka, banning their language and books as well as teachers from certain tribes.

Europeans who broke any of these rules were often "PI'ed"; that is, declared Prohibited Immigrants and deported.

Dress code and conservatism

His government supervised the people's lives very closely. Early in his rule, Banda instituted a dress code which was rooted in his socially conservative predilections. For example, women were not allowed to bare their thighs or to wear trousers. Banda argued that the dress code was not instilled to oppress women but to encourage honour and respect for them.

For men, long hair and beards were banned as a sign of dissent. Men could be seized and forced to have a haircut at the discretion of border officials or police. Kissing in public was not allowed, nor were movies which contained depictions of kissing.

Even foreigners coming in to Malawi were subject to Banda's dress code. In the 1970s, prospective visitors to the country were informed of the following requirement for obtaining visas:

"Female passengers will not be permitted to enter the country if wearing short dresses or trouser-suits, except in transit or at Lake Holiday resorts or National parks. Skirts

376

and dresses must cover the knees to conform with Government regulations. The entry of 'hippies' and men with long hair and flared trousers is forbidden."

Women's issues

Nonetheles, Banda was very supportive of women's rights compared to other African rulers during his reign. He founded Chitukuko Cha Amai m'Malawi (CCAM) to address the concerns, needs, rights and opportunities for women in Malawi. This institution also motivated women to excel both in education and government and encouraged them to play more active roles in their community, church and family.

The foundation's national advisor was Cecilia Tamanda Kadzamira.

Cecelia Tamanda Kadzamira was the official hostess of Malawi during the reign of Kamuzu Banda. Whilst she and Dr. Banda were not officially married, she served as the first lady or official hostess for several years. She was the most powerful woman in Malawi and was fondly referred to as "Mama," or "Mother of the Nation."

She was born in Rhodesia and lived in Old Highfields, Salisbury (now Harare) where she attended school at Mbizi Primary. After her General Certificate of Education (GCE), she enrolled at Salisbury Central Hospital as a cadet nurse where she qualified and was briefly posted to Old Highfields Clinic.

When her father, John Kadzamira, returned to Nyasaland with his family, she joined Dr. Banda at his Limbe medical practice as a staff nurse.

After working for Dr. Banda as a nurse at the Limbe Surgery, she moved to Zomba State House as Dr. Banda's private secretary.

After the cabinet crisis in 1964 where Banda consolidated his political power, she was appointed the Official Government Hostess (OGH).

There is also speculation of her role in the Machiavellian public trial and hanging of Albert Muwalo, the last MCP secretary-general.

In line with her first-lady duties, Dr. Banda announced Mama Tamanda Kadzamira would run an organisation called Chitukuko Cha Amayi muMalawi (CCAM), giving her more influence in Malawian politics and greater control over who had access to Dr. Banda.

She was rumoured as having presidential ambitions. Many point out that during Dr. Banda's reign, she made many decisions for the country when she played her private and public roles.

She became more powerful when Dr. Banda became older and could no longer run the affairs of the country. When Dr Banda turned senile, she unsuccessfully tried to influence him to sponsor her uncle John Tembo as his successor in the party. Although Tembo had been acting in Banda's place in his absence, Dr. Banda handed the MCP political baton to Gwanda Chakuamba.

Her influence over Bamda's political and personal decisions played a significant role in the development of Malawi. The two were inseparable, and she influenced many aspects of his life such as who he had access to, reading materials, knowledge that was passed to him, and policies he approved.

Her influence on the president was so strong that in the 1980s when tension grew between them, Banda banned the Simon and Garfunkel song *Cecilia* from Malawian radio. The lyrics of the song included *"Cecilia/I'm down on my knees/I'm begging you please to come home."*

Controversy grew between Ms. Kadzamira and Banda's relatives after his death when his family accused her of manipulating him to change his will to gain access to his assets.

Ms. Kadzamira and her uncle, John Tembo, were charged with conspiracy to murder after Banda's death, but they were later acquitted due to lack of sufficient evidence.

Banda was also charged but was acquitted because of memory failure caused by his age and progressive senility.

Infrastructure

In 1964, after serving as a government minister in the colonial administration, Banda adopted a macroeconomic policy aimed at accelerating economic development for the betterment of Malawians. He settled on the Rostow model of "Catch Up" Economics under which Malawi would vigorously pursue Import Substitution Industrilaisation (ISI). This entailed both a quest for "self-sufficiency" for Malawi, becoming less reliant on its former colonial master, and growth of an industrial base that could ensure Malawi was capable of producing its own goods and services.

Such capacity would then be used to catch up and even "overtake" the West.

An infrastructure development programme was initiated under the various Development Policies (DEVEPOLs) documents which Malawi adopted from 1964 onwards.

The country's infrastructure benefited through massive road construction programmes. With the decision to shift the capital city from Zomba to Lilongwe (against vociferous objections from the British preference for the economically and well developed Blantyre), a new road was built linking Blantyre and Zomba to Lilongwe. The Capital City Development Corporation (CCDC) in Lilongwe was itself a beehive of infrastructure development, supported by planning and funds from apartheid South Africa.

The British refused to finance the move to Lilongwe. The CCDC became the sole development agent for Lilongwe, putting up roads, the government seat at Capital Hill, and so on. Other infrastructural entities were added, including Malawi Hotels Limited which undertook massive projects such as the Mount Soche, Capital Hotel and Mzuzu Hotel.

On the industrial side, Malawi Development Corporation (MDC) was tasked with setting up industries and other businesses. Meanwhile, Dr. Banda's own Press Corporation Limited and MYP's Spearhead Corporation embarked on various business initiatives which led to an economic boom during the mid- to late 1970s.

However, by 1979/80, the bubble had burst due to the global economic crisis triggered by the Yom Kippur War between Israel and the Arabs in 1973. Rising oil prices and falling global commodity prices combined to wreak havoc on a fragile and landlocked Malawian economy based on an insular and indefensible ISI macroeconomic strategy. Increasingly, the economy was rearranged into a political tool to serve the consumption needs of the emerging Malawian middle-class and thus render it less prone to revolution.

Banda personally founded Kamuzu Academy, a school modelled on Eton, at which Malawian children were taught Latin and ancient Greek by expatriate classics teachers and disciplined if they were caught speaking Chichewa. All the teachers were said to be white. He reportedly did not want any black teachers to teach at the academy.

He spent almost all the country's education budget on that project, while increasingly ignoring the needs and welfare of the greater majority [80%] of Malawians toiling in the rural areas.

And the few urban areas which Dr. Banda's ISI macroeconomic policies had created were now being battered by the arrival of more and more rural people seeking better opportunities.

Eventually, with the collapse of the Cold War, the World Bank and the International Monetary Fund (IMF) arrived, imposing a series of Structural Adjustment Programmes (SAPs) from 1987.

Wealth

It is believed that during his rule, Banda accumulated at least US$320 million in personal assets, thought to be invested in everything from agriculture to mining interests in South Africa. The most controversial part of this is the suspicion that his two grandchildren, who currently reside in the United States and South Africa, are the heirs to the Banda fortune. One of the grandchildren graduated from law school in the United States, while the other remained in South Africa.

Foreign policy

Relations with African countries

Malawi was the only African country which recognised South Africa and established diplomatic relations with it, including a trade treaty which angered other African leaders. They threatened to expel Malawi from the Organisation of African Unity until Banda left power. Banda responded by accusing other African countries of hypocrisy. He ridiculed them by saying in a public speech to his parliament "There is no terror, Cassius, in your threats" (*Julius Caesar*). He told them to concentrate on convincing the South African government that apartheid was unnecessary.

Furthermore, he added: "[African leaders] practise disunity, not unity, while posing as the liberators of Africa. While they play in the orchestra of Pan Africanism, their own Romes are burning."

He became only partially rehabilitated in the eyes of other African leaders after the demise of the apartheid regime in South Africa.

Relations with South Africa

Banda was also the only African ruler to establish diplomatic ties with South Africa during apartheid as well as the oppressive Portuguese regime in Mozambique. Since the cabinet crisis in 1964, Banda became increasingly isolated in African politics.

On the other hand, his antipathy for Roy Welensky and the so called "stupid federation" was a smokescreen he used to reject the proposed Bangula Hydro-electric dam – proposed to be bigger than the Gezira Dam in Khartoum – that Welensky's Federation had sought and obtained funding for from the British government.

Banda went on to blame everything including snails (likely to cause widespread Bilharzias) in order to abort the project.

In turn, the British denied Banda the funding and budgetary support he needed to build his pet dream of a new capital city at Lilongwe in his home region. He then turned to South Africa – itself playing geo-political games in the region – which gave him a soft loan of 300 million rand.

The *quid pro quo* was that Banda had to support South Africa's apartheid policies among fellow African leaders. Hence, on one occasion he paid a state visit to South Africa where he met his South African counterparts at Stellenbosch.

Involvement in Mozambique

Banda's involvement in Mozambique dated back to Portuguese colonial days when Banda supported the Portuguese colonial government. Following Malawi's independence, he strengthened his relationship with the Portuguese colonial government by appointing Jorge Jardim as Malawi's honorary consul in Mozambique in

September 1964. He also worked against the Front for the Liberation of Mozambique (FRELIMO) forces in Malawi in continued support of the Portuguese colonial forces.

By the 1980s, Banda was able to help destabilise neighbouring Mozambique by supporting RENAMO (Mozambique National Resistance), a guerrilla group which was fighting to overthrow the FRELIMO government; FRELIMO came to power after Mozambique won independence from Portugal in June 1975.

Malawi was used to channel foreign aid to RENAMO from South Africa's apartheid regime.

Mozambican President Samora Machel presented evidence to the leaders of the Frontline states showing that Banda was still supporting RENAMO in spite of an agreement signed in 1984 to stop such activities.

In September 1986, Machel, Robert Mugabe and Kenneth Kaunda visited Banda in order to persuade him to stop supporting RENAMO. Machel's successor, Joaquim Chissano, continued to complain of Malawi's lack of willingness to stop supporting RENAMO.

Banda, however, was trying to protect Malawian interests in the Nacala port in Mozambique and did not want to rely on South Africa for Malawian imports and exports because of high cost. Mozambique and Malawi came to an agreement to place troops from both countries in Nayuchi near the port to stop RENAMO attacks.

Incidents of Malawian soldiers being killed over the course of four years angered the army because members of the Malawi Young Pioneers (MYP) were supporting RENAMO insurgents, thus pitting the two against each other.

Tanzania–Malawi dispute over Lake Nyasa

The partition of Lake Nyasa's surface area between Malawi and Tanzania is under dispute. Tanzania claims that the international border runs through the middle of the lake. This is along the lines of the border that were set out between the German and British territories before 1914. On the other hand, Malawi claims the whole of the surface of this lake that is not in Mozambique, including the waters that are next to the shoreline of Tanzania.

The foundations of this dispute were laid when the British colonial government, which had recently captured Tanganyika from Germany, placed all of the water under the jurisdiction of the territory of Nyasaland without a separate administration for the Tanganyikan portion of the surface. This dispute has led to conflicts in the past, although in recent years Malawi has refused to enforce any claims to the disputed portion.

Occasional flare-ups of conflict during the 1990s, and also sometimes in the 21st century, have affected fishing rights, particularly those of Tanzanian fishermen who live on the lake shore and who have occasionally been accused of fishing in Malawian waters.

Political demise

The transition toward democracy in Malawi began in the early 1990s when international aid donors demanded that Banda implement reforms aimed at making his government transparent and accountable to the people and the international community as a condition for aid. The British government also stopped their financial support. This opened up the country to democratic multiparty politics.

In March 1992, Catholic bishops in Malawi issued a Lenten pastoral letter which criticised Banda and his government. Students of the university of Malawi at Chancellor College and the Polytechnic joined protests and demonstrations to support the bishops, forcing authorities to close the campuses.

In April 1992, Chakufwa Chihana, a labour unionist,

openly called for a national referendum on the political future of Malawi. He was arrested before he finished his speech at Lilongwe International Airport.

In May, labour riots in the city of Blantyre turned political with demands that Banda give up power.

This mounting pressure from within and from the international community forced Banda to concede to hold a referendum to decide the future of Malawi's politics in October 1992.

The referendum was held on 14 June 1993, with voters opting for democracy. Banda's one-party state was dismantled.

After this, political parties besides the MCP were formed and preparation for the general elections began.

Banda worked with the newly formed parties and the church and stepped down without protest when a special assembly stripped him of his title of President for Life, along with most of his powers. The transition was relatively peaceful in spite of a very rigid system of rule.

The end of Banda's reign was inevitable after the end of the Cold War helped bring about fundamental changes in many countries round the globe, as despotic regimes were swept out of power.

An eccentric character as well, Banda was profiled in an article by a British journalist as his rule was coming to an end. It was the beginning of the end of an era for Malawi and for a leader whose name was synonymous with Malawi. As Richard Bowden, in his report from Malawi's capital Lilongwe, stated an article appropriately entitled, "Africa's Oldest Despot Faces End of his Strange Journey," in *The Independent*, London, 13 June 1993:

"The final act in an extraordinary African drama will be played out tomorrow in Malawi.

Malawians will vote in a referendum to decide between a one-party state and multi-party democracy. It is the last country in Africa to bend to the demand for a multi-party system, and its ruler, Dr Hastings Kamuzu Banda, is the last president in anglophone Africa to have ruled since independence.

In some ways Dr Banda has been a caricature of an African tyrant. He took over the beautiful but backward protectorate called Nyasaland from the British, locked up his former colleagues, named himself president for life and ruled the country as his personal kingdom.

Dressed in a dark three-piece suit, wearing a black Homburg hat and waving a fly-whisk, he travels the country telling rallies that but for him they would still be living under colonialism.

Back in State House, he appoints, sacks or imprisons like a slave owner. Some who protested were executed or murdered.

Meanwhile the economy, dependent on primary agricultural products, has slid into debt and destitution.

Having achieved independence for Malawi, he turned his back on the black nationalist struggle in the rest of southern Africa and befriended Ian Smith's regime in Rhodesia and the South Africans, who rewarded him by paying for a new capital and a huge palace at Lilongwe. He spurned ideology and grandiose projects - apart from Lilongwe. He believed Malawi's future lay in agriculture and discipline.

Like the British rulers before him, he was ambivalent about education. He built Kamuzu College, a bizarre imitation of Eton, which had only expatriate teachers and taught Latin and Greek. But although he said he believed in schools, he felt threatened by the new elite that emerged from them. He felt happier being the most educated Malawian, caring for the ignorant peasants in paternalistic fashion.

Four years ago Margaret Thatcher visited Malawi, heaped praise on Dr Banda and his government and tipped him some extra aid. The words human rights or democracy never crossed her lips. But, like all other Western powers,

Britain has a new agenda in Africa, and in 1991 cut off aid to force the government to move towards democracy.

Dr Banda grudgingly gave in to the pressure, and last October announced a referendum - but only to prove that those who were calling for multi-party democracy were a tiny, dissident minority, and that most Malawians supported his one-party state.

Since then he has campaigned on this theme, reminding his people of all he has done by rescuing them from colonialism and building schools and clinics. He has identified himself so closely with the one-party state that, if the vote goes against him tomorrow, he will lose everything.

According to those who have known him longest, Dr Banda is now 97. As he grew older, he fell more and more under the influence of the oddly named 'Official Hostess', Cecilia Kadzamira. Dr Banda never married, and he became dependent on this former nurse, who is always at his side and controls access to him.

Ms Kadzamira, or Mama as the President calls her, has an uncle, John Tembo, who is regarded in Malawi as a wicked uncle. With his niece's assistance, Mr Tembo has grown more powerful and is now the most senior minister in the government. He is much feared and many say they will be voting for multi-party democracy on Monday not because they want Dr Banda to go, but because they do not want Mr Tembo and Mama Kadzamira to take over when he dies.

OF ALL African leaders, Dr Banda is the most intriguing. He is a man who has lived in two worlds, Africa and Europe, yet is at home in neither; a man who was known to his friends as a sweet-natured, unassuming and intelligent doctor, but who disintegrated into a vain, paranoid tyrant given to outbursts of rage.

In Britain he was a doctor with a Mother Teresa reputation, yet he was later to be thrown out of Ghana for carrying out abortions. He has never married and appeared to have a fear of sex. Miniskirts, bell-bottoms and long male hair have been banned in Malawi since the permissive Sixties. His one known affair ended when he abandoned the woman who loved him, and their child.

His first wrench was leaving his village in central Malawi to work in the gold mines of South Africa. He was not to return for 43 years, and he lost all contact with the country. He even forgot his mother tongue. His means of escape was education, and even by the standards of his strict Scottish Presbyterian mission education, he pursued it with an astonishing single-mindedness.

He managed to reach America, where he qualified as a doctor, then left to try to make his home in Edinburgh, where he was reportedly shocked to find that dancing was permitted. After retraining as a doctor under the British system, he set up a practice in the poorest part of Liverpool, and soon gained a reputation for free care for the poor, even paying the rent of those facing eviction. When the Second World War broke out, he refused military service as a conscientious objector, but was drafted to the Tyne, where people flocked to his surgery because of his abilities and charm.

From North Shields he moved to Harlesden in north London, where he had an affair with his secretary, Margaret French, who became pregnant. Mrs French was divorced by her husband, and the publicity forced Dr Banda to leave for Ghana. Mrs French followed him with their child, but he rejected them.

In Ghana he seems to have broken down, and those who knew him then said he was depressed and angry. He was forced to leave Ghana after being accused of carrying out illegal abortions at his practice in Kumasi.

Throughout all of this, Dr Banda kept in touch with politics in Africa and in Malawi. Despite his success, he was constantly buffeted by racism. When he became a doctor, the colonial authorities offered to let him return to Nyasaland as long as he had no social contact with whites.

The battle in Nyasaland was over federation. The white rulers of Rhodesia wanted a federation of Southern Rhodesia (now Zimbabwe), Northern Rhodesia (now Zambia) and Nyasaland; but black Africans were against it.

Dr Banda returned to Africa in 1958 to fight federation, and was sent to prison by the colonial authorities. But the tide of history was with him, and on his release, he was treated as a revered statesman and invited to tea at No 10 Downing Street.

As he came to power, Dr Banda realised he no longer knew Malawi; he begged a British friend to advise him about his fellow nationalists. He turned inwards and became suspicious and domineering.

Within weeks of Malawi's independence, he clashed with colleagues who had kept the presidential seat warm for him, sacking and jailing them. Since then he has ruled alone, and become increasingly remote.

But there have been moments of insight into his feelings. Dr Fergus Macpherson, a Presbyterian minister and an old friend, whose father helped Dr Banda to become an elder of the Church of Scotland, met him again in 1977. 'We had talked of the old days in Edinburgh and he was warm and friendly. Then I raised the case of a woman political prisoner. He went berserk. He screamed and ranted, there was saliva coming from his mouth, his feet were dancing up and down, and his eyeballs were rolling alarmingly.'

Within a few minutes, however, he had calmed down and agreed to release the woman. Dr Macpherson met his old friend again a few weeks ago. 'He was very frail, myopic and hard of hearing. I had to get close so he could read my lips. As he talked, he became very affectionate, as he was in the old days.' But when Dr Macpherson spoke about human rights in Malawi, the old man said: 'I know nothing of this.'

'He has become a palace prisoner,' Dr Macpherson

said. 'Four times he told me he did not know what was going on in Malawi. Then he said to me, 'I'm so lonely, so lonely.' ' "

As the tide of democracy swept across Malawi, efforts were made to destroy the institutions Banda had built to keep him power. One of the most feared was the Malawi Young Pioneers (MYP).

An operation was launched to deal with the menace. Known as Operation Bwezani, it was an army operation to disarm the Malawi Young Pioneers at the height of the political transition in December 1993.

Bwezani means "give back," in Chichewa, the main local language of Malawi which was also Banda's native language although he forgot how to speak it after more than 40 years of absence from his homeland.

The MYP had a strong network of spies and supporters countrywide at all levels in society. They were Kamuzu Banda's personal security bodyguards and were all trained and indoctrinated in Kamuzuism. They also had military training.

After some questions about his health, Banda ran in Malawi's first truly democratic presidential election in 1994. He was roundly defeated by Bakili Muluzi, a member of the Yao tribe from the southern region of the country, whose two terms in office were not without serious controversy.

The party Banda led since taking over from Orton Chirwa in 1960, the Malawi Congress Party, remains a major force in Malawian politics.

Mwanza Trials

In 1995, Banda was arrested and charged with the murder, ten years previously, of former cabinet colleagues. He was acquitted due to lack of evidence. He remained quite unrepentant in his opinion of Malawians, calling them "children in politics" and saying they would miss his iron-fisted rule (see *Big Men, Little People* by Alec Russell).

A statement of apology was issued on 4 January 1996 in the name of H. Kamuzu Banda to the people of his nation shortly after being acquitted in the Mwanza Trials. The statement was met with controversy, suspicion and disdain. It was also questioned whether Banda wrote the statement himself or if someone wrote it on his behalf. It stated:

"Systems of government are dynamic and they are bound to change in accordance with the wishes of and aspirations of the people...During my term of office, I selflessly dedicated myself to the good cause of Mother Malawi in the fight against Poverty, Ignorance and Disease among many other issues; but if within the process, those who worked in my government or through false pretence in my name or indeed unknowingly by me, pain and suffering was caused to anybody in this country in the name of nationhood, I offer my sincere apologies.

I also appeal for a spirit of reconciliation and forgiveness amongst us all...

Our beautiful country has been nicknamed "The Warm Heart of Africa" and we have been admired for our warmth and spirit of hardwork. This admiration calls not only for a need for us to look at our past and present and draw lessons from it, but there is even a greater need for us to look forward to the future in our endeavours to reconstruct and reconcile if we have to move forward at all."

Death

Banda died in a hospital in South Africa on 25 November 1997, reportedly aged 101.

Although buried with pomp, in the decade after his death, there were calls for a more substantial memorial for the country's first president. Construction of a mausoleum with provision for a library and a dancing arena was begun in 2005.

When he died, *The New York Times*, in its edition of 27 November 2007, had this report, "Kamuzu Banda Dies: 'Big Man' Among Anticolonialists," from Johannesburg, South Africa:

"Hastings Kamuzu Banda, a founding father in postcolonial Africa who led Malawi to independence in 1964 and then ruled it with a combination of caustic wit, eccentricity and cruelty for 30 years, died on Tuesday (25 November) night in a hospital here....

After a revolt within his cabinet, he declared himself President for Life in 1971 and said his opponents would become 'food for crocodiles.' Hundreds were killed, tortured or forced into exile....

Dr. Banda was perhaps the most idiosyncratic of the 'big men' who led their countries out of colonialism. He held degrees from American and Scottish universities and his London medical offices became a sort of anticolonialist salon frequented by Jomo Kenyatta of Kenya and Kwame Nkrumah of the Gold Coast (now Ghana).

But once in power, Dr. Banda simultaneously affected the lion-tail fly whisk of an African king, the dark suits and homburgs of a British businessman and the arms of a Scottish baron. He refused to make speeches in African languages and established a school modeled on Eton in his birthplace, Mtunthama, where penniless students were taught Latin, Greek and African history from the British point of view. He hired only white foreigners to teach at the school and to run the ministries and businesses that built his personal fortune.

Under his rule, Malawi spurned black nationalist movements and was the only African nation with

392

diplomatic ties to apartheid South Africa and to Israel. He was the darling of cold warriors and big business, and amassed power in his own hands, keeping the Ministries of Justice, Foreign Affairs, Agriculture and Public works to himself, as well as the trusteeship of the state monopolies in tobacco farming, factories, oil and banking....

Victorian in his demands on public morality, he banned women from wearing pants or miniskirts. Long-haired male tourists arriving in Malawi either submitted to shearing by the airport barber or went home.

He also banned television, though he watched it himself by satellite, and prevented the Simon and Garfunkel song 'Cecelia' from being played on local radio, considering it an affront to his consort (Cecilia Kadzamira). He referred to Malawi's 10 million citizens as 'my children' and was said to be deeply embittered when they turned him out in 1994....

His sleek capital, Lilongwe, was built with South African money and South Africa underwrote and trained the red-shirted Young Pioneers, a paramilitary youth group that spied on citizens and terrorized dissidents. And in one of the world's smallest and poorest nations, where the per-capita income was $200 a year, Dr. Banda kept five residences, a fleet of British luxury cars and a private jet....

His first education was at a Church of Scotland mission, but he left at a young age to run away to South Africa....After eight years as a clerk at a Johannesburg gold mine, studying at night, he won help from a Methodist bishop to come to the United States. He studied at the Wilberforce Institute in Xenia, Ohio, and at Indiana University before becoming the only black to graduate from the University of Chicago in 1931.

He received an M.D. from Meharry Medical College in Nashville, then moved to Britain to train at the Universities of Glasgow and Edinburgh and study tropical medicine in Liverpool.

393

He prospered as a physician in suburban London, but in 1953, furious that Britain had allowed the establishment of the Federation of Rhodesia and Nyasaland instead of taking power away from white expatriates, he moved to the Gold Coast, now Ghana, and railed against British treachery. Despite their fear of his firebrand tendencies, the colonial authorities let him return in 1958 to lead the Nyasaland African Congress.

He had apparently forgotten his native tongue, but got an uproarious welcome when he told his audience in English, borrowing from Patrick Henry,'In Nyasaland, we mean to be masters. And if that is treason, make the most of it.'

Riots broke out, and he spent a year in prison in Rhodesia before being released to lead his new Malawi Congress party to victory in a 1961 election. He told white settlers to accept majority rule 'or pack up'....

In 1994, under pressure from Western nations who cut off aid to enforce demands for democratic reforms, he called elections. He was defeated by Bakili Muluzi, a former protege who had resigned from the Cabinet in 1982 suspecting he was about to be killed. His replacement, Mr. Muluzi said, was murdered."

Family

Banda had no known heirs, but had a vast fortune at stake that is run by his family. He was also unmarried when he died.

Cecilia Kadzamira was the official hostess or first lady of Malawi. She also essentially ruled the country together with her uncle, John Tembo, during Banda's last years.

His affair and relationship with Merene French remains largely a mystery. He had rejected companionship and marriage and turned his back on the Englishwoman who bore his son.

394

Jane Dzanjalimodzi, Banda's great grand niece, was appointed in 2003 as the executor of his estate.

In 2010, Jim Jumani Johanssen claimed to be the son of the late president and sought DNA testing through the courts of Malawi. His whole name, legally, is Jim Jumani Immanuel Masauko Kamuzu Banda. He was 37 years old in 2010.

A Malawian Swedish, he claimed to be the son of Dr. Kamuzu Banda. He changed his name to Jim Jumani Immanuel Masauko Kamuzu Banda and said that it was after Banda died in 1997 that 'some government officials' told him about who his father really was.

Officially, Banda died childless and unmarried.

Johansson's claim and resemblance to the former dictator opened up many unanswered questions about the legacy of Banda. Johanssen became a celebrity overnight in Malawi owing to his uncanny resemblance to the former president and his measures to seek legal means of proving his identity.

Malawians are divided on whether he is the true heir but the public is demanding a right to know as well.

Johanssen went to the cabinet to have his name changed officially to Jim Jumani Immanuel Masauko Kamuzu Banda and this was legally granted by the courts who stated that he had the right to call himself any name he wanted in spite of attempts to block this move by the Banda family.

Kamuzu's DNA was secretly taken from the College of Medicine for the purpose of preliminary tests with the help of an unnamed Malawian doctor. Preliminary DNA tests conducted in a private lab in South Africa show that Jim Jumani Johansson is the biological son of Kamuzu Banda. Jumani is still seeking official DNA testing with permission of the Banda estate to prove or disprove his paternity.

Banda was not known to be in any relationships that resulted in heirs but there is evidence of affairs which have mainly been kept confidential.

The official hostess was Cecilia Kadzamira but it is believed it was not a sexual relationship by Malawian historians like John Lwanda. According to Lwanda, Kadzamira cannot be the mother of Jim Jumani Johanssen.

Miriam Kaunda, the adoptive mother of Jim Jumani Johanssen, claims that his father is Muhammad Jogee, an Indian Malawian living outside of Malawi. Jogee, or proof of his existence, however, cannot be located. Banda's family also claim that Jogee is the real father of Jim Jumani Johanssen, obviously to exclude him from any inheritance of Dr. Banda's vast amount of wealth he left behind.

Miriam Kaunda raised Johanssen. But Johanssen insists that she is not his mother, particularly in light of her refusal to take a DNA test for maternity. Miriam Kaunda, a former beauty queen, insists that Banda is not his father.

Although Johanssen is seeking a high court to order DNA testing, Bandas family are denying the use of DNA samples to prove or disprove the claim. Banda's family is skeptical about his claims because of the property claims that his heritage would mean.

A great grand-niece of Dr. Banda, Jane Dzanjalimodzi, noted that "many people will come out of the woodwork to make claims because they know Banda's vast estate is about to be distributed."

In tense court battles, Banda's family members attempted to block Johanssen from legally changing his name to Kamauzu Banda and from visiting the family estates. They also claimed that Johanssen was a Swede, not a Malawian citizen and could not make any claims in Malawian courts without paying court costs.

Johanssen however, insisted on having a court-supervised DNA testing where both himself and Banda's family representatives would be present.

Lawyers from the Centre for Human Rights and Rehabilitation (CHRR) were hired to assist him in his claims.

Although there are people in Malawi who claim to be Banda's blood relatives, and Banda himself said he had such relatives in Malawi, rumours still persist that he was not a Malawian. It is claimed that he "bought" relatives in what was then Nyasaland when he "returned home" to legitimise his identity as someone who was indigenous to Nyasaland.

The lingering suspicion about his identity was further fuelled by claims from some quarters that he was a black American impostor who assumed the identity of the real Banda when Banda died in the United States.

Yet it is difficult to reconcile such claims with some well-known facts. There was not even a trace of an American accent when he spoke. His accent was neither American nor British. And one could easily tell from his pronunciation of some words that there were traces of a distinctly African accent in his speech in spite of the fact that he had lived outside Malawi – mostly in the United States and in the United Kingdom – for more than 40 years.

It could, of course, be argued that he was clever enough to cover up his American accent and imitate an African accent. However, that would be sheer speculation, given the fact that even when he was not in control of his emotions, and spoke naturally in outbursts of rage, there still were traces of an American accent.

But in spite of all that, the suspicion that he was a black American impostor lingers on and is even given credence by some scholars including Professor Terence Ranger, a well-known specialist in African affairs. According to an article in *Malawi News*, 11 December, 1997, "Controversial Biography: Banda 'an American Imposter'":

"Kamuzu Banda, the man who ruled Malawi for 30 years, may not have been Malawian after all.

397

A controversial biography alleges Banda was actually an American impostor who spent his life punishing anyone who questioned his roots, according to a South African newspaper, the *Mail & Guardian*. The allegation is contained in *Postcolonial Identities in Africa*, edited by Richard Werner and Terence Ranger.

In a chapter entitled "Between God and Kamuzu," the book says Banda died young while a medical student in the United States. American Richard Armstrong, whom Banda had befriended, took his place. The book says Armstrong and Banda met as medical students and spent hours talking and sharing stories of their lives. Banda became seriously ill and died before completing his studies.

Armstrong left the United States for Africa and spent some time in Ghana, his mother's ancestral home, before travelling to Nyasaland, as Malawi was then known. The book says that in order to succeed, Banda had to reveal his identity to a small band of collaborators. With their help, he 'bought' relatives in Kasungu District.

However, Banda refused to eat *nsima*, Malawi's staple food, and persisted in speaking only English, with an interpreter translating his messages into the country's languages.

Whoever ruled Malawi, Armstrong or Banda, the book says it was a brutal dictatorship, in which thousands of political opponents were arrested, tortured and killed."

And according to the *Mail & Guardian*, Johannesburg, 28 November 1997, in its article, "Was Kamuzu an American Imposter?":

"The death of former Malawian president Kamuzu Banda invites the following question: who was he really?

President Nelson Mandela seemed in two minds this week. Asked for thoughts on the departed despot, he acknowledged that Banda did not 'have a very good reputation' because of his support of the old apartheid regime, but then had redeemed himself through his subsequent generosity, personally sending him a large sum of money following his release from prison – without his even asking. And then when he did ask for contributions on behalf of the African National Congress, Banda had 'responded magnificently.'

But the identity issue academics have been debating is of a different nature.

It seems the old dictator may not have been the man he appeared to be.

There has been a story circulating for decades in Malawi that Kamuzu Banda died young, while a medical student. And that an American medical student who had befriended him had taken his place.

Who died in the Garden City Clinic this week? Was it Kamuzu Banda, or Richard Armstrong?

In the 1996 book *Postcolonial Identities in Africa*, edited by Richard Werbner and Terence Ranger, the issue is addressed, though left unresolved, in the chapter entitled, 'Between God and Kamuzu.'

According to the counter-biography of Banda, he and Armstrong met as medical students, and spent hours talking and sharing the stories of their lives. Banda became seriously ill and died before completing his studies.

Armstrong departed for Africa and spent some time in Ghana - his mother's ancestral home - before travelling to Nyasaland, as Malawi was then known.

'In order to succeed, he had to reveal his identity to a small band of collaborators ... With their help he bought relatives in Kasungu District. These relatives have been kept well paid ever since, but every once in a while one of them has been detained in order to deter others from revealing the truth,' the book claims.

When Banda returned to Malawi in 1958, he confounded his closest friends by refusing to eat *nsima*, the staple food of the country. He persisted in speaking only English, with an interpreter translating his messages into vernacular languages.

He 'lived like a white man,' his nationalist comrade Kanyama Chiume recalled, insisting on moving into an area declared white residential and never giving up his famous costume of a three-piece suit, black homburg hat, beige raincoat and brown leather gloves.

But whoever ruled Malawi for 30 years, Armstrong or Banda, it was a brutal and isolated dictatorship in which thousands of political opponents were killed, tortured, jailed without trial and hounded into exile.

Banda amassed enormous personal wealth during his reign, building a vast financial empire in an otherwise impoverished nation.

He declared Malawi a one-party state in 1966 and in 1971 made himself president for life.

Malawi was the only independent African nation to foster open and friendly ties with the apartheid government in South Africa.

His age, like his real identity, was under constant question. Some of the obituaries published this week say he was 95, others say 99. For many years, it was a criminal offence to discuss his age in Malawi.

But whichever version of Banda's life story you choose to believe, both recount his past as a 'father and founder' of the Malawian nation.

The official version depicts a hard-working man, imbued with ancient Chewa wisdom, who was called to lead the struggle for independence.

The other version depicts a stranger of mixed parentage who, after failing to realise his medical ambitions abroad, conquered a country through careful planning."

And Banda did look like someone who was racially mixed, a feature common among black Americans – now known as African Americans – during those days when Banda was a student in the United States, and even today; thus fuelling the rumour or suspicion that he may indeed have been or probably was a black American in spite of his non-American accent.

Samora Machel

Samora Moisés Machel (September 29, 1933 – October 19, 1986) was a guerrilla leader and the first president of Mozambique. He led the country from independence in 1975 until his death in 1986 when his presidential aircraft crashed in a mountainous terrain where the borders of Mozambique, Swaziland and South Africa converge.

Early life

Samora Machel was born in the village of Madragoa (today's Chilembene) in Gaza Province in the southern part of Mozambique. Mozambique was also once known as Portuguese East Africa.

His parents were farmers. He was a member of the Shangaan ethnic group which straddles the South African-Mozambican border.

Under Portuguese rule, his father, being a native, was forced to accept lower prices for his crops than white farmers; was compelled to grow labor-intensive cotton which took time away from the food crops needed for his family; and was forbidden to brand his mark on his cattle to discourage theft. However, Machel's father was a successful farmer. He owned four ploughs and 400 head of cattle by 1940.

Coincidentally, Gaza Province was also the home of Dr. Eduardo Mondlane, the first president of the Mozambican liberation movement, FRELIMO, who probably would have become the country's first president had he not been assassinated in Tanzania's capital, Dar es Salaam, on 3 February 1969.

Samora Machel grew up in his home village and attended mission elementary school. In 1942, he was sent to school in the town of Zonguene in Gaza Province. The school was run by Catholic missionaries who educated the children in Portuguese language and culture.

He had primary school education, up to standard four, and never completed his secondary school education. But he had the prerequisite certificate to train as a nurse anywhere in Portugal during that time since the nursing schools were not degree-conferring institutions.

In 1954, he started to study nursing in the capital city of Lourenço Marques (today Maputo).

In the 1950s, he saw some of the fertile lands around his farming community on the Limpopo River appropriated by the provincial government for the white settlers who developed a wide range of new infrastructure for the region.

Like many other Mozambicans near the southern border of Mozambique, some of his relatives went to work in the South African mines where additional job opportunities were found. Shortly afterwards, one of his brothers was killed in a mining accident.

Unable to complete formal training at the Miguel Bombarda Hospital in Lourenço Marques, he got a job working as an aide in the same hospital and earned enough money to continue his education at night school.

He worked at the hospital until he left the country to join the Mozambican nationalist struggle in neighbouring Tanzania where the Mozambican freedom fighters were based and getting ready to start guerrilla warfare against the Portuguese colonial rulers in Mozambique.

Liberation struggle

Machel was attracted to Marxist ideals and began his political activities in the Lourenço Marques hospital where he protested against wage and racial discrimination. Black nurses were being paid less than whites doing the same job. He also protested against poor medical service for blacks. He later told a reporter how bad medical treatment was for Mozambique's poor:

"The rich man's dog gets more in the way of vaccination, medicine and medical care than do the workers upon whom the rich man's wealth is built."

His grandparents and great grandparents had fought against Portuguese colonial rule in the 19th century; so it was not surprising that in 1962 Machel joined the Front for the Liberation of Mozambique (FRELIMO) which was formed in Dar es Salaam, Tanzania, in June same year.

He left his first wife and four children behind. He received military training in 1963 elsewhere in Africa and returned to Mozambique in 1964 to lead FRELIMO's first guerrilla attack against the Portuguese in the northern part of the country.

Samora Machel married his second wife, Josina (née Mutemba), in 1969, who gave birth later that same year.

By 1969, Machel had become commander-in-chief of the FRELIMO army which had already established itself among Mozambique's peasantry. His most important goal, he said, was to get the people "to understand how to turn the armed struggle into a revolution" and to realize how essential it was "to create a new mentality to build a new society."

Two months after the assassination of FRELIMO's president, Eduardo Mondlane, a ruling triumvirate comprising Samora Machel, Marcelino dos Santos, and Frelimo's vice-president, Uria Simango, assumed the leadership of the organisation.

Simango thought he would be president of FRELIMO after Mondlane was assassinated. Unsatisfied, he left for Cairo, Egypt, three months later and founded a rival organisation there in May 1969. He was expelled from FRELIMO in 1970 and Machel became its president.

Independence

After a military coup in Portugal on 25 April 1974, a socialist-oriented military regime replaced the 48-year old dictatorship which had been determined to keep its colonies The new rulers soon decided to grant independence to the five territories administered by Portugal in Africa: Cape Verde; Portuguese Guinea, renamed Guinea-Bissau; São Tomé e Príncipe; Angola, and Mozambique.

When Machel's unelected revolutionary government of FRELIMO took over, he became independent Mozambique's first unelected president on June 25, 1975. Marcelino dos Santos became vice-president. Uria Simango and his wife Celina aa weel as other FRELIMO dissidents such as Adelino Gwambe and Paulo Gumane (former leaders of UDENAMO, one of the national liberation groups in Mozambique) were arrested and later murdered.

In fact, as early as during the transitional government it shared with Portugal, FRELIMO shattered all opposition to its rule.

Former militants Lázaro Kavandame, Uria Simango, Paulo Unhai, Kambeu and Father Mateus Gwengere were arrested under the pretext that they had allied themselves with elements of the white community during the 7 September 1974 upheaval against the transfer of power to FRELIMO (Mateus Gwengere was kidnapped in Kenya where he had sought refuge and was brought secretly to Mozambique).

The same wave of arrests caught Joana Simeão who, in opposition to FRELIMO's one-party system, had created a political party, GUMO (*Grupo Unido de Moçambique* – United Group for Mozambique), proposing a model based on pluralism and free market (which FRELIMO would ironically adopt years later when it eventually renounced Marxism).

They were all accused of "treason" even though Joana Simeão herself had never been a member of FRELIMO.

After a period of internment in *campos de reeducação* (re-education camps), they were executed following a summary trial in the so-called "revolutionary" and "popular" style presided by Samora Machel himself.

Domingos Arouca, Pereira Leite (who had nevertheless had some political activity against the colonial regime), Máximo Dias (GUMO's number 2) and another FRELIMO dissident, Miguel Murupa, managed to escape to Portugal.

Dr Willem Gerard Pott, a lawyer whose resistance to the colonial regime was well-known, was abhorred for not showing unconditional allegiance to FRELIMO. Following a period of detention during which he was subjected to humiliating treatment (such as being displayed half-naked in public), he died in prison.

SNASP (*Serviço Nacional de Segurança Popular* – National Service for People's Security) and PIC (*Polícia de Investigação Criminal* – Criminal Investigation Police) began a wave of arrests, using both traditional prisons and the so-called *campos de reeducação* located randomly in northern and central sparsely populated areas.

Even Machel's first wife, whom he had deserted in 1963, was detained despite her total abstention from political activity.

Citizens were under permanent watch by the *grupos dinamizadores* (movement teams) of control cells set up at

405

neighbourhood and workplace level.

Machel quickly put his Marxist principles into practice by calling for the nationalisation of Portuguese plantations and property, and proposing the FRELIMO government establish schools and health clinics for the peasants.

A land reform was imposed, gathering peasants in *aldeias comunais* (communal villages) in accordance with the kolkhoz and sovkhoz model. For this purpose, the new Mozambican regime did not hesitate to use the old *aldeamentos*, or strategic hamlets, in which the Portuguese army had tried to confine the rural population in order to remove it from FRELIMO's influence in the war-ridden areas of the North (paradoxically, FRELIMO itself then denounced such *aldeamentos* as "concentration camps") during the liberation struggle.

Deeply contrary to the traditional way of life in the Mozambican countryside, which was characterised by single-family units scattered in the bush, the land reform based on the *aldeias comunais* concept soon proved to be a monumental fiasco.

As an internationalist, Machel allowed revolutionaries fighting white minority regimes in Rhodesia (Zimbabwe) and South Africa to train and operate within Mozambique. The regimes retaliated by forming a rebel group called RENAMO – which was also strongly supported by American conservatives including President Ronald Reagan and US senators such Jesse Helms of North Carolina – to destroy the infrastructures built by FRELIMO and to sabotage railway lines and hydroelectric facilities.

The Mozambique economy suffered immensely from these depredations and began to depend on overseas aid, in particular from the Soviet Union.

Nonetheless, Machel remained popular throughout his presidency.

He was awarded the Lenin Peace Prize (1975–76).

Machel's change of attitude
towards the Portuguese

It is widely admitted that one of the main reasons for the economic and financial collapse of post-independence Mozambique was the hasty departure of the majority of about 200,000 Portuguese living in the country on the eve of the Portuguese revolution, which had taken place on 25 April 1974, and that such exodus was caused by a sudden change of attitude by Samora Machel.

Indeed, the transitional government that ruled the country from the cease-fire agreement (signed in Lusaka on 7 September 1974) to independence (set for 25 June of the following year) acted in a very conciliatory fashion. Prime Minister Joaquim Chissano (who would become President of the Republic after Machel's death twelve years later) managed to convince the majority of the white population that only those bearing heavy responsibility for the darkest pages of the colonial era should fear FRELIMO's rule.

However, one month before independence, i.e., in mid-May 1975, Samora Machel crossed over into Mozambique from Tanzania, in the far North, and started a tour heading for the capital city of Lourenço Marques, in the far south, where he would arrive on the eve of Independence Day. Along this tour, he galvanised the masses with bitter speeches, recalling incessantly the most abhorrent and humiliating aspects of colonialism from the standpoint of colonised Mozambicans.

Unease gradually got the upper hand in the Portuguese community, many of whose members then decided to rebuild their lives elsewhere.

Several explanations have been proposed for this change of attitude. In his memoirs, Dr António de Almeida Santos, a renowned lawyer from Lourenço Marques who, after the fall of Caetano's regime, became minister for the coordination of Portuguese-administered territories and who was a close friend of Machel's, states that FRELIMO's president was strongly affected by two outbursts of violence involving the white population.

The first episode was caused by an upheaval in the capital city on 7 September 1974, with the seizing of offices and transmitters of the Rádio Clube de Moçambique in protest against the Lusaka Agreement signed by the Portuguese Provisional Government and FRELIMO which provided for the handover of power exclusively to the nationalist movement.

This upheaval was led by FICO (*Frente Integracionista de Continuidade Ocidental* – Integrationist Front for Western Continuity), a movement mostly composed of whites with which FRELIMO dissidents and other members of the black community unwilling to accept a one-party system had allied themselves.

FRELIMO supporters retaliated with bloody riots in the black shantytowns surrounding the city and, during several days, thousands of people, mostly Portuguese, were killed along with blacks who had allegedly remained loyal to their employers.

The second episode happened a few weeks later, on 21 October 1974, when a quarrel between Portuguese commandos and FRELIMO guerrillas in downtown Lourenço Marques gave rise to another wave of bloody riots in the black shantytown areas, with the murder of dozens of whites.

According to Almeida Santos, Machel possibly became convinced that the presence of a large Portuguese community in Mozambique would always be a source of instability and a potential threat to FRELIMO's rule. To that was allegedly added pressure from the Soviet Union, to which FRELIMO had contracted a heavy debt, namely of a political nature, and which desired to be rid of the Portuguese in order to better exercise its influence at all levels.

Plausible as it may be, this explanation leads us to a surprising conclusion: Since the two outbursts of violence had occurred at the start of the transitional period (the first had even taken place before the inauguration of the government headed by Joaquim Chissano), FRELIMO must therefore have taken its decision to push the Portuguese away at the very moment when its PrimeMinister Chissano seemed to encourage them to stay. But how can it be explained that a transitional government headed by a senior representative of FRELIMO adopts a reconciling approach in such blatant contrast with Machel's hostile and vengeful behaviour later on?

A lack of coordination between the president's policy and that of his delegate in the transitional government seems out of the question.

The most likely explanation is that everything must have been previously arranged at the highest level within FRELIMO: transition would be conducted smoothly during the first stage, until the independence process became irreversible, and as soon as the overwhelming majority of Portuguese colonial officials, in particular the military, left the country (i.e., immediately before independence), Samora Machel's radicalism – in other words, FRELIMO's true face – would reveal itself.

The fatal aircrash and investigations

On 19 October 1986, Samora Machel was on his way back from an international meeting in Lusaka, Zambia, in the presidential Tupolev Tu-134 aircraft when the plane crashed in Lebombo Mountains near Mbuzini, South-Africa. There were ten survivors but President Machel and thirty-three others died, including ministers and officials of the Mozambique government.

The Margo Commission set up by the South African government "investigated" the incident and concluded that the accident was caused by pilot error.

Despite the acceptance of its findings by the International Civil Aviation Organisation, the report was rejected by the Mozambican and Soviet governments. The latter submitted a minority report suggesting that the aircraft was intentionally lured off course by a decoy radio navigation beacon set up specifically for this purpose by the South Africans. Speculation about the accident has therefore continued to the present day, particularly in Mozambique. There is strong suspicion that the accident was caused by the South African government and its security agencies including the military.

Hans Louw, a South African and Civil Cooperation Bureau operative, claims to have assisted in Machel's death. Pik Botha, South African foreign affairs minister at the time who later joined the ruling African National Congress (ANC), said that the investigation into the plane crash should be re-opened.

Portuguese journalist José Milhazes, who lived in Moscow since 1977 and who worked for the Portuguese newspaper *Público* and as a correspondent for the Portuguese television chain *SIC*, stated that the plane crash had nothing to do with any attempt or any mechanical failure but was due to several errors of the Russian crew (including the pilot), who, instead of diligently performing their duties, were busy with things like sharing alcoholic and soft drinks unavailable in Mozambique they had brought from Zambia. In his opinion, both the Soviet and the Mozambican authorities had an interest to spread the thesis of an attempt by the South-African regime to bring down the plane: the Soviets wanted to safeguard their reputation (exempting the plane and the crew from any responsibility), the Mozambicans wanted to create a hero.

In 2007, however, Jacinto Veloso, one of Machel's most unconditional supporters within FRELIMO, stated in his memoirs that Machel's death was due to a conspiracy between the South African and the Soviet secret services, both of which had reasons to get rid of him.

According to Veloso, the Soviet ambassador once asked President Machel for an audience to convey the USSR's concern about Mozambique's apparent "sliding away" towards the West, to which Machel supposedly replied *"Vai à merda!"* (Eat shit!). Having then commanded the interpreter to translate, he left the room. Convinced that Machel had irrevocably moved away from their orbit, the Soviets allegedly did not hesitate to sacrifice the pilot and the whole crew of their own plane.

Graça Machel

Machel's widow, Graça (née Simbine), is convinced the air crash was not an accident and has dedicated her life to tracking down her husband's alleged killers.

In July 1998, Mrs Machel married the then South African President Nelson Mandela. She thus became unique in having been the first lady of two different countries, Mozambique and South Africa.

Memorial

A memorial at the Mbuzini crash site was inaugurated on 19 January 1999 by Nelson Mandela and his wife Graça, and by President Joaquim Chissano of Mozambique. The memorial service is held on the October 19th each year.

Designed by Mozambican architect José Forjaz, at a cost to the South African government of 1.5 million Rand (US$ 300,000), the monument comprises 35 steel tubes symbolising the number of lives lost in the air crash.

At least eight foreigners were killed there, including

the four Soviet crew members, Machel's two Cuban doctors and the Zambian and Zairean ambassadors to Mozambique.

Also, a street in Moscow bears his name. And the Zimbabwean band R.U.N.N. family had a hit song that mourned his loss.

And in neighbouring Tanzania where the Mozambican freedom fighters of FRELIMO were based and had operational bases, there is Samora Machel Avenue in Dar es Salaam, the country's former capital and largest city which still functions as the nation's capital.

Robert Mugabe

Robert Gabriel Mugabe (born 21 February 1924) was the second president of Zimbabwe.

The first president was Canaan Banana from 18 April 1980 to 31 December 1987. But his role was mainly ceremonial.

Mugabe became the first executive president of Zimbabwe.

He was one of the leaders of the liberation movement against white-minority rule and was elected in 1980.

He served as prime minister from 1980 to 1987 and as president since 1987.

He rose to prominence in the 1960s as the secretary-general of the Zimbabwe African National Union (ZANU) during the struggle against the white-minority rule government of Ian Smith. He was a political prisoner in Rhodesia for more than 10 years between 1964 and 1974.

Upon his release with Edgar Tekere, he left Rhodesia in 1975 to re-join the liberation struggle in what was also known as the Rhodesian Bush War – from bases in neighbouring Mozambique.

At the end of the war in 1979, Mugabe emerged as a hero in the minds of many Africans. He won the general elections of 1980, the second in which the majority of Black Africans participated in large numbers (though the electoral system in Rhodesia had allowed Black participation based on qualified franchise). He then became the first prime minister after calling for reconciliation between the former warring parties including white Rhodesians and rival political groups.

The years following Zimbabwe's independence saw a split between the two main leaders – Robert Mugabe and Joshua Nkomo – who had fought alongside each other during the 1970s against the government of Rhodesia.

An armed conflict between Mugabe's government and dissident followers of Joshua Nkomo's Zimbabwe African People's Union (ZAPU) erupted. Following the deaths of thousands, neither warring faction able to defeat the other, the heads of the opposing movements reached a landmark agreement under which was created a new ruling party, ZANU-Patriotic Front (ZANU-PF) as a merger between the two former rivals: ZANU and ZAPU.

In 1998, Mugabe's government supported the intervention by the Southern African Development Community (SADC) in the second Congo war – which started in 1998 – by sending Zimbabwean troops to assist the government of President Laurent Kabila.

And since 2000, Mugabe's government embarked on a controversial fast-track land reform programme intended to correct the inequitable land distribution rooted in colonial injustices during British by colonial rule. The period was marked by the deterioration of the Zimbabwean economy and political violence against Mugabe's opponents..

Mugabe's policies were condemned in some quarters at home and abroad, especially by the British and American governments arguing the policies amounted to violent seizure of land and injustices against white Zimbabweans and their black workers some of whom were also attacked and killed together with their white employers.

413

Eventually a wide range of sanctions were imposed by the Ammmerican government and the European Union against Mugabe himself, individuals, private companies, parastatals and the govvernment of Zimbabwe.

In 2008, his party suffered defeat in national parliamentary elections. But after disputed presidential elections, Mugabe retained power with the signing of a power-sharing agreement with opposition leaders Morgan Tsvangirai and Arthur Mutambara of the Movement for Democratic Change-Tsvangirai (MDC-T) and the Movement for Democratic Change-Mutambara (MDC-M).

Early life

Robert Gabriel Mugabe was born near Kutama Jesuit Mission in the Zvimba District northwest of Salisbury (now Harare) in Southern Rhodesia to a Malawian father Gabriel Matibili and a Shona mother Bona, both Roman Catholic.

He was the third of six children. He had two elder brothers, and one of them, Michael, was very popular in the village. Both his elder brothers died when he was young, leaving Robert and his younger brother, Donato. His father, Gabriel Matibili, a carpenter, abandoned the Mugabe family in 1934, after Michael died, in search of work in Bulawayo in Matebeland in the southwestern part of the country.

Mugabe was raised as a Roman Catholic, studying in Marist Brothers and Jesuit schools including the exclusive Kutama College headed by an Irish priest, Father Jerome O'Hea, who took him under his wing.

Through his youth, Mugabe was never socially popular nor physically active and spent most of his time with the priests or his mother when he was not reading in the school's libraries. He was described as never playing with other children but enjoying his own company. According to his brother Donato, his only friends were his books.

He qualified as a teacher but left to study at Fort Hare University in South Africa graduating in 1951 where he met contemporaries such as Robert Sobukwe. He then studied at Salisbury (1953) and Gwelo (1954).

Originally graduating with a Bachelor of Arts degree from Fort Hare in 1951, Mugabe subsequently earned six further degrees through distance learning including a Bachelor of Administration and Bachelor of Education from the University of South Africa and a Bachelor of Science, Bachelor of Laws, Master of Science and Master of Laws, all from the University of London External Programme. The two Law degrees were earned while he was in prison; the Master of Science degree earned during his premiership of Zimbabwe.

After graduating, Mugabe lectured at Chalimbana Teacher Training College in Zambia from 1955–1958. Thereafter he taught at Apowa Secondary School at Takoradi in the Western region of Ghana after completing his local certification at Achimota School (1958–1960).

During his stay in Ghana, Mugabe was influenced and inspired by Ghana's then prime minister, Kwame Nkrumah. In addition, Mugabe and some of his Zimbabwe African National Union (ZANU) party cadres received instruction at the Kwame Nkrumah Ideological Institute at Winneba in southern Ghana.

When was at Achimota, he met Sally Hayfron whom he married in April 1961. Another article about Sally Hayfron in Wikipedia states:

"She met her future husband, Dr. Robert Mugabe, at Takoradi Teacher Training College where they were both teaching....Hayfron married Robert Mugabe in April 1961 in Salisbury.

She became the first lady of Zimbabwe after Mugabe became president and died on 27 January 1992 from kidney failure. Upon her death she was interred at the

415

National Heroes Acre in the nation's capital Harare....She was popularly known as *Amai* (Mother) in Zimbabwe....She is remembered fondly with love and affection, as she is still considered the founding mother of the nation of Zimbabwe....

The death of Sally is seen by some to be around the time that President Robert Mugabe began indurating his policy in Zimbabwe."

According to Robert Verkaik in his article, "The Love That Made Robert Mugabe A Monster," in *The Independent*, London, 6 April 2008:

"He was a young firebrand locked up in a Rhodesian jail. She was an exile in London, grieving the death of their only son. Here, nearly 40 years on, letters released under the Freedom of Information Act reveal how Robert Mugabe's battle to save his beloved wife from deportation sowed the seeds of his lifelong hatred for the British government....

Think of all the famous modern political love stories: Winston and Clementine Churchill; Tony and Cherie Blair; Margaret and Dennis Thatcher; Nelson and Winnie Mandela; or even the amants de nos jours, the French president and Carla Bruni-Sarkozy. To this glamorous list of leaders, whose relationships inspired their rise to power and helped shape their early years in office, can now be added the unlikely name of international hate-figure Robert Mugabe.

New documents released under the Freedom of Information Act at the National Archives in London reveal for the first time the strength of the bond between the Rhodesian freedom-fighter and his young Ghanaian bride, as Mugabe emerged as a political force in Africa during the 1960s.

In letters and telegrams written to Harold Wilson and his Labour government, Mugabe emerges as a man both sensitive and humble, who was prepared to plead with the British government in order to persuade the Home Office not to deport his wife from London.

The papers also disclose how Westminster mishandled the formative stages of its own relationship with Mugabe and gave the Rhodesian dissident his first lesson in the heartless expediency of British foreign policy. Mugabe watchers will now surely wonder whether this could have been the moment that finally set the Zimbabwean rebel against his former colonial rulers.

Mugabe's political achievements may now be overshadowed by the brutality of his regime, but in his early career he was an inspirational leader among the ranks of the fledgling Zimbabwe nationalist movement in the 1960s.

He was also a man who had recently found love with Sally Hayfron, a Ghanaian national seven years his junior. They had met in 1958 while both were teaching at a college in Ghana, where Mugabe had gone to make something of himself.

Friends say that the attraction between the couple was immediate, though they came from very different worlds. Mugabe's family was poor and his father, Gabriel Mugabe Matibiri, a carpenter, abandoned his wife and Robert in 1934 in search of work in Bulawayo, Rhodesia's second city. Robert is remembered as being bookish and lonely. Hayfron, meanwhile, described by friends as exuberant and beautiful, had been brought up in a political family that was part of the nationalist movement in colonial Ghana. Her family had strong links to Ghana's then-prime minister, Kwame Nkrumah.

It is easy to see why their meeting made such an impression on Mugabe. In Ghana, he had experienced for the first time an African country run by its own people. And in Hayfron, he had met for the first time a woman whose political views were as strong as his own.

In 1960, a proud Mugabe returned home with Hayfron

417

on his arm and immediately introduced her to his mother, to whom he was very close. The next year, with his mother's blessing, the couple were married in a simple church ceremony in St Peter's Catholic Church in Harare, then a black township of Salisbury. Their marriage was not a typical African relationship, where the woman would stay at home cooking and raising children. Rather, a shared political goal for a free Zimbabwe meant they both had key roles to play in Rhodesia's burgeoning independence movement. While Mugabe rose up through the ranks of Joshua Nkomo's Zimbabwe African People's Union (Zapu), Sally helped enfranchise and mobilise the women of Salisbury.

In 1963, Mugabe left Zapu to help establish the rival Zimbabwe African National Union (Zanu), a pan-Africanist movement formed by the Reverend Ndabaningi Sithole and influenced by Maoism. It was an exciting time for the couple and their relationship was strengthened by the news that Sally was pregnant with their first child. Sadly, she lost the baby, but fell pregnant again in 1963 and, to the great delight of Mugabe, gave birth to a boy in September, whom they named Nhamodzenyika.

By the mid-1960s, Mugabe's political activism had brought him to the attention of the Rhodesian state government and, in 1964, he was arrested for "subversive speech" and sentenced to 10 years' imprisonment in the country's notorious Salisbury Prison. For the first time since they had met in 1958, the couple were forced to separate.

A year later, on 11 November 1965, Rhodesia's white-minority government led by Ian Smith officially broke from British rule in what became known as the Unilateral Declaration of Independence (UDI).

It was the same year that Nelson Mandela, already three years into his 18-year prison term, published (?) his seminal work *No Easy Walk to Freedom*. Like Mandela, Mugabe used his time in prison to shape his political thinking. He immersed himself in study and, through correspondence courses, managed to attain seven degrees, including ones in law and engineering to add to his teaching qualifications.

Meanwhile, after her husband's detention, Sally Mugabe had continued to be involved in subversive activities in Rhodesia and spent six weeks in one of Salisbury's prisons for demonstrating against white rule. Later, she was found guilty of organising African women to directly challenge Smith's Rhodesian constitution, which resulted in her being charged with sedition and sentenced to five years' imprisonment, part of which was suspended.

The political climate made it too dangerous for her to stay in Salisbury and so, in 1963, she escaped the security services by fleeing first to Ghana with her son and then, in 1967, to self-imposed exile in London, where she found work as a secretary at the Africa Centre in Covent Garden. From the safety of Britain, she campaigned tirelessly for the release of her husband and other Rhodesian dissidents. She also supported her husband's studies by researching documents that the Salisbury Prison authorities had banned. Sometimes this meant transcribing very dry texts line by line and then posting them to her husband in prison.

There is no doubt that Sally Mugabe's support for her husband helped sustain him during his time as a prisoner in Salisbury. But, in 1970, while still locked up, Mugabe discovered his wife's immigration status was at risk and that the British government was planning to throw her out of the country because her visa had expired.

Now, documents released at the National Archives show that Mugabe was so enraged by the decision that he went to extraordinary lengths to help her. In March of that year, he wrote to James Callaghan, the then-Home Secretary, about his wife's situation. This letter went unanswered, prompting Mugabe to send a telegram to

Harold Wilson on 8 June, asking the Prime Minister to grant his wife British citizenship. Again, there was no official response.

Ten days later, he pursued this request with a three-page, handwritten letter to Wilson setting out the case for reconsideration on the grounds of exceptional circumstances, pleading with the Prime Minister to understand his wife's predicament: shortly before Sally had come to England in 1967, tragedy struck the Mugabes when Nhamodzenyika died after succumbing to a severe attack of malaria. He was just three years old. With her husband in prison, Sally was left to bear the emotional burden of the loss alone. The confidential papers show that she later suffered a mental breakdown while living in London.

One of her supporters, Tony Hughes, secretary of the African rights group Ariel Foundation, wrote at the time that the strain of the bereavement, combined with the stress of her imminent deportation, had taken a great toll on Sally's mental state, and in a letter to the government, he wrote of the proposed deportation: "It is certainly unfair for the British government to add to the misery of her already broken life."

In his letter, Mugabe had told Wilson of the effect the death of his son had had on his wife, explaining that: "My wife, whose health has never been satisfactory since the loss of our son in 1966, is at present suffering serious emotional upset as a result of the decision by the Home Office. Surely then, the fact of my detention is enough suffering for her already. As I stated in my letter to Mr Callaghan, the reason my wife decided to work for the year (September 1969-June 1970) was to enable her to earn a little money for herself until October when she should enter university to do a degree in Household Science. The Home Office decision wrecks even this wholesome plan."

He asked Wilson to reconsider the decision to refuse

420

Sally permission to stay in Britain by politely explaining that his wife had a right to British citizenship because of their marriage, "under Christian rites", in 1961. He added that it was "sheer force of circumstance" that meant his wife had had to use a Ghanaian passport to enter Britain, proclaiming, "She is first and foremost a Rhodesian citizen."

Mugabe explained that, "When I and other nationalist leaders decided in 1963 to return from our temporary exile in Tanganyika, I could not bring my wife, who had just given birth to our late son, back with me as she was liable for imprisonment for a political offence she is alleged to have committed... I therefore decided to take my wife to Ghana, where she was to remain with her parents until our son was about four... When our son died in December 1966 the whole purpose of her stay no longer existed so I arranged that she should go to Britain for her studies."

The letter not only displays Mugabe's incisive intellect but also a talent for elegant and persuasive writing. "Since the British government asserts that it has legally assumed administrative authority for Rhodesia," he added, "then it must place at the disposal of those who come under that authority, as my wife and I do, the procedures it considers valid for the acquisition of nationality as British Rhodesians... More than that, sir, I hold that the British government owes definite moral responsibility not only to persons in my circumstances but their wives and dependents as well... Am I to conclude that merely by virtue of the technicality of her possessing a Ghanaian passport, my wife's Rhodesian citizenship by virtue of her being married to me must cease? Has she ceased being my wife merely because she... cannot produce Rhodesian papers in support of her being Rhodesian?"

Mugabe's brooding frustration and indignation, which would later develop into a naked hatred of all things British, is already clearly marked. "I pose these questions, Mr Prime Minister," he concluded, "because it is clear to me that the Home Office is hanging on to legal technicalities completely deprived of morality."

Mugabe closed his request by appealing to Wilson's sense of humanity, and then apologised for posting the letter from Salisbury Prison, which means that Downing Street had to pay a surcharge for its receipt.

The confidential papers reveal that the Mugabes' case left the Labour government deeply divided. The Foreign Office secretly urged a compassionate approach, while the Home Office insisted on a strict observance of the letter of the law consistent with Labour's immigration policy.

The case of Mrs Mugabe's deportation was taken up by Maurice Foley, a young minister in the Foreign Office who had been corresponding with her supporters. Foley, known for being quick-witted and passionate about his politics, had already served in the Home Office as a minister responsible for immigration, where he was instrumental in introducing measures to help thousands of economic migrants and asylum seekers from post-colonial Africa. Foley even featured in the launch of a BBC TV programme for immigrants, called Apna Hi Ghar Samajhiye (meaning "Make Yourself at Home") that was broadcast on 10 October 1965.

The junior Foreign Office minister decided to raise the matter of Mrs Mugabe with the then-Home Secretary Merlyn Rees. But Rees, who had a reputation for an unbending interpretation of policy and law, wrote back saying that while he sympathised with her "personal problems" he was not prepared to reverse his decision to expel her.

He told Foley: "We deal with large numbers of cases of Commonwealth citizens where there are compassionate elements, and we give full weight to them, but they rarely justify our taking action outside the ordinary rules of immigration control."

After news broke of the Home Office's latest rejection, Sally Mugabe wrote to Foley from her address in Madeley

Road, Ealing Broadway, west London. "I am surprised at this decision in spite of my plight," she said. "I am completely at a loss to know how else I could have written to touch the hearts of the decision makers... My employer has already indicated that she cannot keep me for long and I can understand her fears. But I must live whilst this scrutiny goes on."

Robert Mugabe had every reason to believe the Prime Minister would consider his request favourably. While Mandela had given up believing that South Africa's former colonial rulers would ever come to his aid, Mugabe still clung to the hope that a Labour government would deliver him from Ian Smith's oppressive regime.

His spirits had been raised by Wilson's response to Smith's declaration of UDI in 1965: the British government had adopted a policy of no compromise until there was a commitment to black-majority African rule, dictating that colonies with a substantial population of white settlers would not receive independence except under conditions of universal suffrage and majority rule. And it was at the behest of Wilson that the United Nations Security Council authorised the first use of sanctions.

But Mugabe was not to know that his letter was not processed by Downing Street until 16 July, a full month after Wilson had been defeated by the Conservatives in the snap election of 1970, meaning that the case fell instead to the consideration of Edward Heath's government.

A confidential memo written by a Foreign Office diplomat set out the situation in plain terms: "We know very little about Mr Mugabe except that he is in detention and is the former founder and secretary general of Zanu." Nevertheless, the Foreign Office urged the Home Office to adopt a sympathetic approach on the grounds that they could ill-afford to alienate a potential ally in the road to black independence in Rhodesia: "If Mrs Mugabe has to leave Britain this would have a bad effect on her husband and could be politically embarrassing."

Further correspondence written by Foreign Office minister Lord Lothian to Lord Windlesham, a minister of state at the Home Office, reveals that the Foreign Office had now recognised Mugabe's importance to the nationalist movement in Rhodesia and wanted to bend the immigration rules to preserve good relations, in case he be of use to Britain in the future. Another Foreign Office memo warned that if his wife was not allowed to stay, Mugabe's attitude to the British government could "change completely".

Then, in August 1970, a damaging story appeared in The Observer concerning another politically sensitive immigration case that could be compared unfavourably with the Mugabe request: the Home Office had granted a work visa to Ian Smith's stepson, Robert, a Rhodesian citizen.

Lord Lothian wrote to his colleagues: "The recent agreement by the Home Office that Mr Ian Smith's stepson should be allowed to take up work in the UK can be cited as an example of possible racial discrimination... At the present time we want to avoid as much as possible additional controversy over Southern African issues."

Robert Mugabe, stewing in prison and still without any British government response to his request, must have been incensed by news of the treatment of Ian Smith's stepson.

By now even Number 10 could see the political dangers. "This case," wrote one of Heath's advisers, "is now getting a little ancient. It seems only too likely to me that Mr or Mrs Mugabe may well write to the leader of the Opposition's office to ask what has been done and I think the story we would have to tell would be, to put it mildly, embarrassing."

Towards the end of 1970, Sally Mugabe received further upsetting news that her father had died, and Lord Lothian once again wrote to Lord Windlesham to urge reconsideration of the case: "It is quite evident that this will be a very difficult matter and that topics which bear on Rhodesia will continue to cause us great trouble," he wrote. "We shall not, I think, be assisted in this search for a settlement if any Rhodesian issue attracts more publicity than can be reasonably avoided. There are some new factors in the case of Mrs Mugabe which, in our view, alter its merits to some extent and may well result in further adverse publicity if the present decision is maintained. We would therefore be grateful if you would reconsider the decision in light of these factors and that you would see your way to agreeing that Mrs Mugabe should be treated as a Rhodesian citizen even if... she is not legally so for reasons outside her control."

The need to curry favour with the imprisoned Mugabe was regarded by Lord Lothian as a critical factor. "The issue of detainees in Rhodesia and what we can do for them as part of any settlement is likely to become more sensitive when talk of negotiations is in the air," he wrote. "Critics of the present decision will be able to make some play with the argument that by working in the United Kingdom Mrs Mugabe will be doing the best she can to help her detained husband, and to send her back to Ghana would reduce the possibilities of this and hence cause both him and her further suffering."

Despite mounting pressure, the new Home Secretary, Reginald Maudling, refused to budge, and it was not until after a high-profile media campaign, and a petition signed by more than 400 parliamentarians, that the government finally relented and allowed Sally Mugabe to stay.

Yet, Robert Mugabe would never forget the attempts by the British to deport his wife at a time when she was at her most vulnerable. When his personal entreaties to Britain went unacknowledged for almost a year, the suspicion that neither a Labour nor Conservative government would be prepared to help him topple the Smith government, and install black-majority rule in Zimbabwe, must have hardened. (Indeed, Wilson later famously recounted that he knew the British public would never have countenanced an armed conflict with its "kith and kin" in Rhodesia.)

It was not until 1975 that Mugabe was finally released from prison, and was reunited with his wife in Mozambique, where he had fled to begin a guerrilla war of independence. If anything, however, the years apart had made their relationship stronger, and they set about accomplishing their dream of recreating a free Zimababwe with renewed energy. While he focused on preparing his forces for an armed struggle, his wife found herself in the new role of a mother figure to thousands of Zimbabwean refugees fleeing Smith's regime. Her efforts later earned her the title Amai ("Mother").

Five years later, Mugabe became Zimbabwe's first black Prime Minister, and Sally took her place by his side. As the first lady of Zimababwe, she launched the Zimbabwe Women's Cooperative in the UK and was an active supporter of other London-based African women's organisations.

In the early years of Mugabe's rule, it was his wife who was credited with helping to temper his excesses. She could lighten his mood, said one of his former colleagues, just by entering the room. But the relationship began to falter when they discovered they were unable to have any more children and, as Sally's health failed, Mugabe began to have affairs.

Sally Mugabe died on 27 January 1992 from kidney failure and four years later Mugabe married his South African mistress, Grace Marufu.

Without his first wife there to caution him against his extreme politics, Mugabe began to emerge as a tyrant. But that has not stopped Sally Hayfron from still being remembered affectionately, as the founding mother of the nation of Zimbabwe."

The preceding article states that Mugabe "married his

South African mistress, Grace Marufu." According to Wikipedia, Grace Marufu was not a South African. She was a Zimbabwean by birth.

She was born Grace Marufu in Enkeldoorn (now Chivhu), Southern Rhodesia (now Zimbabwe) on 23 July 1965.

Enkeldoorn is located 91miles south of Harare on the main road south to Masvingo and South Africa. It was founded by Afrikaans-speaking Boer farmers and settlers around 1850. It was the first white settlement in Zimbabwe and it became an Afrikaner stronghold in a predominately English-speaking white Rhodesia.

Early political career

Mugabe returned to Southern Rhodesia from Ghana and joined the National Democratic Party (NDP) in 1960. The administration of Prime Minister Ian Smith banned the NDP when it later became Joshua Nkomo's Zimbabwe African Peoples Union (ZAPU). Mugabe left ZAPU in 1963 to join the rival Zimbabwe African National Union (ZANU) which had been formed in 1963 by the Reverend Ndabaningi Sithole, Edgar Tekere, Edson Zvobgo, Enos Nkala and and lawyer Herbert Chitepo.

Herbert Wiltshire Chitepo (15 June 1923 – 18 March 1975) led the Zimbabwe African National Union (ZANU) until he was assassinated in bomb explosion – his car was rigged with a bomb – Lusaka, Zambia, on 18 March 1975. He was then chairman of ZANU. He moved to Lusaka from Dar es Salaam, Tanzania.

He became the first black citizen of Rhodesia to become a barrister. He was also the first African director of public prosecutions in Tanganyika (renamed Tanzania).

Rhodesian author Peter Stiff says that a former British SAS soldier, Hugh "Chuck" Hind, was responsible for Chitepo's assassination. The SAS – Special Air Service –

is a special forces regiment of the British Army which has served as a model for the special forces of many other countries all over the world.

Hind emigrated from Britain to Rhodesia. He worked with another Rhodesian CIO (Central Intelligence Organisation) operative known only as 'Taffy' Bryce. They performed a series of raids into Zambia against ZANU and ZAPU targets during the Rhodesian Bush War.

'Taffy' and Chuck were assisted in Zambia by a white Zambian farmer, Ian Robert Bruce Sutherland, who was later convicted by Zambian courts of illegally possessing offensive material at his farm in Mazabuka, Zambia.

Herbert Chitepo was assassinated by Chuck Hind and 'Taffy.' They placed a car bomb in his Volkswagen Beetle. He died the following morning. The explosion sent part of the car onto the roof of his house and uprooted a tree next door.

Hind died in a road traffic accident, transporting weapons, whilst driving near Lusaka with Sutherland also in the car. The vehicle skidded and left the road.

Sutherland's farm was raided on 10 November 1978 by Zambian police and in the trial that followed his arrest he was sentenced to 5 years imprisonment.

ZANU was influenced by the Africanist ideas of the Pan African Congress (PAC) in South Africa by Maoism while ZAPU was an ally of the African National Congress (ANC) and was a supporter of a more orthodox pro-Soviet line on national liberation.

There were similar divisions between the MPLA and UNITA in Angola.

It would have been easy for the party to split along tribal lines between the Ndebele and Mugabe's own Shona tribe but cross-tribal representation was maintained by his partners. ZANU leader Sithole nominated Robert Mugabe as his secretary-general.

In 1964 Mugabe was arrested for "subversive speech" and spent the next 11 years in Salisbury prison. When

Mugabe's four-year-old son died, he was denied permission by Smith's government to leave prison to attend the funeral.

In 1974, while still in prison, Mugabe was elected – with the powerful influence of Edgar Tekere – to take over the reins of ZANU after a no-confidence vote was passed on Ndabaningi Sithole. Mugabe himself abstained from voting. His time in prison burnished his reputation and helped his cause.

Following a South African détente initiative, Mugabe was released from prison in November 1974 along with other nationalist leaders. He first went to Zambia where he was ignored by President Kenneth Kaunda. He returned to Rhodesia then left once again in April 1975 for Mozambique assisted by a Dominican nun. After he went to Mozambique, he was later placed in temporary protective custody by President Samora Machel.

According to Eddie Cross who participated in interviews of the leadership at that time to determine their views on the "longer term future", Mugabe's political viewpoint was that "a new 'progressive' society could not be constructed on the foundations of the past [and] that they would have to destroy most of what had been built up after 1900 before a new society, based on subsistence and peasant values, could be constructed."

Mugabe unilaterally assumed control of ZANU after the death of Herbert Chitepo in 1975. Later that year, after squabbling with Ndabaningi Sithole, Mugabe formed a militant ZANU faction, leaving Sithole to lead the moderate ZANU (Ndonga) party. Many opposition leaders mysteriously died during this time (Including one who allegedly died in a car crash, although the car was rumoured to have been riddled with bullet holes at the scene of the accident). Additionally, an opposing newspaper's printing press was bombed and its journalists tortured.

Lancaster House Agreement

Persuasion from South African Prime Minister John Vorster, himself under pressure from US Secretary of State Henry Kissinger, forced Ian Smith, the prime minister of Rhodesia during that time, to accept in principle that white minority rule could not continue indefinitely.

On 3 March 1978, Bishop Abel Muzorewa, Ndabaningi Sithole and other moderate leaders signed an agreement at the Governor's Lodge in Salisbury which paved the way for an interim power-sharing government in preparation for elections.

The elections were won by the United African National Council under Bishop Abel Muzorewa. But the elections were not internationally recognised and sanctions which had been imposed on Rhodesia were not lifted. The two 'Patriotic Front' groups under Mugabe and Joshua Nkomo refused to participate and continued the war.

The incoming government did accept an invitation to talks at Lancaster House in London in September 1979. A ceasefire was negotiated for the talks which were attended by Smith, Mugabe, Nkomo, Zvobgo and others. Eventually the parties to the talks agreed on a new constitution for a new Republic of Zimbabwe with elections in February 1980.

The Lancaster Agreement saw Mugabe make two important and contentious concessions. First, he allowed 20 seats to be reserved for whites in the new parliament, and second, he agreed to a ten-year moratorium on constitutional amendments.

His return to Zimbabwe in December 1979, following the completion of the Lancaster House Agreement, was greeted with enormous supportive crowds.

Prime Minister

After a campaign marked by intimidation from all sides, mistrust from security forces and reports of full ballot boxes found on the road, the Shona majority was decisive in electing Mugabe to head the first government as prime minister on 4 March 1980. ZANU won 57 out of 80 Common Roll seats in the new parliament, with the 20 white seats all going to the Rhodesian Front.

Mugabe, whose political base was in his Shona-speaking homeland in the northern part of the country, attempted to build Zimbabwe on a basis of an uneasy coalition with his ZAPU rivals whose support came from the Ndebele-speaking south, and with the white minority. Mugabe sought to incorporate ZAPU into his ZANU-led government and ZAPU's military wing into the army. ZAPU's leader, Joshua Nkomo, was given a series of cabinet positions in Mugabe's government.

However, Mugabe was torn between this objective and pressures to meet the expectations of his own ZANU followers for a faster pace of social change.

In 1983, Mugabe fired Nkomo from his cabinet, triggering bitter fighting between ZAPU supporters in the Ndebele-speaking region of the country and the ruling ZANU. Mugabe accused the Ndebele tribe of plotting to overthrow him after sacking Nkomo.

Between 1982 and 1985, the military crushed armed resistance from Ndebele groups in the provinces of Matebeleland and the Midlands, leaving Mugabe's rule secure. Mugabe has been accused by the BBC's *Panorama* programme of committing mass murder during this period of his rule after the show investigated claims made by political activist Gary Jones that Mugabe had been instrumental in removing him and his family from his farmland.

A peace accord was negotiated in 1987. ZAPU merged with ZANU to form the Zimbabwe African National Union-Patriotic Front (ZANU-PF) on 22 December 1988; it was virtually absorbed by ZANU. Mugabe brought Nkomo into the government once again as a vice-president.

President

In 1987, the position of prime minister was abolished and Mugabe became executive president, gaining additional powers in the process. He was re-elected in 1990 and 1996, and in 2002 amid claims of widespread vote-rigging and intimidation.

His term of office expired at the end of March 2008, but he was re-elected later in 2008 in another election marred by allegations of election fraud and intimidation.

Mugabe was also the chancellor of the University of Zimbabwe since parliament passed the University of Zimbabwe Amendment Bill in November 1990.

Gukurahundi

There were major outbreaks of violence between ZIPRA and ZANLA awaiting integration into the national army. ZIPRA was the guerrilla army of ZAPU, and ZANLA of ZANU. ZAPU was believed to have been planning an armed revolt to make up for ZAPU's poor showing in the 1980 elections.

Major arms caches were discovered in early 1982 and this caused a final rift between ZANU and ZAPU. Some believe that this was engineered by South African agents. South Africa's policy of destabilising Zimbabwe by military means, while blaming ZAPU for the actions of South African agents, helped to escalate the breakdown between ZAPU and ZANU in the early 1980s. This in turn led Zimbabwe to retain a state of emergency throughout the 1980s.

According to a report by the Catholic Commission for Justice and Peace in Zimbabwe, Zimbabwe's Fifth Brigade killed between 3,000 and 3,750 people. The Fifth Brigade was trained by North Koreans some of whom participated in the war.

Economy

During the 1980s, Mugabe's policies were largely socialist in orientation. In 1980 and 1981, the Zimbabwean economy showed strong growth of the GDP with 10.6% and 12.5%. From 1982–1989 economic growth averaged just 2.7% (1980–1989 average 4.47%). The white minority government maintained (with economic sanctions) from 1966–1972 a 6.7% average growth rate and overall from 1966 till 1979 a 3.8% average growth rate.

Unsuccessful market reform attempts were started in the 1990s and the economy stagnated during that time. Since 2000, GDP declined by roughly 40% in part due to land reform and hyperinflation.

In November 2010, the IMF described the Zimbabwean economy as "completing its second year of buoyant economic growth".

Social programmes

According to a 1995 World Bank report, after independence, "Zimbabwe gave priority to human resource investments and support for smallholder agriculture," and as a result, "smallholder agriculture expanded rapidly during the first half of the 1980s and social indicators improved quickly."

From 1980 to 1990 infant mortality decreased from 86 to 49 per 1000 live births, under five mortality was reduced from 128 to 58 per 1000 live births, and

433

immunisation increased from 25% to 80% of the population. Also, "child malnutrition fell from 22% to 12% and life expectancy increased from 56 to 64. By 1990, Zimbabwe had a lower infant mortality rate, higher adult literacy and higher school enrolment rate than average for developing countries."

In 1991, the government of Zimbabwe, short on hard currency and under international pressure, embarked on an austerity programme. The World Bank's 1995 report explained that such reforms were required because Zimbabwe was unable to absorb into its labour market the many graduates from its impressive educational system and that it needed to attract additional foreign investments.

The reforms, however, undermined the livelihoods of Zimbabwe's poor majority; the report noted "large segments of the population, including most smallholder farmers and small scale enterprises, find themselves in a vulnerable position with limited capacity to respond to evolving market opportunities. This is due to their limited access to natural, technical and financial resources, to the contraction of many public services for smallholder agriculture, and to their still nascent links with larger scale enterprises."

Moreover, these people were forced to live on marginal lands as Zimbabwe's best lands were reserved for mainly white landlords growing cash crops for export, a sector of the economy favoured by the IMF's plan. For the poor on the communal lands, "existing levels of production in these areas are now threatened by the environmental fragility of the natural resource base and the unsustainability of existing farming practices."

The International Monetary Fund (IMF) later suspended aid, saying reforms were "not on track."

According to the World Health Organisation (WHO), life expectancy at birth for Zimbabwean men has since become 37 years and is 34 years for women, the lowest such figures for any nation. The World Bank's 1995 report predicted this decline in life expectancy from its 1990 height of 64 years when, commenting on health care system cuts mandated by the IMF structural adjustment programme, it stated that "The decline in resources is creating strains and threatening the sustainability of health sector achievements."

While Zimbabwe suffered in many other measures under Mugabe, as a former schoolteacher he was well-known for his commitment to education. As of 2008, Zimbabwe had a literacy rate of 90%, the highest in Africa. However, Catholic Archbishop of Zimbabwe Pius Ncube decried the educational situation in the country, saying, among other scathing indictments of Mugabe, "We had the best education in Africa and now our schools are closing."

Prior to its suspension in 2009, the Zimbabwe dollar had suffered from the second-highest hyperinflation rate of any currency in modern times.

Racism

A number of people accused Mugabe of having a racist attitude towards white people. John Sentamu, a Uganda-born Archbishop of York in the United Kingdom, called Mugabe "the worst kind of racist dictator," for having "targeted the whites for their apparent riches."

More than thirty years after ending white-minority rule in Zimbabwe, Mugabe continued to accuse the United Kingdom and the United States of promoting white imperialism. And he regularly accused opposition figures of being allies of white imperialism.

When the United Kingdom once condemned Mugabe's authoritarian policies and alleged racist attitudes as being comparable to those of German Nazi dictator Adolf Hitler, Mugabe responded with an extremely controversial remark, mocking the UK's claims by saying about himself and his policies that "I am still the Hitler of the time. This

Hitler has only one objective, justice for his own people, sovereignty for his people, recognition of the independence of his people, and their right to their resources. If that is Hitler, then let me be a Hitler tenfold."

Views on homosexuality

Mugabe has been uncompromising in his opposition to homosexuality. In September 1995, Zimbabwe's parliament introduced legislation banning homosexual acts. In 1997, a court found Canaan Banana, Mugabe's predecessor and the first president of Zimbabwe, guilty of 11 counts of sodomy and indecent assault.

Second Congo War

Mugabe was blamed for Zimbabwe's involvement in the second Congo war in the Democratic Republic of Congo (DRC). At a time when the Zimbabwean economy was struggling, Zimbabwe responded to a call by the Southern African Development Community (SADC) to help the struggling government of President Laurent Kabila in Congo, a SADC member. The Democratic Republic of Congo had been invaded by Rwanda and Uganda, both of which claimed that their civilians, and regional stability, were under constant threat of attack by Rwandan Hutu militiamen based in Congo.

However, the Congolese government, as well as international commentators, charged that the motive for the invasion was to grab the rich mineral resources of eastern Congo.

The war raised accusations of corruption, with officials alleged to be plundering Congo's mineral reserves. Mugabe's defence minister Moven Mahachi said, "Instead of our army in the DRC burdening the treasury for more resources, which are not available, it embarks on viable projects for the sake of generating the necessary revenue."

Land reform

When Zimbabwe gained independence, 46.5% of the country's arable land was owned by around 6,000 commercial farmers, almost all of whom were white. And white farmers, who made up less than 1% of the country's population, owned 70% of the best farming land.

Mugabe accepted a "willing buyer, willing seller" plan as part of the Lancaster House Agreement of 1979, among other concessions to the white minority. As part of this agreement, land redistribution was blocked for 10 years.

In 1997, the new British government led by Tony Blair unilaterally stopped funding the "willing buyer, willing seller" land reform programme on the basis that the initial £44 million allocated under the Thatcher government was used to purchase land for members of the ruling elite rather than landless peasants.

Furthermore, Britain's ruling Labour Party felt no obligation to continue paying white farmers compensation, or in minister Clare Short's words, "I should make it clear that we do not accept that Britain has a special responsibility to meet the costs of land purchase in Zimbabwe. We are a new Government from diverse backgrounds without links to former colonial interests. My own origins are Irish and as you know we were colonised not colonisers."

Some commentators, such as Matthew Sweet in *The Independent*, London, hold Cecil Rhodes ultimately responsible:

"... It was Cecil Rhodes who originated the racist 'land grabs' to which Zimbabwe's current miseries can ultimately be traced. It was Rhodes who in 1887 told the House Of Assembly in Cape Town, South Africa, that 'the native is to be treated as a child and denied the franchise. We must adopt a system of despotism in our relations with the barbarians of Southern Africa'.'"

According to Sweet, "In less oratorical moments, he put it even more bluntly: 'I prefer land to niggers.'"

From 12 to 13 February 2000, a referendum on constitutional amendments was held. The proposed amendments would have limited future presidents to two terms, but as it was not retroactive, Mugabe could have stood for another two terms. It also would have made his government and military officials immune from prosecution for any illegal acts committed while in office. In addition, it allowed the government to confiscate white-owned land for redistribution to black farmers without compensation. The motion failed with 55% of participants against the referendum.

The referendum had a 20% turnout fuelled by an effective SMS campaign. Mugabe declared that he would "abide by the will of the people". The vote was a surprise to ZANU-PF and an embarrassment before parliamentary elections due in mid-April.

Almost immediately, self-styled "war veterans" led by Chenjerai 'Hitler' Hunzvi began invading white-owned farms. Those who did not leave voluntarily were often tortured and sometimes killed. One was forced to drink diesel fuel as a form of torture.

On 6 April 2000, parliament pushed through an amendment, taken word for word from the draft constitution that was rejected by the voters, allowing the seizure of white-owned farmlands without reimbursement or payment.

On 8 December 2003, in protest against a further 18 months of suspension from the Commonwealth of Nations (thereby cutting foreign aid to Zimbabwe), Mugabe withdrew his country from the Commonwealth. He informed the leaders of Jamaica, Nigeria and South Africa of his decision when they telephoned him to discuss the situation. Zimbabwe's government said the president did not accept the Commonwealth's position, and was leaving the group.

The United Nations provoked anger when its Food and Agriculture Organisation (FAO) invited Mugabe to speak at a celebration of its 60th anniversary in Rome. Critics of the move argued that since Mugabe could not feed his own people without UN assistance, he was an inappropriate speaker for the group, which has a mission statement of "helping to build a world without hunger."

In 2005, Mugabe ordered a raid conducted on what the government termed "illegal shelters" in Harare, resulting in 10,000 urban poor being left homeless from Operation Murambatsvina (Operation Drive Out the Rubbish).

The authorities themselves had moved the poor inhabitants to the area in 1992, telling them not to build permanent homes and that their new homes were temporary, leading the inhabitants to build their own temporary shelters out of cardboard and wood. And since the inhabitants of the shantytowns overwhelmingly supported the Movement for Democratic Change (MDC) opposition party led by Morgan Tsvangirai in the previous election, many alleged that the mass bulldozing was politically motivated.

The UK's *Daily Telegraph* noted that Mugabe's "latest palace," in the style of a pagoda, was located a mile from the destroyed shelters.

The UN released a report stating that the actions of Mugabe resulted in the loss of home or livelihood for more than 700,000 Zimbabweans and negatively affected 2.4 million more.

As of September 2006, Mugabe's family owned three farms: *Highfield Estate* in Norton, 45 kilometres west of the capital Harare; *Iron Mask Estate* in Mazowe, about 40 kilometres from Harare; and *Foyle Farm* in Mazowe, formerly owned by Ian Webster and adjacent to Iron Mask Farm, renamed *Gushungo Farm* after Mugabe's own clan name. These farms were seized forcibly from their previous owners.

Mugabe blamed the food shortages on drought and the cumulative effect of sanctions imposed on the country by Western countries.

In November 2010, the Institute of Development Studies at Sussex University in England released a comprehensive study on the effects of Zimbabwean land reform. The study suggested that the consequences were mixed but that previous claims that the reform was a failure, and that its primary recipients were political "cronies" or that it caused rural collapse were unfounded.

One of the study's authors, Professor Ian Scoones, stated: "What comes through from our research is the complexity, the differences in experience, almost farm by farm; there is no single, simple story of the Zimbabwe land reform as sometimes assumed by press reports, political commentators, or indeed much academic study."

Elections

In April 1979, 64% of the black citizens of Rhodesia (now Zimbabwe) lined up at the polls to vote in the first democratic election in the history of that southern African nation. Two-thirds of them supported Abel Muzorewa, a bishop in the United Methodist Church. He was the first black prime minister of a country only 4% white. Muzorewa's victory put an end to the 14-year political odyssey of outgoing prime minister Ian Smith who had infamously announced in 1976, "I do not believe in black majority rule – not in a thousand years."

Less than a year after Muzorewa's victory, however, in February 1980, another election was held in Zimbabwe. This time, Robert Mugabe, who had fought a seven-year guerrilla war against Rhodesia's white-led government, won 64% of the vote, after a campaign marked by widespread intimidation, outright violence, and Mugabe's threat to continue the civil war if he lost.

Mugabe became prime minister and was toasted by the international community and media as a new sort of African leader.

Mugabe continued to win elections, although frequently he was criticised by outsiders for violating electoral procedures.

Mugabe faced Tsvangirai of the Movement for Democratic Change (MDC) in presidential elections in March 2002. He defeated Tsvangirai by 56.2% to 41.9% amid violence and the prevention of large numbers of citizens in urban areas from voting. The conduct of the elections was widely viewed internationally as having been manipulated. Many countries including the United Kingdom and the United States, and the European Union (EU) as well as Tsvangirai's party, asserted that the elections were rigged.

Mugabe's ZANU-PF party won the 2005 parliamentary elections with an increased majority. The elections were said by (again) South African observers to "reflect the free will of the people of Zimbabwe" despite accusations of widespread fraud from the MDC.

On 6 February 2007, Mugabe orchestrated a cabinet reshuffle, ousting ministers including five-year veteran finance minister Herbert Murerwa.

On 11 March 2007, opposition leader Morgan Tsvangirai was arrested and beaten following a prayer meeting in the Harare suburb of Highfields. Another member of the Movement for Democratic Change was killed while other protesters were injured. Mugabe claimed that "Tsvangirai deserved his beating-up by police because he was not allowed to attend a banned rally" on 30 March 2007.

General elections 2008

Mugabe launched his election campaign on his birthday in Beitbridge, a small town on the border with

South Africa on 23 February 2008 by denouncing both the opposition MDC and Simba Makoni's candidacy. He was quoted in the state media as saying: "Dr Makoni lacked majority support while Mr Tsvangirai was in the presidential race simply to please his Western backers in exchange for money." These are the charges he has used in the past to describe the leader of the opposition.

In the week Dr. Makoni launched his campaign for the presidency, he accused Mugabe of buying votes from the electorate. This was a few hours after Dumiso Dabengwa had come out and endorsed Dr. Makoni's candidature.

The presidential elections were conducted on 29 March 2008, together with the parliamentary elections. On 2 April 2008, the Zimbabwe Electoral Commission confirmed that Mugabe and his party, known as ZANU-PF, had lost control of parliament to the main opposition party, the Movement for Democratic Change. This was confirmed when the results were released.

Both the opposition and his party challenged the results in some constituencies. According to unofficial polling, Zanu-PF took 94 seats, and the main opposition party MDC took 96 seats.

On 3 April 2008, Zimbabwean government forces began cracking down on the main opposition party and arrested at least two foreign journalists who were covering the disputed presidential election, including a correspondent for *The New York Times*.

On 30 March 2008, Mugabe convened a meeting with his top security officials to discuss his defeat in the elections. According to *The Washington Post*, he was prepared to concede but was advised by Zimbabwe's military chief Gen. Constantine Chiwenga to remain in the race, with the senior military officers "supervising a military-style campaign against the opposition."

The first phase of the plan started a week later, involving the building of 2,000 party compounds across Zimbabwe to serve as bases for the party militias.

On an 8 April 2008 meeting, the military plan was given the code name, "CIBD," which stood for "Coercion. Intimidation. Beating. Displacement."

The official results of the presidential elections would be delayed for five weeks. When British Prime Minister Gordon Brown attempted to intervene in the election controversy, Mugabe dismissed him as "a little tiny dot on this planet."

When the official results were finally published by the Zimbabwe Electooral Commission on 2 May 2008, they showed that Mr. Mugabe had lost in the first round, getting 1,079,730 votes (43.2%) against 1,195,562 (47.9%) won by Tsvangirai. Therefore no candidate secured final victory in the first round, and a presidential run-off was needed.

The opposition called the results "scandalous daylight robbery," claiming an outright victory in the first round with 50.3% of the votes. However, closer analysis of the opposition MDC's own figures, as published on the party's website at time, showed they had secured 49.1% of the vote and not the claimed requiste of +50% to avoid a run-off election.

Mugabe's run-off campaign was managed by Emerson Mnangagwa, a former security chief of the conflict of Gukurahundi.

The Washington Post stated that the campaign of violence was bringing results to the ruling party by crushing the opposition MDC and coercion of its supporters.

By 20 June 2008, the Zimbabwe Association of Doctors for Human Rights had "recorded 85 deaths in political violence since the first round of voting."

News organisations reported that, by the date of the second-round election, more than 80 opposition supporters had been killed, hundreds more were missing, in addition to thousands injured and hundreds of thousands driven from their homes.

Zimbabwean officials alleged that activists of the MDC, disguised as ZANU-PF members, had perpetrated violence against the people, mimicking the tactics of the Selous Scouts during the liberation struggle. They alleged that there was a "predominance" of Selous Scouts in the MDC.

The *Sunday Mail* published an article which claimed that former Selous Scouts were training MDC youth activists in violent tactics at locations near Tswane (Pretoria) and Pietermaritzburg in South Africa.

In addition, at least 100 officials and polling officers of the Zimbabwe Electoral Commission were arrested after the first round election.

Tsvangirai initially agreed to a presidential run-off with Robert Mugabe but later withdrew (on 22 June 2008), citing violence targeted at his campaign. He complained that the elections were pointless, as the outcome would be determined by Mugabe himself.

The run-off election was held on 27 June 2008, and Zimbabwe's Electoral Commission released the results two days later. The official results showed that Mugabe had managed to double his votes since the first round, to 2,150,269 votes (85.5%), while his opponent Tsvangirai obtained only 233,000 (9.3%). However Tsvangirai had pulled out previously because of widespread violence from the ZANU-PF's forces.

The violence included beating, rape and others. Many voted because if they did not they could face violence against them. Although witnesses and election monitors had reported a low turnout in many areas of the country, the official tally showed that the total vote had increased from 2,497,265 votes in the first round to 2,514,750 votes in the second round.

Two legal opinions commissioned by the Southern African Litigation Centre (SALC) declared the run-off election illegal because it occurred outside the 21-day period within which it had to take place under

444

Zimbabwean law. Under item 3(1)(b) of the Second Schedule of the Electoral Act, if no second election is held within 21 days of the first election, the candidate with the highest number of votes in the first election has been duly elected as president and must be declared as such. According to the figures released by Zimbabwe's Electoral Commission, that would have meant that Morgan Tsvangirai was the *de jure* president.

Mugabe's inauguration to his sixth presidential term of office was a hastily arranged ceremony, convened barely an hour after the electoral commission declared his victory on 29 June 2008. None of his fellow African heads of state were present at his inauguration; there were only family members, ministers, and security chiefs in the guests' tent.

The Zimbabwean military, and not president Robert Mugabe, was now running the troubled country, according to a South Africa-based NGO called the Zimbabwe Solidarity Forum (ZSF) – 10 July 2008.

The United Kingdom announced a policy of seizing foreign assets belonging to Mugabe. Mugabe replied that he has no foreign assets to seize. HSBC proceeded to seize the bank account of Sam Mugabe, a 23-year old British subject of Zimbabwean origin, no relation to Robert Mugabe. The HSBC bank which carried out the seizure of her account (yes, *her* account *not his* account) subsequently apologised.

On 20 December 2008, despite increased criticism and pressure to resign, Mugabe averred during ZANU-PF's tenth annual conference in Bindura about 50 miles north of Harare that he would brook no such thing.

Criticism and opposition

Since 1998, Mugabe's policies have increasingly provoked domestic and international denunciation. They have been denounced as racist against Zimbabwe's white minority. Mugabe has described his critics as "born again

445

colonialists" and both he and his supporters claim that Zimbabwe's problems are the legacy of imperialism aggravated by Western economic meddling. According to *The Herald*, a Zimbabwean newspaper owned by the government, the U.K. is pursuing a policy of regime change.

Mugabe's critics accuse him of conducting a "reign of terror" and of being an "extremely poor role model" for the continent whose "transgressions are unpardonable."

In solidarity with the April 2007 general strike called by the Zimbabwe Congress of Trade Unions (ZCTU), Britain's Trades Union Congress general secretary Brendan Barber said of Mugabe's regime: 'Zimbabwe's people are suffering from Mugabe's appalling economic mismanagement, corruption, and brutal repression. They are standing up for their rights, and we must stand with them."

Lela Kogbara, Chair of ACTSA (Action for Southern Africa) expressed similar sentiments, stating: "As with every oppressive regime women and workers are left bearing the brunt. Please join us as we stand in solidarity with the people of Zimbabwe in their struggle for peace, justice and freedom."

Robert Guest, the Africa editor for *The Economist* for seven years, argued that Mugabe was to blame for Zimbabwe's economic freefall: "In 1980, the average annual income in Zimbabwe was US$950, and a Zimbabwean dollar was worth more than an American one. By 2003, the average income was less than US$400, and the Zimbabwean economy was in freefall. Mugabe has ruled Zimbabwe for nearly three decades and has led it, in that time, from impressive success to the most dramatic peacetime collapse of any country since Weimar Germany."

In *The Daily Telegraph*, London, Mugabe was criticised for comparing himself to Hitler. He was quoted as saying "This Hitler has only one objective: justice for his people, sovereignty for his people, recognition of the independence of his people and their rights over their resources. If that is Hitler, then let me be a Hitler tenfold."

Western governments also condemned Mugabe's government. On 9 March 2003, U.S. President George W. Bush approved measures for economic sanctions to be levelled against Mugabe and other high-ranking Zimbabwe politicians, freezing their assets and barring Americans from engaging in any transactions or dealings with them.

Justifying the move, Bush's spokesman stated that the President and Congress believe that "the situation in Zimbabwe endangers the southern African region and threatens to undermine efforts to foster good governance and respect for the rule of law throughout the continent."

The bill was known as the Zimbabwe Democracy Act.

In reaction to human rights violations in Zimbabwe, students at universities from which Mugabe got honorary doctorates sought to get the degrees revoked. The University of Edinburgh in Scotland and the University of Massachusetts, in the United States stripped him of his honorary degrees after two years of campaigning.

And the student body (ASMSU) at Michigan State University in the United States unanimously passed a resolution aimed at stripping him of his honorary degree. ASMSU stands for Associated Students of Michigan State University.

Mugabe's office forbade the screening of the 2005 movie *The Interpreter* claiming it was propaganda by the CIA and fearing that it could incite hostility towards him.

In 2007, *Parade* magazine ranked Mugabe the 7th worst dictator in the world. Two years later, the same magazine ranked him worst dictator of the year 2009.

An official from Chatham House suggested that Mugabe was unlikely to leave Zimbabwe but that if he were to leave, he might go to Malaysia where some believe that he has "stashed much of his wealth."

In response to Mugabe's critics, former Zambian president, Kenneth Kaunda, was quoted blaming not Mugabe for Zimbabwe's troubles but successive British governments. He wrote in June 2007 that "leaders in the West say Robert Mugabe is a demon, that he has destroyed Zimbabwe and he must be got rid of – but this demonising is made by people who may not understand what Robert Gabriel Mugabe and his fellow freedom fighters went through."

Similarly, Senegalese President Abdoulaye Wade responded to Mugabe's critics by saying that Zimbabwe's problems are the legacy of colonialism.

Mugabe's supporters characterise him as a true Pan-Africanist and a dedicated anti-imperialist who stands strong against forces of imperialism in Africa. According to Mugabe's supporters, the Western media are not objectively reporting on Zimbabwe but are peddling falsehoods. Mugabe's supporters accuse certain Western governments of trying to undermine and eradicate pan-Africanism in order to deny real independence for African countries by imposing client regimes on them.

The Times, London, charged that on 12 June 2008, Mugabe's militia murdered Dadirai Chipiro, the wife of Mugabe's political opponent, Patson Chipiro, by burning her alive with a petrol bomb after severing her hands and feet.

Sanctions

After the start of the fast track land reform programme in 2000, the US Senate put a credit freeze on the government of Zimbabwe under the Zimbabwe Democracy and Economic Recovery Act (ZDERA) of 2001. Signed into law on 21 December 2001, ZDERA froze the Zimbabwean government's lines of credit at international financial institutions through Section 4C entitled Multilateral Financing Restriction.

The credit freeze forced the Zimbabwean government to operate on a cash only basis and caused high inflation in 2001 to turn into hyperinflation in 2002 and beyond. It caused the first export deficit, the first big drop in tobacco exports, and a greater fall of the Zimbabwe dollar against the US dollar than in the previous 6 years, in the year 2002:

"SEC. 4. SUPPORT FOR DEMOCRATIC TRANSITION AND ECONOMIC RECOVERY. (c) MULTILATERAL FINANCING RESTRICTION- ... the Secretary of the Treasury shall instruct the United States executive director to each international financial institution to oppose and vote against-- (1) any extension by the respective institution of any loan, credit, or guarantee to the Government of Zimbabwe; or (2) any cancellation or reduction of indebtedness owed by the Government of Zimbabwe to the United States or any international financial institution."

ZDERA was sponsored by Senator Bill Frist (Republican-Tennessee). It was co-sponsored by then senators Hillary Clinton, Joe Biden, Russ Feingold and Jesse Helms.

In 2010, Russ Feingold introduced a new law – called the Zimbabwe Transition to Democracy and Economic Recovery Act of 2010 (ZTDERA) – that would continue the credit freeze on Zimbabwe.

Senator James Inhofe (Republican-Oklahoma) introduced the Zimbabwe Sanctions Repeal Act of 2010) specifically to repeal ZDERA through Section 2 article 26.

After observers from the European Union (EU) were barred from monitoring Zimbabwe's 2002 elections, the EU imposed sanctions on Mugabe and 94 members of his government, banning them from travelling to participating countries and freezing any assets held there. The United States instituted similar restrictions.

But the EU's ban had a few loopholes, enabling Mugabe to take a few trips to Europe despite the ban.

And he was still permitted to travel to UN events within European and American borders.

On 8 April 2005, Mugabe attended the funeral of Pope John Paul II, a move which seemed to be a defiance of the European Union travel ban. But the ban did not apply to Vatican City.

He was granted a transit visa by the Italian authorities, as obliged to under the Concordat.

However, the Catholic hierarchy in Zimbabwe had always been very vocal against his tyrannical rule. The senior Catholic cleric, Pius Ncube, was a major critic of Mugabe and even called for Western governments to help overthrow him.

Mugabe surprised Prince Charles by shaking his hand during the service at the Pope's funeral. Afterwards, the Prince's office issued a statement saying: "The Prince of Wales was caught by surprise and not in a position to avoid shaking Mr. Mugabe's hand. The Prince finds the current Zimbabwean regime abhorrent. He has supported the Zimbabwe Defence and Aid Fund which works with those being oppressed by the regime. The Prince also recently met Pius Ncube, the Archbishop of Bulawayo, an outspoken critic of the government".

Robert Mugabe and senior members of the Harare government were not allowed to travel to the United States because it was the position of the American government that he undermined democracy in Zimbabwe and restricted freedom of the press.

But in spite of the strained political relations between the two countries, the United States remained a leading provider of humanitarian assistance to Zimbabwe, providing roughly US$900 million in humanitarian assistance from 2002–2008, mostly food aid.

Mugabe also attended the Food and Agriculture Organisation (FAO) summit in Rome because United

Nations events are exempt from travel bans. African leaders threatened to boycott the event if Mugabe were blacklisted. The United Kingdom refused to send a representative. British and Australian officials denounced the presence of Mugabe at the FAO summit.

Succession

Speculation built over the years relating to Mugabe's succession because of his age. He was also one of Africa's longest-ruling leaders.

Joyce Mujuru was elevated to vice-president of ZANU-PF during the December 2004 party congress. Considerably younger than Joseph Masika, the other vice-president, she was touted as a likely successor to Mugabe. Her candidacy for the presidency was strengthened by the backing of her husband, Solomon Mujuru, who once was the head of the Zimbabwean army.

In October 2006, a report prepared by Zimbabwe's ministry of economic development acknowledged lack of coordination among critical government departments in Zimbabwe and the overall lack of commitment to end the crisis. The report implied that the infighting in ZANU-PF over Mugabe's successor was also hurting policy formulation and consistency in implementation.

In late 2006, a plan was presented to postpone the next presidential until 2010, at the same time as the next parliamentary election, thereby extending Mugabe's term by two years. It was said that holding the two elections together would be a cost-saving measure but the plan was not approved: there were reportedly objections from some in ZANU-PF to the idea.

In March 2007, Mugabe said that he thought that the feeling was in favour of holding the two elections together in 2008 instead of 2010. He also said that he would be willing to run for re-election again if the party wanted him to do so.

Other leaders in southern Africa were rumoured to be less warm on the idea of extending his term to 2010.

On 30 March 2007, it was announced that the ZANU-PF central committee had chosen Mugabe as the party's candidate for another term in 2008, that presidential terms would be shortened to five years, and that the parliamentary election would also be held in 2008. Mugabe was chosen by acclamation as the party's presidential candidate for 2008 by ZANU-PF delegates at a party conference on 13 December 2007.

At Zanu-PF's tenth annual conference in Bindura in December 2008, Mugabe spoke of his determination not to follow US president George W. Bush to his "political death" and urged the party to ready itself for new polls. He also took the opportunity once more to cite Britain as the source of Zimbabwe's woes.

At the 50th anniversary of Ghana's independence in Accra in March 2007, South African President Thabo Mbeki was rumoured to have met with Mugabe in private and told him that "he was determined that South Africa's hosting of the Football World Cup in 2010 should not be disrupted by controversial presidential elections in Zimbabwe."

As of 10 September 2010 there was considerable speculation that Mugabe was dying of cancer. It was rumoured that his choice of successor was Simba Makoni.

Power-sharing Agreement Facilitated by SADC

On 11 September 2008, at the end of the fourth day of negotiations, South African President and mediator to Zimbabwe, Thabo Mbeki, announced in Harare that Robert Mugabe of ZANU-PF, Professor Arthur Mutambara and Morgan Tsvangirai (both of MDC) finally signed the power-sharing agreement – "memorandum of understanding." Mbeki stated:

"An agreement has been reached on all items on the agenda ... all of them [Mugabe, Tsvangirai, Mutambara] endorsed the document tonight, and signed it. The formal signing will be done on Monday 10 am. The document will be released then.

The ceremony will be attended by SADC and other African regional and continental leaders. The leaders will spend the next few days constituting the inclusive government to be announced on Monday. The leaders will work very hard to mobilise support for the people to recover.

We hope the world will assist so that this political agreement succeeds."

In the signed historic power deal, Mugabe, on 11 September 2008 agreed to surrender day-to-day control of the government. The deal was also expected to result in a *de facto* amnesty for the military and ZANU-PF party leaders.

Opposition sources said "Tsvangirai will become prime minister at the head of a council of ministers, the principal organ of government, drawn from his Movement for Democratic Change and the president's ZANU-PF party; and Mugabe will remain president and continue to chair a cabinet that will be a largely consultative body, and the real power will lie with Tsvangirai."

South Africa's *Business Day* reported, however, that Mugabe was refusing to sign a deal which would curtail his presidential powers.

The New York Times said Nelson Chamisa, a spokesman for the opposition Movement for Democratic Change, announced: "This is an inclusive government. The executive power would be shared by the president, the prime minister and the cabinet. Mugabe, Tsvangirai and Arthur Mutambara have still not decided how to divide the ministries. But Jendayi E. Frazer, the American assistant secretary of state for African affairs, said: "We don't know what's on the table, and it's hard to rally for an agreement when no one knows the details or even the broad outlines."

On 15 September 2008, the leaders of the 14-member SADC witnessed the signing of the power-sharing agreement brokered by South African leader Thabo Mbeki. With symbolic handshake and warm smiles at the Rainbow Towers hotel in Harare, Mugabe, Mutambara and Tsvangirai signed the deal to end violent political crisis provides. As provided, Robert Mugabe would be recognised as president, Morgan Tsvangirai would become prime minister, the MDC would control the police, Mugabe's ZANU-PF would control the army, and Arthur Mutambara would become deputy prime minister.

Violence, however, did not entirely subside with the power-sharing agreement. As *The New Your Times* reported, Mugabe's top lieutenants started "trying to force the political opposition into granting them amnesty for their past crimes by abducting, detaining and torturing opposition officials and activists."

Dozens of members of the opposition and human rights activists were abducted and tortured in the months since October 2008, including Roy Bennett, the opposition's third-highest ranking official and Tsvangirai's nominee for deputy agriculture minister (arrested just two days after Tsvangirai was sworn in as prime minister on 11 February 2009) and Chris Dhlamini, the opposition's director of security.

Personal life

Mugabe's first wife, Sally Hayfron, died in 1992 from a chronic kidney ailment. Their only son, Michael Nhamodzenyika Mugabe, born 27 September 1963, died on 26 December 1966 from cerebral malaria in Ghana where Sally was working while Mugabe was in prison.

Sally Mugabe was a trained teacher who asserted her

position as an independent political activist and campaigner who was seen as Mugabe's closest friend and advisor. Some critics suggest that Mugabe began to misrule Zimbabwe after her death.

On 17 August 1996, Mugabe married his former secretary, Grace Marufu, 41 years his junior, with whom he already had two children; she first became pregnant by Mugabe while he was still married to his first wife, Sally, and while Grace was married to another man, Stanley Goreraza, a senior officer in the Zimbabwean air force who later served as defence attaché at the Zimbabwean embassy in China.

Mugabe and Marufu were married in a Roman Catholic wedding Mass at Kutama College, a Catholic mission school he previously attended. Nelson Mandela and Mugabe's two children by Grace were among the guests.

The Mugabes have three children: Bona, Robert Peter Jr. (although Robert Mugabe's middle name is Gabriel) and Bellarmine Chatunga.

As first lady, Grace has been the subject of criticism for her lifestyle. Her sometimes lavish European shopping sprees have led to the nickname "Gucci Grace."

When she was included in the 2002 European Union (EU) travel sanctions on her husband, one EU parliamentarian was quoted as saying that the ban "will stop Grace Mugabe going on her shopping trips in the face of catastrophic poverty blighting the people of Zimbabwe."

Seretse Khama

Seretse Khama (1 July 1921 – 13 July 1980) was the first leader of independent Botswana. Born into one of the powerful royal families of what was then the British protectorate of Bechuanaland, and educated in neighbouring apartheid South Africa and in the United Kingdom, he returned home – with a popular but controversial bride – to lead his country's independence movement.

He founded the Botswana Democratic Party (BDP) in 1962 and became prime minister in 1965.

In 1966, Botswana became independence and Khama became its first president.

During his presidency, the country underwent rapid economic and social progress.

Childhood and education

Seretse Khama was born in 1921 in Serowe in what was then the Bechuanaland Protectorate. He was the son of Sekgoma Khama II, the paramount chief of the Bamangwato people, and the grandson of Khama III, their king.

The name "Seretse" means "the clay that binds together" and was given to him to celebrate the recent reconciliation of his father and grandfather; this reconciliation assured Seretse's own ascension to the throne with his aged father's death in 1925.

Seretse became *kgosi* (king) at the age of four, with his uncle Tshekedi Khama as his regent and guardian.

After spending most of his youth in South African boarding schools, Seretse Khama attended Fort Hare University College there, graduating with a general B.A. in 1944. He then travelled to the United Kingdom and spent a year at Balliol College, Oxford, before joining the Inner Temple in London in 1946 to study to become a barrister.

Marriage and exile

In June 1947, Khama met Ruth Williams, an English clerk at Lloyd's of London, and after a year of courtship, married her.

The interracial marriage sparked a furore among both the apartheid government of South Africa and the tribal elders of the Bamangwato.

After he was told about the marriage, Khama's uncle Tshekedi Khama demanded his return to Bechuanaland and the annulment of the marriage. Khama did return to Serowe but after a series of *kgotlas* (public meetings), was re-affirmed by the elders in his role as the *kgosi* in 1949. Ruth Williams Khama, travelling with her new husband, proved similarly popular. Admitting defeat, Tshekedi Khama left Bechuanaland, while Khama returned to London to complete his studies.

However, the international ramifications of his marriage would not be so easily resolved. Having banned interracial marriage under the apartheid system, South Africa could not afford to have an interracial couple ruling just across their northern border. As Bechuanaland was then a British protectorate, the South African government immediately exerted pressure to have Khama removed from his chieftainship.

Britain's Labour government, then heavily in debt from World War II, could not afford to lose cheap South African gold and uranium supplies. There was also a fear that South Africa might take more direct action against Bechuanaland through economic sanctions or a military incursion. The British government therefore launched a pparliamentary enquiry into Khama's fitness for the chieftainship.

Although the investigation reported that he was in fact eminently fit to rule Bechuanaland, "but for his unfortunate marriage," the government ordered the report suppressed (it would remain so for thirty years), and exiled Khama and his wife from Bechuanaland in 1951.

Return to politics

The sentence would not last nearly so long. Various groups protested against the government decision, holding it up as evidence of British racism. In Britain itself, there was widespread anger at the decision and calls for the resignation of Lord Salisbury, the minister responsible. A deputation of six Bamangwato travelled to London to see the exiled Khama and Lord Salisbury, in an echo of the 1895 deputation of three Bamangwato *kgosis* to Queen Victoria, but with no success. However, when ordered by the British High Commission to replace Khama, the people refused to do so.

In 1956, Seretse and Ruth Khama were allowed to return to Bechuanaland as private citizens after he had renounced the tribal throne. Khama began an unsuccessful stint as a cattle rancher and dabbled in local politics. He was elected to the tribal council in 1957. In 1960, he was diagnosed with diabetes.

In 1961, however, Khama leapt back onto the political scene by founding the Bechuanaland Democratic Party (BDP).

His exile had given him an increased credibility with an independence-minded electorate and the BDP swept aside its socialist and pan-Africanist rivals to dominate the 1965 elections.

Now prime minister of Bechuanaland, Seretse Khama continued to push for Botswana's independence from the newly-established capital of Gabarone.

A 1965 constitution delineated a new Botswana government   and on 30 September 1966, Botswana became independent.

Presidency

At the time of its independence, Botswana was among the world's poorest countries, even poorer than most other African countries. Khama launched a vigorous economic programme intended to transform the country into an export-based economy built around beef, copper and diamonds. The 1967 discovery of Orapa's diamond deposits helped a lot in fuelling economic growth.

Botswana's achievements were remarkable in sharp contrast with those of many other African countries which had abundant resources but still remained poor because of bad leadership, wrong policies, corruption, tribalism, nepotism, and mismanagement of the economy.

Between 1966 and 1980, Botswana had the fastest-growing economy in the world. Much of the money earned was reinvested in infrastructure, health and education, resulting in further economic development. Khama also instituted strong measures against corruption, the bane of so many other newly-independent African nations.

And unlike many other countries in Africa which adopted socialist policies or tried to build state-run economies, Khama's government pursued market-friendly policies to foster economic development. He promised low and stable taxes to mining companies, liberalised trade and increased personal freedom. He maintained low marginal income tax rates to deter tax evasion and corruption. He also upheld liberal democracy and non-racialism in the midst of a region embroiled in civil war, racial enmity and corruption.

In foreign policy, Khama exercised caution and did not

allow militant groups to operate from within Botswana. According to Richard Dale "The Khama government had authority to do so by virtue of the 1963 Prevention of Violence Abroad Act, and a week after independence, Sir Seretse Khama announced before the National Assembly his government's policy to ensure that Botswana would not become a base of operations for attacking any neighbor."

Shortly before his death, Khama would play a major role in negotiating the end of the Rhodesian civil war wwhich eventually led to Zimbabwe's independence.

On a personal level, he was known for his intelligence, integrity and sense of humour.

Legacy

Khama remained president until his death from pancreatic cancer in 1980. He was succeeded by vice president Quett Mmasire.

Forty thousand people paid their respects while his body lay in state in the nation's capital Gaborone. He was buried in the Khama family graveyard on a hill in Serowe, Central District.

Twenty-eight years after Seretse Khama's death, his son Ian Khama succeeded Festus Mogae as the fourth president of Botswana.

In the 2009 general election, Ian Khama won a landslide victory. His younger brother, Tshekedi Khama II, was elected as a member of parliament representing Serowe North West.

Agostinho Neto

António Agostinho Neto (September 17, 1922 – September 10, 1979) was the first president of Angola (1975–1979).

He led the Popular Movement for the Liberation of Angola (MPLA) during the struggle for independence and during the civil war. His birthday is a public holiday in and is celebrated as the Day of the National Hero.

Early life

Neto was born at Ícolo e Bengo, in Bengo Province in northern Angola and attended high school in the capital city, Luanda. His father, also called Agostinho Neto, was a Methodist pastor.

The younger Neto left Angola for Portugal where he studied medicine at the universities of Coimbra and Lisbon. He combined his academic life with covert political activity of a revolutionary kind. The security police force – PIDE – of Portuguese Prime Minister António Salazar arrested him in 1951 for his activism. He was released from prison seven years later and finished his studies. He married Maria Eugénia da Silva the same day he graduated. He returned to Angola in 1959.

His arrest and imprisonment further galvanised him into action and played a role in shaping his political thinking. Harassment by PIDE during his years in Portugal never damped his enthusiasm and his interest in politics.

PIDE was notorious for harassing students from the Portuguese colonies who were studying in Portugal. Others included Marcelino dos Santos from Mozambique who later became vice president of his country after it won independence from Portugal in 1975.

PIDE – *Polícia Internacional e de Defesa do Estado* which means International and State Defence Police – was the main tool of repression used by the authoritarian regime of Salazar.

Although the name PIDE was only used from 1945 to 1969, the whole network of secret police forces which existed during the 40 years of the regime are commonly known as PIDE.

Political career

In December 1956 the Angolan Communist Party (PCA) merged with the Party of the United Struggle for Africans in Angola (PLUA) to form the Popular Movement for the Liberation of Angola (MPLA) with Viriato Clemente da Cruz, the President of the PCA, as secretary-general and Neto as president.

MPLA is an acronym for *Movimento Popular de Libertação de Angola.*

The Portuguese authorities in Angola arrested Neto on 8 June 1960. His patients and supporters marched for his release from Bengo to Catete but were stopped when Portuguese soldiers shot at them, killing 30 and wounding 200 in what came to be known as the Massacre of Icolo e Bengo.

At first, Portugal's government exiled Neto to cape Verde. Then, once more, he was sent to jail in Lisbon. After international protests were made to Salazar's administration urging Neto's release, Neto was freed from prison and put under house arrest. He escaped from there and went to Morocco and then to Zaire (later renamed the Democratic Republic of Congo – DRC).

In 1962, Dr. Neto visited Washington, D.C. and asked the Kennedy administration for some help in his war against the Portuguese colonial rulers in Angola. But the American government turned him down. Instead, the

Americans chose to support Dr. Holden Roberto, the leader of another liberation group in Angola, the FNLA, because of its anti-communist stand. The United States considered Neto to be a communist sympathiser because he was said to be a Marxist.

Neto met Che Guevara in 1965 and began getting support from Cuba. He visited Havana many times and he and Fidel Castro shared similar ideological views.

Following the Carnation Revolution in Portugal in April 1974 which deposed Salazar's successor Marcelo Caetano, there was a struggle for power in Angola involving three political groups: the MPLA, FNLA, and UNITA.

The MPLA, led by Dr. Neto, was the most powerful.

On 11 November 1975, Angola achieved full independence from Portugal and Neto became the nation's leader. His government was also recognised by the Organization of African Unity (OAU), hence by the majority of the African countries whose collective will was expressed by the OAU.

Neto's government developed close links with the Soviet Union and other nations in the Eastern bloc as well as other communist states, especially Cuba which helped the MPLA win its war against the FNLA, UNITA, and eventually against apartheid South Africa.

Neto died in a hospital in Moscow while undergoing surgery for cancer, shortly before his 57th birthday.

Jose Eduardo dos Santos succeeded him as president. But the Angolan civil war continued to rage for almost a quarter of a century more.

Legacy

The Soviet Union awarded Neto the Lenin Peace Prize for 1975-76.

The public university of Luanda, the Agostinho Neto

University, is named after him.

A poem by Chinua Achebe entitled *Agostinho Neto* was written in his honor.

An airport in Santo Antão, Cape Verde, is named after him, due to the beloved work he performed there as a doctor. There is also a morna dedicated to him.

A street in New Belgrade in Serbia, the Dr. Agostina Neta Street, is named after him.

In 1973, during one of his few unofficial visits to Bulgaria, Neto met a woman with whom he had a daughter called Mihaela Marinova. Unfortunately Neto's sudden death did no favour for his daughter who had been raised in orphanages in Bulgaria. Neto's family has not recognised the child.

Sam Nujoma

Samuel Daniel Shafiishuna Nujoma (born 12 May 1929) was the first president of Namibia. He was simply known as Sam Nujoma.

He was inaugurated as president of Namibia on 21 March 1990. He was re-elected in 1994 and 1999 and served until 2005.

He was also president of the South-West Africa People's Organisation (SWAPO) from its founding in 1960 until 2007. SWAPO led the struggle for independence and became the ruling party after the country attained sovereign status.

Early life

Nujoma was born at Etunda village in Ongandjera in the northern part of South West Africa. Ongandjera was renamed Omusati Region. And the country South West Africa was renamed Namibia.

Omusati is an integral part of the ethno-cultural region

known as Ovamboland which is inhabited by the members of the Ovambo ethnic group, the largest in the country.

President of SWAPO

In 1960, Sam Nujoma became the first president of the South-West Africa People's Organisation (SWAPO). He was a co-founder of its forerunner, the Ovamboland People's Organisation in the late 1950s.

Before independence, Namibia was a virtual colony of apartheid South Africa. The apartheid regime extended its racist policies to South West Africa which was a Germany colony until the end of World War I.

When the South African apartheid regime assumed control of the former Germany colony under the League of Nations mandate, it brutally suppressed the indigenous people and reserved for whites the country's best resources including land. Blacks and other non-whites were treated as inferior. They were forbidden from active participation in the political process and government of their country.

After years of campaigning and pleading with the United Nations to force the apartheid regime to relinquish control of South West Africa failed to produce results, Sam Nujoma and his colleagues started waging guerrilla warfare in 1966 to free their country. That was the beginning of the Namibian war of independence. The war went on for 24 years and was conducted by SWAPO.

During the liberation struggle, Nujoma took the combat name "Shafiishuna" which means "lightning." The name was also already in his family on his father's side.

For years, the South African armed forces fought SWAPO guerrillas in brutal campaigns inside Namibia and in southern Angola where SWAPO had some of its operational bases.

The apartheid regime was also involved in other

conflicts in the region to destabilise countries which were helping the freedom fighters including those who were fighting the apartheid regime in South Africa itself.

And it was successful in most of those campaigns but later suffered a serious setback at the Battle of Cuito Cuanavale when its army fought Cuban soldiers who were helping the MPLA army of Angola.

Victory against the South Africans at Cuito Cuanavale – some people, especially the South Africans of the apartheid era, said it was a stalemate – led to negotiations between the two sides and finally to the independence of Namibia. It also accelerated the collapse of the apartheid regime in South Africa itself.

President of Namibia

As head of SWAPO, Nujoma was unanimously declared president upon the victory of SWAPO in a United Nations-supervised election in 1989, and was sworn in on 21 March 1990.

But his government, although democratic, faced some criticism which was justified.

In 1992, Norway decided to stop drought relief to Namibia in response to the purchase of an expensive new presidential jet and two new VIP helicopters. The planes were bought just a few weeks after Sam Nujoma had appealed to the international community for drought aid.

Many years later after leaving office, Nujoma was still being criticised for excessive luxury and perks he got in a country which, although potentially rich, was considered to be poor and one of the least developed in the world.

But he also introduced some popular reforms. For example, he launched a programme for land reform under which land would be redistributed from whites (who, despite constituting only a small percentage of the population, owne a disproportionately large amount of the nation's farmland) to blacks, although it is being implemented on a more gradual and long-term basis than what is being done in nearby Zimbabwe.

Nujoma was a vocal supporter of land redistribution in Zimbabwe. He also strongly supported Zimbabwe's President Robert Mugabe who faced strong criticism from Western countries because of his policy of land reform which entailed seizing land from whites without compensation and giving it to blacks. Mugabe said blacks were the rightful owners of the land. He also once bluntly stated that whites don't belong in Africa.

The seizure of land from whites in Zimbabwe started in earnest in 2003. Nothing of the sort took place in Namibia under Nujoma.

Nujoma was re-elected president of Namibia in December 1994 with 76.3% of the vote.

The constitution of Namibia was changed to allow Nujoma to run for a third five-year term in 1999; this was justified on the grounds that he had not been directly elected for his first term, and the change applied only to Nujoma. He won the 1999 election with 76.8% of the vote.

The constitution did not allow Nujoma to run in November 2004 for a fourth term and there was not much enthusiasm even within SWAPO itself to change it again.

Hifikepunye Pohamba, described by some people as Nujoma's "hand-picked successor," was chosen as the candidate for the presidential election during the SWAPO congress held on the 30 May 2004. He defeated two other contenders: Nahas Angula and Hidipo Hamutenya.

Hamutenya had been dismissed from his post as foreign affairs minister by Nujoma barely two days before the congress.

Pohamba was elected as president of Namibia with a large majority and was sworn in on 21 March 2005.

Post-presidency

While Pohamba replaced Nujoma as the president of Namibia, Nujoma retained his post as president of the ruling party SWAPO. There was speculation that he would be re-elected as SWAPO leader in 2007 and that he was planning to run for president again in 2009.

In early October 2007, however, Nujoma said that he had no intention of seeking re-election as SWAPO president and would stand aside later in the year in favour of Pohamba, the SWAPO's vice president. Nujoma led SWAPO for 47 years.

Pohamba was accordingly elected unopposed as SWAPO president on 29 November 2007 at a party congress. Nujoma said that he was "passing the torch and mantle of leadership to comrade Pohamba."

The party congress also decided to give Nujoma the title, Leader of the Namibian Revolution, in addition to his other title, Founding Father of the Namibian Nation.

Choosing to leave active politics, Nujoma was not re-elected to SWAPO's central committee or politburo. But the congress granted him permission to attend meetings of the Central Committee and Politburo "at his discretion."

Nujoma's son, Utoni Nujoma, deputy minister of justice, was elected to the central committee and politburo of SWAPO at its November 2007 congress.

The director of the National Security for Human Rights (NSHR) in Namibia stated that Nujoma had connections to the CIA.

The NSHR asked the International Criminal Court to investigate Nujoma and what they claimed was his role in the disappearance of a number of individuals during his term.

But none of the claims were substantiated.

In 2009, Sam Nujoma earned a master's degree in geology from the University of Namibia.

Despite stepping down from the presidency and other positions of leadership, Nujoma remained active in the political sphere and regularly campaigned for SWAPO at various rallies and functions across the country.

Nelson Mandela

Nelson Rolihlahla Mandela (born 18 July 1918) was the first democratically elected president of South Africa.

He won the presidency in an election in which South Africans of all races, including the black majority, participated on equal basis for the first time in the nation's history. He served as president from 1994 to 1999. All the other presidential candidates before Mandela had been white. And all the elections had been exclusively for white voters to elect white leaders for the whole country.

Before he became president, Mandela was an anti-apartheid activist. He was also the leader of Umkhonto we Sizwe, the armed wing of the African National Congress (ANC).

In 1962 he was arrested and convicted of sabotage and other charges. He was sentenced to life in prison in June 1964.

Mandela served 27 and a half years in prison. He spent many of those years on Robben Island.

Following his release from prison on 11 February 1990, he led his party, the African National Congress (ANC), in negotiations with the white rulers which led to multi-racial democracy in 1994. As president from 1994 to 1999, he frequently gave priority to racial reconciliation and became an icon and symbol of unity for South Africans of all races.

In South Africa, Mandela is often known as *Madiba*, his Xhosa clan name, or as *tata* which in his native Xhosa language means "father."

He received more than 250 awards in a period

spanning more than four decades. One of those awards was the Nobel Peace Prize in 1993 which he shared with the last white president of apartheid South Africa, F.W. de Klerk, who also played a role in ending white minority rule in the country.

Early life

Nelson Mandela belonged to a cadet branch of the Thembu dynasty which reigns in the Transkei region of South Africa's Eastern Cape Province.

He was born in Mvezo, a small village on the banks of the Mbashe River, known today as the Bashee River, in the district of Umtata in Transkei. He had Khoisan ancestry on his mother's side, clearly visible in his facial features which gave him a somewhat "Oriental" appearance as is the case with all Khoisans or so-called Bushmen, or "Hottentots," a pejorative name given to them by whites – Afrikaners.

His patrilineal great-grandfather Ngubengcuka (who died in 1832) ruled as the *Inkosi Enkhulu*, or king, of the Thembu people. One of the king's sons, named *Mandela*, became Nelson's grandfather and the source of his surname.

However, because he was only the *Inkosi's* child by a wife of the Ixhiba clan, the so-called "Left-Hand House," the descendants of his branch of the royal family were not eligible to succeed to the Thembu throne.

Mandela's father, Gadla Henry Mphakanyiswa, served as cchief of the town of Mvezo. However, upon alienating the colonial authorities, they deprived Mphakanyiswa of his position and moved his family to Qunu.

In spite of that, Mphakanyiswa remained a member of the *Inkosi's* privy council and played a major role in Jongintaba Dalindyebo's ascension to the Thembu throne. Dalindyebo would later return the favour by informally adopting Mandela upon Mphakanyiswa's death.

Mandela's father had four wives with whom he fathered thirteen children (four boys and nine girls). Mandela was born to his third wife ('third' by a complex royal ranking system), Nosekeni Fanny. Fanny was a daughter of Nkedama of the Mpemvu Xhosa clan, the dynastic Right Hand House in whose *umzi* or homestead Mandela spent much of his childhood. His given name *Rolihlahla* means "to pull a branch of a tree," or more colloquially, "troublemaker."

Rolihlahla Mandela became the first member of his family to attend a school where his teacher Miss Mdingane gave him the English name "Nelson."

When Mandela was nine, his father died of tuberculosis and the regent, Jongintaba, became his guardian.

Mandela attended a Wesleyan mission school located next to the palace of the regent. Following Thembu custom, he was initiated at age sixteen and attended Clarkebury Boarding Institute. He completed his Junior Certificate in two years instead of the usual three. Designated to inherit his father's position as a privy councillor, in 1937 Mandela moved to Healdtown, the Wesleyan college in Fort Beaufort which most Thembu royalty attended. At nineteen, he took an interest in boxing and running at the school.

Mandela later went to Fort Hare University to study for a Bachelor of Arts (B.A.). It was when he was at Fort Hare that he met Oliver Tambo for the first time. The two became lifelong friends and compatriots in the struggle for freedom and racial equality.

Mandela also became a close friend of his kinsman, Kaiser ("K.D.") Mantazima who, as royal scion of the Thembu Right Hand House, was in line for the throne of Transkei, a role that would later lead him to embrace Bantustan policies.

During the apartheid era, Mantazima became prime

minister of Transkei in 1976 when Transkei became the first Bantustan to gain nominal independence which was not recognised by any country except the apartheid regime itself within South Africa. His support of those policies would place him and Mandela on opposing political sides.

At the end of his first year at Fort Hare University, Mandela became involved in a Students' Representative Council boycott against university policies and was told to leave and not return unless he accepted election to the SRC.

Later in his life while in prison, Mandela studied for a Bachelor of Laws (LL.B.) from the University of London External Programme.

Shortly after leaving Fort Hare, Jongintaba announced to Mandela and Justice (the regent's son and heir to the throne) that he had arranged marriages for both of them. The young men, displeased by the arrangement, decided to move to Johannesburg.

After arriving in Johannesburg, Mandela first got a job as a guard at a mine. But his employer quickly sacked him after learning that he was the regent's runaway ward.

Mandela later started work as an articled clerk at a Johannesburg law firm, Witkin, Sidelsky and Edelman, through connections with his friend and mentor, realtor Walter Sisulu.

While working at Witkin, Sidelsky and Edelman, Mandela completed his B.A. degree at the University of South Africa via correspondence, after which he began law studies at the University of Witwatersrand (Wits) where he first befriended fellow students and future anti-apartheid political activists Joe Slovo, Harry Schwarz and Ruth First.

Ruth First was assassinated by the apartheid regime in Mozambique in 1982 when she opened a letter bomb addressed to her.

Slovo become minister of housing under Mandela after the end of apartheid, and Schwarz became South

Africa's ambassador to Washington during the same period.

During his student days at Wits, Mandela lived in Alexandra township north of Johannesburg.

Political activity

After the 1948 election victory of the Afrikaner-dominated National Party which supported the apartheid policy of racial segregation and separation, Mandela began actively participating in politics. He led prominently in the ANC's 1952 Defiannce campaign and the 1955 Congress of the People whose adoption of the Freedom Charter provided the fundamental basis of the anti-apartheid cause.

During this time, Mandela and fellow lawyer Oliver Tambo operated the law firm of Mandela and Tambo providing free or low-cost legal counsel to many blacks who lacked attorney representation.

Mahatma Gandhi influenced Mandela's approach and subsequently the methods of succeeding generations of South African anti-apartheid activists. Mandela later took part in the 29–30 January 2007 conference in New Delhi marking the 100th anniversary of Gandhi's introduction of satyagraha (non-violent resistance) in South Africa.

Initially committed to nonviolent resistance, Mandela and 150 others were arrested on 5 December 1956 and charged with treason. The marathon treason trial of 1956–1961 followed, with all defendants being acquitted.

From 1952–1959, a new class of black activists known as the Africanists disrupted ANC activities in the townships, demanding more drastic steps against the National Party regime. The ANC leadership under Albert Luthuli, Oliver Tambo and Walter Sisulu felt not only that the Africanists were moving too fast but also that they challenged their leadership. The ANC leadership consequently bolstered their position through alliances with small White, Coloured, and Indian political parties in an attempt to give the appearance of wider appeal than the Africanists.

The Africanists ridiculed the 1955 Freedom Charter Kliptown Conference for the concession of the 100,000-strong ANC to just a single vote in a Congressional alliance. Four secretaries-general of the five participating parties secretly belonged to the reconstituted South African Communist Party (SACP).

In 2003 Blade Nzimande, the SACP general secretary, revealed that Walter Sisulu, the ANC secretary-general, secretly joined the SACP in 1955 which meant all five secretaries-general were SACP and thus explains why Sisulu relegated the ANC from a dominant role to one of five equals.

In 1959, the ANC lost its most militant support when most of the Africanists, with financial support from Kwame Nkrumah in Ghana and significant political support from the Transvaal-based Basotho, broke away to form the Pan Africanist Congress (PAC) under the leadership of Robert Sobukwe and Potlako Leballo.

Armed anti-apartheid activities

In 1961, Mandela became the leader of the ANC's armed wing, Umkhonto we Sizwe (translated *Spear of the Nation*, and also abbreviated *MK*), which he co-founded. He coordinated sabotage campaigns against military and government targets, making plans for a possible guerrilla war if the sabotage failed to end apartheid. He also raised funds for MK abroad and arranged for paramilitary training of the group.

Fellow ANC member Wolfie Kadesh explains the

bombing campaign led by Mandela: "When we knew that we [sic] going to start on 16 December 1961, to blast the symbolic places of apartheid, like pass offices, native magistrates courts, and things like that ... post offices and ... the government offices. But we were to do it in such a way that nobody would be hurt, nobody would get killed." Mandela said of Wolfie: "His knowledge of warfare and his first hand battle experience were extremely helpful to me."

Mandela described the move to armed struggle as a last resort. Years of increasing repression and violence from the state convinced him that many years of non-violent protest against apartheid had not and could not achieve any progress.

Later, mostly in the 1980s, MK waged a guerrilla war against the apartheid government in which many civilians became casualties. Mandela later admitted that the ANC, in its struggle against apartheid, also violated human rights, sharply criticising those in his own party who attempted to remove statements supporting this fact from the reports of the Truth and Reconciliation Commission (TRC).

Until July 2008, Mandela and ANC party members were barred from entering the United States – except to visit the United Nations headquarters in Nnew York – without a special waiver from the US secretary of state because of their designation as terrorists by the South African government during the apartheid era.

Arrest and Rivonia trial

On 5 August 1962, Mandela was arrested after living on the run for seventeen months and was imprisoned in the Johannesburg Fort. The arrest was made possible because the U.S. Central Intelligence Agency (CIA) tipped off the security police about Mandela's whereabouts and disguise.

Three days later, the charges of leading workers to strike in 1961 and leaving the country illegally were read to him during a court appearance. On 25 October 1962, Mandela was sentenced to five years in prison.

While he was in prison, police arrested prominent ANC leaders on 11 July 1963 at Liliesleaf Farm, Rivonia, north of Johannesburg. Mandela was brought in and he and his colleagues were charged – at the Rivonia Trial – by the chief prosecutor Dr. Percy Yutar with four charges of the capital crimes of sabotage (which Mandela admitted) and crimes which were equivalent to treason but easier for the government to prove. They were also charged with plotting a foreign invasion of South Africa, which Mandela denied.

The specifics of the charges to which Mandela admitted complicity involved conspiring with the African National Congress and South African Communist Party to use explosives to destroy water, electrical, and gas utilities in the Republic of South Africa.

Bram Fischer, Vernon Berrange, Joel Joffe, Arthur Chaskalson and George Bizos were part of the defence team that represented the main accused. Harry Schwarz represented Jimmy Kantor who was not a member of the ANC or MK. Kantor was acquitted long before the end of the trial. Harold Hanson was brought in at the end of the case to plead mitigation.

In his statement from the dock at the opening of the defence case in the trial on 20 April 1964 at Pretoria Supreme Court, Mandela laid out the reasoning in the ANC's choice to use violence as a tactic.

His statement described how the ANC had used peaceful means to resist apartheid for years until the Sharpeville Massacre. That event coupled with the referendum establishing the Republic of South Africa and the declaration of a state of emergency along with the banning of the ANC made it clear to Mandela and his compatriots that their only choice was to resist through

476

acts of sabotage and that doing otherwise would have been tantamount to unconditional surrender.

He went on to explain how they developed the Manifesto of Umkhonto we Sizwe on 16 December 1961 intent on exposing the failure of the National Party's policies after the economy would be threatened by foreigners' unwillingness to risk investing in the country. He closed his statement with these words:

:During my lifetime I have dedicated myself to the struggle of the African people. I have fought against white domination, and I have fought against black domination. I have cherished the ideal of a democratic and free society in which all persons live together in harmony and with equal opportunities. It is an ideal which I hope to live for and to achieve. But if needs be, it is an ideal for which I am prepared to die."

All except Rusty Bernstein were found guilty. But they escaped the gallows and were sentenced to life imprisonment on 12 June 1964.

Imprisonment

Mandela was imprisoned on Robben Island where he remained for the next eighteen of his twenty-seven years in prison. While in jail, his reputation grew and he became widely known as the most significant black leader in South Africa.

On the island, he and others performed hard labour in a lime quarry.

Prison conditions were very basic. Prisoners were segregated by race, with black prisoners receiving the fewest rations. Political prisoners were kept separate from ordinary criminals and received fewer privileges. Mandela describes how, as a D-group prisoner (the lowest classification), he was allowed one visitor and one letter every six months. Letters, when they came, were often delayed for long periods and made unreadable by the prison censors.

Whilst in prison, Mandela undertook study with the University of London by correspondence through its external programme and received the degree of Bachelor of Laws (LL.B.). He was subsequently nominated for the position of chancellor of the University of London in the 1981 election but lost to Princess Anne.

In his 1981 memoir, *Inside BOSS,* secret agent Gordon Winter describes his involvement in a plot to rescue Mandela from prison in 1969: this plot was infiltrated by Winter on behalf of South African intelligence who wanted Mandela to escape so they could shoot him during recapture. The plot was foiled by British Intelligence.

In March 1982, Mandela was transferred from Robben Island to Pollsmoor Prison along with other senior ANC leaders Walter Sisulu, Andrew Mlangeni, Ahmed Kathrada and Raymond Mhlaba. It was speculated that this was to remove the influence of these senior leaders on the new generation of young black activists imprisoned on Robben Island, the so-called "Mandela University." However, National Party cabinet member Kobie Coetsee said the move was to enable discreet contact between them and the South African government.

In February 1985, President P.W. Botha offered Mandela his freedom on condition that he 'unconditionally rejected violence as a political weapon.' Coetsee and other ministers had advised Botha against this, saying that Mandela would never commit his organisation to giving up the armed struggle in exchange for personal freedom. Mandela indeed spurned the offer, releasing a statement via his daughter Zindzi saying: "What freedom am I being offered while the organisation of the people remains banned? Only free men can negotiate. A prisoner cannot enter into contracts."

The first meeting between Mandela and the National Party government came in November 1985 when Kobie Coetsee met Mandela in Volks Hospital in Cape Town where Mandela was recovering from prostate surgery. Over the next four years, a series of tentative meetings took place, laying the groundwork for further contact and future negotiations. But little real progress was made.

In 1988, Mandela was moved to Victor Verster Prison and would remain there until his release. Various restrictions were lifted and people such as Harry Schwarz were able to visit him.

Schwarz, a friend of Mandela, had known him since their student days when they were in the same law class at Witwatersrand Univevrsity. He was also a defence barrister at the Rivonia Trial and became South Africa's ambassador to Washington during Mandela's presidency. He died on 5 February 2010. He was 86.

Throughout Mandela's imprisonment, local and international pressure mounted on the South African government to release him, under the resounding slogan *Free Nelson Mandela!* In 1989, South Africa reached a crossroads when Botha suffered a stroke and was replaced as president by Frederick Willem de Klerk who was simply known as F.W. de Klerk. De Klerk, the seventh and last president of apartheid-era South Africa, announced Mandela's release in February 1990.

Mandela was visited several times by delegates of the International Committee of the Red Cross while at Robben Island and later at Pollsmoor Prison. He had this to say about the visits: "To me personally, and those who shared the experience of being political prisoners, the Red Cross was a beacon of humanity within the dark inhumane world of political imprisonment."

Release

On 2 February 1990, President F.W. de Klerk reversed the ban on the ANC and other anti-apartheid organisations and announced that Mandela would shortly be released from prison. Mandela was released from Victor Verster Prison in Paarl on 11 February 1990. The event was broadcast live all over the world.

On the day of his release, Mandela made a speech to the nation in which he declared his commitment to peace and reconciliation with the country's white minority. But he made it clear that the ANC's armed struggle was not yet over when he said:

"Our resort to the armed struggle in 1960 with the formation of the military wing of the ANC (Umkhonto we Sizwe) was a purely defensive action against the violence of apartheid. The factors which necessitated the armed struggle still exist today. We have no option but to continue. We express the hope that a climate conducive to a negotiated settlement would be created soon so that there may no longer be the need for the armed struggle."

He also said his main focus was to bring peace to the black majority and give them the right to vote in both national and local elections.

Negotiations

Following his release from prison, Mandela returned to the leadership of the ANC and, between 1990 and 1994, led the party in the multi-party negotiations which led to the country's first multi-racial elections.

In 1991, the ANC held its first national conference in South Africa after its unbanning and elected Mandela as president of the organisation. His old friend and colleague,

Oliver Tambo, who had led the organisation in exile during Mandela's imprisonment, became national chairman.

Mandela's leadership through the negotiations, as well as his relationship with President F.W. de Klerk, was recognised when they were jointly awarded the Nobel Peace Prize in 1993.

However, the relationship was sometimes strained, particularly so in a sharp exchange in 1991 when he furiously referred to De Klerk as the head of "an illegitimate, discredited, minority regime."

The talks broke down following the Boipatong massacre in June 1992 when Mandela took the ANC out of the negotiations, accusing De Klerk's government of complicity in the killings.

However, talks resumed following the Bishop massacre in September 1992 when the spectre of violent confrontation made it clear that negotiations were the only way forward.

Following the assassination of ANC leader Chris Hani in April 1993, there were renewed fears that the country would erupt in violence. Mandela addressed the nation appealing for calm in a speech regarded as 'presidential' even though he was not yet president of the country at that time. He said:

"Tonight I am reaching out to every single South African, black and white, from the very depths of my being. A white man, full of prejudice and hate, came to our country and committed a deed so foul that our whole nation now teeters on the brink of disaster. A white woman, of Afrikaner origin, risked her life so that we may know, and bring to justice, this assassin.

The cold-blooded murder of Chris Hani has sent shock waves throughout the country and the world. ...Now is the time for all South Africans to stand together against those who, from any quarter, wish to destroy what Chris Hani gave his life for – the freedom of all of us."

While some riots did follow the assassination, the negotiators were galvanised into action and soon agreed that democratic elections should take place on 27 April 1994 just over a year after Hani's assassination.

Presidency of South Africa

South Africa's first multi-racial elections in which full enfranchisement was granted were held on 27 April 1994. The ANC won 62% of the votes and Mandela, as leader of the ANC, was inaugurated on 10 May 1994 as the country's first black president, with the National Party's de Klerk as his first deputy and Thabo Mbeki as the second in the Government of National Unity (GNU). As president from May 1994 until June 1999, Mandela presided over the transition from minority rule and apartheid, winning international respect for his advocacy of national and international reconciliation.

He encouraged black South Africans to get behind the previously hated Springboks (the South African national rugby team) as South Africa hosted the 1995 Rugby World Cup; this is the theme of the 2009 film *Invictus*.

After the Springboks won an epic final over New Zealand, Mandela presented the trophy to captain Francois Pienaar, an Afrikaner, wearing a Springbok shirt with Pienaar's own number 6 on the back. This was widely seen as a major step in the reconciliation of white and black South Africans.

After assuming the presidency, one of Mandela's trademarks was his use of Batik shirts, known as "Madiba shirts," even on formal occasions.

In South Africa's first post-apartheid military operation, Mandela ordered troops into Lesotho in September 1998 to protect the government of Prime Minister Pakalitha

Mosisili. This came after a disputed election prompted fierce opposition threatening the unstable government.

Commentators and critics including AIDS activists such as Edwin Cameron criticised Mandela for his government's ineffectiveness in handling the AIDS crisis. After his retirement, Mandela admitted that he may have failed his country by not paying more attention to the HIV/AIDS epidemic. And he continued to speak out on several occasions about the AIDS epidemic.

Lockerbie trial

President Mandela took a particular interest in helping to resolve the long-running dispute between Gaddafi's Libya, on the one hand, and the United States and Britain on the other, over bringing to trial the two Libyans who were indicted in November 1991 and accused of sabotaging Pan Am Flight 103 which crashed at the Scottish town of Lockerbie on 21 December 1988, with the loss of 270 lives.

As early as 1992, he informally approached President George H.W. Bush with a proposal to have the two indicted Libyans tried in a third country. Bush reacted favourably to the proposal, as did President Francois Mitterrand of France and King Juan Carlos of Spain.

In November 1994 – six months after his election as president – Mandela formally proposed that South Africa should be the venue for the Pan Am Flight 103 bombing trial.

However, British Prime Minister John Major flatly rejected the idea saying the British government did not have confidence in foreign courts.

A further three years elapsed until Mandela's offer was repeated to Major's successor, Tony Blair, when Mandela visited London in July 1997. Later the same year, at the Commonwealth Heads of Government Meeting

(CHOGM) in Edinburgh, Scotland, in October, Mandela warned:

"No one nation should be complainant, prosecutor and judge."

A compromise solution was then agreed upon for a trial to be held at Camp Zeist in the Netherlands, governed by Scots law, and President Mandela began negotiations with Colonel Gaddafi for the handover of the two accused (Megrahi and Fhimah) in April 1999.

At the end of their nine-month trial, the verdict was announced on 31 January 2001. Fhimah was found not guilty but Megrahi was convicted and sentenced to 27 years in a Scottish jail.

Megrahi's initial appeal was turned down in March 2002, and former president Mandela went to visit him in Barlinnie prison on 10 June 2002.

"Megrahi is all alone," Mandela told a packed press conference in the prison's visitors room. "He has nobody he can talk to. It is psychological persecution that a man must stay for the length of his long sentence all alone. It would be fair if he were transferred to a Muslim country – and there are Muslim countries which are trusted by the West. It will make it easier for his family to visit him if he is in a place like the kingdom of Morocco, Tunisia or Egypt."

Megrahi was subsequently moved to Greenock jail and out of solitary confinement. In August 2009, suffering from cancer and expected to have only 3 months left to live, he was released on compassionate grounds and allowed to return to Libya. The Nelson Mandela Foundation expressed its support for the decision to release Megrahi in a letter sent to the Scottish government on behalf of Mandela.

Marriage and family

Mandela was married three times, had six children, twenty grandchildren, and a growing number of great-grandchildren. He was grandfather to Chief Mandla Mandela.

First marriage

Mandela was first married to Evelyn Ntoko Mase who, like Mandela, also came from what later became the Transkei area of South Africa. But they met in Johannesburg.

The couple broke up in 1957 after 13 years of marriage. They divorced under the multiple strains of his constant absences, devotion to revolutionary agitation, and the fact that she was a Jehova's Wintess, a religion which requires political neutrality. As Mandela stated in his autobiography, *Long Walk to Freedom*:

"I could not give up my life in the struggle, and she could not live with my devotion to something other than herself and her family....I never lost my admiration for her, but in the end we could not make our marriage work."

Evelyn Mase died on 30 April 2004. She was 82. The couple had two sons, Madiba Thembekile (Thembi) (1946–1969) and Makgatho Mandela (1950–2005), and two daughters, both named Makaziwe Mandela (known as Maki; born 1947 and 1953).

Their first daughter died aged nine months. They named their second daughter in her honour.

All their children were educated at the United World College of Waterford Kamhlaba.

Thembi was killed in a car crash in 1969 at the age of 23 while Mandela was imprisoned on Robben Island.

Mandela was not allowed to attend his son's funeral. Makgatho died of AIDS in 2005. He was 54.

Second marriage

Mandela's second wife, Winnie Madikizela-Mandela, also came from the Transkei area although they, too, met in Johannesburg where she was the city's first black social worker.

They had two daughters, Zenani (Zeni), born 4 February 1958, and Zindziswa (Zindzi) Mandela-Hlongwane, born 1960.

Zindzi was only 18 months old when her father was sent to Robben island.

Later, Winnie would be deeply torn by family discord which mirrored the country's political strife. While her husband was serving life sentence on the Robben Island prison, her father became the agriculture minister in the Transkei.

The marriage ended in separation (April 1992) and divorce (March 1996), fuelled by political estrangement.

Mandela was still in prison when his daughter Zenani was married to Prince Thumbumuzi Dlamini in 1973, elder brother of King Mswati III of Swaziland. Although she had vivid memories of her father, from the age of four up until sixteen, South African authorities did not permit her to visit him.

The Dlamini couple live and run a business in Boston, Massachusetts, the United States. One of their sons, Prince Cedza Dlamini (born 1976), educated in the United States, has followed in his grandfather's footsteps as an international advocate for human rights and humanitarian aid.

Zindzi Mandela-Hlongwane made history worldwide when she read out Mandela's speech refusing his conditional pardon in 1985. She is a businesswoman in South Africa with three children, the eldest of whom is a son, Zondwa Gadaffi Mandela.

Third marriage

Mandela was remarried, on his 80th birthday in 1998, to Graça Machel *née* Simbine, widow of Samora Machel, the former Mozambican president and ANC ally who was killed in an air crash 12 years earlier.

The wedding followed months of international negotiations to set the unprecedented bride price to be remitted to Machel's clan. Negotiations were conducted on Mandela's behalf by his traditional sovereign, King Buyelekhaya Zwelibanzi Dalindyebo. The paramount chief's grandfather was the regent Jongintaba Dalindyebo who had arranged a marriage for Mandela which he eluded by fleeing to Johannesburg in 1940.

After retirement, Mandela still maintained a home in his home village of Qunu in the realm of his royal nephew (second cousin thrice-removed in Western reckoning) whom he helped to educate; he paid for his university education and remained his privy councillor.

Retirement

Mandela became the oldest elected president of South Africa when he took office at the age of 75 in 1994. He was also one of the oldest in Africa to become president. He decided not to stand for a second term and retired in 1999. He was succeeded by Thabo Mbeki.

After his retirement as president, Mandela went on to become an advocate for a variety of social and human rights organisations. He has expressed his support for the international Make Poverty History movement of which the ONE Campaign is a part.

The Nelson Mandela Invitational charity golf tournament hosted by Gary Player has raised more than twenty million rand for children's charities since 2000 when it started. It is a special annual event and has become South Africa's most successful charitable sports gathering and benefits both the Nelson Mandela Children's Fund and Gary Player Foundation equally for various children's causes around the world.

Mandela was a vocal supporter of SOS Children's Villages, the world's largest organisation dedicated to raising orphaned and abandoned children.

He also appeared in a televised advertisement for the Winter Olympics in 2006 and was quoted for the International Olympic Committee's *Celebrate Humanity* campaign:

"For seventeen days, they are roommates. For seventeen days, they are soulmates. And for twenty-two seconds, they are competitors. Seventeen days as equals. Twenty-two seconds as adversaries. What a wonderful world that would be. That's the hope I see in the Olympic Games."

Three organisations associated with Mandela were established during his lifetime: the Nelson Mandela Foundation, the Nelson Mandela Children's Fund, and the Mandela Rhodes Foundation.

Post-retirement health

In July 2001, Mandela was diagnosed and treated for prostate cancer. He was treated with a seven-week course of radiation.

In 2003, Mandela's death was incorrectly announced by CNN when his pre-written obituary (along with those of several other famous figures) was inadvertently published on CNN's web site due to a fault in password protection.

In 2007, a fringe right-wing group distributed hoax email and SMS messages claiming that the authorities had covered up Mandela's death and that white South Africans would be massacred after his funeral. Mandela was on holiday in Mozambique at the time.

In June 2004, at age 85, Mandela announced that he would be retiring from public life. His health had been declining and he wanted to enjoy more time with his family. He said that he did not intend to hide away totally from the public but wanted to be in a position "of calling you to ask whether I would be welcome, rather than being called upon to do things and participate in events. My appeal therefore is: Don't call me, I will call you."

Since 2003, he appeared in public less often and became less vocal on topical issues.

He was white-haired and walked slowly with the support of a stick. There were reports that he may be suffering from age-related dementia.

Mandela's 90th birthday was marked across the country on 18 July 2008, with the main celebrations held at his home town of Qunu. A concert in his honour was also held in Hyde Park, London. In a speech to mark his birthday, Mandela called for the rich people to help poor people across the world.

Despite maintaining a low-profile during the 2010 FIFA World Cup in South Africa, Mandela made a rare public appearance during the closing ceremony, where he received a "rapturous reception."

In January 2011, he was admitted to the private Milpark Hospital in Johannesburg for what were at the time described as "routine tests" by his foundation, leading to intense media speculation about the health condition of the increasingly frail Mandela. It later emerged that he had been suffering from a respiratory infection which had responded well to treatment. He was discharged after two and a half days in hospital in a stable condition and returned to his Houghton, Johannesburg home in an ambulance.

Elders

On 18 July 2007, Mandela, his wife Graça Machel, and Archbishop Desmond Tutu convened a group of world leaders in Johannesburg to contribute their wisdom and independent leadership to address the world's toughest problems. Mandela announced the formation of this new group, The Elders, in a speech he delivered on the occasion of his 89th birthday.

Archbishop Tutu served as the chair of The Elders. The founding members of this group also included Graça Machel, Kofi Annan, Ela Bhatt, Gro Harlem Brundtland, Jimmy Carter, Li Zhaoxing, Mary Robinson and Muhammad Yunus.

"This group can speak freely and boldly, working both publicly and behind the scenes on whatever actions need to be taken", Mandela commented. "Together we will work to support courage where there is fear, foster agreement where there is conflict, and inspire hope where there is despair."

AIDS engagement

Since his retirement, one of Mandela's primary commitments was to the fight against AIDS. He gave the closing address at the XIII International AIDS Conference in 2000 in Durban, South Africa. In 2003, he had already lent his support to the 46664 AIDS fundraising campaign, named after his prison number.

In July 2004, he flew to Bangkok, Thailand, to speak at the XV International AIDS Conference. His son, Makgatho Mandela, died of AIDS on 6 January 2005.

Mandela's AIDS activism was chronicled in Stephanie

Nolen's book, *28: Stories of AIDS in Africa.*

Criticism of US and UK foreign policy

Nelson Mandela had strongly opposed NATO's intervention in Kosovo in 1999 and called it an attempt by the world's powerful nations to police the entire world.

In 2002 and 2003, Mandela criticised the foreign policy of the administration of US President George W. Bush in a number of speeches. Criticising the lack of UN involvement in the decision to start the war in Iraq, he said: "It is a tragedy, what is happening, what Bush is doing. But Bush is now undermining the United Nations."

Mandela stated he would support action against Iraq only if it was ordered by the UN. He also insinuated that the United States may have been motivated by racism in not following the UN and its secretary-general Kofi Annan on the issue of the war. "Is it because the secretary-general of the United Nations is now a black man? They never did that when secretary-generals [*sic*] were white."

General Colin Powell, the first of two African-Americans appointed by Bush to the position of US secretary of state, presented to the United Nations General Assembly the case for the war in Iraq and overthrow of Saddam Hussein.

Mandela urged the people of the United States to join massive protests against Bush and called on world leaders, especially those with veto power in the UN Security Council, to oppose him. "What I am condemning is that one power, with a president who has no foresight, who cannot think properly, is now wanting to plunge the world into a holocaust."

He attacked the United States for its record on human rights and for dropping atomic bombs on Japan during World War II. "If there is a country that has committed unspeakable atrocities in the world, it is the United States of America. They don't care."

Nelson Mandela also harshly condemned British Prime Minister Tony Blair and referred to him as the "foreign minister of the United States."

Mandela, and Kofi Annan, also strongly criticised George W Bush's PEPFAR initiative at an international AIDS conference in 2004.

PEPFAR – the President's Emergency Plan For AIDS Relief (PEPFAR/Emergency Plan) – was a commitment of $15 billion over five years (2003–2008) from President George W. Bush to fight the global HIV/AIDS pandemic.

The programme initially aimed to provide anti-retroviral treatment (ART) to 2 million HIV-infected people in resource-limited settings, to prevent 7 million new infections, and to support care for 10 million people (the "2–7–10 goals") by 2010.

PEPFAR increased the number of Africans receiving ART from 50,000 at the start of the initiative in 2004 to at least 1.2 million in early 2008.

PEPFAR has been called the largest health initiative ever initiated by one country to address a disease. The budget presented by President Bush for the fiscal year 2008 included a request for $5.4 billion for PEPFAR.

The U.S. Leadership Against HIV/AIDS, Tuberculosis, and Malaria Act of 2003 (or the Global AIDS Act) established the State Department Office of the Global AIDS Coordinator to oversee all international AIDS funding and programming.

In July 2008, PEPFAR was renewed, revised and expanded as the "Tom Lantos and Henry J. Hyde United States Global Leadership Against HIV/AIDS, Tuberculosis, and Malaria Reauthorization Act of 2008." The expansion more than tripled the initiative's funds to $48 billion through 2013.

On June 23, 2009, Ambasssador Eric Goosby was sworn in as the United States Global AIDS Coordinator.

The massive funding increases made anti-retrovirals widely available, saving millions of lives.

Critics contended that spending a portion of funding on abstinence-until-marriage programmes was unjust. Others felt that foreign aid is generally inefficient. According to a 2009 study published in *Annals of Internal Medicine*, the programme had averted about 1.1 million deaths in Africa and reduced the death rate due to AIDS in the countries involved by 10%.

PEPFAR focused on resource-limited countries with high HIV/AIDS prevalence rates. The first 15 "focus countries" were Botswana, Ivory Coast (Côte d'Ivoire), Ethiopia, Guyana, Haiti, Kenya, Mozambique, Namibia, Nigeria, Rwanda, South Africa, Tanzania, Uganda, Vietnam, and Zambia. While most of the $15 billion for the programme would be spent on these focus countries, $4 billion was allocated for programmes elsewhere and for HIV/AIDS research. The other $1 billion was contributed to the Global Fund.

Ismail Ayob controversy

Ismail Ayob was a trusted friend and personal attorney of Mandela for over 30 years.

In May 2005, Ayob was asked by Mandela to stop selling prints signed by Mandela and to account for the proceeds of their sale. This bitter dispute led to an extensive application to the High Court of South Africa by Mandela that year.

Ayob denied any wrongdoing and claimed that he was the victim of a smear campaign orchestrated by Mandela's advisors, in particular, lawyer George Bizos.

In 2005 and 2006, Ayob, his wife, and son were subjected to a verbal attack by Mandela's advisors. The dispute was widely reported in the media, with Ayob being portrayed in a negative light, culminating in the action by Mandela to the High Court.

There were public meetings at which Mandela associates attacked Ayob and there were calls for Ayob and his family to be ostracised by society. The defence of Ismail and Zamila Ayob (his wife, and a fellow respondent) included documents signed by Mandela and witnessed by his secretaries, that, they claimed, refuted many of the allegations made by Nelson Mandela and his advisors.

The dispute again made headlines in February 2007 when, during a hearing in the Johannesburg High Court, Ayob promised to pay R700 000 to Mandela which Ayob had transferred into trusts for Mandela's children and apologised, although he later claimed that he was the victim of a "vendetta" by Mandela. Some media commentators expressed sympathy for Ayob's position, pointing out that Mandela's iconic status would make it difficult for Ayob to be treated fairly.

Allegations

Ayob, George Bizos and Wim Trengove were trustees of the Nelson Mandela Trust which was set up to hold millions of rands donated to Nelson Mandela by prominent business figures including the Oppenheimer family for the benefit of his children and grandchildren.

Ayob later resigned from the Trust. In 2006, the two remaining trustees of the Nelson Mandela Trust launched an application against Ayob for disbursing money from the trust without their consent. Ayob claimed that this money was paid to the South African Revenue Service, to Mandela's children and grandchildren, to Mandela himself, and to an accounting company for four years of accounting work.

Bizos and Trengrove refused to ratify the payments to the children and grandchildren of Nelson Mandela and the payments to the accounting firm. A court settlement was reached in which the money, totalling over R700,000, was paid by Ismail Ayob to the trust on the grounds that Ayob had not sought the express consent of the other two trustees before disbursing the money.

It was also alleged that Ayob made defamatory remarks about Mandela in his affidavit, for which the court order stated that Ayob should apologise.

It was pointed out that the remarks, which centred on Nelson Mandela holding foreign bank accounts and not paying tax on these, had not originated from Ayob's affidavit but from Nelson Mandela's and George Bizos's own affidavits.

Blood Diamond controversy

In an article in *The New Republic* in December 2006, Nelson Mandela was criticised for a number of positive comments he had made about the diamond industry. There were concerns that this would benefit suppliers of blood diamonds. In a letter to Edward Zwick, the director of the motion picture *Blood Diamond*, Mandela stated:

"...It would be deeply regrettable if the making of the film inadvertently obscured the truth, and, as a result, led the world to believe that an appropriate response might be to cease buying mined diamonds from Africa. ...

We hope that the desire to tell a gripping and important real life historical story will not result in the destabilisation of African diamond producing countries, and ultimately their peoples."

The *New Republic* article claims that this comment, as well as various pro-diamond-industry initiatives and statements during his life and during his time as president of South Africa, were influenced by both his friendship with Harry Oppenheimer, former chairman of De Beers, as well as an outlook for 'narrow national interests' of South Africa (which is a major diamond producer).

Zimbabwe and Robert Mugabe

Robert Mugabe, the president of Zimbabwe who led the country since independence in 1980, was widely criticised internationally for the 1980s' fighting in which about 3,000 people were killed in Matebeleland in the southern part of the country. He was also criticised for corruption, incompetent administration, repression and favouritism which ultimately led to the country's economic collapse.

In spite of their common background as freedom fighters and national liberators, and the fact that Mugabe demanded the release of Mandela when Mandela was in prison, the two leaders were seldom seen as close after they came into power.

Mandela criticised Mugabe in 2000, referring to African leaders who had liberated their countries but had then overstayed their welcome. But after his retirement, Mandela spoke out less often on Zimbabwe and other international and domestic issues, sometimes leading to criticism for not using his influence to greater effect to persuade Mugabe to moderate his policies.

His lawyer George Bizos revealed that Mandela had been advised on medical grounds to avoid engaging in stressful activity such as political controversy. Nonetheless, in 2007, Mandela attempted to persuade Mugabe to leave office "sooner than later," with "a modicum of dignity," before he was hounded out like Augusto Pinochet of Chile. Mugabe did not respond to that.

In June 2008, at the height of the crisis over the Zimbabwean presidential election, Mandela condemned the "tragic failure of leadership" in Zimbabwe.

Acclaim

According to an article in *Newsweek* magazine, "Mandela rightly occupies an untouched place in the South African imagination. He's the national liberator, the savior, its Washington and Lincoln rolled into one."

In November 2009, the United Nations General Assembly announced that Mandela's birthday, 18 July, was to be known as Mandela Day to mark his contribution to world freedom.

Orders and decorations

Mandela received many South African, foreign and international honours including the Nobel Peace Prize in 1993 (which he shared with South African President Frederik Willem de Klerk), the Order of Merit from, and creation as, a Baliff Grand Cross of the Order of St. John by Queen Elizabeth II, and the Presidential Medal of Freedom from US President George W. Bush.

In July 2004, the city of Johannesburg bestowed its highest honour on Mandela by granting him the freedom of the city at a ceremony in Orlando, Soweto.

As an example of his popular foreign acclaim, during his tour of Canada in 1998, 45,000 school children greeted him with adulation at a speaking engagement in the SkyDome in the city of Toronto.

In 2001, he was the first living person to be made an honorary Canadian citizen (the only previous recipient, Raoul Wallenberg, was awarded honorary citizenship posthumously). While in Canada, he was also made an honorary Companion of the Order of Canada, one of the few foreigners to receive the honour.

In 1990, he received the Bharat Ratna Award from the government of India and also received the last ever Lenin Peace Prize from the Soviet Union.

In 1992 he was awarded the Atatürk Peace Award by Turkey. He refused to accept the award citing human rights violations committed by Turkey at the time but later accepted it in 1999.

In 1992 he received the Nishan-e-Pakistan, the highest civil service award of Pakistan.

Musical tributes

Many artists have dedicated songs to Mandela. One of the most popular was from The Specials who recorded the song *Free Nelson Mandela* in 1983.

Stevie Wonder dedicated his 1985 Oscar for the song *I Just Called to Say I Love You* to Mandela, resulting in his music being banned by the South African Broadcasting Corporation during that period of apartheid.

Also in the same year, 1985, Youssou N'Dour's album *Nelson Mandela* was the Senegalese artist's first United States release.

In 1988, the Nelson Mandela 70th Birthday Tribute concert at London's Wembley Stadium was a focal point of the anti-apartheid movement, with many musicians voicing their support for Mandela.

Jerry Dammers, the author of *Nelson Mandela*, was one of the organisers of the concert.

Simple Minds recorded the song *Mandela Day* for the concert. Santana recorded the instrumental *Mandela*. Tracy Chapman performed *Freedom Now*, dedicated to Mandela and released on her album *Crossroads*. Salif Keita from Mali, who played at the concert, later visited South Africa and in 1995 recorded the song *Mandela* on his album *Folon*. And Whitney Houston performed and dedicated the gospel song *He I Believe*.

In South Africa, *Asimbonanga (Mandela)* ("We Have Not Seen Him") became one of Johnny Clegg's most famous songs, appearing on his *Third World Child* album in 1987. Hugh Masekela, in exile in the UK, sang *Bring Him Back Home* (Nelson Mandela) in 1987.

Brenda Fassie's 1989 song *Black President*, a tribute to Mandela, was hugely popular even though it was banned in South Africa.

Nigerian reggae musician Majek Fashek released the single, *Free Mandela*, in 1992, making him one of many Nigerian recording artists who had released songs related to the anti-apartheid movement and to Mandela himself.

In 1990, a Hong Kong rock band, Beyond, released a popular Cantonese song, *Days of Glory*. The anti-apartheid song featured lyrics referring to Mandela's heroic struggle for racial equality.

The group Ladysmith Black Mambazo accompanied Mandela to the Nobel Peace Prize ceremony in Oslo, Norway, in 1993, and performed for his inauguration in 1994.

In 2003, Mandela lent his weight to the 46664 campaign against AIDS, named after his prison number. Many prominent musicians performed in concerts as part of the campaign.

A summary of Mandela's life story is featured in the 2006 music video *If Everyone Cared* by Nickelback.

Raffi's song *Turn This World Around* is based on a speech given by Mandela where he explained the world needs to be "turned around, for the children."

A tribute concert for Mandela's 90th birthday took place in Hyde Park, London, on 27 June 2008.

Musician Ampie du Preez and cricketer AB de Villiers wrote a song called *Madibaland* in honour of Mandela. It was featured as the 4th and 14th tracks on their album, *Maak Jou Drome Waar*.

Published biographies

Mandela's autobiography, *Long Walk to Freedom*, was published in 1994. It was an extended version of *No Easy Walk to Freedom*, which was first published by Heinemann in 1965. Mandela had begun work on it secretly while in prison.

In that book, Mandela did not reveal anything about

the alleged complicity of F.W. de Klerk in the violence of the eighties and nineties or the role of his ex-wife Winnie Mandela in that bloodshed. However, he later co-operated with his friend, journalist Anthony Sampson, who discussed those issues in *Mandela: The Authorised Biography*.

Another detail that Mandela omitted was the allegedly fraudulent book, *Goodbye Bafana*. Its author, Robben Island warder James Gregory claimed to have been Mandela's confidant in prison and published details of the prisoner's family affairs.

Sampson maintained that Mandela had not known Gregory well, but that Gregory censored the letters sent to the future president and thus discovered the details of Mandela's personal life. Sampson also averred that other warders suspected Gregory of spying for the government and that Mandela considered suing Gregory.

Cinema and television

The film *Mandela and De Klerk* told the story of Mandela's release from prison. Mandela was played by Sidney Poitier.

Goodbye Bafana, a feature film which focuses on Mandela's life, had its world premiere at the Berlin film festival on 11 February 2007. The film starred Dennis Haysbert as Mandela and chronicled Mandela's relationship with prison guard James Gregory.

On the American television series *The Cosby Show*, Cliff and Claire Huxtable's grandchildren were named Nelson and Winnie in honour of Mandela and his then wife Winnie. In real life, Cliff was the renowned African American actor Bill Cosby. And his wife on the show, Claire Huxtable, was in real life Phylicia Rashād (born Phylicia Ayers-Allen), also an African American best known for her role in that show.

In the final scene of the 1992 movie *Malcolm X*,

Mandela – then recently released after 27-and-a-half years in prison – appeared as a schoolteacher in a Soweto classroom. He recited a portion of one of Malcolm X's most famous speeches including the following sentence:

"We declare our right on this earth to be a human being, to be respected as a human being, to be given the rights of a human being in this society, on this earth, in this day, which we intend to bring into existence...."

The famous final phrase of that sentence is "by any means necessary."

Mandela informed director Spike Lee that he could not utter the phrase on camera fearing that the apartheid government would use it against him if he did. Lee obliged, and the final seconds of the film feature black-and-white footage of Malcolm X himself delivering the phrase.

Mandela and Springboks captain, François Pienaar, were the focus of a 2008 book by John Carlin, *Playing the Enemy: Nelson Mandela and the Game that Made a Nation*, which spotlighted the role of the 1995 Rugby World Cup win in post-apartheid South Africa.

Carlin sold the film rights to Morgan Freeman. The film, entitled *Invictus*, was directed by Clint Eastwood and featured Freeman as Nelson Mandela and Matt Damon as Pienaar.

In the BBC television one-off drama *Mrs Mandela*, Nelson Mandela was portrayed by David Harewood and Sophie Okonedo played his former wife Winnie Mandela.

Statues and civic tributes

On 30 April 2001, Nelson Mandela Gardens in Millennium Square, Leeds, was officially opened and Nelson Mandela was awarded the freedom of the city and a commemorative 'golden owl' (the heraldic symbol of

Leeds). In a speech outside Leeds Civic Hall in front of 5000 people, Mandela famously and mistakenly thanked "the people of Liverpool for their generosity."

On 31 March 2004, Sandton Square in Johannesburg was renamed Nelson Mandela Square after a 6-metre statue of Nelson Mandela was installed on the square to honour the famous South African statesman.

On 29 August 2007, a statue of Nelson Mandela was unveiled at Parliament Square in London by Richard Attenborough, Ken Livingstone, Wendy Woods (widow of Donald Woods),and British Prime Minister Gordon Brown.

Donald Woods was a white South African journalist and anti-apartheid activist who died of cancer in London on 19 August 2001. He was forced to flee into exile on New Year's Eve, 1978, first in Lesotho and then in Britain because of his anti-apartheid activities.

The campaign to erect Mandela's statue was started in 2000 by Donald Woods. Mandela stated that the statue represented not just him but all those who had resisted oppression, especially those in South Africa. He added:

"The history of the struggle in South Africa is rich with the stories of heroes and heroines, some of them leaders, some of them followers. All of them deserve to be remembered."

An earlier London statue of Mandela is on the South Bank of the Thames. It was erected in 1985.

On 27 August 2008, a statue of Nelson Mandela was unveiled at Groot Drakenstein Correctional Centre between Paarl and Franshhoek on the R301 road near Cape Town. Formerly known as Victor Verster, that was where Mandela spent the last few years of his 27 years in prison in relative comfort as he and other ANC stalwarts negotiated with the apartheid government on the terms of his release and the nature of the new South Africa.

The statue stands on the very spot where Mandela took

his first steps as a free man.

In the United States, after the 1989 Loma Prieta earthquake demolished the Cypress Street Viaduct portion of the Nimitz Freeway in Oakland, California, the city renamed the street-level boulevard which replaced it Mandela Parkway in his honour.

In Leicester, England, there is a Nelson Mandela Park with the slogan "South Africa belongs to all those who live there, Black and White." It is opposite Leicester Tigers ground which is located between Aylestone Road and Welford Road on the edge of the city centre.

Mandela Day

Mandela Day, on his birthday, 18 July, is an annual international day adopted by the United Nations. Individuals, communities and organisations are asked to donate 67 minutes to doing something for others, commemorating the 67 years that Nelson Mandela gave to the struggle for social justice.

Other honours

Nelson Mandela has been honourded in many other ways around the world. Schools and streets have been named after him in many countries.

In the town of Arusha in northern Tanzania, there is The Nelson Mandela African Institute of Science and Technology (NM-AIST) which is one in a network of Pan-African Institutes of Science and Technology located across the continent.

And in Tanzania's largest city and former capital Dar es Salaam, there is a road named after Nelson Mandela. It's popularly known as Mandela Road.

Some indigenous people in the Andes Mountains in South America who were demanding their rights named their village after Nelson Mandela.

In 2004, zoologists Brent E. Hendrixson and Jason E. Bond named a South African species of trapdoor spider in the family Ctenizidae as *Stasimopus mandelai*, "honouring Nelson Mandela, the former president of South Africa and one of the great moral leaders of our time."

Thabo Mbeki

Thabo Mvuyelwa Mbeki (born 18 June 1942) was the second president of post-apartheid South Africa after Nelson Mandela. He served as president for almost two terms from 14 June 1999 to 24 September 2008.

He was also the elder brother of Moeletsi Mbeki, a political economist who served as deputy chairman of the South African Institute of International Affairs, an independent think tank based at the University of the Witwatersrand in Johannesburg.

They were the sons of prominent anti-apartheid activist Govan Mbeki who was imprisoned for life on Robben Island together with Nelson Mandela, Walter Sisulu and others. The Govan Mbeki Health Building at Glasgow Caledonian University in Scotland which was inaugurated in 2001 at a ceremony featuring his son Thabo was, at Nelson Mandela's suggestion, renamed in his honour.

On 20 September 2008, Thabo Mbeki announced his resignation as president of South Africa after being recalled by the National Executive Committee of the ruling African National Congress (ANC) following a conclusion by Judge Nicholson of Mbeki's improper interference in the National Prosecuting Authority (NPA) including the prosecution of (future president) Jacob Zuma for corruption. On 12 January 2009, the Supreme Court of Appeal unanimously overturned Judge Nicholson's judgment but Mbeki's resignation stood.

Thabo Mbeki was the executive face of government in

South Africa from 1994 when Nelson Mandela first became president. Mbeki served as deputy president.

During Mbeki's time in office as president, the economy grew at an average rate of 4.5% per annum. He created employment in the middle sectors of the economy and oversaw a fast-growing black middle class with the implementation of Black Economic Empowerment (BEE).

Black Economic Empowerment was a programme launched by the government to redress the inequalities created during apartheid by giving previously disadvantaged groups of South African citizens – black Africans, Coloureds, Indians and some Chinese – economic opportunities previously not available to them. It included measures such as employment equity, skills development, ownership, management, socioeconomic development and preferential procurement.

The economic growth the country enjoyed during Mbeki's tenure exacerbated the demand for trained professionals – strained by emigration due to violent crime – but failed to address unemployment amongst the unskilled bulk of the population.

Mbeki attracted the bulk of Africa's Foreign Direct Investment (FDI) and made South Africa the focal point of Africa's economic growth. He was one of the architects of NEPAD – New Partnership for Africa's Development, an economic development programme of the African Union (AU) – whose aim was to develop an integrated socio-economic development framework for Africa.

He also oversaw the successful building of economic bridges to BRIC (Brazil, Russia, India and China) nations with the eventual formation of the India-Brazil-South Africa (IBSA) Dialogue Forum to "further political consultation and co-ordination as well as strengthening sectoral co-operation, and economic relations."

Mbeki mediated in difficult and complex issues on the African continent especially those dealing with conflicts in Burundi, the Democratic Republic of Congo (DRC), and

Ivory Coast, as well as some important peace agreements.

He also oversaw the transition from the Organisation of African Unity (OAU) to the African Union (AU) during the last OAU summit held in Lusaka , Zambia, from 9 July to 11 July 2001. The OAU was officially disbanded on 9 July 2001 by Mbeki as its last chairman. It was replaced by the African Union (AU).

Mbeki's 'quiet diplomacy' in Zimbabwe, however, was blamed for delaying the removal of President Robert Mugabe's regime at a cost of many lives and intense economic pressure on Zimbabwe's neighbours.

Mbeki was also an outspoken leader of the Non-Aligned Movement in the United Nations and called for reform of the Security Council. He campaigned for an African seat on the UN Security Council and wanted South Africa to get the seat because of its status as the African "super power."

He was also strongly criticised around the world for his position on AIDS. He questioned the link between viruses and AIDS and believed that the correlation between poverty and the AIDS rate in Africa was a challenge to the viral theory of AIDS. His fate was not helped by Health Minister Manto Tshabalala-Msimang and the overhaul of the pharmaceutical industry in South Africa. According to a report, "Manto Tshabalala-Msimang Dies," in a South African newspaper, *Mail & Guardian*, 16 December, 2009, the day the health minister died:

"Never far from controversy, Tshabalala-Msimang's views on the treatment of HIV/Aids drew international condemnation, especially her advocacy of beetroot, garlic, and African potatoes as nutritional supplements to fight the disease.

This led to her being dubbed 'Dr Beetroot' by critics.

Her views on the use of antiretroviral (ARV) drugs in the treatment of Aids often provoked vehement opposition from both Aids activists and experts alike.

In 2004, she said: 'I have always said there are three options – and we must remember that ARVs are not a cure and they do have side-effects.'

She said at the time that garlic, lemon, olive oil and beetroot 'are absolutely critical -- first of all to have a beautiful face and beautiful skin -- but they also protect you from disease.'

Tshabalala-Msimang was widely seen as championing former President Thabo Mbeki's views on Aids, and was supportive of so-called Aids dissidents, who questioned the link between HIV and Aids, and pinned the cause of the disease on nutritional deficiencies.

Her statements on this matter often appeared contradictory.

On more than one occasion she vehemently denied suggestions she believed the herbs and vegetables she championed were a substitute for ARVs, and was often at pains to make it clear good nutrition was an important part of fighting the virus.

An incident at the International Aids Conference in Canada, when Aids activists vandalised a South African department of health exhibition displaying samples of Tshabalala-Msimang's vegetables, left the South African government red-faced.

Calls were made to Mbeki to remove his health minister, but these were not heeded by the president.

These calls reached a peak after Tshabalala-Msimang's hospitalisation.

During her absence, former deputy president, Phumzile Mlambo-Ngcuka, and former deputy health minister, Nozizwe Madlala-Routledge, began talks with civil society groups on the treatment of Aids.

Another controversial issue during Tshabalala-Msimang's tenure as health minister were her efforts to reduce the cost of medicines to the public.

These raised the ire of pharmacists around South

Africa, who took her to court, claiming she was threatening their continued existence.

She also created a media ethics debate over the reporting of information deemed to be between a doctor and a patient when she was in hospital.

The *Sunday Times* had reported that in spite of her condition she was consuming alcohol, and had sent hospital staff to purchase wine.

Tshabalala-Msimang was born on October 9, 1940, in Durban, KwaZulu-Natal.

She matriculated from Inanda Seminary, and went on to earn a BA degree from the University of Fort Hare in the Eastern Cape, graduating in 1961.

In 1962, shortly after the African National Congress was banned, Tshabalala-Msimang was one of a group of 27 young members of the organisation ordered to go into exile by the ANC leadership. She remained abroad for 28 years.

She went to the then Union of Soviet Socialist Republics (USSR) where she enrolled at the First Leningrad Medical Institute. She graduated from that institution with a medical degree in 1969.

Tshabalala-Msimang later moved to Tanzania, where in 1972 she completed a diploma in obstetrics and gynaecology at the University of Dar es Salaam.

One legacy of her time spent in these two countries was an ability to speak fluent Russian and Swahili.

Tshabalala-Msimang went on to work in health services in Tanzania and Botswana. She returned to South Africa in 1990, and at first worked in community health organisations in KwaZulu-Natal.

She was first elected to Parliament in 1994. She served as chairperson of the National Assembly's health committee, and on July 1 1996, was appointed deputy justice minister.

She was appointed minister of health in Mbeki's administration on June 17 1999.

She was married to ANC veteran Mendi Msimang. She had two daughters, Zuki and Pulane."

The delay in distributing antiretroviral drugs was attributed to the ban President Thabo Mbeki placed on their use in public state hospitals and was linked to the deaths of thousands of people in South Africa during his tenure as president.

Mbeki was also criticised for the way he responded to negative comments made about poor governance in South Africa and other parts of the continent in general. He accused his critics of being racist.

Early life

Thabo Mbeki was born and brought up in Idutywa, Transkei – what is now the Eastern Cape Province of South Africa. He was one of four children of Epainette and Govan Mbeki.

His father was a stalwart of the African National Congress (ANC) and the South African Communist Party. He was a member of the Xhosa ethnic group. His parents were both teachers and activists in a rural area of ANC strength, and Mbeki describes himself as being "born into the struggle." A portrait of Karl Marx sat on the family mantelpiece, and a portrait of Mahatma Gandhi was on the wall.

Mbeki attended primary school in Idutywa and Butterworth and acquired a high school education at Lovedale in Alice.

Lovedale was a mission station and educational institute in the Victoria East division of the Cape Province, in what is now the Eastern Cape Province, located about 2 miles north of Alice.

Alice, also home to the University of Fort Hare, was the administrative and magisterial capital of the old district of Victoria East.

In 1959, Thabo Mbeki was expelled from school as a result of student strikes and was forced to continue studies at home. In the same year, he sat for matriculation examinations at St. John's High School, Umtata. In the ensuing years, he completed British Advanced levels – also known as "A" levels – examinations and undertook studies for an economics degree as an external student with the University of London.

During that time, the African National Congress (ANC) was banned and Mbeki was involved in underground activities in the Pretoria-Witwatersrand area. He was also involved in mobilising students in support of the ANC's call for a stay-at-home to be held in protest against South Africa becoming a republic.

In December 1961, Mbeki was elected secretary of the African Students Association in his home country. He left South Africa in 1962 on instructions from the ANC leadership.

His father Govan Mbeki had moved to the rural Eastern Cape as a political activist after earning two university degrees and urged his family to make the ANC their family. Of all Govan Mbeki's children, it was Thabo Mbeki who clearly followed that instruction. He joined the ANC when he was 14 years old and devoted his life to the party thereafter.

Marriage and family

Mbeki married his wife Zanele (née Dlamini) at Farnham Castle, in the United Kingdom, in 1974.

Farnham Castle is a castle in Farnham, Surrey, England. It overlooks the historic town of Farnham on the western border of Surrey.

Exile and return

After leaving the Eastern Cape, Thabo Mbeki lived in Johannesburg, working with Walter Sisulu. After the arrest and imprisonment of Sisulu, Mandela and his father -- and facing a similar fate -- he left South Africa as one of a number of young ANC militants (Umkhonto we Sizwe cadres) sent abroad to continue their education and their anti-apartheid activities. He ultimately spent 28 years in exile, returning to his homeland only after the release of Nelson Mandela.

Mbeki spent the early years of his exile in the United Kingdom. In 1962, aged 19, he arrived at the University of Sussex where he earned a BA degree in economics and later a M. A. degree in African studies. While at Sussex he saw himself as a representative of the ANC and helped motivate the university population against apartheid.

He later worked in the ANC office in London on Penton Street.

He received military training in the Soviet Union and lived at different times in Botswana, Swaziland and Nigeria. But his primary base was in Lusaka, Zambia.

The ANC also had an office in Dar es Salaam, Tanzania, on Nkrumah Street. Other African liberation liberation movements were also based in Dar es Salaam which was the headquarters of all the African liberation movements under the auspices of the OAU Liberation Committee.

In 1973, Mbeki was sent by the ANC to Botswana where he engaged the Botswana government in discussions to open an ANC office there. He left Botswana in 1974.

In 1975, he became a member of the National Executive Committee of the ANC. In December 1976, he was sent to Nigeria as a representative of the ANC.

While in exile, his brother Jama Mbeki, a supporter of

the rival Pan Africanist Congress (PAC) led by Robert Mangaliso Sobukwe, was killed by the agents of the Lesotho government in 1982 while attempting to assist the Lesotho Liberation Army (LLA).

The Lesotho Liberation Army was a military wing and guerrilla force of the Basotho Congress Party (BCP) – formerly known as the Basutoland Congress Party – which waged an unsuccessful campaign against the Basotho National Party (BNP) after the BCP was cheated by the BNP in the first post-independence general elections in January 1970. The BCP won the election but was denied power.

Thabo Mbeki's son Kwanda – the product of a liaison in Mbeki's teenage years – was killed while trying to leave South Africa to join his father. He went missing in 1981when he was about 20 years old and was assumed to have been killed by the agents of the apartheid regime. Thabo Mbeki's brother and cousin also disappeared in the 1980s.

But they were never forgotten. And according to a report by Raymond Whitaker, "Fresh Inquiry Ordered into Death of Mbeki's son," in *The Independent*, London, 13 September 2006:

"Memories of the 'dirty war' waged by South Africa's apartheid regime against its opponents have been revived by a fresh attempt to discover what happened to President Thabo Mbeki's son.

Kwanda Mbeki disappeared in South Africa in 1981 while attempting to join his father and other anti-apartheid activists in exile. He is assumed to have been killed by agents of the white government, but his body, like those of hundreds of others who disappeared while resisting minority rule, was never found.

Fresh leads have been developed in the case and will be followed 'very soon,' according to Makhosini Nkosi, spokesman for the National Prosecuting Authority.

512

South Africa's first democratically-elected president, Nelson Mandela, set up the Truth and Reconciliation Commission (TRC) under Archbishop Desmond Tutu to investigate apartheid-era crimes on both sides of the struggle, but it wound up its work in 2003 with many cases unresolved. Among them were the disappearances not only of Kwanda Mbeki, born when his father was a teenager, but the president's brother and cousin.

Mr Mbeki has rarely spoken of his own family's losses, and referred to them only in general terms when he gave evidence to the TRC. Last week, however, the president wrote in his weekly ANC newsletter: 'I too, and especially my mother, regret that the TRC process did not succeed to unearth the truth about what happened to our own loved ones who disappeared without trace - my brother Jama Mbeki, my son Kwanda Mbeki and my cousin, Phindile Mfeti.'

Mr Mbeki did not ask the TRC to investigate the disappearances, but the case of Kwanda Mbeki was referred to the TRC by his mother, Olive Mpahla. She said he disappeared when on his way to visit his uncle, Mr Mfeti, although accounts exist of him having been seen in exile. But the TRC did not have the time or resources to investigate a large proportion of cases, including those of the president's family.

According to South Africa's *Sunday Independent*, the names of Mr Mbeki's son and cousin are on a list of 477 political disappearances that the TRC forwarded to the National Prosecuting Authority. It has a missing persons' task force which is pursuing the cases, along with about 1,000 others.

Most of the disappearances date from the late 1970s onwards, when the apartheid government resorted to undercover methods to quell the black militancy which erupted in Soweto and other townships in 1976. It staged raids into neighbouring countries to attack ANC training camps and assassinate key opponents in exile. Although the example of the TRC has been copied in many other countries emerging from conflict, there is lingering frustration and bitterness in South Africa at the many agents of apartheid who escaped unpunished or refused to admit their guilt.

The main theme of Mr Mbeki's newsletter, however, was a remarkable ceremony of repentance which took place recently at the Union Buildings in Pretoria, when Adriaan Vlok, a hardline law and order minister in the old regime, publicly washed the feet of the Rev Frank Chikane, the director general in the presidency. 'What his [Mr Vlok's] words and actions said to me was that our society, which includes those who matured under circumstances very different from today's, is gradually growing out of its traumatic past,' Mr Mbeki wrote."

When Thabo Mbeki finally was able to return home, to South Africa, and was reunited with his own father, the elder Mbeki told a reporter: "You must remember that Thabo Mbeki is no longer my son. He is my comrade!" A news article pointed out that this was an expression of pride, explaining, "For Govan Mbeki, a son was a mere biological appendage; to be called a comrade, on the other hand, was the highest honour."

Thabo Mbeki devoted his life to the ANC and during his years in exile was given increased responsibility. Following the 1976 Soweto riots – a student uprising in the township outside Johannesburg – he initiated a regular radio broadcast from Lusaka, Zambia, tying ANC followers inside the country to their exiled leaders. Encouraging activists to keep up the pressure on the apartheid regime was a key component in the ANC's campaign to liberate their country.

In the late 1970s, Mbeki made a number of trips to the United States in search of support among U.S. corporations. Literate and funny, he made a wide circle of friends in New York City.

He was appointed head of the ANC's information department in 1984 and then became head of the international department in 1989, reporting directly to Oliver Tambo, then president of the ANC. Tambo was Mbeki's long-time mentor.

In 1985, Mbeki was a member of a delegation which began meeting secretly with representatives of the South African business community. And in 1989, he led the ANC delegation which conducted secret talks with the South African government. The talks led to the unbanning of the ANC and the release of political prisoners. He also participated in many other important negotiations between the ANC and the apartheid regime which eventually led to the democratisation of South Africa.

He became one of the two deputy presidents of South Africa in May 1994 on the attainment of universal suffrage and sole deputy-president in June 1996.

The other deputy president was F.W. de Klerk, the last president of the apartheid regime who freed Mandela. He became deputy president in the government of national unity under Nelson Mandela after the first free elections in 1994 and kept the post until 1996 when Thabo Mbeki became the only deputy president under Mandela.

Thabo Mbeki succeeded nelson Mandela as ANC president in December 1997 and as president of South Africa in June 1999 when he was inaugurated on the 16th. He was reelected for a second term in April 2004.

Role in African politics

Thabo Mbeki was a powerful figure in African politics, positioning South Africa as a regional power broker and also promoting the idea that African political conflicts can and must be solved by the Africans themselves.

He played a major role in formulating the programme of NEPAD – n New Partnership for Africa's Development

– and in establishing the African Union (AU), a successor to the OAU. He also played influential roles in brokering peace deals in Rwanda, Burundi, Ivory Coast and the Democratic Republic of Congo (DRC).

Mbeki also tried to popularise the concept of an African Renaissance. He saw African dependence on aid and foreign intervention as a major barrier to the continent being taken seriously in the international arena. He believed that programmes and institutions such as NEPAD and the African Union (AU) were a part of the process in which Africa would be able to solve its own problems without relying on external help.

Economic policies

Mbeki, as an ANC insider and while president, was a major force behind the continued neoliberal structure of the South African economy.

He drew criticism from the left for his perceived abandonment of state-interventionist social democratic economic policies – such as nationalisation, land reform, and democratic capital controls – prescribed by the Freedom Charter, the ANC's seminal document.

Political style

Mbeki was often characterised as remote and academic, although in his second campaign for the presidency in 2004, many observers described him as finally relaxing into a more traditional campaign mode, sometimes dancing at events and even kissing babies. Yet, the fact that this was remarkable confirms the broader observation that Mbeki values the exercise of centralised policy over demonstrations of grassroots populism.

Mbeki used his weekly column in the ANC newsletter, *ANC Today*, to stimulate discussions on a variety of topics.

516

He sometimes used his column to deliver pointed invectives against political opponents, and at other times used it as a kind of professor of political theory, educating ANC cadres on the intellectual justifications for ANC policy.

Although the columns were remarkable for their dense prose, they often were used to influence news.

Mbeki did not generally make a point of befriending or courting reporters. But his columns and news events often produced good results for his administration by ensuring that his message was a primary driving force of news coverage. Indeed, in initiating his columns, Mbeki stated his view that the bulk of South African media sources did not speak for or to the South African majority, and stated his intention to use *ANC Today* to speak directly to his constituents rather than through the media.

Mbeki and the Internet

Mbeki was comfortable with the Internet and was willing to quote from it. For instance, in a column discussing Hurricane Katrina, he cited Wikipedia, quoted at length a discussion of Katrina's lessons on American inequality from the Native American publication *Indian Country Today*, and then included excerpts from David Brooks's column in *The New York Times* in a discussion of why the events of Katrina illustrated the necessity for global development and redistribution of wealth.

His penchant for quoting diverse and sometimes obscure sources, both from the Internet and from a wide variety of books, made his column an interesting parallel to political blogs.

Also, his views on AIDS were supported by Internet searching which led him to so-called "AIDS denialist" websites. In this particular case, his use of the Internet was roundly criticised and was even ridiculed by opponents.

Global apartheid

Mbeki used his position on the world stage to call for an end to global apartheid, a term he used to describe the disparity between a small minority of rich nations and a large number of impoverished countries in the world. He argued that a "global human society based on poverty for many and prosperity for a few, characterised by islands of wealth, surrounded by a sea of poverty, is unsustainable."

Controversies

Zimbabwe

South Africa's proximity, strong trade links, and similar struggle credentials placed South Africa in a unique position to influence politics in Zimbabwe during President Mugabe's rule.

Zimbabwe's hyperinflation since 2000 was a matter of increasing concern to Britain (as the former colonial power) and other donors to that country.

High-ranking diplomatic visits to South Africa repeatedly attempted to persuade Mbeki to take a harder line with Robert Mugabe over violent state-sponsored attacks on political opponents and opposition movements, expropriation of white-owned farms by ZANU-PF allied "war veterans," suppression of the media, and infringements on the independence of the judiciary.

But, rather than publicly criticise Mugabe and his government, Mbeki chose 'quiet diplomacy' over 'megaphone diplomacy' - his term for the West's increasingly forthright condemnation of Mugabe's rule. Mbeki was even quoted claiming "there is no crisis" in Zimbabwe despite increased evidence of political violence and murders, hyperinflation, and the influx of political refugees into South Africa from Zimbabwe. As he bluntly stated:

"The point really about all this from our perspective has been that the critical role we should play is to assist the Zimbabweans to find each other, really to agree among themselves about the political, economic, social, and other solutions that their country needs.

We could have stepped aside from that task and then shouted, and that would be the end of our contribution....

They would shout back at us and that would be the end of the story.

I'm actually the only head of government that I know anywhere in the world who has actually gone to Zimbabwe and spoken publicly very critically of the things that they are doing."

2002 Presidential elections

Mugabe faced a critical presidential election in 2002. The run-up was shadowed by a difficult decision to suspend Zimbabwe from the Commonwealth. The full meeting of the Commonwealth had failed in a consensus to decide on the issue and they tasked the previous, present (at the time), and future leaders of Commonwealth (respectively President Olusegun Obasanjo of Nigeria, John Howard of Australia, and Mbeki of South Africa) to reach a consensus among themselves over the issue.

On 20 March 2002 (10 days after the elections, which Mugabe won), Howard announced that they had agreed to suspend Zimbabwe for a year.

2005 Parliamentary Elections

In the face of laws restricting public assembly and freedom of the media, and restricting campaigning by the Movement for Democratic Change (MDC) for the 2005

Zimbabwe parliamentary elections, President Mbeki was quoted as saying:

"I have no reason to think that anything will happen ... that anybody in Zimbabwe will act in a way that will militate against the elections being free and fair. [...] As far as I know, things like an independent electoral commission, access to the public media, the absence of violence and intimidation ... those matters have been addressed."

Minerals and Energy Minister Phumzile Mlambo-Ngcuka led the largest foreign observer mission, the SADC Observer Mission, to oversee the Zimbabwe elections. Contrary to other international missions and parts of the South African Parliamentary Mission, the SADC mission congratulated "the people of Zimbabwe for holding a peaceful, credible and well-mannered election which reflects the will of the people."

The Democratic Alliance delegation (which was a part of the South African A Parliamentary Observer Mission) clashed with Phumzile Mlambo-Ngcuka and eventually submitted a separate report contradicting her findings.

The elections were widely denounced and many people and organisations accused ZANU-PF of massive and often violent intimidation, using food to buy votes, and large discrepancies in the tallying of votes.

Dialogue between ZANU-PF and MDC

Mbeki attempted to restore dialogue between President Mugabe and the opposition Movement for Democratic Change (MDC) in the face of denials from both parties.

A fact-finding mission in 2004 by the Congress of South African Trade Unions (COSATU) to Zimbabwe led to their widely-publicised deportation back to South Africa which reopened the debate, even within the ANC, as to whether Mbeki's policy of 'quiet diplomacy' was constructive.

On 5 February 2006, Mbeki said in a televised interview with the South African Broadcasting Corporation (SABC) that Zimbabwe had missed a chance to resolve its political crisis in 2004 when secret talks to agree on a new constitution ended in failure. He claimed that he saw a copy of a new constitution signed by all the parties involved.

The job of promoting dialogue between the ruling party and the opposition was likely made more difficult by divisions within the MDC, splits to which President Mbeki alluded when he stated that the MDC were "sorting themselves out."

The MDC unanimously rejected that assertion. MDC-Mutambara faction's secretary general Welshman Ncube said: "We never gave Mbeki a draft constitution - unless it was ZANU-PF which did that. Mbeki has to tell the world what he was really talking about."

In May 2007, it was reported that Mbeki had been partisan and taken sides with ZANU-PF in his role as mediator. He had given pre-conditions to the opposition Movement for Democratic Change before the dialogue could resume while giving no conditions to the ZANU-PF government. He required the MDC to accept and recognise Robert Mugabe as the president of Zimbabwe, and for the the MDC to accept the 2002 presidential election results despite wide-spread belief of being unfree, unfair, and fraudulent.

Business response

On 10 January 2006, businessman Warren Clewlow, on the board of four of the top-10 listed companies in South Africa including Old Mutual, Sasol, Nedbank and Barloworld, said that the government should stop its

521

unsuccessful behind-the-scenes attempts to resolve the Zimbabwean crisis and start vociferously condemning what was happening in that country.

Clewlow's sentiments reflected the South African private sector's increasing impatience with Mbeki's "quiet diplomacy" and were echoed by Business Unity South Africa (BUSA), the umbrella body for business organisations in South Africa.

As the company's chairman, he said in Barloworld's latest annual report that South Africa's efforts to date were fruitless and that the only means for a solution was for South Africa "to lead from the front. Our role and responsibility is not just to promote discussion... Our aim must be to achieve meaningful and sustainable change."

Position on Mugabe

Mbeki was frequently criticised for having failed to exert pressure on Mugabe to relinquish power but chaired meetings in which the Zimbabwean leader's departure from power was being negotiated.

He rejected calls in May 2007 for tough action against Zimbabwe ahead of a visit by the then-UK Prime Minister Tony Blair. He said on 29 July 2007 that Zimbabwe's elections in March 2008 must be 'free and fair.'

An article critical of Mbeki's handling of Mugabe appeared in *Forbes* and claimed a peaceful transfer of power in Zimbabwe "will not be because of [Mbeki], but in spite of him."

Ebrahim Fakir, a researcher at the Johannesburg-based Centre for Policy Studies, and Susan Booysen, political analyst at the University of the Witwatersrand, said Mbeki had botched his legacy over his cautious approach to Mugabe.

The media also was very critical. *The Washington Post* published a commentary describing Mbeki as a bankrupt democrat and accused him of complicity in "stealing" the

Zimbabwean election. *The Economist* called Mbeki's actions "unconscionable."

SADC facilitator of Zimbabwe
power-sharing agreement

At the end of the fourth day of negotiations, South African president and mediator to Zimbabwe, Thabo Mbeki, announced in Harare that President Robert Mugabe of ZANU-PF, Professor Arhtur Mutambara of MDC-M, and Morgan Tsvangirai of MDC-T, finally signed the power-sharing agreement – "memorandum of understanding." Mbeki stated:

"An agreement has been reached on all items on the agenda ... all of them [Mugabe, Tsvangirai, Mutambara] endorsed the document tonight, and signed it. The formal signing will be done on Monday 10 am. The document will be released then.

The ceremony will be attended by the SADC and other African regional and continental leaders. The leaders will spend the next few days constituting (sic) the inclusive government to be announced on Monday.

The leaders will work very hard to mobilise support for the people to recover. We hope the world will assist so that this political agreement succeeds."

In the signed historic power deal, President Mugabe agreed on 11 September 2008 to surrender day-to-day control of the government. The agreement was also expected to result in a *de facto* amnesty for the military and ZANU-PF party leaders.

Opposition sources said "Tsvangirai will become prime minister at the head of a council of ministers, the principal organ of government, drawn from his party and the president's ZANU-PF party; and Mugabe will remain president and continue to chair a cabinet that will be a largely consultative body, and the real power will lie with Tsvangirai."

South Africa's *Business Day* reported, however, that Mugabe was refusing to sign a deal which would curtail his presidential powers.

The New York Times stated that Nelson Chamisa, a spokesman for MDC-T, announced: "This is an inclusive government. The executive power will be shared by the president, the prime minister and the cabinet. Mugabe, Tsvangirai and Arthur Mutambara have still not decided how to divide the ministries."

But Jendayi E. Frazer, the American assistant secretary of state for African affairs, said: "We don't know what's on the table, and it's hard to rally for an agreement when no one knows the details or even the broad outlines."

On 15 September 2008, the leaders of the 14-member Southern African Development Community (SADC) witnessed the signing of the power-sharing agreement, brokered by Mbeki. With symbolic handshakes and warm smiles at the Rainbow Towers hotel in Harare, Mugabe and Tsvangirai signed the deal to end violent political crisis. According to the agreement, Mugabe was to remain president, Morgan Tsvangirai was to become prime minister, the MDC would control the police, Mugabe's ZANU-PF would command the army, and Arthur Mutambara would become deputy prime minister.

AIDS

Mbeki's views on the causes of AIDS, and in particular the link between HIV and AIDS, and the treatment of AIDS were also much criticised.

In 1995, the International Conference for People Living with HIV and AIDS was held in South Africa, the first time that the annual conference had been held in Africa. Mbeki was then oeputy president and in his official capacity acknowledged the seriousness of the epidemic.

The South African ministry of mealth announced that about 850,000 people – 2.1% of the total population – were believed to be HIV-positive. In 2000 the department of health outlined a five-year plan to combat AIDS, HIV and sexually transmitted infections. A National AIDS Council was established to oversee the implemenation of the plan.

However, after becoming president, Mbeki changed his position and represented the views of a small group of dissident scientists who claimed that AIDS was not caused by HIV. On 9 July 2000, at the International AIDS Conference in Durban, South Africa, President Mbeki made a speech which drew much criticism. In his speech, he avoided making references to HIV and instead focused mainly on poverty as a powerful co-factor in AIDS diagnosis.

His government was repeatedly accused of failing to respond adequately to the AIDS epidemic. It also refused to authorise and implement an overall national treatment programme for AIDS which included anti-retroviral medicines and in particular an anti-retroviral programme to prevent HIV transmission from pregnant mothers to babies while in the womb.

Mbeki's government did, however, introduce a law allowing cheaper locally-produced generic medicines and in April 2001 succeeded in defending a legal action brought by transnational pharmaceutical companies to set aside the law. AIDS activists, particularly the Treatment Action Campaign and its allies, thought that the law was intended to support a cheap antiretroviral drugs programme and applauded Mbeki's government.

However, the Treatment Action Campaign and its allies were eventually forced to resort to the South African Courts which in 2002 ordered the government to make the drug nevirapine available to pregnant women to help prevent mother-to-child transmission of HIV. Notwithstanding and despite international drug companies offering free or cheap antiretroviral drugs, until 2003, South Africans with HIV who used the public sector health system could only get treatment for opportunistic infections they suffered because of their weakened immune systems, but could not get antiretrovirals designed to specifically target HIV.

In November 2003, the government finally approved a plan to make antiretroviral treatment publicly available. And that was only after the cabinet had overruled the president.

In November 2008, *The New York Times* reported that due to Thabo Mbeki's rejection of scientific consensus on AIDS and his embrace of AIDS denialism, an estimated 365,000 people had perished in South Africa.

2006 Zuma rape trial

In 2006, Jacob Zuma (who became president of South Africa in 2009) went on trial for allegedly raping an HIV-positive woman. He argued that she had consented to sex and he was eventually found not guilty, but attracted controversy when he stated that he had showered after sex in the belief that this would reduce his chances of becoming infected with HIV.

Criticism of the government's response to AIDS heightened, with UN special envoy Stephen Lewis attacking the government as "obtuse and negligent" at the International AIDS Conference in Toronto. At the end of the year, the South African government announced a draft framework to tackle AIDS and pledged to improve anti-retroviral drug access.

Mbeki and the Cabinet

The South African constitution allows the cabinet to override the president. The secret ballot appears to have gone against the president when cabinet policy declared that HIV is the cause of AIDS. Again in August 2003, the cabinet promised to formulate a national treatment plan that would include ARVs.

During that time, the health ministry was still headed by Dr. Manto Tshabalala-Msimang who had served as health minister since June 1999 and was promoting nutritional approaches (the infamous "African potatoes and garlic") to AIDS while highlighting the toxicities of antiretroviral drugs. That led critics to question whether the same leadership which opposed ARV treatment would effectively carry out the treatment plan.

Implementation was slow, requiring a court judgement eventually to force government to distribute ARV's. Delivery was further improved when Thabo Mbeki was ousted, Dr. Manto Tshabalala-Msimang was re-assigned and became minister of the presidency, and Barbara Hogan was appointed minister of health.

AIDS denialist connections

Mbeki's more inclusive stance led some to connect him to AIDS denialism. While serving as deputy president, AIDS was in his portfolio, and he customarily wore a red ribbon while specifically promoting AIDS prevention measures. He did preside over a controversial and brief embrace of a South African experimental drug called Virodene which later proved to be ineffective; the episode appeared to have increased his skepticism about the scientific consensus which quickly condemned the drug.

After he became president, he appeared to have articulated more clearly his understanding that poverty is a significant co-factor in the prevalence of AIDS and other health problems. He urged political attention be directed to addressing poverty generally rather than only against

527

AIDS specifically.

Some speculate that the suspicion engendered by a life in exile and by the colonial domination and control of Africa led Mbeki to react against a portrayal of AIDS as another Western characterisation of Africans as promiscuous and Africa as a continent of disease and hopelessness. For example, speaking to a group of university students in 2001, he struck out against what he viewed as the racism underlying how many in the West characterised AIDS in Africa:

"Convinced that we are but natural-born, promiscuous carriers of germs, unique in the world, they proclaim that our continent is doomed to an inevitable mortal end because of our unconquerable devotion to the sin of lust."

Additionally, his views dovetailed with some broader themes in African politics. Many Africans find it suspicious that black Africans bear the largest share of the AIDS burden, and that the drugs to treat it are expensive and sold mainly by Western pharmaceutical companies.

The history of malicious and manipulative health policies of the colonial and apartheid governments in Africa, including biological warfare programmes set up by the apartheid state, also help to fuel views that the scientific discourse of AIDS might be a tool for European and American political, cultural or economic agendas.

ANC rules and Mbeki's commitment to the idea of party discipline meant that he could not publicly criticise the government policy that HIV causes AIDS and that antiretrovirals should be provided.

Some critics of Mbeki continued to assert that, notwithstanding, he continued to influence AIDS policy through his personal views behind the scenes, a charge which his office regularly denied. However, in a 2007 published biography *Thabo Mbeki: The Dream Deferred*, author Mark Gevisser described how the president, knowing that he was writing the biography, contacted him earlier in 2007 to ask whether the author had seen a 100-page paper secretly authored by Mr. Mbeki and distributed anonymously among the ANC leadership six years ago.

The paper compared orthodox AIDS scientists to latter-day Nazi concentration camp doctors and portrayed black people who accepted orthodox AIDS science as "self-repressed" victims of a slave mentality. It described the "HIV/AIDS thesis" as entrenched in "centuries-old white racist beliefs and concepts about Africans."

In the biography of Mbeki, Mr Gevisser described the president's view of the disease as apparently shaped by an obsession with race, the legacy of colonialism and "sexual shame."

From the time the biography was released, President Mbeki's defenders tried hard to clarify his position as being an AIDS "dissident" as opposed to being an AIDS "denier"; that is, he accepted that HIV caused AIDS but was a dissident in that he was at odds with prevailing AIDS-focused public health policies, stating that it was only one of many immune deficiency diseases, many of which were associated with poverty, and that political attention and resources should be directed to fight poverty and immune deficiency diseases in general rather than AIDS specifically.

Power crisis

In January 2008, the South African government announced that it would introduce electricity rationing. On 25 January 2008, the country's deepening power crisis was such that South Africa's (and the world's) largest gold and platinum mining companies were forced to shut down operations. Eskom (the national power supplier) and the government both apologized for the blackouts and in his next-to-last state of the nation speech, Mbeki devoted nearly three pages to the power crisis, repeating the apologies of Eskom and the government.

President Mbeki blamed the power shortages on increased demand caused by years of economic growth and the provision of electricity to black townships which were not connected in the apartheid era. But Mbeki also admitted the government had failed to heed warnings from Eskom (the earliest 10 years previously) that without new power stations, Eskom might not be able to meet demand by 2007.

Each year over the preceding 10 years, Eskom had produced annual Integrated Strategic Electricity Plans each setting out scenarios of future investment requirements to cope with projected increased demand. But although projections of average demand growth in the period 2001–2005 had been accurate, no investment had been forthcoming.

Mbeki failed to respond to allegations that the government's black empowerment strategy had been a root cause of the problem in that small and medium-sized black entrepreneurs, in preference to large corporations, had been awarded coal supply tenders.

The policy of giving preference to small suppliers had caused problems in securing reliable supplies of coal and had also, because small suppliers did not have the capital to invest in rail or conveyor belts infrastructure but used coal trucks, accelerated the wear and tear damage to the roads around the power stations.

Warnings highlighted in several of Eskom's annual reports, starting in 2003, had been ignored not only by the Eskom board but also by its political masters, Mbeki's government.

The power problems were further exacerbated by Mbeki's government policy of attracting energy-intensive industry (such as aluminium smelters) through the carrot of cheap electricity. This meant that, as Eskom's excess capacity ran out and became a deficit, the South African government found itself contractually bound to provide power to energy-intensive industries; despite this meaning the rest of the country experienced traffic problems and business disruption due to the blackouts.

For South Africa to remain a desirable foreign investment destination the country must be seen to honour its contractual obligations. To shut down the smelters is not a simple process, said one analyst. Government would be paying the cost of effects all through the relevant parties aluminium value chain – its aluminium refineries and bauxite ore mines in other countries.

Crime

In 2004, President Thabo Mbeki made an attack on commentators who argued that violent crime was out of control in South Africa, calling them white racists who wanted the country to fail. He said crime was falling but some journalists distorted reality by depicting black people as "barbaric savages" who liked to rape and kill.

Annual statistics published in September 2004 showed that most categories of crime were down. But some had challenged the figures' credibility and said that South Africa remained extremely dangerous, especially for women.

In a column for the African National Congress website, the president rebuked the doubters. Mbeki did not name journalist Charlene Smith who had championed victims of sexual violence since writing about her own rape but quoted a recent article in which she said South Africa had the highest rate of rape and referred (apparently sarcastically) to her as an "internationally recognised expert on sexual violence." He said: "She was saying our cultures, traditions and religions as Africans inherently make every African man a potential rapist ... [a] view which defines the African people as barbaric savages."

Mbeki also described the newspaper *The Citizen* and other commentators who challenged the apparent decline in crime rates, as pessimists who did not trust black rule.

In January 2007, the African Peer Review Mechanism (APRM) draft report on South Africa was released. This noted that South Africa had the world's second-highest murder rate, with about 50 people a day being killed, and that although serious crime was reported as falling, security analysts said that the use of violence in robberies, and rape, were more common. Mbeki in response said in an interview that fears of crime were exaggerated.

In December 2007, the final African Peer Review Mechanism (APRM) report on South Africa, again suggested that there was an unacceptably high level of violent crime in the country. President Mbeki said the suggestion of unacceptably high violent crime appeared to be an acceptance by the panel of what he called "a populist view."

He challenged some of the statistics on crime, which he noted may have resulted from a weak information base, leading to wrong conclusions. Although rape statistics had been obtained from the South African Police Service, "this only denotes the incidents of rape that were reported, some of which could have resulted in acquittals," Mbeki indicated.

2008 Xenophobia attacks

In May 2008, a series of riots took place in a number of townships, mainly in Gauteng Province, which left 42 dead, several hundred injured and several thousand displaced.

The root cause of the riots was xenophobia against

black foreigners from other African countries, including Zimbabweans who had fled their country following the collapse of the Zimbabwean economy. The migrants were blamed for high levels of unemployment, housing shortages, crime, lowering wages by accepting low pay South African workers will not accept, getting "assistance" from the government they are not entitled to, and even for "taking our women."

Following the riots, President Mbeki was criticised for ignoring the scale of the problem and failing to deal with the causes of it. The Zimbabwe Exiles Group accused him of being "more concerned with appeasing Mr. Mugabe than recognising the scale of the problem caused by the flood of Zimbabweans into South Africa."

In response to the violence, Mbeki announced he would set up a panel of experts to investigate the riots and authorised the use of military force against the rioters. That was the first time that such an authorisation was used by the government since the end of apartheid.

Debate with Archbishop Tutu

In 2004, the Archbishop Emeritus of Cape Town, Desmond Tutu, criticised President Mbeki for surrounding himself with "yes-men", for not doing enough to improve the position of the poor, and for promoting economic policies which only benefited a small black elite. He also accused Mbeki and the ANC of suppressing public debate.

Mbeki responded by saying that Tutu had never been an ANC member and defended the debates which took place within ANC branches and other public forums. He also asserted his belief in the value of democratic discussion by quoting the Chinese slogan "let a hundred flowers bloom," referring to the brief Hundred Flowers Campaign within the Chinese Communist Party in 1956–1957.

The *ANC Today* newsletter featured several analyses of the debate, written by Mbeki and the ANC. The latter suggested that Tutu was an "icon" of "white elites," thereby suggesting that his political importance was overblown by the media. And while the article took pains to say that Tutu had not sought this status, it was described in the press as a particularly pointed and personal critique of Tutu.

Tutu responded by saying that he would pray for Mbeki as he had prayed for the officials of the apartheid government.

Mbeki, Zuma, and succession

In 2005, Mbeki removed Jacob Zuma from his post as deputy president of South Africa after Zuma was implicated in a corruption scandal.

In October 2005, some supporters of Zuma (who remained deputy president of the ANC) burned T-shirts portraying Mbeki's picture at a protest. In late 2005, Zuma faced new rape charges which dimmed his political prospects. There was visible split between Zuma's supporters and Mbeki's allies in the ANC.

In February 2006, Mbeki told the South African Broadcasting Corporation (SABC) that he and the ANC had no intention of changing the constitution of the country in order to permit him a third term in office. He stated: "By the end of 2009, I will have been in a senior position in government for 15 years. I think that's too long."

Although he was barred by the constitution of South Africa from seeking a third term as president of the country, Mbeki entered, in 2007, the race to be president of the ANC (no term limit exists for the position of ANC president), for a third term, in a close battle with Jacob Zuma. He lost on the 18 December 2007 at the ANC conference at Polokwane in Limpopo Orovince. Zuma went on to be the ANC's presidential candidate in the 2009 general election.

Appeal

On 12 September 2008, Pietermaritzburg High Court Judge Chris Nicholson ruled that Zuma's corruption charges were unlawful on procedural grounds and added that there was reason to believe the charges against Zuma had been politically motivated, thereby clearing the way for Zuma to run for president.

Mbeki filed an affidavit and applied to the Constitutional Court to appeal the ruling:

"It was improper for the court to make such far-reaching 'vexatious, scandalous and prejudicial' findings concerning me, to be judged and condemned on the basis of the findings in the Zuma matter. The interests of justice, in my respectful submission would demand that the matter be rectified.

These adverse findings have led to my being recalled by my political party, the ANC – a request I have acceded to as a committed and loyal member of the ANC for the past 52 years. I fear that if not rectified, I might suffer further prejudice."

Tlali Tlali, the National Prosecuting Authority spokesman, stated by telephone from Pretoria on 23 September: "We have received the papers. It's under consideration."

Resignation

Note: Unless otherwise specified, the terms "president" and "deputy president" refer to roles in government, whereas "ANC president" or "ANC deputy president" refer to roles in the ANC political party.

Having "made it a point not to contest this decision" of the ANC National Executive Committee (NEC) that Mbeki was no longer fit to lead South Africa, he formally announced his resignation on 21 September 2008 as a result of the ANC National Executive Committee's decision no longer to support him in parliament. This came a few days after the dismissal of a trial against ANC president Jacob Zuma on charges of corruption due to procedural errors.

Allusions were made in the ruling to possible political interference by Mbeki and others in his prosecution. Parliament convened on 22 September and accepted his resignation with effect from 25 September. However, because an MP for the Freedom Front opposition party declared his objection to the resignation, a debate was set to take place the following day.

In cases of such a void in the presidency, the constitution regulates the replacement to serve as the interim president: either the deputy president, the speaker of parliament or any MP (Member of Parliament), as chosen by parliament, can take the role of president of the country until the next election. ANC president Jacob Zuma, who was elected president after the next general election, was not eligible as he was at the time none of these.

The then deputy president, Phumzile Mlambo-Ngcuka, was unlikely to be chosen either, apparently due to her close ties to Mbeki and because her husband, Bulelani Ngcuka, was involved in the decision to charge Zuma with corruption. As a result, the speaker of parliament, Baleka Mbete, had been cited as the likely caretaker president. However, speaking on behalf of the ANC, Zuma strongly hinted at ANC deputy president, Kgalema Motlanthe, who was an MP, becoming Mbeki's replacement for the remainder of the term of parliament which ended in early 2009.

Although Zuma could put pressure on the government and his party to choose Motlanthe, the replacement president had to be decided by parliament.

Deputy President Phumzile Mlambo-Ngcuka, Minister in the Presidency Essop Pahad, and Minister of Science and Technology Mosibudi Mangena all announced their intentions of resigning after Mbeki lost the presidency.

Nathi Mthethwa, chief chip of the ruling African National Congress (ANC) stated that Mbeki's resignation would take effect on 25 September 2008.

ANC president, Jacob Zuma, said that his deputy, Kgalema Motlanthe, would become acting president until 2009 general elections: "I am convinced – if given that responsibility – he (Motlanthe) would be equal to the task."

The ANC confirmed that "Kgalema Motlanthe is to become caretaker president until 2009 elections, with Baleka Mbete being appointed deputy president."

2009 general election

The direction of Mbeki's vote in South Africa's 2009 general election was a matter of moot discussion amongst the press and the public alike.

Although Mbeki had completely disassociated himself from party politics subsequent to his resignation, many suggested that the new party, the Congress of the People (COPE) composed in large part of Mbeki loyalists, would secure his mark on the ballot paper.

COPE was led by one of its founders, Mosiuoa Lekota, who was also known as "Terror Lekota" because of his agility and prowess on the football – soccer – field. He had been one of the prominent leaders of the ANC before he left the party to form COPE.

On election day, 22 April, Mbeki announced that his vote was a secret and called on the electorate to exercise its democratic right not out of fear or historical loyalty but for a future that it desired and a party that would further its ends.

Those sentiments were widely interpreted as being pro-COPE. Indeed, Mbhazima Shilowa, COPE's first deputy president, confirmed on his Facebook page that "i [*sic*] liked TM's message." .It was noted, though, that, despite having been invited, Mbeki had failed to attend a COPE rally the week before.

Winnie Madikizela-Mandela

Winnie Madikizela-Mandela (born Nomzamo Winfreda Madikizela on 26 September 1936) was once the wife of Nelson Mandela and one of the most prominent leaders of the anti-apartheid movemnt inside South Africa.

Although still married to Nelson Mandela when he became president of South Africa in May 1994, she was never the first lady of South Africa because the couple had separated two years earlier after it was revealed that

Winnie had been unfaithful to her husband when he was in prison.

Their divorce was finalised on 19 March 1996, with an unspecified out-of-court settlement. Winnie Mandela's attempt to obtain a settlement equivalent to about 5 million US dollars, half of what she claimed her ex-husband was worth, was dismissed when she failed to appear in court for a financial settlement hearing.

A fiery and highly controversial activist, Winnie was very popular among her supporters who called her the 'Mother of the Nation.' Yet she was reviled by others, mostly because of her alleged involvement in several human rights abuses including the 1989 kidnapping of a 14-year old ANC activist, Stompie Moeketsi Seipei, who was later murdered. He was reportedly kidnapped and murdered on 29 December 1988 by members of Winnie Mandela's bodyguards known as the Mandela United Football Club.

In March 2009, the Independent Electoral Commission ruled that Winnie Mandela, who was selected as an ANC candidate, could run in the April general election that year in spite of the fact that she was convicted of fraud.

Early life

Winnie Mandela's name in her Xhosa language was Nomzamo wwhich means "trial (having a hard time in life)."

She was born in the village of eMbongweni, Bizana, in the Pondo region of what is now South Africa's Eastern Cape Province and experienced racism from both sides at an early age.

She said her grandmother, on her father's side, was the first racist she ever knew because she did not accept Winnie's mother who looked almost white although she was identified as a coloured. She was "half-white."

From the way she looked, some people might think she could have been more white than black, or she had other non-black blood, as well as white, making her more non-black or more white-looking than black. – if she had any black blood at all. But some records do show that her mother was a Pondo, or probably a Pondo, a group which is a part of the Xhosa ethnic group. As Anné Mariè du Preez Bezdrob states in her book, *Winnie Mandela: A Life*:

"Winnie's mother, Gertrude Mzaidume was the first domestic science teacher in the Bizana district....Fair skinned with blue eyes and straight hair, her lineage was thought to include a liaison between a Pondo woman and a white trader....

Makhulu (Winnie's paternal grandmother whose name was Seyina but was simply called Makhulu which means 'grandmother' in Xhosa) enjoyed entertaining the children with her stories of how white men with blue eyes, long beards and straight hair came to Pondoland, warning the little ones that with their Bibles and their money, the strangers had come to steal their people's cattle and destroy their customs. Her obvious resentment of the whites made a strong impression on the children.

Makhulu's affection for (her son and Winnie's father) Columbus and his children did not extend to Gertrude....Makhulu's resentment was further fuelled by the fact that Gertrude was a Christian, and she held her daughter-in-law responsible for the fact that her son was barred from taking more wives.

Moreover, Gertrude was a schoolteacher, and when Columbus had announced that he wanted to marry her, his mother undiplomatically told him he was mad to wed someone who not only wasn't a *muntu* [black], but more of a man than a woman. 'Marry a wife,'she advised, 'not a fellow teacher.'

Her counsel was to no avail, and Makhulu never hid

her displeasure over her eldest son's choice of wife. Winnie and her siblings (nine altogether, Winnie being fifth-born) were always aware of the tension between their mother and grandmother....

Seyina had long decided that the best way of dealing with her son's 'affliction' was by keeping him close to her, while at the same time making it clear that she did not respect Gertrude's position as his wife....

More than anything else, Makhulu could never forgive Columbus for the constant reminder that Gertrude had brought white blood into her family. Columbus was in a difficult position. He was a Christian and an active member of the church, but he dared not openly defy his mother. In deference to her, and to Winnie's puzzlement, he sometimes joined in the cruel jibes about Gertrude's white blood, reminding his children that she was a *mlungu* [white]."

The racial turmoil in Winnie's family has been addressed by other writers as well. As Mary Ann French stated in her article, "The Resurrected Winnie Mandela," in *The Washington Post*, 30 April 1994:

"The personal has always been political for (Winnie) Mandela, according to a new biography by Emma Gilbey, an English journalist who covered Mandela's kidnapping trial.

She was born in a rural southeastern corner of South Africa to a father who had wanted a boy, and a mother who was ostracized because she was half-white.

Her mother's blood had been 'polluted' by her European father, a settler who had cohabited with a Xhosa woman.

Mandela's mother had pale skin, blue eyes and long red hair that she kept hidden, Gilbey writes. Nevertheless, her appearance was a constant reminder to Mandela's people, the Pondos, of the land they had lost to the white man.

Mandela's paternal grandmother was particularly hard

on her daughter-in-law -- to the extent that Mandela would later refer to her grandmother as the first racist she ever knew.

'Her childhood,' Gilbey writes, 'was a blistering inferno of racial hatred.'"

Years later, Winnie Mandela held a number of jobs in various parts of what was then the Bantustan of Transkei, including some with the black Transkei government, living at various times in Bizana, Shawbury and Johannesburg.

She met lawyer and anti-apartheid activist Nelson Mandela in 1957. He was almost 18 years older. They were married in 1958 and had two daughters: Zenani, also called Zeni, born in 1959; and Zindzi, born in 1960.

In June 2010, Winnie was treated for shock after the death of her great granddaughter, Zenani, who was killed in a car accident on the eve of the opening of South Africa's World Cup. Winnie also had diabetes.

Despite restrictions on education for blacks during apartheid, Winnie Mandela earned a degree in social work from the Jan Hofmeyer School in Johannesburg. Several years later, she earned a bachelor's degree in international relations from the University of Witwatersrand, also in Johannesburg. She was also a qualified social worker.

Apartheid

Winnie Mandela emerged as a leading opponent of white minority rule in South Africa during the later years of her husband's long imprisonment (August 1963 – February 1990). For many of those years, she was exiled to the town of Brandfort in the Orange Free State and was confined to the area except for the times she was allowed to visit her husband on at the prison Robben Island. Beginning in 1969, she spent eighteen months in solitary confinement at Pretoria Central Prison.

In a leaked letter to Jacob Zuma in October 2008, Thabo Mbeki who then had just resigned as president of South Africa alluded to the role the ANC created for her in the anti-apartheid struggle:

"In the context of the global struggle for the release of political prisoners in our country, our movement took a deliberate decision to profile Nelson Mandela as the representative personality of these prisoners, and therefore to use his personal political biography, including the persecution of his then wife, Winnie Mandela, dramatically to present to the world and the South African community the brutality of the apartheid system."

Violent rhetoric and murder allegations

Winnie Mandela's reputation was damaged by her bloodthirsty rhetoric, the most noteworthy example of this being a speech she gave in Munsieville on 13 April 1986 when she endorsed the practice of necklacing (burning people alive using tyres and petrol) in the struggle to end apartheid. She said: "With our boxes of matches and our necklaces we shall liberate this country."

Further tarnishing her reputation were accusations by her bodyguard, Jerry Musivuzi Richardson, that Winnie Madikizela-Mandela ordered kidnapping and murder.

On 29 December 1988, Richardson, coach of the Mandela United Football Club (MUFC) – which acted as Mrs. Mandela's personal security detail – abducted 14-year-old James Seipei (also known as Stompie Moeketsi) and three other youths from the home of Methodist minister, Reverend Paul Verryn.

Mrs. Mandela claimed that she had the youth taken to her home because she suspected the reverend was sexually abusing them.

The four were beaten in order to get them to admit to

having sex with the reverend. Seipei was also accused of being an informer.

Seipei's body was found in a field with stab wounds to the throat on 6 January 1989.

Stompie Moeketsi joined the street uprising against apartheid in the mid-1980s at the age of 10 and soon took on a leading role. He became the country's youngest political detainee when he spent his 12th birthday in jail without trial. At the age of 13, he was expelled from school.

Moeketsi was kidnapped on 29 December 1988 after a school rally, accused of being a police informer and murdered at the age of 14. His body was found in Soweto with his throat slit Stompie's body was recovered by the police.

The brutal murder of Stompie became a *cause célèbre* for the apartheid government and opponents of the ANC, and Winnie Mandela's iconic status suffered a heavy blow.

In 1991, Winnie Mandela was convicted of kidnapping and being an accessory to assault in connection with the death of Seipei. Her six-year jail sentence was reduced to a fine and a two-year suspended sentence on appeal.

Appearing before the Truth and Reconciliation Commission in 1997, she said allegations that she was involved in at least 18 human rights abuses including eight murders were "ridiculous." She claimed that her main accuser, former comrade Katiza Cebekhulu, was a former "mental patient'""and that his allegations against her were "hallucinations."

The final report of the South African Truth and Reconciliation commission issued in 1998 found "Ms Winnie Madikizela Mandela politically and morally accountable for the gross violations of human rights committed by the MUFC."

Her chief bodyguard was convicted of killing Stompie. According to a report by The New York Times News Service from Johannesburg, South Africa, published in the

Chicago Tribune, 26 May 1990, headlined "Winnie Mandela's Bodyguard Convicted In Slaying":

"The chief bodyguard of Winnie Mandela, wife of South African nationalist leader Nelson Mandela, was found guilty Friday of murdering James ``Stompie`` Mokhetsi Seipei, a 14-year-old who had been abducted with three men and held in Mrs. Mandela's home in late 1988.

Jerry Musivuzi Richardson, 41, the coach of the Mandela United Football Club, a soccer team whose principal activity was protecting Mrs. Mandela during part of her husband's imprisonment, was also convicted of kidnapping and assaulting the three other men and of trying to kill yet another man in an unrelated case.

Justice Brian O'Donovan of the Rand Supreme Court further ruled Mrs. Mandela participated in part of the initial beating inflicted on the four abducted youths, contradicting her contention and that of Richardson that she was absent.

The three survivors-Kenneth Kgase, 30, Barend Thabiso Mono, 20, and Gabriel Pelo Mekgwe, 21-had testified that Mrs. Mandela was the first to beat them, using her fists and a whip.

Mrs. Mandela was not a defendant in the case, but Friday's verdict raised the possibility that she could be charged with assaulting Seipei and his companions after their abduction.

Conviction would carry a prison sentence as long as 10 years.

At the least, Mrs. Mandela's image is likely to be further tarnished among her fellow residents of the black township of Soweto, where she lives and where the events leading to the murder took place.

At a news conference Tuesday, Mandela asserted his wife had not been given the opportunity to defend herself.

'They don't want to charge her and give her the

opportunity of proving she is innocent,' he said.

According to trial testimony, Seipei and the three others were abducted on Dec. 29, 1989, from the house of a Methodist minister, Rev. Paul Verryn, ostensibly because Mrs. Mandela suspected the minister was sexually abusing them.

Taken by Richardson back to Mrs. Mandela`s house, the four were beaten to persuade them to admit sexual encounters with the minister.

Seipei was also accused of being a police informer.

O`Donovan cleared Verryn of the allegations.

The four were kept inside Mrs. Mandela`s house until Seipei, who had been beaten so badly he could neither speak nor eat, was taken away by Richardson on the night of Jan. 1, 1989, the judge said.

His body was discovered on Jan. 6 in a field with stab wounds in the throat."

Stompie's murder became one of the defining moments in the history of the struggle against apartheid. And it continued to haunt the nation for a long time. As Mary Braid stated in her article, "Stompie's Ghost Refuses to Rest in Peace," in *The Independent*, London, 29 June 1997:

"In 1989, the battered body of Stompie Moeketsi Seipei was found, his throat slit, in a field near the sprawling township of Soweto. Just 14, Stompie was already both veteran ANC activist and suspected police snitch. His murder was testimony to the dark days of apartheid that so often robbed children of their childhood, and sometimes their lives.

The deaths of these children cast long shadows, as the hearings of the Truth and Reconciliation Commission, charged with exposing the atrocities of the apartheid years, have illustrated.

In Stompie's case, however, his shadow has fallen not

across the perpetrators of apartheid, but on those who claimed to be resisting it. And events at the TRC this week have again shown that while his body has been laid to rest, the controversy surrounding his death has not.

Stompie was kidnapped from a church home in Soweto and taken to the home of Winnie Mandela, then wife of the imprisoned ANC leader and now President, Nelson Mandela, where he was severely beaten.

Ms Madikizela-Mandela, as she is now known, claimed she took the teenager from the church home because he was being sexually abused. Although charged with murder, she was convicted only of kidnapping and beating the boy. She was sentenced to six years in jail but this was later reduced to a fine.

This week Stompie rose from the veld to haunt her again, this time with the encouragement of the commission. She may yet regret her decision to ignore the TRC's closing date last month for amnesty applications for politically motivated crimes.

Emma Nicholson is among the forces gathering against the President's ex-wife. The former British MP is the self-styled 'champion' of Katiza Cebekhulu, a former member of Ms Madikizela-Mandela's thuggish bodyguards who, under the nickname Mandela United Football Club, terrorised Soweto in the late 1980s. The club was 'captained' by Jerry Richardson, currently serving life for Stompie's murder.

This week TRC officials revealed a fresh inquiry into Mandela United was drawing to a close and Ms Nicholson was expected to fly to Johannesburg to discuss the whereabouts of Mr Cebekhulu who disappeared while on trial with Ms Madikizela-Mandela over the death.

He surfaced in a Zambian jail claiming he had been spirited away from South Africa by ANC members anxious that he did not give evidence. It was there that he met Ms Nicholson, a parliamentary spokesperson on human rights. She taped an interview with him, later

547

described as 'sensational.' She is one of the few people who have any idea where he is now hiding, apparently too terrified to return: some reports say his 'safe house' is in London, some in Lusaka.

'We are very keen to talk to Mr Cebekhulu so we have to go through Ms Nicholson who guards him rather jealously,' said a TRC insider, after information leaked earlier this week that a subpoena would soon be issued, summoning Ms Madikizela-Mandela to a private hearing. That leak led Commissioner Dumile Ntsebeza to admit new allegations about the football club which went far beyond what was known before.

The TRC insider dismissed as 'way off the mark' a report that it now had a map showing where other children's bodies could be found - but another allegation involving a mineshaft where children were dumped was still under investigation.

The inquiry seems to have been prompted in part by pressure from the families of children who went missing after being threatened by Ms Madikizela-Mandela's 'team.' A few years ago the father of Lolo Sono, 21, claimed that in 1988 he saw his son, battered and bleeding in the back of a minibus driven by her. When the distraught father implored her to let Lolo go, he said, she refused and drove off insisting Lolo was a 'sell-out.' He was never seen again.

In addition, the family of Dr Abu-Bakr Asvat, who was murdered during a robbery at his home four weeks after Stompie died, have pressed the Commission to investigate links with Mandela United. Dr Asvat is believed to have examined Stompie shortly before he died.

Ms Nicholson has previously claimed to have evidence about Dr Asvat's murder. But this week she said that she felt Mr Cebekhulu's importance to the current investigation was being exaggerated. His evidence, she said, amounted to corroboration of what others already knew.

Ms Madikizela-Mandela remained tight-lipped last week. Despite attempts to stem the flow of leaks on one of its most politically sensitive investigations, Commission officials have said privately that former associates of hers are 'singing' about the past in their bid for amnesty.

They apparently include Richardson and Xoliswa Falati, who served a two-year jail sentence for her part in Stompie's death. In court she provided her then best friend with an alibi against murder charges but, like Richardson, she has since given newspaper interviews where she claims she committed perjury.

Ms Madikizela-Mandela, affectionately referred to as 'mummy' by the old football team, has claimed a political smear campaign has been launched against her. She has even appealed to Mr Cebekhulu to come home, insisting he has nothing to fear.

But his elderly mother Joyce, who claims not to have heard a whimper from her son in eight years, warned that 'the killers' will get him if he returned. So far he appears to prefer his biological mother's advice to that of his former political 'mummy.'"

Transition to democracy

During South Africa's transition to democracy, Winnie Mandela adopted a far less conciliatory attitude than her husband towards the dominant white community.

And despite being on her husband's arm when he was released in 1990, the first time the two had been seen in public for nearly thirty years, the Mandelas' 38-year marriage ended when they separated in April 1992 after it was revealed that she had been unfaithful to Nelson during his imprisonment.

One of her lovers was Dali Mpofu who was young enough to be her son and even grandson. He was about 30 years younger than she was. If she had a child at 15, she would have been old enough to be his grandmother.

There was damning evidence against her about her infidelity with Dali Mpofu. According to *The Independent*, 7 September 1992, in an article entitled, "Letter to Lover Spells Trouble for Winnie":

"WINNIE MANDELA'S persistent denial of accusations that she misappropriated African National Congress funds and had an affair with a young lawyer were contradicted yesterday by publication in the South African press of a letter she wrote to her lover.

The letter, dated 17 March and signed 'It's me', reveals how Mrs Mandela's relationship with Dali Mpofu - who at 30 is about half her age - helped wreck her marriage to Nelson Mandela. It discloses that at one point Mr Mandela, whom she calls by his family nickname 'Tata', refused to speak to her for five months because of the affair. The letter was authenticated using a copy of her handwriting.

Mrs Mandela lays bare her obsession with Mr Mpofu, who was part of her defence team during her trial for the kidnap and assault of a child activist and who later worked in the ANC's social-welfare department, which she headed.

Mrs Mandela refers to the mother of his child as a 'white hag' and accuses him of betraying her (Mrs Mandela) by 'running around fucking at the slightest emotional excuse'.

'The only time you have time to talk to me is about women *ofeba nabo* (a Xhosa term meaning 'women you are having sex with'), as you are doing right now. You are supposed to care so much for me that the fact that I haven't been speaking to Tata for five months now over you is no longer your concern.

'I keep telling you the situation is deteriorating at home, you are not bothered because you are satisfying yourself every night with a woman,' the letter said, adding: 'I won't be your bloody fool, Dali.'

Less than a month later, Mr Mandela announced his separation from his wife.

But it is likely to be a later section of the letter that Mrs Mandela will have most cause to regret. She admits giving 160,000 rand (about pounds 30,000) to Mr Mpofu, and talks of her fear of an investigation into the accounts of the social welfare department of the ANC.

'You think you can just wish away certain things Dali, not with me. I tell you I'm in trouble with the Simmonds Street a/c which reflects over R160,000 drawn over a period for you. You don't even bother to check how we can overcome this. I tell you (ANC lawyer Ismael) Ayob has been sent by Tata to get an accountant to investigate my a/c. I tell you Ntombi (a woman in the ANC welfare department) is gossiping about the cheques we used to ask her to cash in the name of the Dept and how I gave you all that money,' the letter says.

Two months later the ANC said it was investigating alleged fraud involving 400,000 rand while Mrs Mandela and Mr Mpofu were running the department. In May, Mr Mpofu was sacked by the ANC after Mrs Mandela resigned from the welfare department. He is suing for wrongful dismissal

The newspapers which published the letter – the *Sunday Star* and the *Sunday Times* – said both people declined opportunities to comment.

Yesterday, telephone calls to Mrs Mandela's Soweto home were not answered, and Mr Mpofu's home number was not listed.

The ANC's information chief, Pallo Jordan, declined to comment on the letter other than to suggest it had been intercepted and leaked by government intelligence officials. However, there is no shortage of candidates within the ANC if the organisation wants to consider Mrs Mandela's other enemies.

The Zulu leader, Mangosuthu Buthelezi, called on Inkatha's youth wing to 'stop the ANC in its tracks' after

551

the murder of 10 Inkatha supporters on Friday. Chief Buthelezi said the ANC was obsessed with seizing power. He subsequently denied that he was advocating violence."

Nelson and Winnie Mandela were divorced in March 1996. She then adopted the surname Madikizela-Mandela. Appointed deputy minister of arts, culture, science and technology in the first post-apartheid government (May 1994), she was dismissed eleven months later following allegations of corruption.

She remained popular among many ANC supporters and, in December 1993 and April 1997, she was elected president of the ANC Women's League, although she withdrew her candidacy for ANC deputy president at the movement's Mafikeng conference in December 1997.

In 1997, she appeared before the Truth and Reconciliation (TRC). Archbishop Desmond Tutu as chairman of the commission recognised her importance in the anti-apartheid struggle but also begged her to apologise and to admit her mistakes. In a guarded response, she echoed his words, admitting that "things went horribly wrong."

Legal problems

On 24 April 2003, she was found guilty on 43 counts of fraud and 25 of theft, and her broker, Addy Moolman, was convicted on 58 counts of fraud and 25 of theft.

Both had pleaded not guilty to the charges which related to money taken from loan applicants' accounts for a funeral fund but from which the applicants did not benefit. Madikizela-Mandela was sentenced to five years in prison.

Shortly after the conviction, she resigned from all leadership positions in the ANC, including her parliamentary seat and the presidency of the ANC Women's League.

In late 2003, her close friend and socialite Hazel Crane, was murdered. Crane previously offered to buy Madikizela-Mandela a house.

In July 2004, an appeal judge of the Pretoria High Court ruled that "the crimes were not committed for personal gain." The judge overturned the conviction for theft but upheld the one for fraud, handing her a three years and six months suspended sentence.

In June 2007, the Canadian High Commission in South Africa declined to grant Winnie Mandela a visa to travel to Toronto, Canada, where she was scheduled to attend a gala fund-raising concert organised by an arts organisation, MusicaNoir, which included the world premiere of *The Passion of Winnie*, an opera based on her life.

Return to politics

When the ANC announced the election of its National Executive Committee on 21 December 2007, Winnie Mandela placed first with 2845 votes.

Apology to riot victims

Winnie Mandela criticised the anti-immigrant violence in May–June 2008 which began in Johannesburg and spread throughout the country and blamed the government's lack of suitable housing provisions for the sentiments behind the riots. She also apologised to the victims of the riots and visited the Alexandra township.

She also offered her home as a shelter for an immigrant family from the Democratic Republic of Congo (DRC). She warned that the perpetrators of the violence could strike at the Gauteng train system.

2009 general election

Winnie Mandela secured fifth place on the ANC's electoral list for the 2009 general election behind party president and current president of South Africa Jacob Zuma, former president of South Africa Kgalema Motlanthe, deputy president of South Africa Baleka Mbete, and finance minister Trevor Manuel.

An article in *The Observer*, London, suggested that her position near the top of the list indicated that the party's leadership saw her as a valuable asset in the election with regard to solidifying support among the party's grassroots and the poor.

2010 interview with Nadira Naipaul

In 2010, Winnie Madikizela-Mandela was interviewed by Nadira Naipaul.

In the interview, she attacked her ex-husband, claiming that he had "let blacks down," claiming that he was only "wheeled out to collect money" and that he is "nothing more than a foundation."

She further attacked his decision to accept the Nobel Peace Price with the last president of apartheid South Africa, F.W. de Klerk.

Among other things, she also claimed that Mandela was no longer "accessible" to her daughters. She referred to Archbishop Desmond Tutu, in his capacity as the head of the Truth and Reconciliation Commission (TRC), as a "cretin."

The interview attracted media attention and the ANC announced it would ask her to explain the apparent attack on Nelson Mandela.

On 14 March 2010, a statement was issued on behalf of Winnie Mandela claiming that the interview was a "fabrication."

In media

Winnie Mandela was first portrayed by Alfre Woodard in the TV movie *Mandela*.

Tina Lifford portrayed Winnie Mandela in the 1997 TV drama *Mandela and De Klerk*.

Sophie Okonedo portrayed her in the BBC television drama *Mrs Mandela*, first broadcast on BBC Four on 25 January 2010.

Jennifer Hudson played Winnie Mandela in the biopic film, *Winnie*, directed by Darrell J. Roodt and released in Canada by D Films in December 2011.

Andre Pieterse, Roodt and Paul L. Johnson based the film's script on Anne Marie du Preez Bezdrob's biography, *Winnie Mandela: A Life*.

The Creative Workers Union of South Africa opposed the choice, stating that they would push for a moratorium on the film if the casting was not reversed.

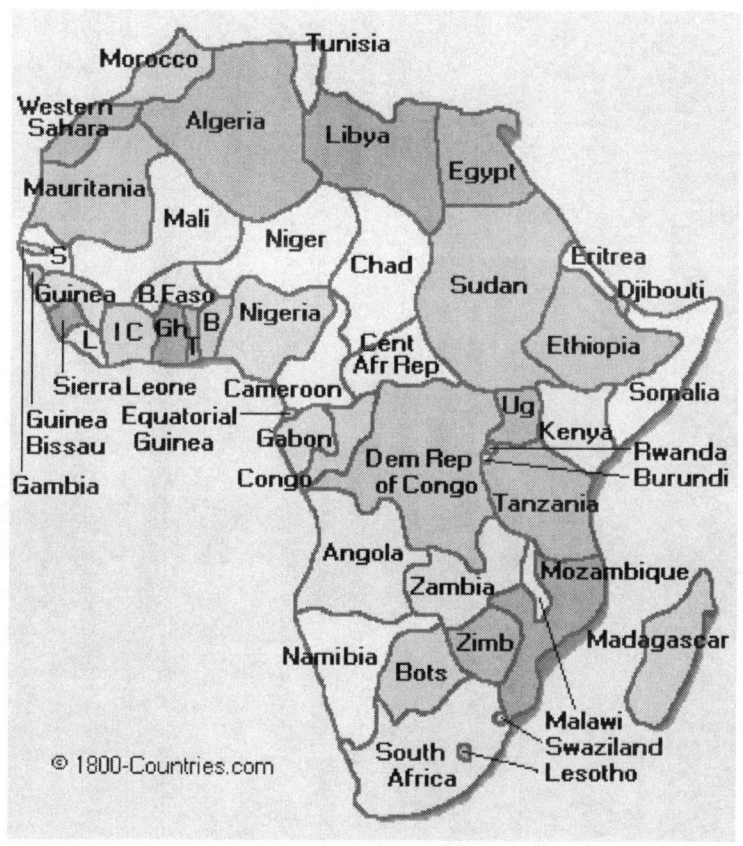

Lightning Source UK Ltd.
Milton Keynes UK
UKOW03f1135060814

236449UK00001B/46/P